D-Day Gunners

Firepower on the British Beaches and Landing Grounds

Frank Baldwin

Pen & Sword
MILITARY

First published in Great Britain in 2022 by
Pen & Sword Military
An imprint of
Pen & Sword Books Ltd
Yorkshire – Philadelphia

ISBN 978 1 47383 493 4

A CIP catalogue record for this book is available from the British Library.

Typeset by Mac Style
Printed and bound in the UK by CPI Group (UK) Ltd,
Croydon, CR0 4YY

MIX
Paper from responsible sources
FSC® C013604

Pen & Sword Books Limited incorporates the imprints of Atlas, Archaeology, Aviation, Discovery, Family History, Fiction, History, Maritime, Military, Military Classics, Politics, Select, Transport, True Crime, Air World, Frontline Publishing, Leo Cooper, Remember When, Seaforth Publishing, The Praetorian Press, Wharncliffe Local History, Wharncliffe Transport, Wharncliffe True Crime and White Owl.

For a complete list of Pen & Sword titles please contact

PEN & SWORD BOOKS LIMITED
47 Church Street, Barnsley, South Yorkshire, S70 2AS, England
E-mail: enquiries@pen-and-sword.co.uk
Website: www.pen-and-sword.co.uk

Or

PEN AND SWORD BOOKS
1950 Lawrence Rd, Havertown, PA 19083, USA
E-mail: Uspen-and-sword@casematepublishers.com
Website: www.penandswordbooks.com

D-Day Gunners

Contents

Preface		vi
Acknowledgements		viii
Chapter 1	The Background to D-Day	1
Chapter 2	The Royal Artillery in 1944	5
Chapter 3	The Germans	29
Chapter 4	Preparing For D-Day	43
Chapter 5	Overview of D-Day	59
Chapter 6	Orne Bridgehead, D-Day	85
Chapter 7	Sword Beach	107
Chapter 8	Juno Beach	145
Chapter 9	Gold Beach	174
Chapter 10	After D-Day	208
Chapter 11	Touring the D-Day Beaches	243
Appendix A: Artillery Technical Terms and Glossary		246
Appendix B: Artillery Equipment		253
Appendix C: Artillery on the British Beaches and Landing Grounds		257
Index		260

Preface

This is the first part of a two-part work on artillery on the D-Day beaches and landing grounds. Artillery is an overlooked and critical part of the D-Day assault and the Battle of Normandy. This volume covers the story of the British beaches and landing grounds, with a second volume in production focusing on the American beaches and landing grounds.

While it is widely recognized that Allied firepower was key to success, the ubiquity of the Gunners has resulted in their story being taken for granted. Their contribution has become anonymous, if not invisible.

Whether field, AA or anti-tank/tank destroyers, artillerymen are largely absent from popular media portrayals of D-Day and Normandy. Three feature films have been made about D-Day, but there is no individual gunner of any Allied nationality portrayed in *The Longest Day, Band of Brothers* or *Saving Private Ryan*. Popular computer games set in the Normandy campaign almost invariably set the player as an infantryman of some sort.

There are memoirs by British and Canadian artillerymen from the Normandy campaign, but far fewer than from the other arms. There are even fewer by American artillerymen, whose story has been particularly neglected.

The dominant images from the newsreels are of air power and tanks, the iconic weapons of the Second World War. Artillery is more associated with the First World War. There are few if any publicly available images of many key artillery activities or equipment. There are more photographs of the interior of Bletchley Park than of heavy AA guns, anti-aircraft early warning or gun-laying radars in Normandy. Nor are there photographs of sound ranging units or surveyors at work. Field artillery command posts, artillery signallers, observers and artillery commanders rarely caught the photographer's eye.

Some of these omissions are understandable. Photographs of the latest radars would be highly classified, and it was not easy to photograph forward observers at work. Small parties of artillerymen carrying out technical work may not have caught the photographer's attention. It is easy to understand why video game players are not faced with scenarios that invite them to run a fire direction centre, calculate firing data, establish radio nets or lay out a survey scheme.

These books are battlefield guides. They are intended to tell the artillery story with reference to the locations and exhibits to be found on the D-Day beaches and landing zones. There are three unique elements to these books. The D-Day fire plan was a key part of the Operation Overlord Plan. This work includes a detailed study of the D-Day fire plan and a systematic examination of its effects in order to give a new interpretation of the D-Day landings. The works tell the story from the artillery's point of view, with the often-overlooked stories of the artillerymen. It also uses examples to explain in simple terms how artillery worked.

This first volume covers the events on the British and Canadian beaches (Sword, Juno and Gold) and Landing Grounds.

Several parts of this story should be of interest to American readers. The heavy day bombers of the Eighth Air Force were an important part of the D-Day fire plan. However, their contribution has been misunderstood and unfairly maligned. In fact, the pre-landing D-Day assault was a masterpiece of precision bombing undertaken by a force that had neither been equipped nor trained for this purpose.

The book also tells the story of the 987th Field Artillery Battalion. This force was unique in being the only American unit to land on the British beaches and it was scheduled to land on D-Day. The battalion was equipped with self-propelled tracked 155mm howitzers. Originally scheduled to land long after D-Day, in March 1944 the 987th were ordered across the Atlantic and found themselves trained as assault troops scheduled to land through the surf on D-Day.

The book will focus on the story of the Royal Artillery on D-Day and for the following few days, and on the related sites close to the Normandy D-Day beaches. It will have two elements not covered in more general guides to Normandy.

It also tells the stories of artillerymen themselves. These stories deserve to be told, for the sake of their families.

Acknowledgements

The original inspiration for this book came from Nigel Cave, the series editor for the Pen & Sword Battleground series of books, and it could not have been written without his support and guidance. A second inspiration was the late Will Townend, whose history of the Royal Artillery in Normandy I completed as co-author for the Royal Artillery Institution. Will was a fellow battlefield guide and had lectured and guided tours of the D-Day beaches. He had originally intended to write a more focused work on D-Day and had identified much more primary source material than could be included in the wider work on the Normandy campaign. I also owe a debt to General Martin Farndale, whose battlefield study notes have been an inspiration.

I am very grateful for the assistance of the old Firepower Museum and archives, in particular Paul Evans, whose expertise as an archivist was invaluable. Phil Jobson and the late Nigel Evans have been very generous with their support and assistance in respect of artillery terminology, organization and methods. Fellow Gunner Tim 'Bertie' Morris has been a great help as an informed and knowledgeable critic. I owe thanks to the online elves who contribute to ww2talk.com, the internet forum dedicated to the British and Commonwealth experience of the Second World War and who have been an invaluable sounding board and research resource. I also owe thanks to Michael Mannix, my navigator and photographer on our expedition to Normandy.

This book could not have been published without the expertise and support of Heather Williams at Pen & Sword, and George Chamier, my copy editor.

Finally, I owe everything to the patience, tolerance and good humour of my wife Helen.

Chapter 1

The Background to D-Day

At the Casablanca Conference in January 1943, the British and Americans agreed to invade Western Europe in 1944. The planners determined that the landings should take place in Normandy, between the rivers Vire and Orne; and the plan was subsequently accepted by military and political leaders at the Quadrant Conference in Quebec held between 17 and 24 August 1943. However, the plans were not finalized until General Eisenhower was appointed in overall command of the Anglo-American forces, and General Montgomery was appointed to command the 21st Army Group, which was to tackle the assault.

The British Army had not been idle since the disastrous events of May and June 1940. With strong encouragement from Winston Churchill, soldiers had formed specialist forces to raid the French coast. The Royal Artillery had provided many volunteers to serve as commandos, and some of their key leaders. Lieutenant Colonel Dudley Clarke suggested the name 'Commando' for these specialist troops and took part in the first raid. Captain John Durnford Slater was an early volunteer who formed No 3 Commando and would be the Deputy Commander Special Forces on D-Day. Captain Pat Porteus was awarded the Victoria Cross for gallantry in a large-scale raid on Dieppe in August 1942. On the night of 12 September 1942, Major Augustus 'Gus' March-Phillips, who had already been awarded the MC and MBE, would be one of the first of the Allied troops to die on what would later be the D-Day beaches. The experience gained from raiding was invaluable in planning the D-Day landings. It also deflected German efforts away from an invasion by an army to counter-measures against raids against targets that would never be attacked in force.

The plan for the D-Day landings, Operation Overlord, threw up major challenges. By June 1944 the Allied armies had already made amphibious landings in 1943 in North Africa, Sicily and Italy. But these had been launched against thinly defended coasts, at night and with the advantage of surprise. This would not be possible against the French coast, as demonstrated by the failure of the Dieppe Raid in the summer of 1942 to obtain tactical surprise. The Germans had been preparing the defences on the Channel coast since 1942. Operation Overlord, the lodgement of the Allied armies in occupied France, would inevitably begin with a large-scale attack on a well-fortified position held by an alert enemy.

The Allies had identified Normandy as the target for their lodgement by July 1943, with much of the initial planning led by an artillery general, Frederick Morgan, appointed as Chief of Staff to the Supreme Allied Commander, nine months before Eisenhower's appointment as Supreme Commander.

The plan adopted was to land the equivalent of over five infantry divisions and their supporting arms on five beaches between the Orne Canal and halfway up the eastern side of the Cotentin Peninsula. The flanks of the seaborne assault were to

THE BRITISH ASSAULT AREA
MILES
Main roads
Railways; Double line, Single line
Woods and orchards
Port en Bessin
Longues
Arromanches les Bains
Tracy sur Mer
le Hamel
Hable de Heurtot
les Roquettes
Asnelles sur Mer
Meuvaines
Mont Fleury
Ver sur Mer
la Rivière
Bernières sur Mer
Courseulles sur Mer
Graye sur Mer
St Aubin sur Mer
Langrune sur Mer
Luc sur Mer
Lion sur Mer
la Brèche
Ouistreham
Hermanville sur Mer
Colleville sur Orne
Franceville Plage
Merville
Buhot
la Rosière
Crépon
Ste Croix sur Mer
Banville
Tailleville
Reviers
Douvres la Délivrande
Bény sur Mer
Basly
Fontaine Henry
Colombiers sur Seulles
Tierceville
Villers le Sec
Creully
St Gabriel
Bazenville
Sommervieu
St Sulpice
Sully
Vaux sur Aure
Ste Anne
BAYEUX
Esquay sur Seulles
Brécy
Rucqueville
Coulombs
St Léger
le Fresne Camilly
Thaon
Colomby sur Thaon
Anguerny
Anisy
Villons les Buissons
les Buissons
Cambes
Périers sur le Dan
St Aubin d'Arquenay
Beuville
Biéville
Bénouville
le Port
Blainville
Ranville
le Mariquet
Amfreville
Bréville
St Côme
Hérouvillette
Escoville
Bois de Bavent
Longueval
Ste Honorine la Chardonnerette
Colombelles
Cuverville
Touffréville
Sannerville
Démouville
Lebisey
CAEN
Faubourg de Vaucelles
Cormelles
Galmanche
Buron
St Contest
Authie
la Villeneuve
Carpiquet
AIRFIELD
Secqueville en Bessin
Ste Croix Grand Tonne
Duoy Ste Marguerite
Loucelles
Bronay
Putot en Bessin
Bretteville l'Orgueilleuse
Norrey en Bessin
Audrieu
le Haut d'Audrieu
Cristot
le Mesnil Patry
St Manvieu
Fontenay le Pesnel
Saint Pierre
Tilly sur Seulles
Bucéels
la Belle Épine
Juaye Mondaye
Subles
R. Aure
R. Seulles
R. Mue
R. Orne
R. Odon
Verson
Rauray
le Haut du Bosq
Grainville sur Odon
Hottot
Lingèvres

be protected by airborne landings. The British Second Army would be responsible for the eastern half of the assault, from the River Dives to Port-en-Bessin, while the American First Army would be responsible for the western half from west of Port-en-Bessin to St Marcouf. The coastline was divided into codenamed sectors. The British were responsible for the sector between the rivers Dives and Orne, officially known as Band, and west of the Orne Canal, Sword, Juno and Gold.

Once ashore, the assaulting troops would expect to face opposition from the full might of the German army in the west. In broad terms, it would be a race between trains and vehicles across the Continent on the one hand and shipping across the Channel on the other. The Germans aimed to make landing as difficult as possible for the Allies, with coastal defences backed by reserves that could be expected to concentrate where the invader had landed. The Allies would need to rely on fire power to destroy or suppress defences for long enough for Allied troops to deal with them at close quarters.

The three service branches were all mutually at their most helpless during the assault. Aircraft could not give prolonged help. They could deal with targets on the day before and with targets inland or away from the landing places. The navy would be standing too far out to sea to offer more than coastal artillery assistance. The Army was the most exposed because its men would be in landing craft, waiting to disembark and deploy their weapons for the land battle. At the same time, the Army needed intense artillery close support, just as on land. Soldiers would need to land on the beaches, breach obstacles and assault and defeat enemy defenders strongly entrenched and in formidable shelters.

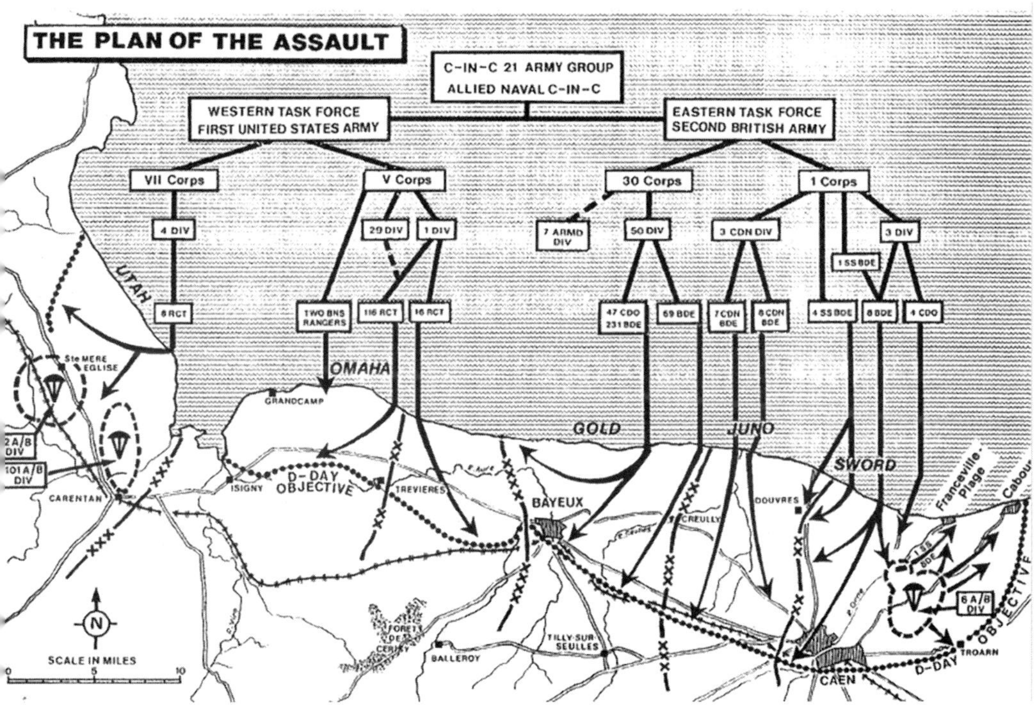

The Germans would be deployed in concrete or field defences sited to engage troops to the front and the flanks. They would be protected with barbed wire, mines and anti-tank obstacles. These positions were sited in depth, supported by mortars and artillery. There would be mobile reserves ready to regain any lost ground. They would be supported by the Luftwaffe's fighters, bombers and anti-aircraft defences.

The assaulting force would need to 'drench' the beaches with fire as the assault force approached them. The density of fire provided would need to be of a similar weight to that in the barrage at El Alamein in October 1942, equivalent to one 25-pounder gun per 17 yards. As one of the few successful assaults mounted by the British Army against German-held positions, El Alamein was the best benchmark. Engineers built full-scale models of the German defences and designed equipment to gap obstacles and demolish defences. Drills were developed to capture strong points using battle groups of infantry, armour artillery and engineers.

These techniques were developed during the first half of 1943 by Combined Operations. This was a force of sailors, soldiers and airmen established in 1940 to carry out raids and develop amphibious warfare techniques for landings on an enemy-held coast.

Once ashore, both sides would race to reinforce the invasion area, the Allies reinforcing the beachhead by sea and air against the Germans moving by rail and road. Although the Allied forces outnumbered the Germans, most of the land forces remained in the UK or USA. The build-up would take several months before the Allies outnumbered the total German force in Western Europe. The Allied Expeditionary Force would need to be ready to defend as well as attack.

Chapter 2

The Royal Artillery in 1944

The Royal Artillery was the dominant arm of the British Army in 1944. Artillery had grown from around 10 per cent at the start of the war to over 25 per cent of the Army. Together with its logistic support, it was the biggest single component of the British Liberation Army of 1944. Artillery firepower was key to Montgomery's tactical methods developed in North Africa. Anti-tank guns blunted the German panzers at the battles of El Alamein and Medenine. Field and medium artillery pulverized defences, suppressed enemy artillery and broke up counter-attacks, minimizing infantry casualties and bolstering confidence. Anti-aircraft artillery had improved dramatically in quality and quantity during the war years. The Blitz had promoted innovative technology that made heavy AA guns over one hundred times as effective as in 1940. It would play a decisive part in the 1944 Blitz, Hitler's gamble to win the war in 1944 with V1 missiles. Artillery is a technical arm; there is a glossary of terms and abbreviations at Appendix A.

The British Army in 1944 classified artillery as air landing, field, anti-tank, medium, heavy and anti-aircraft. A proportion of field, light anti-aircraft and anti-tank artillery was allocated to the divisional artillery, under the Commander Royal Artillery of the division (CRA). The Brigadier Royal Artillery at Corps (CCRA) and Army Headquarters (BRA) was attached to the headquarters to provide advice to the commander. Medium and heavy artillery and most field regiments not part of a division were grouped into Army Groups Royal Artillery. These were commanded by a brigadier with a similar establishment to the HQRA and provided the staff work for counter bombardment plans.

Field artillery

The Royal Artillery was organized in regiments, commanded by a lieutenant colonel; these were organized into batteries, commanded by a major. Field regiments had three batteries of eight guns; medium regiments had two batteries of eight guns; and heavy regiments had four batteries of four guns. Field and medium batteries were organized into two troops of four guns, with a captain troop commander.

A field artillery regiment provided artillery fire units and a network of liaison officers and observers to enable fire to be commanded at the highest level while controlled at the lowest practical. In battle, the commanding officer of a field regiment of the divisional artillery would join their affiliated brigade headquarters, while battery commanders joined the headquarters of the infantry battalion or armoured regiments. Troop commanders would typically deploy with the forward companies or squadrons. Linked by wireless and line communications, artillery fire could be applied flexibly and concentrated where it was needed most. Behind the scenes, guns were surveyed on a common map grid, and firing calculations were based on the best

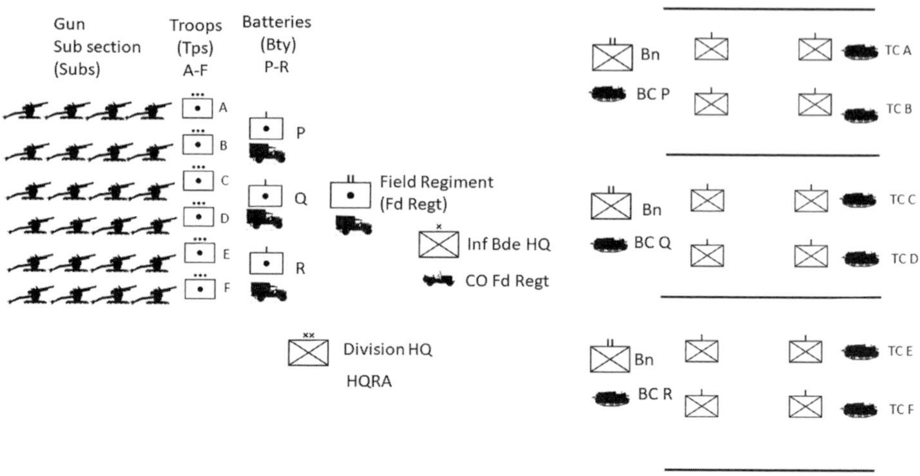

Field artillery regiment affiliations.

information about meteorological conditions and wear on the guns. The regiment's second-in-command was responsible for its gun area. The Regimental HQ (RHQ) was there, operated by the adjutant where it could best communicate with the OPs. The image above illustrates how the regimental, battery and troop commanders and staff were deployed in direct support (DS) of an infantry brigade. Troops in a Regiment were usually lettered A to F, while batteries would have their own unique number or letter rather than P, Q and R. The term 'direct support' might give the misleading impression that each battalion could count on the support of 'their' DS battery. This was not so. The communications network between the gunners meant that the whole regiment could be concentrated in support of the battalion or even company that faced the weight of the enemy attacks and be switched quickly if necessary. Twenty-four guns when they were needed were more use than eight when they were not.

The 25-pounder gun howitzer was the main field artillery equipment used by Field artillery regiments. This ordnance had a calibre of 3.45 inches (89mm) and fired a 25lb shell to a range of 13,400 yards. This was a lighter and less lethal shell than that of the 105mm howitzers used by the German or US armies but outranged both. While it had little physical effect on armoured vehicles, fortifications or dug in troops, the massed fire from 25-pounder artillery was capable of inflicting heavy casualties on troops in the open and of neutralizing German defenders. The turntable allowed large switches of targets to be made by one man lifting the trail. This equipped most of the field regiments of the Royal Artillery.

The tractor for the 25-pounder was the Morris Commercial C8 Field Artillery Tractor (FAT), often known as a 'Quad'. The FAT towed a limber and gun as well as carrying the six-man detachment at a maximum speed of 50 mph. It was seriously under-powered. Its 3.5 litre petrol engine developed 70bhp (52.2 kW), which is less than that of the economy versions of modern small cars such as the Ford Fiesta or Vauxhall Corsa.

The 25-pounder SP (Sexton) mounted a 25-pounder gun howitzer on a Canadian Ram chassis. The armour gave some protection to those of the detachment from

Field Artillery tractor, limber and 25-pounder gun on exercise in the UK.

shell and mortar splinters. The 25-pounder SP could engage targets between 25° left and 15° right of the centre line by traversing the gun. If the target was outside this arc, the gun would need to track left or right. This equipped the self-propelled field regiments that supported the armoured Brigades in each armoured division and some independent regiments.

The US M7 (Priest) mounted an M1 105mm howitzer on an M3 chassis. It had a maximum range of 10,500 yards and fired a 37lb round. It also had a white phosphorous smoke round. The field regiments of 3rd British and Canadian divisions were equipped with the M7 so they could provide support from the surf on D Day.

The American-manufactured 75mm M8 pack howitzer equipped 53 (Worcester Yeomanry) Airlanding Light Regiment, seen here on exercise in spring 1944. A single battery of these guns was air landed on the evening of D-Day.

The fire of field artillery was usually directed by forward observers. The image on page 8 taken in training in the UK shows the walking party of a Forward Observation Party. The Forward Observation Officer (FOO), carrying essential items of equipment, is listening on the wireless headset. Around his neck are a pair

Forward observation party. The No 11 radio set dates this as many months before D-Day.

of binoculars; these will have graticules expressed in degrees that allow the observer to estimate angles – and the range. The small web pouch is for a prismatic compass. To the right is a signaller. In the background the OP Assistant, known in short as 'Ack' or 'Alpha' is studying the map.

The orders to the guns to hit a particular target are translated by the command post into a bearing (azimuth), elevation, ammunition order and firing rates. This involved manual trigonometry calculations to take account of the target location and altitude, charge temperature and wind direction and speed. These calculations were carried out often by tired men, sometimes under fire.

The Royal Artillery had also developed effective and responsive fire control techniques using wireless communications. This relied on the skills of the signallers

A Canadian battery command post training in the UK in the months before D-Day. A technical assistant is working on the artillery board, where firing data is calculated using a 1:25,000 map. A signaller monitors the wireless net while the Command Post Officer talks on the telephone, probably to the guns.

The final link in the communications chain is the Gun No 1 noting the firing data he received over the gun's Tannoy loudspeaker.

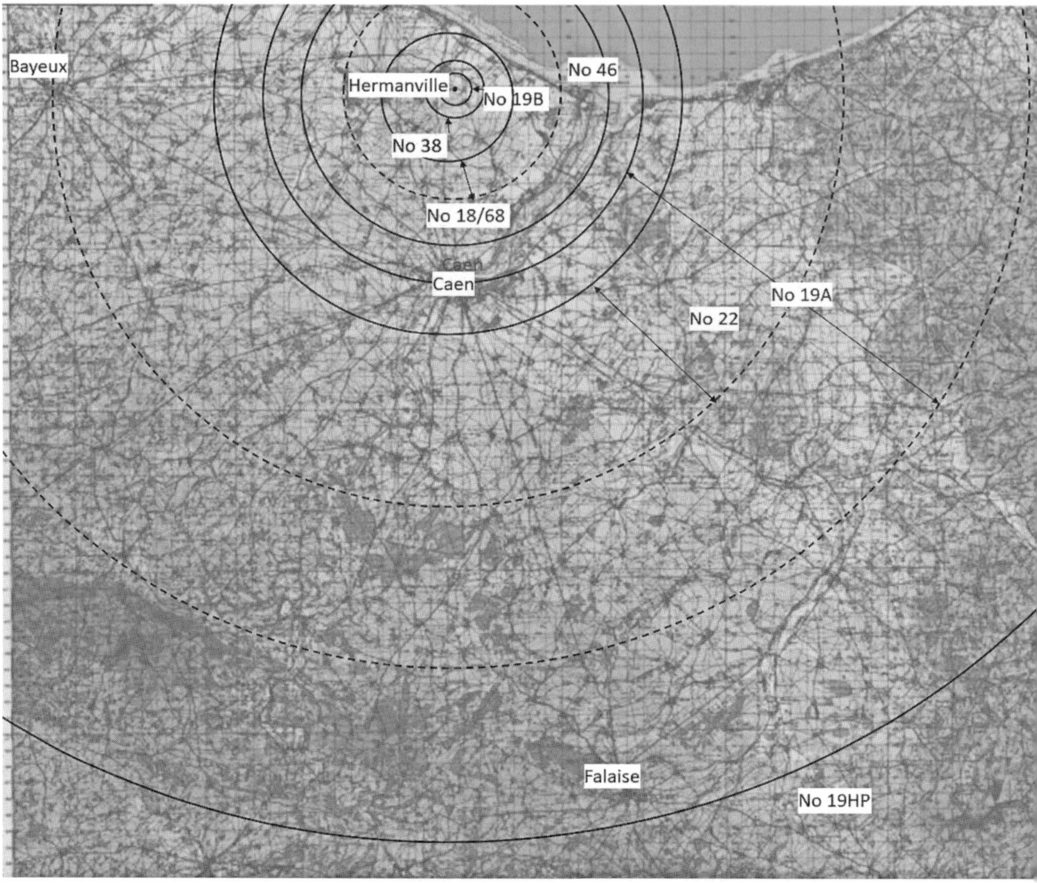

The range of radio sets was a key limitation on the effectiveness of field artillery. The solid lines indic the approximate ranges for working when using voice transmissions, while the dotted lines show the rang for carrier wave (CW), which allowed for transmission in Morse code. The ranges are based on quo performance figures, but in practice wireless range depended on the aerial used, trees and buildin atmospheric conditions and operator skill.

who, besides knowing Morse code, needed to coax the best performance from the valve technology available at the time. Radios would drift off frequency, and it was easy to lose communication with some or all of the other stations on the net. It was not easy to work with 1940s era wireless sets, particularly at night, when wireless reception was at its worst. Atmospheric and other types of interference were deafening and continuous at their worst, a sort of 'juddle-diddle-juddle-diddle' on a high-pitched note.

Non-divisional field medium and heavy artillery was grouped into Army Groups Royal Artillery (AGRA). An AGRA was assigned to each army corps. Most AGRA included a heavy regiment, a field regiment and a medium regiment per division, plus one. An Air OP Squadron would be assigned to each corps, vitally important in flat, close country of Normandy. For major operations several AGRA might support the operations of a single corps.

The 15cwt half-tracked M14 was supplied under Lend Lease as a self-propelled AA gun mounting four 0.5 inch calibre machine guns. The British converted these back to load-carrying vehicles and they were used extensively by the Royal Artillery as ammunition vehicles, 17-pounder gun tractors, command posts and armoured OP vehicles for Forward Observation Bombardment parties.

The Universal Carrier was used by the field artillery as an Armoured OP and for starting and charging batteries. Fitting an OP Party of four and their kit into an Armoured OP was a tight squeeze, and with an engine hardly much more powerful than an economy saloon, it was underpowered. **(Myer Malin)**

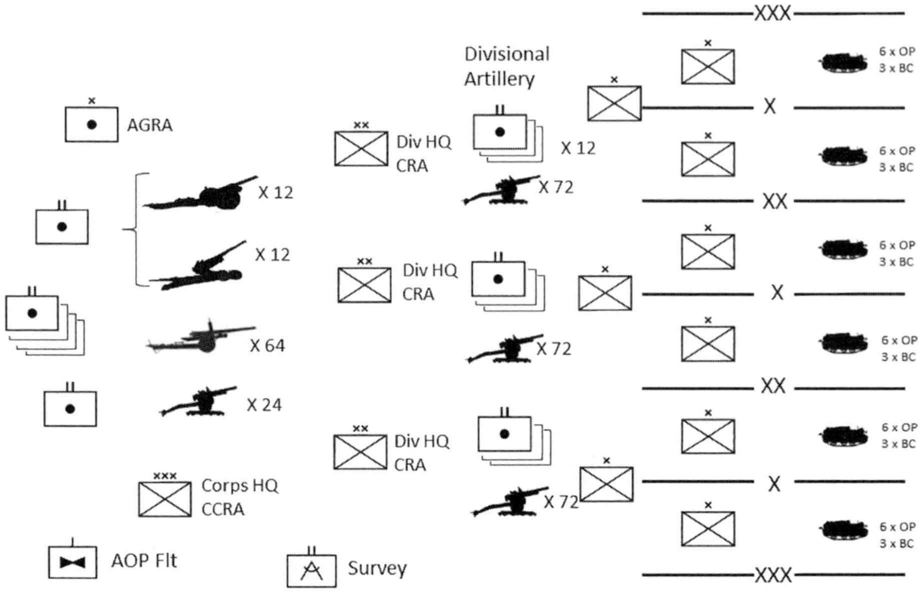

This diagram shows three divisions of a corps with 240 field, 64 medium and 16 heavy guns that could be, and sometimes were, fired as if one big battery.

This is one of several 5.5-inch guns in Normandy – a testimony to the long service of this equipment post war.

The 5.5-in gun was the workhorse of the medium artillery. Its 80lb and 100lb HE rounds contained enough high explosive to damage entrenchments, and its splinters would penetrate light armour. With a 100lb shell its range was an unimpressive 16,500 yds. The lighter 80lb shell extended the range to 18,100 yds. It was towed by the Matador 3-ton 4x4 truck. For counter-battery fire, four batteries were equipped with the 4.5″ gun, which looked similar but had a barrel two feet longer. It was mounted on the same carriage as the 5.5 and fired a 55lb round 20,500 yds.

Heavy regiments were equipped with two types of guns. Each heavy regiment included two batteries of four Ordnance BL 7.2-in howitzers. These were the First World War vintage 8in howitzer relined and fitted with modern sights, pneumatic tyres and brakes. It fired a 202lb HE projectile to 16,900 yds. These were the guns to engage hardened targets. The US M1 155mm 'Long Tom' equipped the other two batteries in heavy regiments. This fired a 100lb shell to a maximum range of 24,050 yds. These were for counter-battery fire.

Each corps was also assigned a survey regiment. All the guns were surveyed to a common grid and azimuth, which was vital to ensure that calls for fire from lots of batteries hit the same target. Survey regiments also deployed flash spotting and sound ranging teams to locate hostile batteries. Royal Air Force tactical reconnaissance aircraft flew artillery photo reconnaissance missions and could conduct shoots, typically against targets well beyond the front line. Air OP squadrons had largely replaced RAF TAC (R) aircraft as artillery spotters close to the front line. It was easier to train an experienced gunner officer to fly an aircraft than to train an RAF pilot to apply artillery tactically. It was also easier to see ground detail from a slow light aircraft than a high-performance fighter.

The Long Tom was the first gun in British service that could match the range of German long-range artillery.

P51 B Mustang III equipped the Tactical Reconnaissance Squadrons of the RAF, who were trained to conduct artillery shoots.

Combined Operations Bombardment Units were the link between naval firepower and the land battle. A special organization was needed because the navy used different procedures and had different communications equipment. Each Combined Operations Bombardment Unit supported an army corps, with a troop supporting a division. Each troop provided seven Forward Observers Bombardment (FOB) and seven Naval Liaison Officers (NLO). The Forward Observers Bombardment were deployed to Battalions or Regiments.

The Auster Mk III light aircraft, flown by artillery officer pilots, was much less vulnerable than feared.

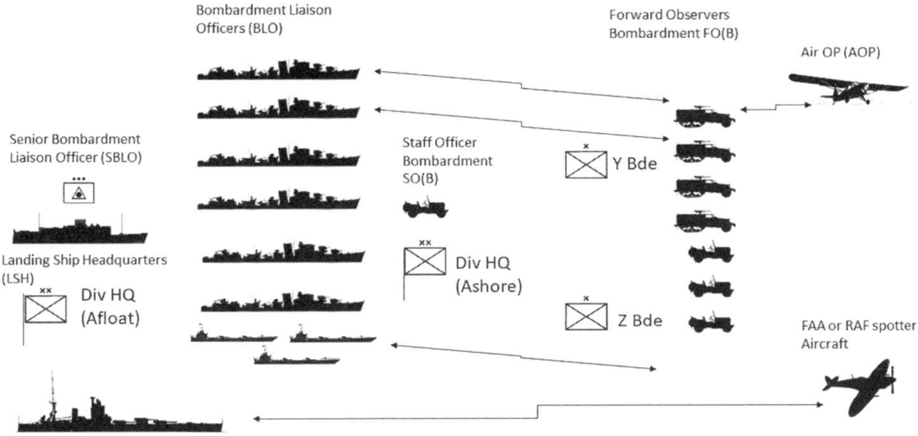

Deployment and communications for naval gunfire.

Each FOB party consisted of an Artillery officer and NCO assistant, and three naval ratings wireless telegraphers. The Troop was equipped with four M14 armoured half-tracks and eight jeeps. Neither was ideal as an OP vehicle. The Naval Liaison officers on ship were key to explaining to the navy what was happening on land, preventing friendly fire incidents and solving communications problems.

Aircraft could be used to direct naval gunfire in two ways. Fleet Air Arm and RAF aircraft were fitted with radios that could communicate directly to warships. The Auster aircraft of the Air OP Squadrons could not communicate directly with a warship so would work with an FOB which would relay messages.

The firepower of the fleet offshore dwarfed the field artillery available for the first few weeks after D-Day.

The Landing Craft Gun (Large) mounted two 4.7–in BL or QF guns on a reinforced deck over the tank well. Its firepower was equivalent to a battery of field guns.

HMS Scourge *fired on targets of Sword Beach. She mounted four 4.7-inch guns.*

HMS Orion, *with her six 6-inch guns that fired a 112lb round to 24,480 yds, was considered the equivalent of a medium regiment.*

HMS **Roberts** ***was a shallow draft craft especially designed for land bombardment. Her 15-inch guns fired a 1,938lb shell 33,500yds. One of her guns is now displayed outside the Imperial War Museum in London.***

- Each of the twenty-seven Landing Craft Gun (Large) mounted two 4.7in (120mm) guns firing a 50 lb HE shell to just under 17,000 yds, and was considered equivalent to a battery of 25-pounder guns.
- A destroyer with four to eight 4in or 4.7in guns with a range of 15,000–17,000 yds was considered the equivalent of a regiment of field artillery
- A light cruiser with six 6in guns fired 112lb rounds 24,480 yds and was considered the equivalent of a medium regiment.
- There was no land artillery equivalent to the 15in and 16in guns of the battleships and monitors that could throw 1-ton projectiles around 32km (20 miles).

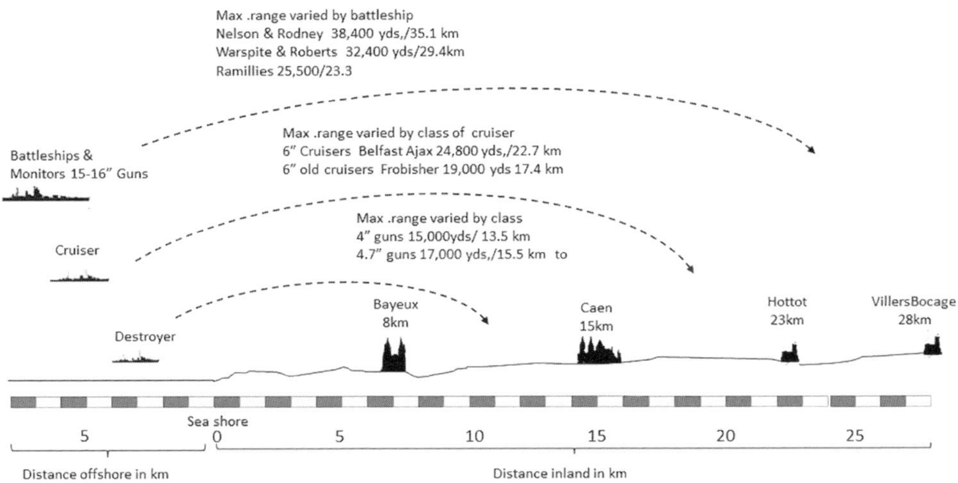

Sketch showing approximate maximum range inland of naval guns off the Normandy coast. One of the furthest inland was a shot by HMS **Rodney** ***on 11 June at a range 33,100 yards against German tanks forming up near Hottot.***

Anti-tank Artillery

Three types of anti-tank guns were used by the Royal Artillery in Normandy: the 6-pounder and 17-pounder towed anti-tank guns, and the M10 tank destroyer, armed with the US 3-in anti-tank gun or the 17-pounder.

The 6-pounder anti-tank gun had a calibre of 57mm and could engage a German tank with an effective range of 500 to 1,000 yards. It was easy to manhandle and easy to conceal. The introduction of Armour Piercing Discarding Sabot (APDS) ammunition made it even more effective. It was manned by both the gunners and the infantry. The cross-country performance of a Universal Carrier towing a 6-pounder gun was described by one senior officer as 'paralytic'.

The 17-pounder anti-tank gun could penetrate any German tank armour at up to about 1,000 yards with Armour Piercing Ballistic Cap Ammunition and up to 2,000 yards with the APDS ammunition that was introduced in August 1944. However, the 17-pounder was an unwieldy weapon, large, heavy and hard to conceal. It took twelve hours for the detachment to dig a hole big enough to conceal the gun. The British struggled to find a suitable tractor. The unarmoured FAT left the detachment vulnerable to mortar and shell splinters and random rounds in a forward area. M14 half-tracks were used in armoured divisions, while turretless Crusader tanks were used by the towed batteries of the corps anti-tank regiments.

The anti-tank regiments of the assault divisions were issued twelve American M10 tank destroyers. These were armed with the US 3in gun. The AP rounds from these could penetrate all but the German Pz VI Tiger and the frontal armour of the Pz V Panther. Although their main role was anti-tank, half their ammunition was HE and they were used extensively as assault guns whenever tanks were unavailable.

Armed with the 17-pounder, the M10 was a terror, capable of knocking out any tank hit.

The M10 was even more effective when the 3in gun was replaced by the 17-pounder. Twenty-four had been converted by D-Day, and half were issued to each of the two corps anti-tank regiments that landed on D-Day (62 and 73 Anti-tank Regiments). Industrial action slowed the delivery of this important equipment.

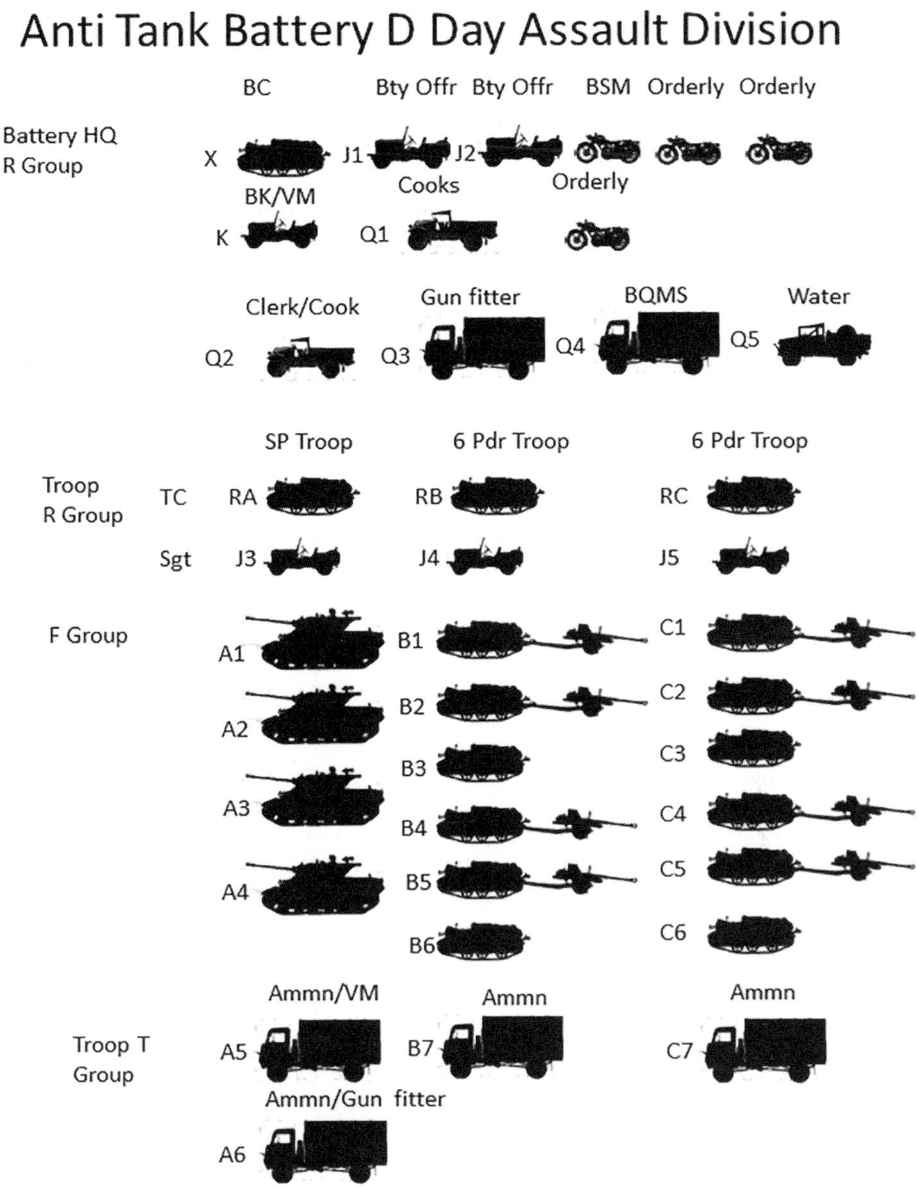

The vehicles of an anti-tank battery in an assault division. Follow on divisions such as 51st Highland would not have had M10 SP guns, but 17-pounder guns towed by field artillery tractors.

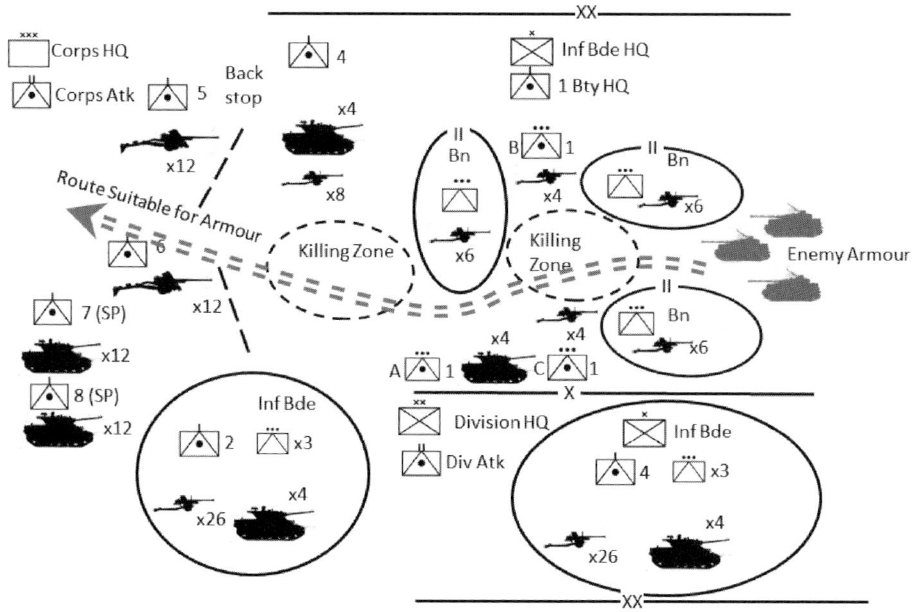

Anti-tank deployment to defend an assault division.

Anti-tank artillery was organized in regiments, consisting of four anti-tank batteries, each of which had three troops of four anti-tank guns. Each troop was commanded by a lieutenant troop commander. There were three types of anti-tank regiment. Anti-tank regiments of infantry divisions were established for thirty-two towed 17-pounders and sixteen 6-pounders, with each battery organized into two troops of towed 17-pounder guns and one 6-pounder troop. However, the anti-tank regiments of the assault divisions (3rd, 3rd Canadian and 50th) were equipped with sixteen 3in M10 SPs and thirty-two 6-pounders, organized in the reverse proportion of troops.

The above diagram illustrates how the divisional and corps anti-tank regiments were organized to support one of the D-Day assault divisions. The 6-pounder-equipped anti-tank platoons of infantry battalions were sited to protect the infantry positions. Gunner 6-pounders and M10s from the divisional regiment were to be sited to kill tanks in brigade killing zones, while 17-pounders were normally used as a final stop line, with the corps M10s anti-tank guns as a reserve. However, there were problems in the attack, which envisaged anti-tank guns deployed soon after an infantry assault to defeat an armoured counter-attack over ground which might be swept by small arms fire or subject to mortar or artillery fire.

The diagram on p.21 shows the main tactical vehicles of 62nd or 73rd Anti-Tank Regiments. Headquarters battery vehicles have been omitted. The corps anti-tank regiments and armoured divisions were equipped with twenty-four 3in or 17-pounder SP M10 and twenty-four towed 17-pounders. The two corps regiments that took part in D-Day (62 and 73) received Crusader gun tractors. The anti-tank regiments of the armoured divisions used M14 half-tracks, while the other corps regiments had to make do with the Quad Field Artillery Tractor.

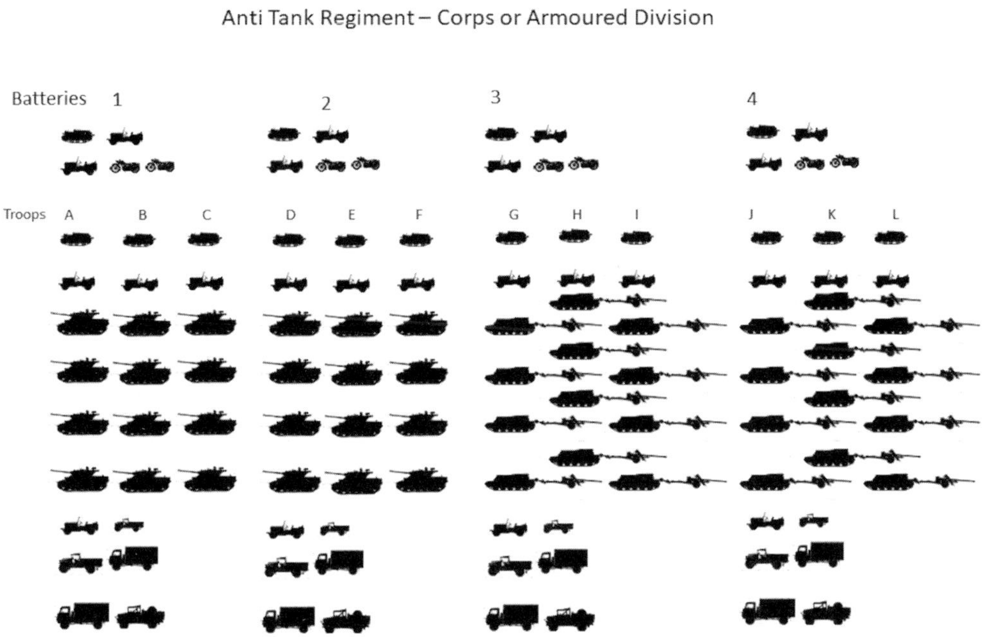

Principal fighting and command vehicles in a corps or divisional anti-tank regiment.

Anti-Aircraft Artillery

Anti-aircraft (AA) artillery was the largest branch of the artillery in the British Army. AA Regiments were formed into AA Brigades, with operational control of AA guns exercised through AA Operations Rooms. AA guns were part of an integrated air defence system, with early warning provided by radar and observer teams, and the AA guns and fighters controlled by sector control centres and a network of AA operations rooms. Anti-aircraft artillery was organized into heavy, light and searchlight regiments.

Each Heavy AA Regiment was formed of three batteries, each of four troops. Heavy AA regiments were equipped with the 3.7in gun. Their main role was to defend vulnerable areas, such as ports and the landing beaches against attacks from high-flying aircraft. Heavy AA was landed early in the Normandy campaign in preference to medium guns, as this gun, like the German Flak 88, was versatile. It had an anti-tank range of about 1,600 yards. Its HE rounds were fitted with mechanical time fuses. In the ground role its range of 16,500 yards was comparable to the 5.5in medium gun and outranged the 25-pounder. The 3.7in AA gun was highly effective against tanks, but its height and weight made it too vulnerable to be used in that role except as a final defence.

The QF 3.7-inch AA gun was the standard British Heavy AA equipment. It was towed by an AEC Matador 4x4 tractor. It was part of a weapon system, including the ammunition, warning, detection and fire control technology. Progressive alterations greatly improved its effectiveness over the course of the war. In its original form the 3.7in gun fired a 28lb (12.7kg) HE shell fitted with a powder-burning fuse, Time No 199, to an effective ceiling of 23,500ft using Predictor No.1 at a maximum eight

SPECIMEN A.A.LAYOUT OF BEACH GROUP AREA

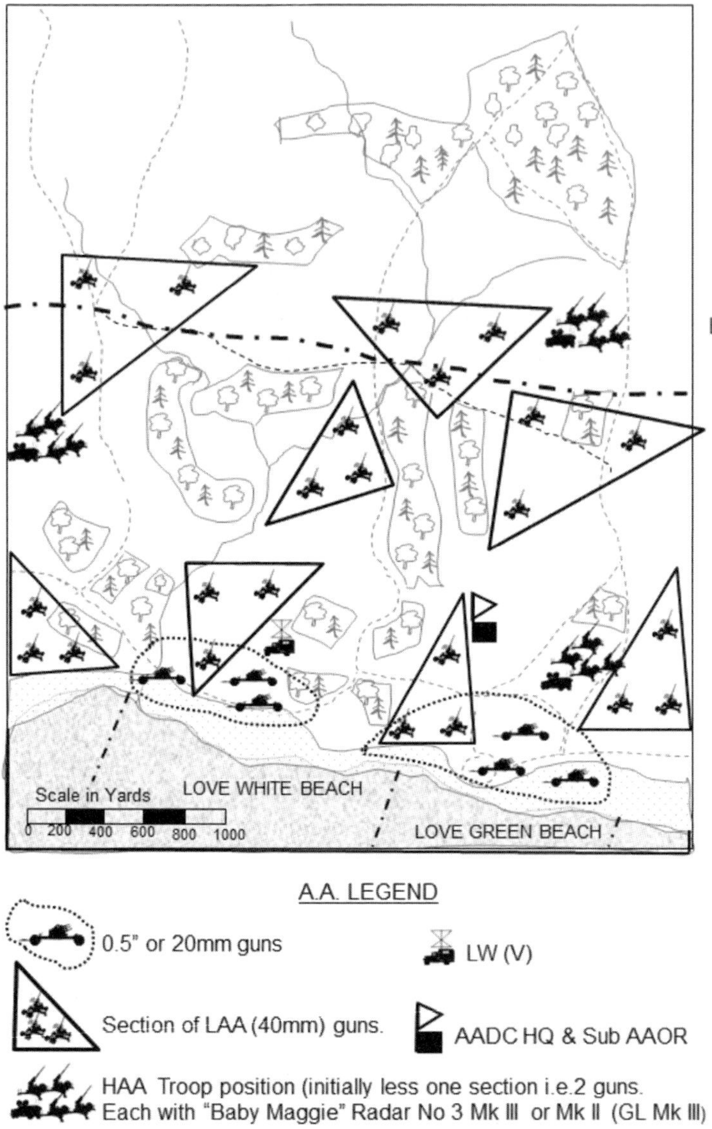

Based on Appendix J to Combined Training Centre Largs Lecture Beach Organisation

This diagram shows an idealised defence of a beachhead by a battery of twelve Heavy AA guns, twenty-four 40mm guns and six 20mm Light AA guns. Guns formed part of an integrated air defence system, with early warning provided by radar and observer teams. The AA guns and fighters were controlled by sector control centres and a network of AA operations rooms. The air defences had their own early warning radar (Light Warning Vehicle mounted: LW (V)). The Sub AAOR was the operations room controlling all AA in the beach subsector, while the AADC was the Anti-Aircraft Defence Commander. The heavy AA guns were also the last line of anti-tank defence for each beach.

The 3.7-inch AA gun was a versatile piece of equipment and was effective against aircraft, ground targets, tanks and ships.

The AA Radar No 3 Mk II GL No 3 was a skilled operator that could detect the splash made by a sea mine dropped by aircraft 10 miles out to sea, or a mortar bomb in flight.

rounds per minute with manual fuse setting and loading. By the end of the war the Mk1-3 equipment firing the same shell with a proximity fuse and predictor No.11 and autoloading had an effective ceiling of 32,000ft and a rate of fire of thirty-two rounds per minute. In the 1940 blitz 18,500 rounds were fired for each aircraft shot down. By 1944 the guns only needed an average of 156 rounds per V1 brought down. Proximity fuses were not used until after the Normandy campaign. In the Normandy campaign the standard fuse was the mechanical, clockwork, time Fuse No. 208, with a maximum running time of 43 seconds. These guns were landed early in the Normandy campaign in preference to medium guns, since they, like the German Flak 88, were versatile. They had an anti-tank range of about 1,600, their HE rounds were fitted with mechanical time fuses, and in the ground role their range of 16,500 yards was comparable to the 5.5in medium gun and outranged the 25-pounder.

The AA Radar No3 Mk II, commonly known as GL (Gun Laying) III, provided unseen fire control for AA guns, enabling them to engage targets at night and through cloud. It was based on the cavity magnetron, a major step forward in radar technology. This allowed for narrower radar beams and smaller antennae. It could pick up and engage targets at a range of 25km (27,000 yards) but had a narrow beam and needed to be pointing in the right direction.

The Anti-Aircraft Radar No.4 Marks II and III had the role of local warning and 'putting on' the GL III radars, that is, pointing them in the right direction with a pick-

This earlier AA Radar No 4 Marks II & III was the equivalent radar to those used to detect enemy aircraft in the Battle of Britain. The presence of classified radars on Heavy AA sites is probably the main reason why there are so few images of Heavy AA in Normandy.

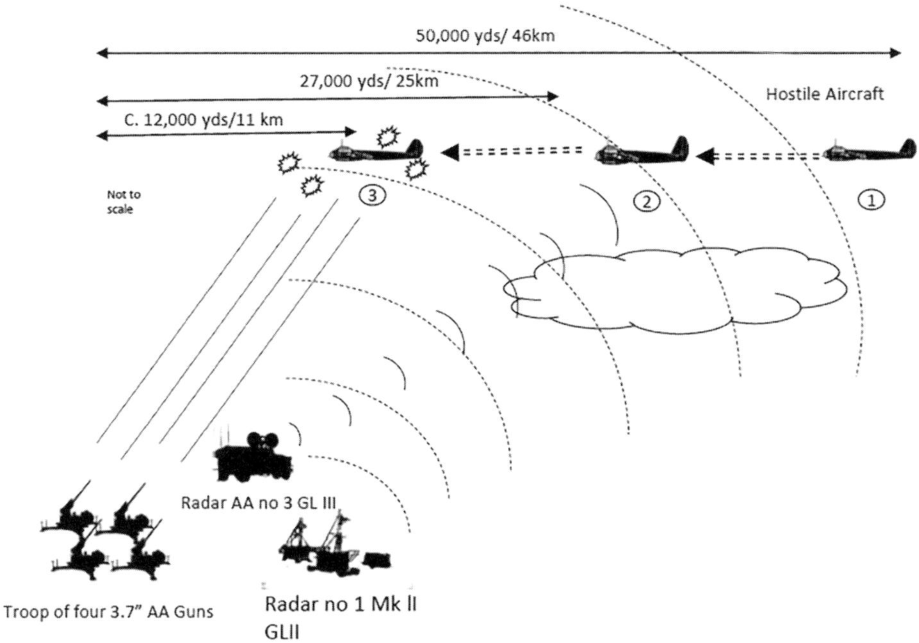

Each heavy AA Troop of four 3.7-inch guns included an Early Warning Radar and a Gun Laying Radar. These were to enable the guns to engage targets at night and through cloud. The set in the diagram is the AA No 1 Mk II, comprising a transmitter and receiver mounted in separate trailers. These had a wide beam and could pick up a target at 50,000yds (28 miles/49km). (1) The AA Radar No 3, known as GL III, was based on centimetric radar and could pick up and control fire at a range of 27,000 yards (25Km) (2). GL III had a directional beam and needed to be oriented by an early warning radar. The firing data for the guns would be calculated by a mechanical predictor and fire at the expected position of the aircraft.

up range of 25 miles (40km) at 3,000ft and 45 miles (72.4km) for targets at 15,000 ft. The GL Mk II Radar consisted of a transmitter and receiver in separate cabins.

Light AA Regiments were to protect against attacks by low-flying aircraft. The main equipment was the 40mm Bofors Light Anti-Aircraft Gun, mainly as towed equipment. Self-propelled versions were based on the Quad Field Artillery Tractor chassis and the Crusader tank. Light AA regiments were established for fifty-four guns, organized into three batteries, each of nine troops of six guns.

The most numerous artillery piece of equipment in Normandy was the 40mm Bofors light anti-aircraft gun. It had a horizontal range of 10,800 yards, but its HE rounds detonated after 3,400 or 5,500 yards. It could engage targets to an altitude of 5,000ft.

As the Allies achieved air superiority, the Germans resorted to attacks at very low level. To meet this threat, and for low-level defence of vulnerable points such as the Mulberry Harbour, the British deployed 20mm calibre Oerlikon cannon, in troops within each Light AA Regiment as well as in AA tanks manned by the Royal Armoured Corps. However, the ammunition for these guns, unlike the 40mm

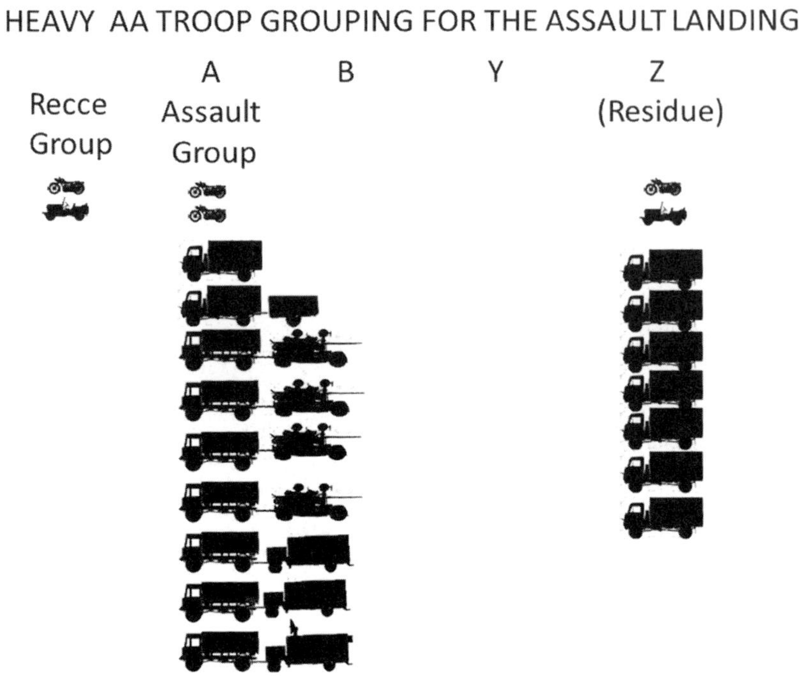

This shows the grouping for a Heavy AA Troop by landing priorities. Limited shipping space forced each unit to prioritise the vehicles. The recce parties reconnoitred the deployment positions. The assault echelon landing with the initial assault consisted of the essential vehicles and equipment needed for up to four days. The Z Group was the balance of vehicles to bring the unit up to the War Establishment. For a Heavy AA Troop, the recce group was the troop commander in a jeep and a dispatch rider. The A Group consisted of the guns, radars, generators, tractors and command vehicles and a single administration vehicle. The remaining ammunition vehicles might only be needed if the unit deployed at some distance from the beachhead.

The Bofors Gun was towed by the Bedford QLB Bofors Tractor. This image from the North African campaign shows some of the detachment travelling on the gun, which could be fired from its carriage.

The SP Bofors mounted the Bofors Gun on a modified chassis of a Morris Field Artillery Tractor. It was faster in and out of action than the towed equipment and popular with the gunners.

Half of the Bofors Guns that landed on the D-Day beaches to protect the beachheads were mounted on Crusader tank chassis, which allowed the gun to be used in the surf.

The Polsten 20mm AA gun entered service in 1944 for point defence against very low-flying aircraft. It was far superior than the 20mm Oerlikon AA guns used on ships as the latter lacked self-destructing ammunition, thus limiting its use on land. There were enough Polsten guns to equip the three batteries of the 93 Light AA regiment, in triple mountings on modified Bofors carriages and Crusader tank chassis.

Bofors, did not self-destruct after a set time. This was a severe restriction in the crowded beachhead, and the guns could only be entrusted to well-disciplined AA troops. There were enough Polsten guns to equip the three batteries of the 93 Light AA regiment, in triple mountings on modified Bofors carriages and Crusader tank chassis. This unit landed on D-Day as part of the AA Brigades.

Chapter 3

The Germans

Gerd v. Rundstedt (Commander-in Chief in the West) in the centre, with Erwin Rommel (Commander Army Group B) on the left.

The German High Command did not agree on its defensive tactics. Hitler had ordered the coast itself to form the main defensive positions, based on the fortifications of the Atlantic Wall. General von Rundstedt, the Commander West, and his staff argued that the Germans lacked the troops to cover every section of coastline; therefore, panzer divisions and other mobile troops should be held centrally to deliver a counter-blow.

Colonel General Friedrich Dollman, Commander of the Seventh Army and a former Inspector of Artillery. Although all the German generals in command on the British sector were artillerymen, German artillery was largely ineffective on D-Day.

General Erich Marcks, German General of Artillery, Commander LXXXIV Army Korps.

Generalleutnant Wilhelm Richter, Commander 716th Infantry Division, another German gunner.

Generalleutnant Edgar Feuchtinger, Commander 21st Panzer Division, was an artillery not a panzer officer.

Major Alfred Becker was the inspirational engineer behind 21st Panzer Division's scrapyard artillery.

Hitler appointed Field Marshal Erwin Rommel to inspect the Atlantic Wall defences in late 1943. Rommel's experience was that Allied air superiority would prevent the kind of manoeuvres that von Rundstedt's staff envisaged. He recommended an extreme form of coastal defence, gambling on stopping the invaders at the waterline itself. Rommel's views were in line with those of Hitler and his Supreme Command of the Armed Forces, the *Oberkommando der Wehrmacht* (OKW). On 1 January 1944 Rommel was appointed to command the two armies on the Channel coast, the most likely invasion front, combined as Army Group B. This appointment galvanized activity on the Channel front, and defenders spent the next six months building obstacles and fortifications, even to the neglect of training.

Five of the seven German generals in the chain of command in the British Second Army sector were artillery officers: 716th Infantry Division was commanded by Lieutenant General Friedrich-Wilhelm Richter, who had commanded non-mechanized Artillery Regiment No 30 in Belgium, France and Russia. Richter reported to General of Artillery Erich Marcks, the commander of LXXXIV Army Corps, responsible for the defence of Lower Normandy and the Cotentin peninsula. On D-Day Marcks reported to Generaloberst Dollmann, who commanded the Seventh Army, responsible for the defence of Normandy and Brittany. Dollmann was another artilleryman, who had served in the First World War as an aerial observer. At the top of the Nazi regime, two of Hitler's closest staff officers; Wilhelm Keitel, the Chief of Staff of OKW, and Alfred Jodl, Chief of the Operations Staff of OKW, were also gunners. None of these men had commanded mechanized troops.

The German defences

Owing to the shortage of manpower, defences would be organized in strong points at the expense of depth. Each strongpoint (*Stützpunkt*) might be based on a company of 50–120 men. A defence post (*Widerstandsnest* – WN) might contain a section of ten to twenty men and one to three anti-tank guns. The scarcity of men might mean additional small posts were required, with perhaps one light machine gun, to maintain observation without a break over the whole coastal sector. At night, patrols would be undertaken as far as possible on bicycles.

The coastline to be attacked by the Anglo-Canadian force was low in the German defensive priorities. The Channel Islands, the Port of Cherbourg and the Eastern Cotentin coast all had a higher priority than the coast between the Vire and the Orne. The German Navy had advised that reefs offshore made this sector an unlikely invasion zone. Only the rocky western Cotentin coast had a lower priority in German preparations.

Engaging ships at sea was the responsibility of the Coastal Artillery, under the command of the German Navy. Army Coastal Artillery Battalion (HKK) 1260, with three four-gun batteries, was responsible for the sector between the Vire and Dives, and HKK 1255 was situated to its east between the Dives and the Seine, with three six-gun and one four-gun batteries.

German positions were strengthened with a mix of field defences and concrete fortifications. Many anti-tank guns and some infantry weapons were emplaced in concrete bunkers. Standardized open concrete 'Tobruk' posts were provided for machine guns, mortars and light anti-tank guns, as were concrete shelters to protect

The Fw 190 was the principal German ground-attack aircraft in the West in 1944. It was armed with cannon and bombs or cluster bomb and minelets.

troops from a bombardment. Concrete circular artillery emplacements allowed artillery pieces to be traversed to hit targets inland as well as on the coast. During 1944 many artillery embrasures were built for field and coastal artillery pieces. These provided overhead protection for the gun detachment, but at the expense of a limited arc of fire and concealment. Each position was supported by a reserve. Companies were expected to keep a section as a reserve, regiments a company, and divisions a battalion.

Until March 1944 the sector between the Dives and the Vire had been the responsibility of the 716th Infantry Division. This was one of the weakest formations on the invasion coast and formed of only two infantry regiments: 726 Infantry Regiment on the west covered the Bayeux Sector, while 736 was responsible for the Caen sector on the eastern half of the Division's area of responsibility. In the six months before D-Day, an additional force, the 352nd Infantry Division, took over the Bayeux area and superimposed two of its regiments on the positions of 726 Regiment.

As a result of Rommel's emphasis on coastal defence, the Caen sector was further reinforced. The 716th Infantry Division was reinforced with Heavy Artillery Battalion No.989 deployed in the Caen sector. This was equipped with twelve ex-Soviet 12.2cm heavy howitzers. Half of the 21st Panzer Division's infantry – two panzer grenadier battalions, the anti-tank battalion, part of the divisional AA battalion and an artillery battalion of twelve guns – all deployed north of Caen, where they would come under the command of the 716th Division. Richter could call on a total of seventy field artillery pieces. These could provide a defensive barrage 3,500m long, not much shorter than the 4km assault frontages of the ten battalions that would make the seaborne assault. For every 200m of assault, a German battery could create a pattern of shells criss-crossing the beach with supersonic fragments.

The Germans had not agreed where to deploy the armoured reserves by D-Day. Rommel wanted to deploy the panzer divisions as close to the coast as possible, while Von Rundstedt's OB West staff argued for a central reserve. Hitler's solution was to assign three of the panzer divisions to Rommel as Army Group B Reserve, while retaining a further four as an OKW Reserve. The resulting compromise satisfied

A 7.5cm PAK 40 manned by SS men from the 12th SS Hitlerjugend Division.

neither party. The immediate reserves in the Caen sector were the 21st Panzer Division, which was deployed between Caen and Falaise, and the 12th SS Panzer Division near Liseaux.

The 21st Panzer Division owed its existence to the initiative and engineering talents of Major Alfred Becker, an artillery officer and professional engineer, and the political influence of Major General Edgar Feuchtinger, another artilleryman. As a *Hauptmann* (Captain), Becker mechanized his own battery by mounting his howitzers on to the chassis of AFVs captured in 1940. Impressed by the performance of these improvised weapons and Becker's initiative, Hitler sent Becker to Paris to oversee the renovation and conversion of the stocks of captured vehicles and scrap. *Baustab* Becker (Becker's construction staff) restored or converted approximately 1,800 vehicles, including self-propelled anti-tank guns, self-propelled howitzers, armoured observation posts, armoured personnel and munitions carriers, supply vehicles, multiple rocket launchers and self-propelled flak (AA) guns. Many of these were sent to other fronts.

Those retained in the West were manned with troops deemed surplus to requirements by infantry and artillery units. In spring 1943 these were designated the Schnell Brigade West. Manpower was recruited from the artillery and infantry units on the Channel coast. In July 1943 these were designated the 21st Panzer Division, which had been destroyed in Tunisia, and received approximately 2,000 reinforcements from its survivors. Its establishment table was based on the equipment provided by Becker.

One of Major Becker's creations: a Hotchkiss H39 based GW H39 7.5cm Pak 40.

A 5cm KwK/Pak 38 emplaced at Courseulles-sur-Mer. Several of these obsolescent anti-tank guns were sited in fixed mountings. Capable of penetrating allied tanks landing on D-Day, they would make a mess of a landing craft.

The 21st Panzer Division was extremely strong in artillery. The two panzer grenadier regiments each had six SP 15cm guns and four SP multiple 8cm mortars, while 155 Artillery Regiment was equipped with two rather than one battalion of self-propelled guns; its observation troops were mounted in armoured OP vehicles, and it possessed an additional section of two self-propelled *Nebelwefer* multiple rocket launchers.

The Division had an assault artillery battalion (*Sturm-Artillerie Abteilung* 200) with fifty self-propelled guns, four batteries each of six 7.5cm anti-tank guns and four 10.5cm howitzers mounted on a Hotchkiss chassis, and two more commanded by Becker himself. Two, rather than one, of its infantry battalions were mounted in half-tracked Armoured Personnel Carriers. The panzer regiment was relatively weak. Its original obsolescent French tanks were only replaced by Panzer IV tanks weeks before D-Day. It was well equipped for defensive rather than offensive operations.

Feuchtinger had few of the leadership qualities expected of a panzer division commander. However, he was shrewd enough to recruit competent panzer commanders as subordinates, including *Ritterkreutz* holder and Olympic medal winner *Oberst* (Colonel) Opplen-Brokinski to command the 22 Panzer Regiment, and Lieutenant Colonel Hans von Luck to command 125 Panzer Grenadier Regiment.

German Artillery

The Germans had an artillery system that looked superficially like the British. A division had an integral divisional artillery regiment, commanded by an *Oberstleutnant* (Lieutenant Colonel). A regiment was divided into two to four *Abteilungen* (battalions) commanded by a major. Each *Abteilung* of three batteries could provide a liaison officer to an affiliated Regiment. Each *Batterie* had a battery commander and an observation section capable of providing an OP party.

A German *Batterie* was the equivalent of a British troop with four guns and one OP Party. The Germans had around half as many artillery observers and were less

A pak 41/43 88mm anti-tank gun of the type deployed on the D-Day beaches.

lavishly equipped with communications. Nor did they have the communication and technical staff, counter-battery target location organization or survey teams of the British. They lacked air support and were unable to make use of air OPs. Crucially, the Germans lacked artillery ammunition. For every shell they fired the British could return ten.

The Germans also had a class of artillery not adopted by the British Army. Each infantry regiment had a gun company as its 15th company. These were equipped with 15cm and 7.5cm howitzers manned by infantrymen and providing guaranteed artillery support for the regiment.

The main German field artillery piece was the 10.5cm Field Howitzer; 352 Artillery Regiment, of 352nd Infantry Division was equipped with thirty-six of these pieces and a further twelve 15cm howitzers. This was a non-motorized formation reliant on horse transport. The Germans also used captured Czech, French, Italian and Russian artillery, which was issued to static formations manning the Atlantic Wall. This complicated ammunition supplies.

The Germans also made use of assault artillery, *Sturmgeschutz.* (StuG). These armoured artillery pieces, manned by the artillery arm, were used to support infantry with direct and sometimes indirect fire. Self-propelled artillery and anti-tank guns were used interchangeably in the anti-tank role. The anti-tank battalion of the 352nd Infantry Division was equipped with ten *Sturmgeschutz* assault guns.

One of the 10cm leFH 14/19 of 3./AR 1716 captured at the Daimler position at Coleville. This Czech artillery piece also equipped the batteries at Merville, Breville, Ver-sur-Mer and Crépon.

Mortars and multiple rocket launchers (*Nebelwerfers*) which could deliver a high volume of fire quickly enabled the Germans to make the best use of their limited ammunition and move before the Allies could retaliate. Each German infantry battalion included a heavy weapons company which operated mortars. The Germans deployed some multiple rocket launchers on the beaches. The 21st Panzer Division's rocket projector company was deployed in support of the 716th Division.

German observation parties were equipped with binocular periscopes, which allowed the observer to remain behind cover. The Germans did use sound ranging and flash spotting to locate enemy batteries, but there were no units of this type close to the D-Day beaches in the first week after the invasion.

The Germans used wireless radio and telephones, backed up by dispatch riders and pigeons. German equipment was good. However, the Germans reported many difficulties using wireless in the trees and hedges of Normandy. The wirelesses used a VHF frequency range which overlapped with those used by the US Army, resulting in interference. They were also inhibited by a widespread belief that the Allies had well developed tactical radio direction-finding to locate German OP parties using wireless. Static formations were short of radios, although many of their defence posts were linked by secure voice communications using modulated light or infra-red waves (*Lichtsprechgerät*). This had a range of 3–4km but would be interrupted by mist or smoke.

German indecision about their armoured reserves would hamper the effectiveness of their artillery in Normandy. There was a shortage of 1:25,000 maps. The Germans did not survey artillery positions to support a fight inland from the beaches, because Rommel's and Hitler's plan was to defeat the Allies on the beaches themselves. Nor did the armoured reserves have the logistics to support a sustained battle. They would be commanded by an operational headquarters (*Panzer Gruppe West*) and for supplies they were dependent on the Seventh Army.

Anti-tank Artillery

The 5cm *PanzerAbwehrKanone* (Anti-tank gun, or PAK) 38 had been superseded as the standard anti-tank gun. However, it would penetrate the armour of an M4 Sherman, and 5cm PAK were deployed in static mounts in the Atlantic Wall defences, manned by the anti-tank companies of the static infantry regiments.

The 7.5cm PAK 40 was the standard anti-tank gun in 1944. It was mounted on a towed gun carriage and on a variety of self-propelled mounts. The anti-tank battalion of 716th division had nine 7.5cm towed anti-tank guns and ten on self-propelled chassis.

The 8.8cm AA gun was one of the most effective German anti-tank weapons of the Second World War. It was adapted as an anti-tank gun, mounted on a field gun carriage, as the PAK 41/43. Several of these were deployed on the beaches. The 21st Panzer Division's anti-tank battalion was equipped with twenty-four 8.8cm anti-tank guns, and the anti-tank battalion of the 716th Infantry Division had a further two or three.

Some obsolete 3.7cm anti-tank guns and a variety of captured Italian, Russian and Czech anti-tank guns were also deployed in static positions as part of the Atlantic Wall.

A Panzer IV H of the 21st Panzer Division. The armoured skirts and turret screen gave this 23-ton tank a similar appearance to the 56-ton Mk VI Tiger tank.

Anti-Aircraft

The Germans had an extensive *FliegerAbwehrKanone* (anti-aircraft, or Flak) arm. There were three main anti-aircraft weapons used.

The 8.8cm Flak 36/37 AA gun was the standard heavy AA gun. It was used in the AA role in conjunction with anti-aircraft fire control equipment that enabled the guns to be trained to deliver air-burst shells at the point where an aircraft was predicted to be. The Flak 36/37 was rarely used in the anti-tank role in Normandy. It was not as effective as the 7.5cm PAK 40 in the anti-tank role, and in any case, flak gunners

Easy to deploy and hard to detect, German mortars caused the Allies more problems than field artillery.

Another creation from Major Becker's workshop. German gunners loading a self-propelled multiple mortar for a demonstration at the chateau at Lion-sur-Mer before D-Day.

A self-propelled multiple rocket launcher of the 21st Panzer Division.

The 2cm Flak 30 was widely deployed for low level air defence. This example, on Meuvaines ridge overlooking Gold Beach, is being examined by British servicemen.

were fully employed protecting the Germans from air attack. The 8.8cm Flak played a more important role in supplementing German field artillery. In the ground role, 8.8 cm Flak had a longer range than the British 25-pounder. Flak units had good communications, were better supplied with ammunition than the field artillery and enjoyed a high proportion of time and mechanical fuses to support air burst shoots.

The 3.7cm Flak 38 was roughly comparable to the British Bofors. It was lighter and had a higher rate of fire, but had a shorter range and fired a lighter projectile. These guns were often mounted on half-tracked vehicles.

The 2cm Flak 30/38 was the most widely deployed German light AA gun. Individual guns were added to the establishments of field and coastal gun batteries. They were the armament of the Flak sections of panzer grenadier regiments. The 2cm Flak ammunition would self-destruct after between four and five and a half seconds, which created less collateral damage than the Allied 20mm Oerlikon.

German Flak was reasonably effective in providing air defence for the German army. It could not prevent Allied aircraft from attacking but could exact a toll on the Allied air forces and disturb a pilot's aim.

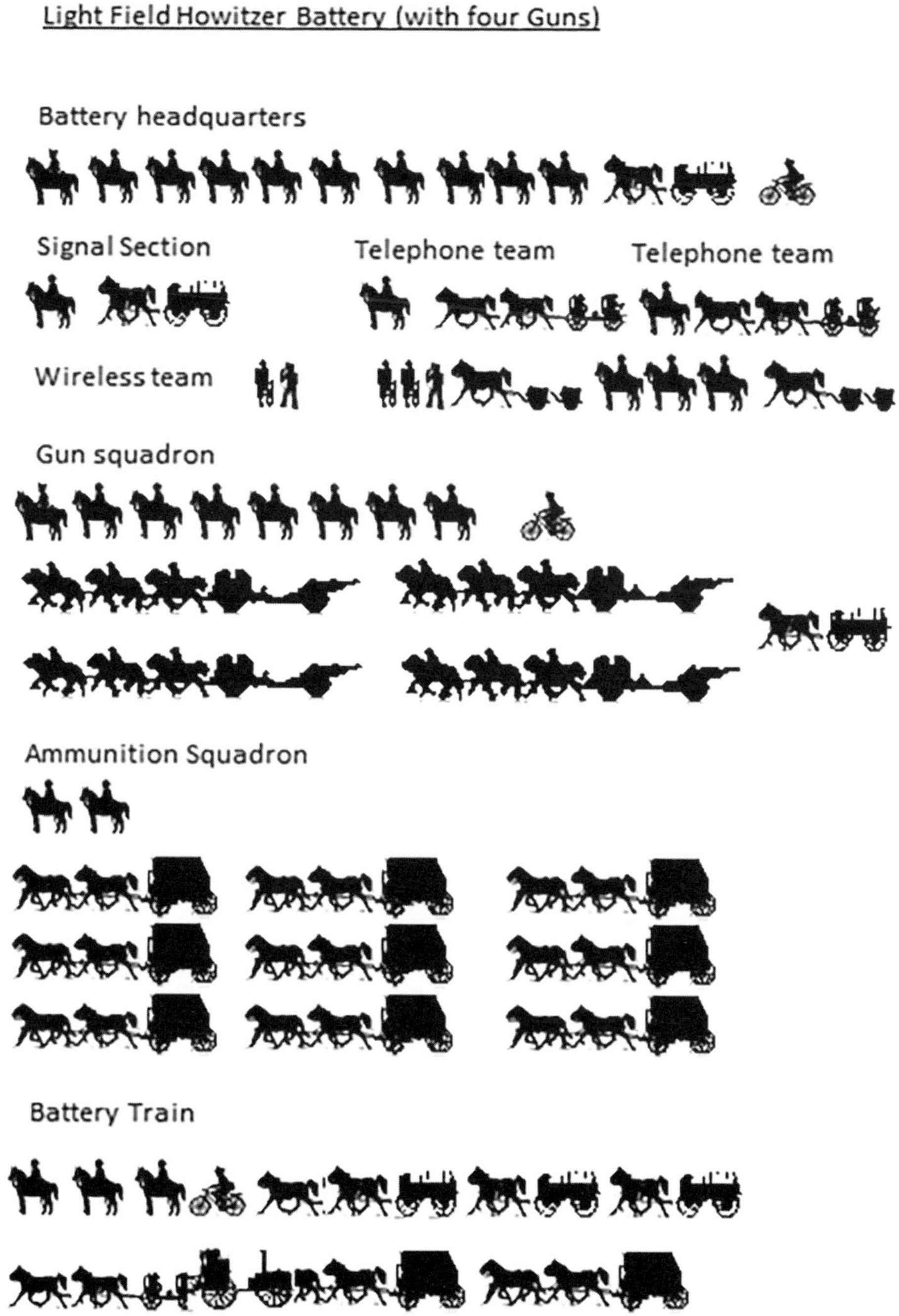

The authorised organization of a four-gun light howitzer battery in a non-motorised infantry division such as the 352nd. It has comparable firepower to a British field artillery troop, but with more manpower, mostly to look after the battery's 102 horses. The artillery of static formations such as 716th Infantry Division needed to borrow or hire horses to move.

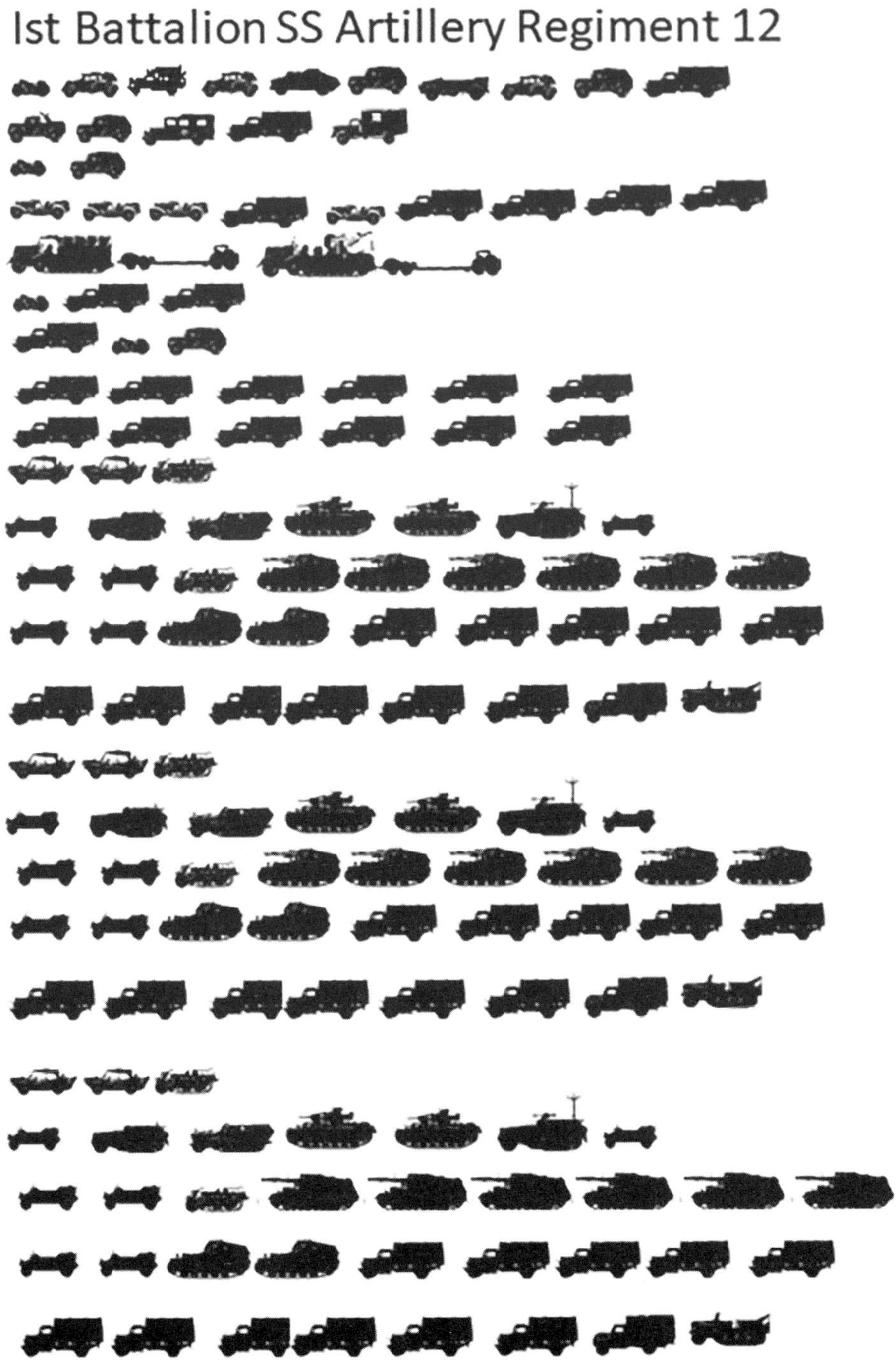

The 1st Battalion of SS Artillery Regiment 12 was motorised and equipped with self-propelled guns, half-tracked carriers as command posts and tanks as armoured observation posts. It was comparable to a British SP regiment, but with only eighteen larger calibre, guns.

Chapter 4

Preparing For D-Day

There were several tasks for the artillery. The army would need firepower to breach Fortress Europe by destroying or neutralizing defences. The advance inland would need indirect firepower to neutralize defenders and anti-tank guns to protect against armoured attack. The beachheads would need protection from air, ground and sea attack.

The navy's warships would take on coastal batteries and could provide special craft, based on landing-craft hulls, such as gun craft designed to give similar fire to that of the army's field guns. Fighter aircraft could provide fleeting direct close support. Heavy bombing could help in a period of preparation or deliver a sudden smashing blow to fill the gaps in fire support during the initial stage of the landings. One of the most important functions of the Air Force would be to help slow up enemy movements towards the area of assault. But what could the army do while still afloat?

The 86th (Hertfordshire Yeomanry) Field Regiment was given the task of experimenting with firing self-propelled field guns from landing craft. They started by evolving drills to load guns and vehicles into Landing Craft Tanks (LCT), which

A 3.7-inch Heavy AA gun on manoeuvres in the United Kingdom.

A huge park of Bofors guns at the ordnance depot, Bicester. There were reserves in place to replace the anticipated potentially heavy losses.

could only be entered in reverse through the bow ramp. Replicas were staked out on the ground at Blandford, and time was spent placing the guns accurately in relation to the centre line of the vessel and working out how to use every inch of space: for the four guns in a troop as two sections 'forward' and 'aft'; for the vehicles needed on the gun position (especially the GPO's tank, the wireless sets of which were needed to control the run-in shoot); and for OP tanks and carriers.

The first experiments shooting on to the shore were carried out by 341 and 342 Batteries in Studland Bay, near Poole, in the second half of July and the first half of August 1943. The GPO would align his guns to the centre line of the vessel and apply any 'switch' necessary to compensate for sailing 'up-tide', but the vessel's heading, which was the captain's responsibility, would determine the direction in which the shells departed. (The captain had some help; all six LCTs travelled in a tight group on a common heading dictated by a radar-equipped motor-launch, which accompanied the group). Range was set on the gun sights in accordance with a 'range clock', which was synchronized to a speed of six knots (200 yards per minute). The range clock became known as the 'Coventry Clock' after the artillery officer who thought of the idea.

Gunners did not begin to train with the craft from which they would land in Europe until a few weeks before the invasion. By the time all the necessary trials and training were finished, it was proved to everybody' s satisfaction that a self-propelled regiment loaded by troops in six LCT Mk. IV could produce a concentration covering an area of 300 by 300 yards.

Corrections to the predicted fire would be made by a control FOO travelling with the navigation leader. A FOO would travel with each assault company and control the fire of the SP artillery and tank guns on the LCT(A) when ashore. There might

This sketch shows guns of A Troop 90th Field Regiment on LCT 2144, Leslie Herbert 357 battery.

be FOOs travelling with reserve companies and an additional FOO per regiment in an independent craft. An artillery officer travelled with the deputy senior officer of the assault group. Another artillery officer would travel with the navigation officer to brief the Gun Position Officers on the craft. The two regiments supporting an assault brigade were grouped under the senior regimental commander and travelled with the assault brigade commander.

The guns would open fire from 11,000 yards (10,050m) until the range shortened to 3,000 yards (2,740m). With the LCTs travelling at 6 knots this would take 45 minutes. The operation was controlled on four radio nets, three RA and one Royal Navy.

The field army in Britain started undertaking exercises to simulate a landing on a foreign shore in spring 1943. Until then, major exercises had been focused on defending Britain against a German landing.

By mid-1943 the procedures for landing an infantry brigade group supported by armour, artillery and engineers had been developed. Combined Operations established a training course for commanders and staff officers to enable them to plan their part in a landing by a brigade group.

Artillery units needed to practise the technical drills of moving, deploying and firing. They also needed to train with the armour and infantry with whom they would work. Training was built up with larger and larger organizations. Troops would train under the troop commander, then the batteries, then the whole regiment and then the regiments within a division. Training might be 'dry', in other words without ammunition, or 'live firing' on artillery ranges.

Some training could take place in barracks or billets. Gun detachments could practise gun drill on any flat ground. Signallers practised Morse code and establishing communications, and technicians calculated firing data. It was even possible to practise observing and correcting the fall of shot on a 'puff range' – a sheet of cloth stretched over a frame, painted to represent countryside. Trainee observers would give the fire orders as if sent to the guns. A technician under the frame would calculate where the shot would fall and blow cigarette smoke through the cloth. The trainee would then order a correction also applied via cigarette puffs.

Not everything could be practised in camp. Drivers needed skills beyond simply driving safely, since 1940s vehicles lacked synchromesh gearboxes, and changing gear took technique. So did driving cross-country, towing a trailer or gun, driving a tank, driving at night in convoy with only a faint light at the rear, or deploying as a troop, battery and regiment at night quietly. If equipment changed, then these skills might need re-learning.

Training exercises with whole units would practise movement and deployment, while communications and fire orders might be practised with a command post exercise, which just involved the observation posts and command posts, often practising over realistic communications distances. In wartime Britain these exercises could take place over the countryside, with due regard for avoiding damage to crops.

Guns would practise engaging tanks on anti-tank ranges, many firing out to sea. Indirect live firing by field and medium artillery needed a target area of many square miles, mainly on the ranges at Okehampton, Sennybridge, Otterburn and Salisbury Plain. Anti-aircraft ranges were typically sited on the coast, where firing could take place safely, usually against a drone target towed by an aircraft on a long line.

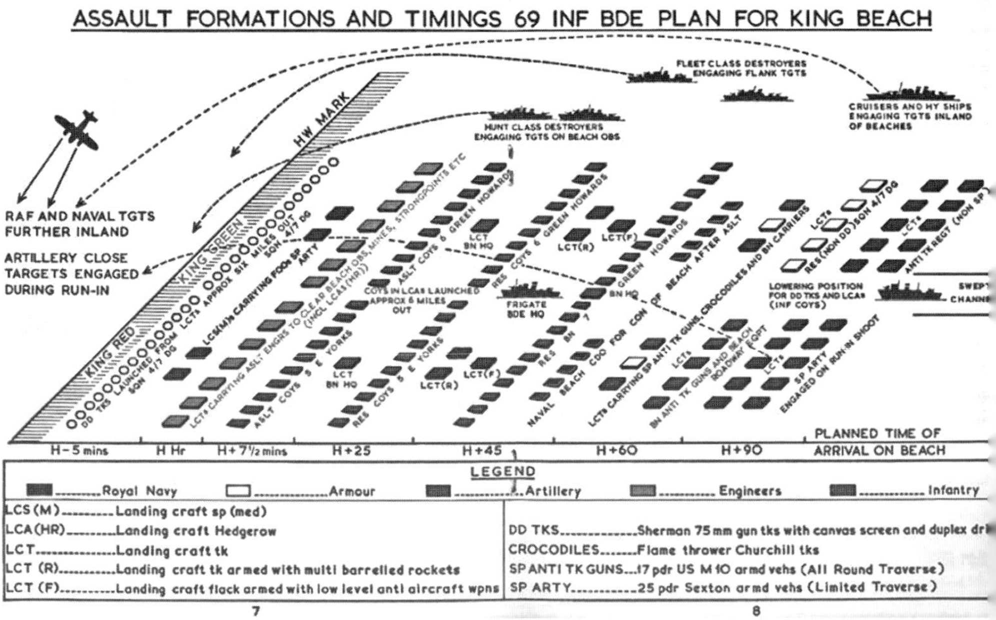

This much-reproduced sketch shows the assault brigade landing on King Beach. It omits the Centaur tanks operated by the Royal Marine Armoured Support Group. This is because the sketch was prepared from a handout on a training course produced before the decision was made to add the Centaurs.

Gun detachment maintaining a Priest of 3 British Division before D-Day. The M7 Priest, based on an M3 tank chassis, was a reliable vehicle, a feature much appreciated by gun detachments. The only item to wear was the rubber on the bogie wheels.

Gunners were soldiers first. The soldiers who landed on D-Day were given some of the most rigorous training devised for a mass army. At battle schools, troops trained with live ammunition and were exposed to incoming fire. Training was physically hard, and living conditions were basic, to inure soldiers to the deprivations of active service.

Artillery would need to learn to work with the infantry and armour. Troop and battery commanders tried to spend time with their affiliated infantry battalion or armoured regiment, understanding how their officers worked and gaining their confidence. Infantry and armoured commanders learned to make the best use of artillery support in different tactical settings. This was accomplished through study days, map exercises and field training.

Training was a continual process. There were always changes. In January 1943 the Hertfordshire Yeomanry needed to train a completely new 462 battery, after most of their battery was taken for a new field regiment. In the next eighteen months they would be re-equipped three times before D-Day. Their 25-pounder towed equipment was replaced in March 1943 with Bishop SP guns, which they trained to fire from landing craft. In September 1943 they were replaced by US-made M7 Priest SP equipment mounting a US 105mm howitzer. This used different ammunition with different firing characteristics to the 25-pounder. Then in March 1944 these were replaced by the 'Sexton' SP equipment mounting the 25-pounder.

How Liverpool and London's Ack Ack prepared to assault Europe

The 103rd Heavy AA Regiment formed in May 1940 in Oswestry was part of Liverpool's air defences, and 393 Liverpudlians joined the regiment to defend their homes. In July 1941 it was given the vehicles to become a mobile unit and assigned an anti-tank role in case the Germans landed heavy tanks. By the end of 1942 103rd Heavy AA Regiment had fired 39,532 rounds, mostly in defence of Liverpool, and had lost twelve killed and thirteen wounded in action.

In December 1942 it was transferred from AA Command to the field force, with the task of protecting landing beaches. Soldiers retrained in the skills needed, including fieldcraft, small arms and camouflage. Wireless sets were issued, and signallers trained. Anti-tank and coastal defence shooting were practised, and detachments practised firing from the wheels as well as their platforms. Radars needed to be persuaded to work in the field. From January 1943, 103rd Regiment practised loading and unloading vehicles and equipment on to dummy Tank Landing Craft (LCT) built on the regimental square.

In April 1943, the 103 HAA Regiment joined the newly formed 80th AA Brigade along with 86th (HAC) Heavy AA, and 73rd and 114th Light AA Regiments. These would be responsible for the air defence of a beachhead and the beach maintenance

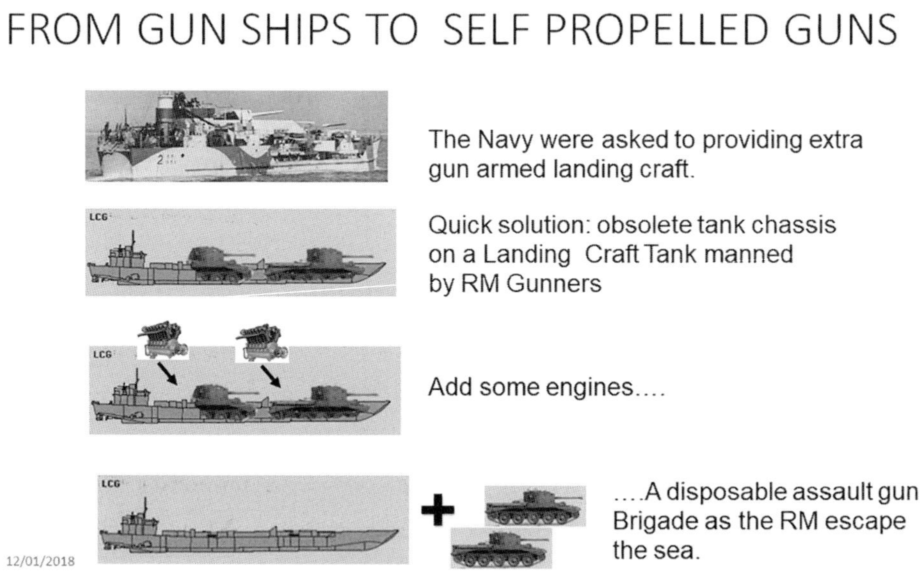

The evolution of the Royal Marines Armoured Support Group. Starting from the idea of using obsolescent tanks as gun turrets on a landing craft, through dropping the tanks as static pill boxes to a disposable self-propelled artillery brigade. One key factor was the enthusiasm and fighting spirit of the Royal Marine artillerymen: 'A fine bunch of chaps'.

Canadian artillerymen on a command post exercise, practising technical procedures until they become second nature.

area inland. Soon after landing, the expeditionary force would recreate the Great Britain air defence system, with its radar and communications integrated with the Air Force. The summer of 1943 was spent in amphibious training, embarking and disembarking from real landing craft and working with other units. In December 1943 80th AA Brigade was organized into two battlegroups of combined heavy and light anti-aircraft artillery, one for each sector of the beach.

The 86th HAC Heavy AA Regiment had a similar story. The Honourable Artillery Company is an unusual, very British institution. Originally founded in 1537 to provide officers for the Trained Bands of London, it was a civic organization until it became part of the British Army in 1902.

The Worcestershire Hussars take to the air

The 53rd (Queens Own Worcestershire Hussars Yeomanry) Regiment RA had also been originally raised as cavalry and only converted to artillery in the 1920s, although they were an anti-tank regiment with a heroic history. Some of their soldiers had been sacrificed defending the hilltop town of Cassel, others were executed by the SS after ambushing German tanks outside Wormhout.

By October 1943, the regiment was apparently surplus to requirements, after their armoured division had been disbanded. Their task was testing one of every type of vehicle to be landed on the D-Day beaches on a similar beach in the UK. The CO, Lieutenant Colonel Teacher, was summoned to an interview with the Director Royal Artillery. He feared the decision might have been taken to disband the regiment. Instead, he was made a proposition: 'The 6th Airborne Division is a new division. Would the Worcestershire Yeomanry care to join it as its only field artillery?' There was only one possible answer.

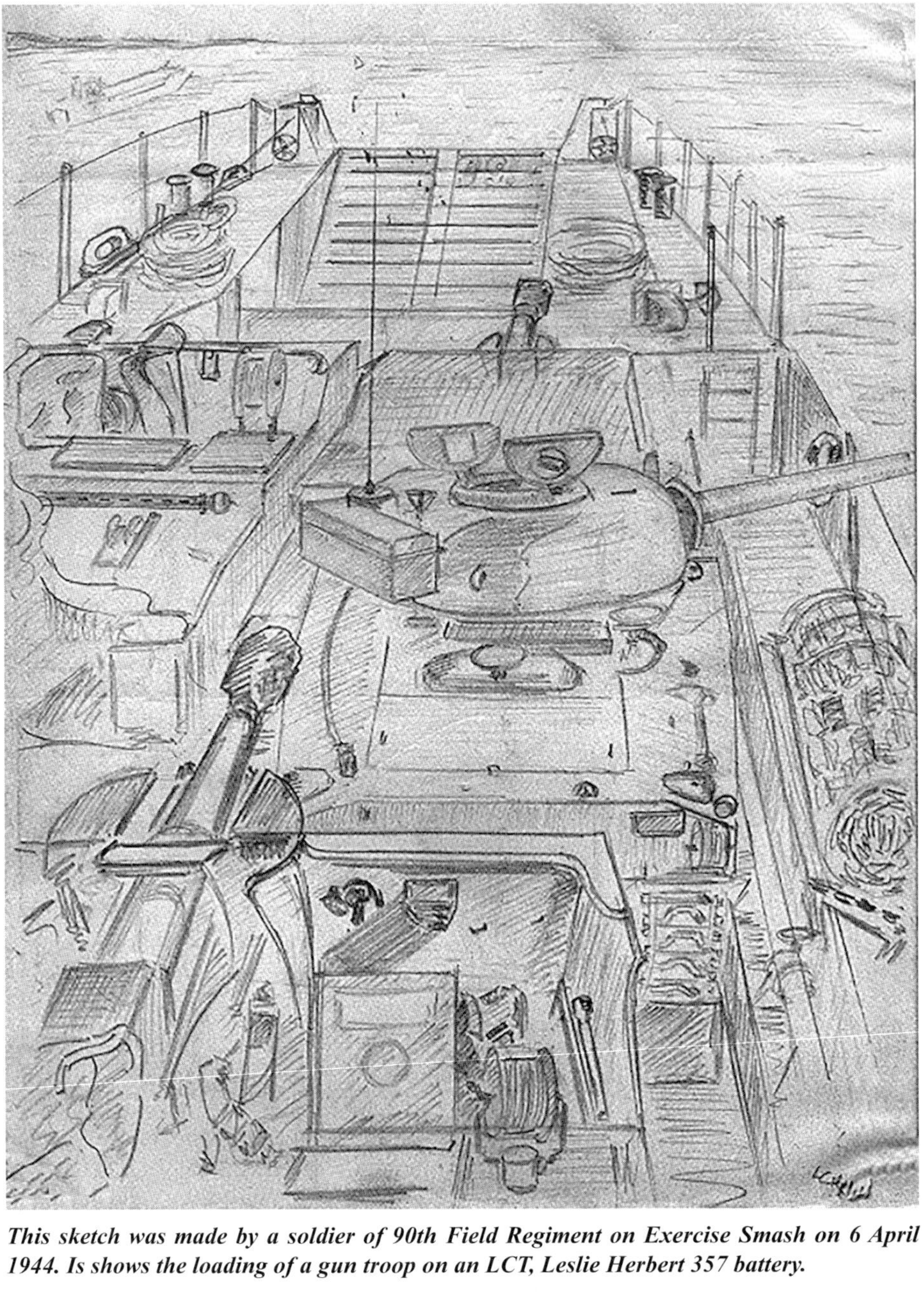

This sketch was made by a soldier of 90th Field Regiment on Exercise Smash on 6 April 1944. Is shows the loading of a gun troop on an LCT, Leslie Herbert 357 battery.

The seven months from 3 November 1943 to 5 June 1944 were hectic. There was much to learn. Indirect field artillery is technically more complicated than anti-tank gunnery. Air landing training started on 13 March 1944 with instruction in loading, lashing and unloading equipment from gliders. On the night of 15 March, ten of the regiment's signallers took part in a massed parachute jump. Then on 9 March the whole regiment was taken into the air in eighty gliders – one of which crashed in the sea, killing two gunners. In April 1944 the 6th Airborne Division deployed on a rehearsal, protecting the flank of an infantry division landing by sea and the gunners practised ferrying guns on rafts across the River Avon at Amesbury.

The Brigadier's problem – the D-Day fire plan

Despite his relatively junior rank, H. J. 'Hatchet Jack' Parham was one of the most influential British artillerymen of the Second World War. He had commanded 10th Field Regiment in France in 1940, when he foresaw the potential of wireless communications to control artillery and trained his unit to use radios in a new disciplined way to concentrate the fire of the twenty-four guns of his regiment on to the Germans. After Dunkirk, as the Commander Royal Artillery of the 38th Division in the UK Home Forces, he demonstrated a method of concentrating the fire of the seventy-two guns of a division quickly and switching it between targets. Despite calculation errors resulting in senior officer casualties in a disastrous firepower demonstration, he had proved his point. This was a turning point for the techniques of massed artillery fire which were a characteristic feature of British Army doctrine.

HM King and Queen inspect the newly converted 53 Air Landing Regiment before D-Day. There were many inspections and pep talks like this, and every witness seems to have been impressed by the King.

Parham was a qualified pilot and convinced of the value of aerial observation. In his view, the fighter aircraft used by the RAF flew too fast to observe the battlefield. It was easier to teach a trained artillery officer to fly than teach an airman to understand the ground battle. As the senior artillery officer of the British First Army, he had supported the use of Air OPs during the Tunisia campaign, which demonstrated its value and survivability.

At the start of 1944 Parham became involved in planning Operation Overlord, as the Brigadier Royal Artillery adviser to Lieutenant General Miles Dempsey, GOC Second Army. The corps commanders and their CCRAs and the commanders and CCRAs of the assaulting divisions decided where they wanted their fire to come down, before and during the assault, and planned this with the naval forces allocated to their sectors. The elimination of the major enemy batteries was the concern of the Army and Army Group, who had call on Bomber Command and then Eighth US Air Force. Parham considered that this would require some co-ordination, not least with the navies and air forces.

The British anticipated that the Germans would attempt to destroy the assault on the beaches, and if that failed, deny access to Caen. The Germans were expected to deploy the guns of reinforcing units in the Orne and Dives valleys and the hilly ground south of Caen. Field and coastal guns sited in 711st Division's area east of the Dives were also identified as posing a threat. The Allies were confident that they had identified all the units that they were expecting to find. However, the Germans had far more troops in the D-Day beach areas than had been anticipated, and the Allies were not aware of many of them.

Fire plans for the assaulting brigades followed the templates developed by Combined Operations staff and were essential in tackling the strongly defended beaches. Each was envisaged as an integral part of the assault, included all services and was divided into four phases:

Phase 1 – Long term preparation
Phase 2 – Preliminary bombardment
Phase 3 – Direct support of the assault
Phase 4 – Support of the advance inland

The most dangerous moments would be immediately before and after initial touchdown. This is when the assaulting infantry and armour would be at their most vulnerable, as they emerged from landing craft or were on the exposed beaches. German artillery batteries would need to be suppressed. This was a harder task than if mounted on land against an enemy in contact, whose positions might be exposed by preliminary operations. Ammunition supply would need to be calculated to ensure that sufficient was available, while without taking up more transport space than needed. The artillery fire plan was planned to provide a similar weight of fire to that at the Battle of El Alamein in October 1942.

The fire plan was the result of a series of planning conferences that took place between February and April 1944. The divisions and corps bid for targets and for the effects they wanted. The plan was agreed and published in mid-May. It was based on the best information on German positions as known in early 1944.

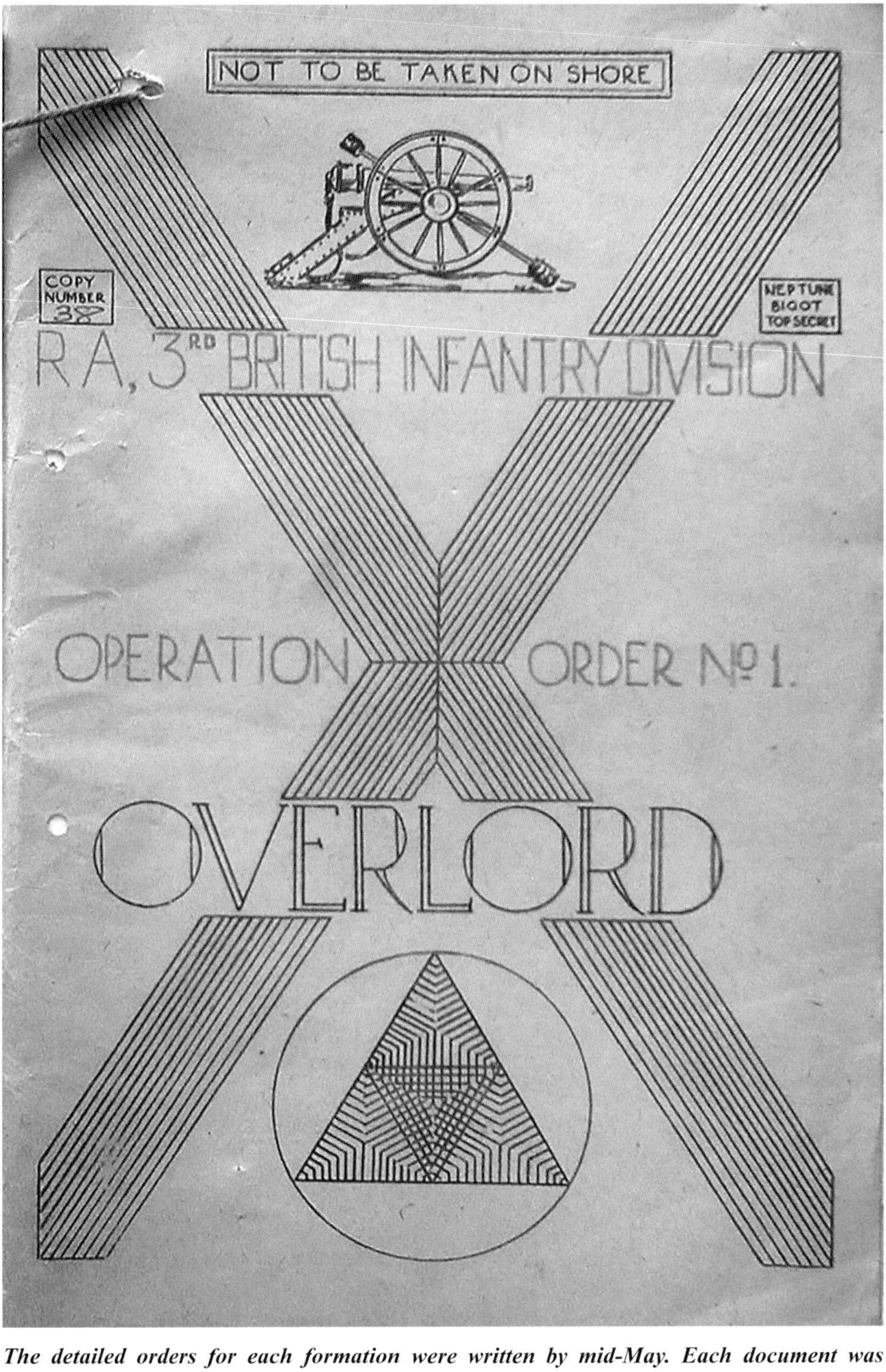

The detailed orders for each formation were written by mid-May. Each document was reproduced using manual duplicating machinery. All copies were numbered and accounted for. All waste was destroyed.

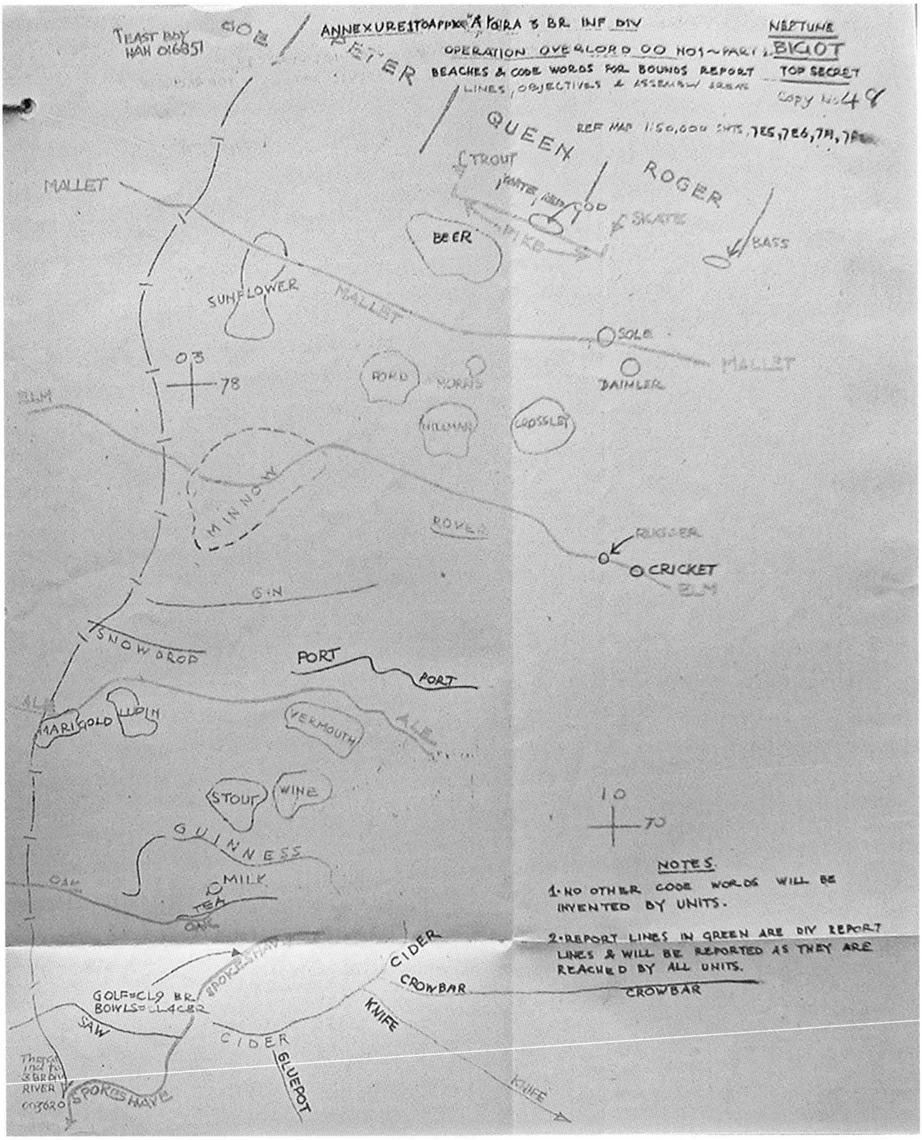

Graphic information such as report lines was circulated as hand-drawn traces.

Air support

The Air Force would play a key role, pushing the Luftwaffe from their forward airfields and attacking enemy naval bases, headquarters and lines of communications. Aircraft would be used in the assault to pulverize enemy defences in the area selected for assault. Once the invaders landed, the Air Force would need their control systems and airfields to support he forces ashore. On D-Day, fighter-bombers were arranged through the chain of command, with some assigned to each assaulting beach and a series of pre-arranged targets.

Naval gunfire

Naval bombardment would provide much of the firepower for bombarding the beach and coastal batteries. Battleships, cruisers and monitors would provide indirect fire on coastal batteries spotted by RAF, USN and FAA pilots in Mustang and Seafire aircraft. Destroyers would engage defended localities on the flanks of the assault using direct fire.

Light craft fitted with guns and rockets, and field artillery firing from landing craft would drench the beach area with fire. Each sector of beach attacked by each assault brigade would receive the equivalent of around 0.1lb/sq. yard of equivalent of 25-pounder fire, roughly the same weight as for the attack at El Alamein.

The Royal Marine Armoured Support Group

Immediately following the assault and before the SP artillery was deployed ashore, close support was to be provided by direct or indirect fire from the 95mm howitzers of obsolescent Centaur CS tanks mounted on Landing Craft Tanks (A). These were Mk V landing craft with a ramp fitted so that five tanks loaded on each could fire over the ramp of the landing craft. This made the landing craft top heavy and less than fully seaworthy in rough water. This force was manned by the Royal Marines. Tank drivers were from the Royal Armoured Corps, while the command structure was from the Royal Artillery. There were four Centaurs in each troop and a Sherman tank for the GPO. The GPO would be in radio contact with the FOOs of the field regiment, and the troop could act as an extra field artillery troop. Four troops made a battery and two batteries a regiment. Each assaulting brigade would receive the support of a battery of twenty tanks trained for direct or indirect fire. Thus, two batteries (one regiment) were deployed on each of Gold and Juno Beaches, and a single battery on Sword Beach.

Copy No 37.

APPENDIX "E" TO RA 3 BR INF DIV OPERATION ORDER NO 1 DATED 15 MAY 44

PRE-ARRANGED TARGETS INLAND

Target No	Co-ordinates E	N	Ht	Description
U 101	403000	176900	52	Buildings CAPELLO (and)
U 102	403300	175910	55 m	Buildings at road junction
U 103	403730	174320	50 m	Buildings
U 104	405590	173990	50 m	HQ in village
U 105	405100	172300	35 m	Corner of orchard WEST of road
U 106	403750	172460	50 m	Cross tracks
U 107	400680	172030	63 m	Cross roads in village
U 108	403760	170300	62 m	Buildings

These targets had been identified ahead of the landings. Every command post would calculate the firing data (Azimuth, elevation and charge) to hit these targets.

Airborne OP Parties

An airborne division had only a single artillery regiment. Limited airlift would restrict how much of the unit could be landed by air. The three batteries of 53rd Regiment could provide three battery commanders' and six troop commanders' parties, which was enough to support three out of the 6th Airborne division's nine battalions. They would be dependent on artillery support from neighbouring formations landed by sea. In order to give each battalion access to artillery support, additional liaison parties and OP parties were recruited from across the artillery and trained to parachute, as would forward observer teams be to call on naval gunfire.

Air OPs

Air OPs were invaluable in Normandy, where there were few good observation positions not obscured by hedges, orchards, woods and villages. However, the D-Day beaches were 100 miles from the English coast and there could be no guarantee that any landing strips would be available by the end of the day. Despite Parham's efforts to obtain aircraft carriers and even the prototype Sikorsky helicopters, none would be available on D-Day itself.

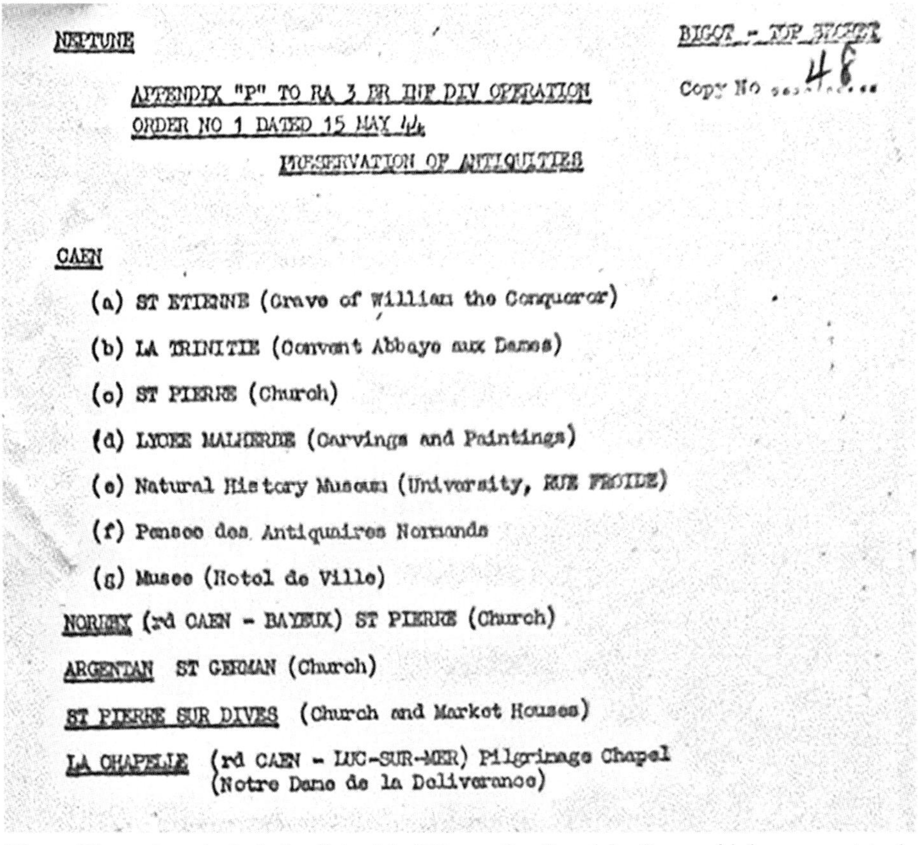

NEPTUNE — BIGOT - TOP SECRET

Copy No ...48...

APPENDIX "P" TO RA 3 BR INF DIV OPERATION ORDER NO 1 DATED 15 MAY 44

PRESERVATION OF ANTIQUITIES

CAEN

(a) ST ETIENNE (Grave of William the Conqueror)

(b) LA TRINITIE (Convent Abbaye aux Dames)

(c) ST PIERRE (Church)

(d) LYCEE MALHERBE (Carvings and Paintings)

(e) Natural History Museum (University, RUE FROIDE)

(f) Pensee des Antiquaires Normands

(g) Musee (Hotel de Ville)

NORREY (rd CAEN - BAYEUX) ST PIERRE (Church)

ARGENTAN ST GERMAN (Church)

ST PIERRE SUR DIVES (Church and Market Houses)

LA CHAPELLE (rd CAEN - LUC-SUR-MER) Pilgrimage Chapel (Notre Dame de la Deliverance)

The artillery plans included a list of buildings of cultural heritage which were not to be targeted. There was a similar list covering hospitals and utilities that should be avoided.

Medium Artillery

Naval gunfire could undertake counter-battery and harassing fire tasks normally provided by medium and heavy artillery. However, XXX Corps' D-Day objectives were well beyond the range of naval guns. There were no British self-propelled medium guns, nor any tracked gun tractors for medium artillery, so the British approached the Americans to borrow M12 self-propelled guns. Omar Bradley's generous response was to offer a complete field artillery battalion. The 987th Field Artillery Battalion and its 155mm SP guns were shipped across the Atlantic to join 5 AGRA with less than a month's preparation before landing on D-Day.

Anti-tank

German tanks were a major threat. The anti-tank platoons of the assaulting infantry brigade would be supported by an anti-tank battery from the divisional anti-tank regiment and the corps anti-tank regiment. These would be equipped with self-propelled M10 guns that could operate from the surf. A proportion of the M10s were up-gunned

This 40mm Bofors SP on a Crusader towing a Bofors gun is on its way to load into LCT 220 for exercise or D-Day itself. This gun and its detachment from 395th Light AA Battery would land at H+45 on Sword Beach.

with 17-pounders which could defeat the armour of the heaviest tanks. The latest anti-tank ammunition, Armour Piercing Discarding Sabot, enabled 6-pounder anti-tank guns to take on the heavier armed tanks. Firepower demonstrations were staged to give anti-tank gunners confidence in the efficacy of the ammunition. The APDS was allocated to those units most likely to need it, especially the Airborne division.

Anti-aircraft

The Germans had responded to the landings in Sicily, Salerno and Anzio with vigorous day and night bombing as well as technological surprises such as air-to-surface guided missiles. Regardless of Allied air superiority, German fighter-bombers were expected to be able to make low-level raids by day and medium bomber attacks by night. AA battle groups would land on D-Day itself with the aim of establishing air defences by the end of the day. A lot of thought was given to command and control for air defence of the landings and the beachhead, both to engage the Luftwaffe and to avoid friendly fire casualties to Allied aircraft.

Expectations from the fire plan

The Second Army Overlord Planning diary contains a file note in Parham's handwriting dated 31 May 1944, with a summary of the fire plan and predictions about D-Day.

> As a personal matter of opinion, I suspect that the fire plan will – with perfect weather and freedom from cloud (which is essential) – go as follows when it comes off in a few days' time.
>
> (a) A vast quantity of moderately aimed and highly assorted missiles will fall on or near or not so near the beach localities from H-30 to H.
> (b) There will be a vast pall of smoke. As a result, the very high proportion of our fire which is dependent on direct laying will go haywire. And so, will the Huns.'
> (c) Defiladed A/T guns on beaches cause a lot of trouble as many will survive. They will be hard to K/O and will account for a lot of our DDs and Centaurs on some beaches.
> (d) Counter battery and counter mortar will be our biggest headache.
> (e) The successful engagement of hull down tanks, (Tigers and Panthers) lying back 3,000-4,000 yards from beaches and covering our painful progress through minefields will be difficult.
> (f) We shall be badly short of air observation early on.
> (g) The battle on D-Day and for the next few days will be a very rough house indeed. On it the war depends. BUT we are absolutely certain to get ashore in enough places to stay there. Nothing else matters and we then win the war, sooner or later and we hope sooner. The Hun commanders on the spot are in for an interesting, exciting and highly depressing day.

It is not often that senior officers document their predictions about an imminent battle. The next few chapters will look at what happened on the landing grounds and the beaches and see how well the plan worked.

Chapter 5

Overview of D-Day

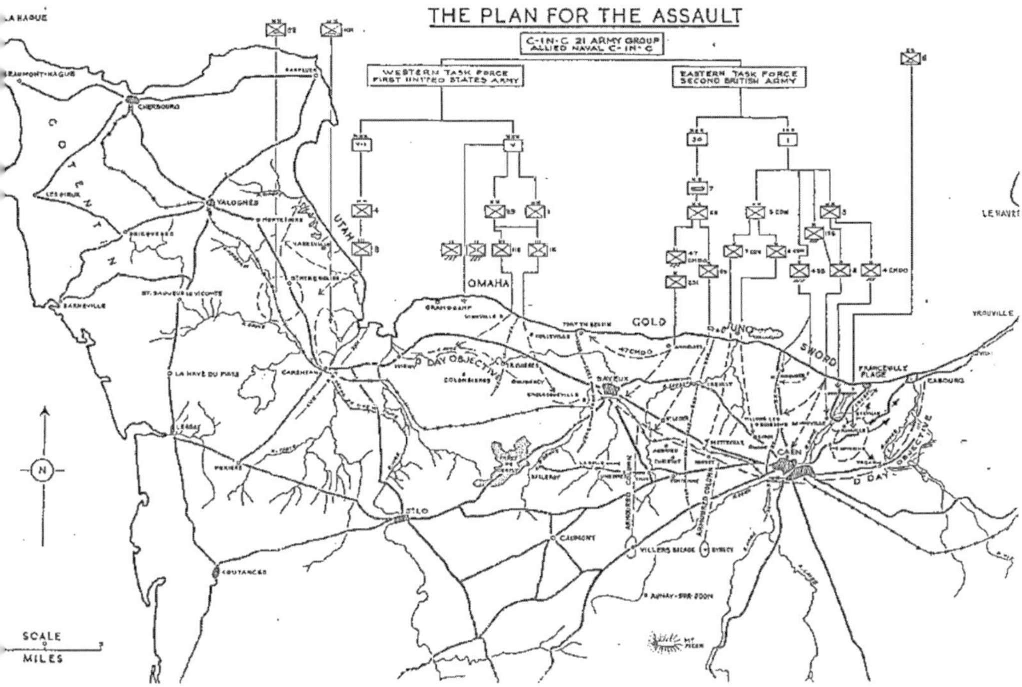

Allied landing plan.

D-Day was an Allied success, but how much of this was due to the fire plan? How well did artillery help or hinder the Allies or the Germans? What happened to the artillery deploying by air and sea? Once ashore, how did artillery support the operations inland from the beaches and landing sites?

The operation was carried out by the 1st and 30th Army Corps of the Second British Army as part of the 21st Army Group. On the left, 1st British Corps assaulted the beaches between Ouistreham and Graye-sur-Mer, with the intention on D-Day of securing a position between the River Orne, Caen and Putot-en-Bessin, preparatory to advancing south-east towards Falaise. On the right, the 30th Army Corps was to assault the coast between Graye-sur-Mer and Port-en-Bessin, capturing Bayeux before an advance towards Villers Bocage.

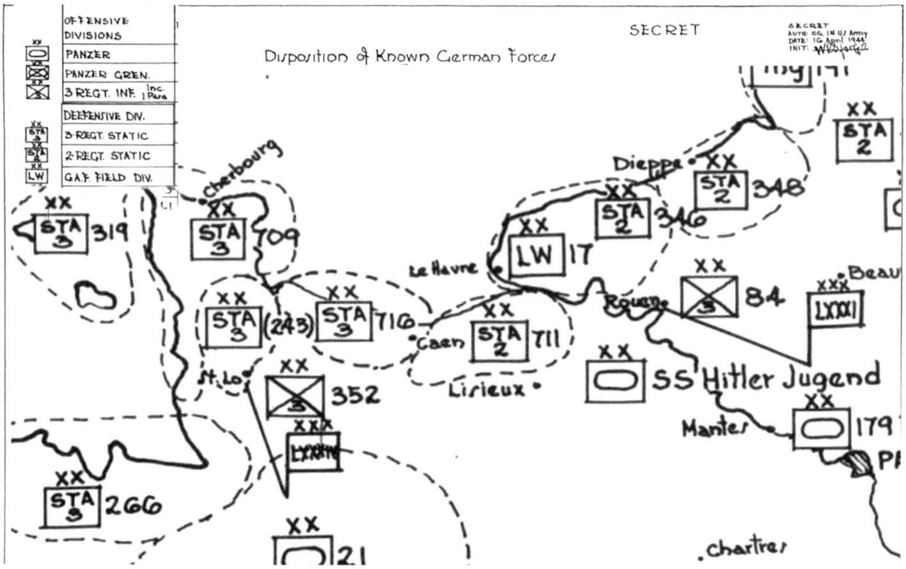

This intelligence map shows the information known about German dispositions at the time the fire plan for Operation Overlord was written and was the result of a series of planning conferences that took place between February and April 1944. The divisions and corps bid for targets and the effects they wanted before the plan was agreed and published in mid-May.

The British 1st Corps assault sector between Bayeux and Caen in 1944.

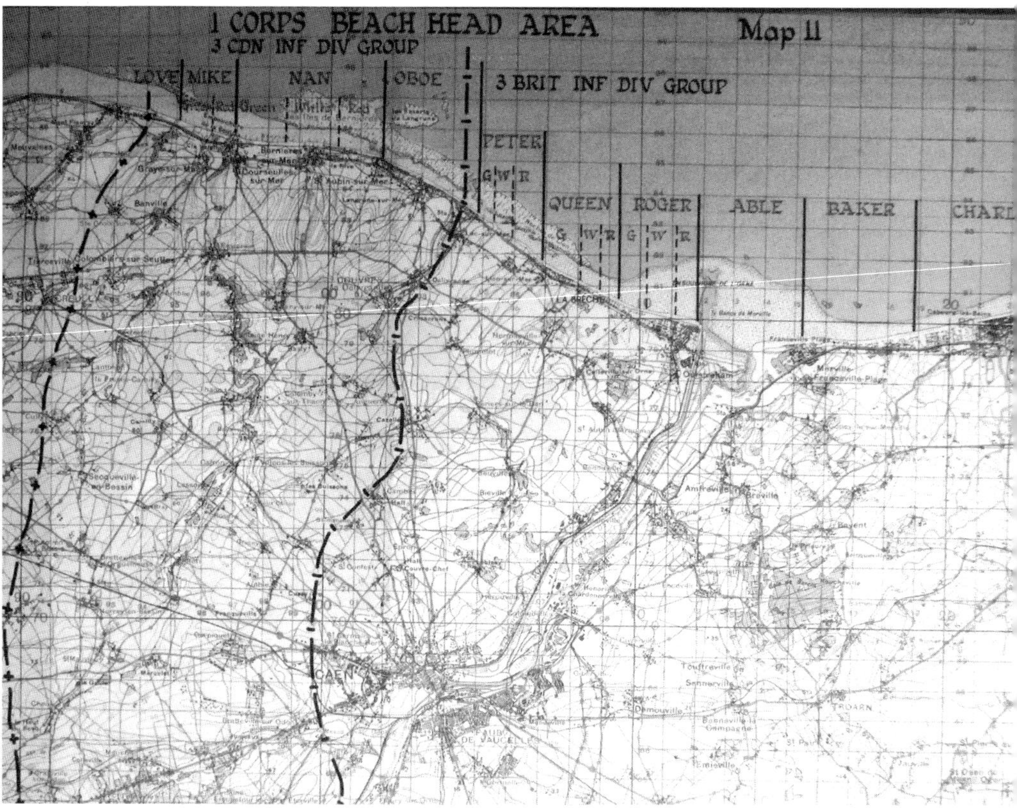

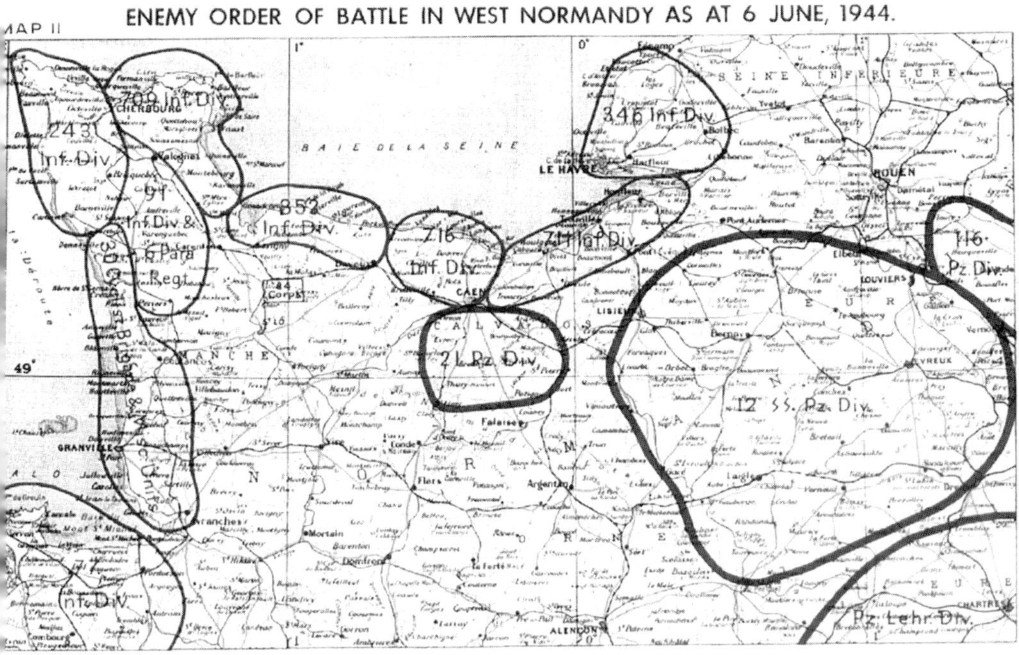

This map shows the German dispositions on 6 June 1944 after the adjustments Rommel had made. The move of the 21st Panzer and 352nd Infantry divisions were not identified early enough to be included in the fire plan.

Preparatory aerial bombardment

Thousands of sorties were flown by the fighters and twin-engine bombers of the tactical air forces and by the four-engine bombers of the strategic air forces in the month before D-Day. The Allied air forces lost 2,000 aircraft and aircrew, while 210 French civilians were reported as dead or missing and 190 wounded. The physical results were unimpressive. Between 15 May and 3 June 1944, German Seventh Army losses were four field positions, one gun, three buildings, four vehicles and two field kitchens destroyed, and six guns and seven pillboxes or bunkers damaged. Ninety-two German soldiers and two civilians were killed or missing, and 198 soldiers and twelve civilians wounded.

More important was the damage to seven Luftwaffe radar installations, the telephone system, 107 railway locomotives and enormous quantities of freight material and railway track. The damage to the rail system devastated the Germans' logistic support. The Seventh Army received only 200 out of 1,600 freight cars of cement expected, resulting in unfinished fortifications on the landing beaches. Less visible was the damage to the telephone network that led to much confusion and delay during the invasion.

Naval and aerial bombardment

A major part of the fire plan was to suppress German artillery batteries that could engage ships or the landing beaches. This was separate to the fire directed at the

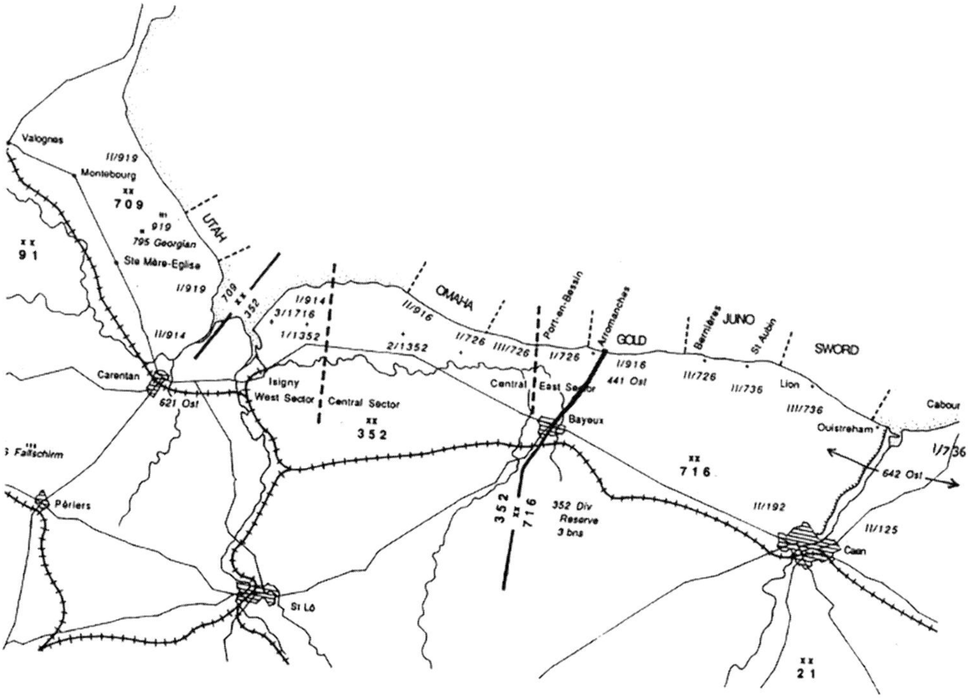

The German deployment at battalion level was more complicated than can be shown by divisional boundaries.

German positions in the 1 BR Corps sector from the Canadian official history.

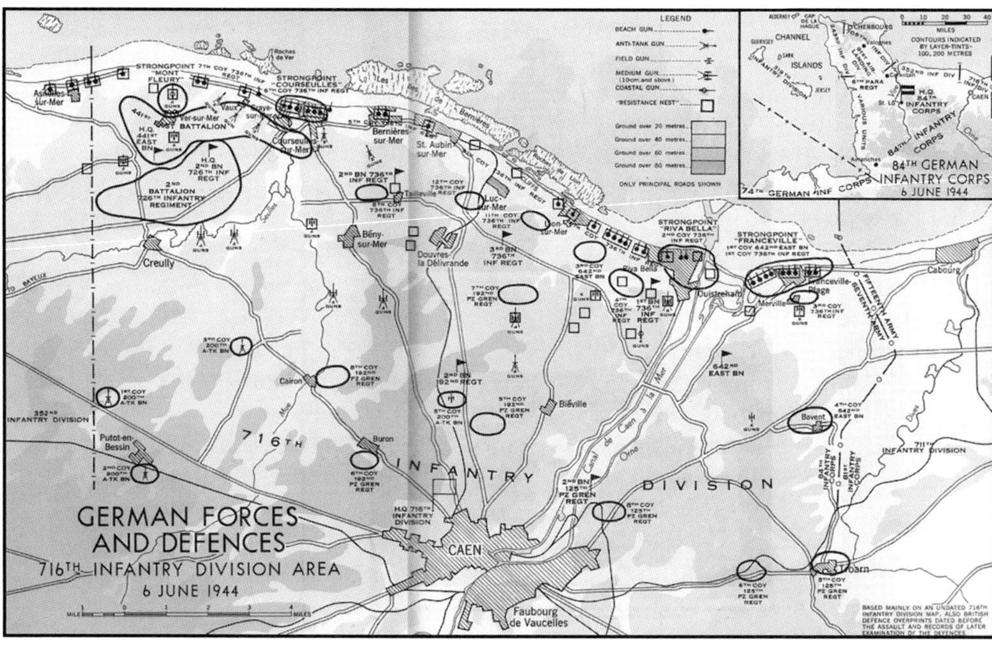

beach defences being attacked. Only two batteries in the British sector, at Merville and Riva Bella, were singled out for a ground assault. The remainder were to be suppressed by aerial and naval bombardment. Heavy day and night bombers would bomb the batteries an hour before H-Hour. Of the eleven installations identified by the Allies as coastal batteries, only five had been correctly identified as trained and equipped to engage ships. The other six consisted of the artillery of the local infantry division deployed to engage troops landing on the beach itself.

The diagram on p.68 shows the location of the German guns and defences identified by the Allies and included in the fire plan, as well as those that had been missed by Allied intelligence.

The preliminary bombardment began with overnight bombing by 1,056 Halifax, Lancaster and Mosquito bombers on ten coastal batteries, an average of 100 aircraft and 500 tons of bombs on each target. This ended just after dawn on 6 June. Targets close to the assault beaches would only be bombed with 100lb bombs fitted with instantaneous fuses, to avoid creating craters. Targets inland, in particular batteries with concrete bunkers, were attacked with bigger bombs fused to create craters.

B26 Marauder medium bombers from the Ninth US Air Force equipped with Oboe navigation equipment set out to bomb six of the most important batteries, three in the British Army sector at Ouistreham and Ouistreham II, also known as Daimler, and at Benerville, as soon as possible after civil twilight, 0515 hours Double BST. This was an unusual mission for day bombers. Difficulties in navigation and unfamiliarity with the methods resulted in only one aircraft actually attacking the battery.

Heavy bombers of the Eighth Air Force were allocated to attack beach targets in support of the landings; 125 squadrons, each of six B17 or B24 bombers, were assigned to attack thirty-two targets across the three British beach areas between 0645 hours and 0720 hours – except the Longues-sur-Mer battery, where bombing was extended to 0735 hours. Each squadron would be led by an aircraft with H2X air-to-ground radar to enable bombing to take place through cloud. This was the first occasion on which strategic bombers would be used in close support of the army in North-West Europe. In the event of cloud cover, the bombers were not to engage targets closer than 1,000 yards from the landing beaches. The scatter of bombs from heavy bombers was such that a proportion would fall on the target.

RAF Boston bomber aircraft laid a smokescreen over the sea east of the task forces, screening the fleet from the coastal guns ashore.

From civil twilight the batteries were engaged by warships for six hours as part of a timed programme, with the fire spotted by Spitfire or Mustang aircraft manned by the RAF or FAA. After this programme ended, the targets were all on call. The details of the targets and schedule for the bombardment can be seen in the table on pp.64-66.

Several targets might need to be engaged by the air forces during the day. These were on-call targets, listed in the table on p.67.

Although the munitions used were unable to destroy hardened bunkers, and some batteries had not been located, the bombardment of the German artillery was remarkably effective. Only one German battery, at Longues-sur-Mer, engaged the fleet. Despite possessing sufficient artillery to cover the landing beaches with defensive fire, German artillery played little part in responding to the initial assault. The bombardment does seem to have disrupted communications between observation posts on the coast and the German guns.

Fire Plan Scheduled Targets

Targets	Bombing	Naval Gunfire	Comments
Ouistrhem Riva Bella WN08 1/HKA 1260 4x155mm sFH414(f)	Heavy night bombers 0502–0515 Medium day bombers 05.15	HMS Frobisher 7 × 7.5″ HMS Scorpion HMNor S Stord	Position abandoned. Battery in field position Aubin-d'Arquenay
Longues sur Mer WN48 M.K.B. Longues: 4x 15 cm SKL/C36	Heavy night bombers 04.14–04.28 36 heavy day bombers 06.45–07.35	HMS Ajax 6 × 6″	
Mont Fleury WN(35A) 3./HKA 1260 4x 12.2 cm K390/1(r)	Heavy night bomber 04.29–04.49 12 heavy day bombers 07.15–07.25 20 medium bombers	HMS Orion, 8 × 6″	
Bernerville 2./HKA 1255: 6x 15.5 cm K420(f)	100 × heavy night bombers 20 medium bombers	HMS Ramillies 6 × 15″	
Villerville Battery 1./HKA 1255: 6x15.5 cm K420(f))		HMS Warspite 6 × 15″	
1000m NW Beny -sur Mer (WN28A) 7./AT 1716 4x10 cm leFH 14/19(t)	C. 20 medium bombers Fighter bombers 07.50–08.00	HMS Diadem 8 × 5.25″	
Ouistrehem II "Daimler" 4./AR 1716; 4 × 10 cm leFH 14/19(t)	20 medium bombers 05.15 12 heavy day bombers 0655–0720	HMS Danae 6 × 6″	AP 1000 yards south (1)
Coleville-sur-Mer "Morris" 2./AR 1716; 4x10 cm leFH 14/19(t)	12 heavy day bombers 0655–0720	ORP Dragon 6 × 6″	
Merville Salennelles (WN01) 1./AR 1716 4x10cm leFH 14/19(t)	100 heavy night bombers 00.25–00.39	HMS Arethusa 6 × 6″	Naval bombardment to be cancelled if parachute assault succeeded
Ver-sur-Mer Battery 6./AR 1716 4x10 cm leFH 14/19(t)	48 heavy day bombers	HMS Belfast 12 × 6″	

Targets	Bombing	Naval Gunfire	Comments
Vaux sur Aure 10./AR 1716 4x15,5 cm sFH 414(f)	Fighter bombers 07.45–07.50 & 10.00	HMS Argonaut 10 × 5.25″	
Houlgate Battery (StPVIII 033) 3./HKA 1255 6x155 mm K420 (f)	Heavy night bombers 0345–0359	HMS Roberts 2 × 15″	
Arromanches III Battery St Come-du-Fresne WN39	Heavy day bombers 0655–0720	HMNS Flores 3 × 5.9″	
Battery 1500yds S Arromanches Abandoned gun position	Heavy day bombers 0655–0720	HMS Emerald 7 × 6″	
Arromanches Strong point	Heavy day bombers 0655–0720		AP 1000 yards south
Le Hamel 1	Heavy day bombers 0655–0715		AP 1000 yards south
Le Hamel 2	Heavy day bombers 0655–0715		AP 1000 yards south
Rocket projector	Heavy day bombers 0655–0715		
Ver-Sur Mer Bty (WN34)	Heavy day bombers 0655–0720		AP 1000 yards south
Ver-Sur Mer (WN33)	Heavy day bombers 0655–0720		AP 1000 yards south
La Riviere I (WN33)	Heavy day bombers 0655–0715		AP 1000 yards south
La Riviere II (WN34)	Heavy day bombers 0655–0715		AP 1000 yards south
Courseulles I (WN31)	Heavy day bombers 0655–0720		AP 1000 yards south
Courseulles II (WN29)	Heavy day bombers 0655–0720		AP 1000 yards south
Bernieres sur Mer (WN28)	Heavy day bombers 0655–0720		AP 1000 yards south
St Aubin-sur-Mer (WN27)	Heavy day bombers 06.55–07.20		AP 1000 yards south
Periers-sur-Dan Battery (2./ Pz Art 155)	Heavy day bombers 06.55–07.20 Fighter bombers 07.50–08.03		AP 1000 yards south
Petit Enfer. (WN24)	Heavy day bombers 06.55–07.20		AP 1000 yards south

Targets	Bombing	Naval Gunfire	Comments
Lion-sur-Mer (WN 21 "Trout")	Heavy day bombers 06.55–07.20		AP 1000 yards south
Ouistrehem (WN20 "Cod")	Heavy day bombers 06.55–07.20		AP 1000 yards south
Ouistrehem (WN10)	Heavy day bombers 06.55–07.20		AP 1000 yards south
Merville Franceville I	Heavy day bombers 06.55–07.20		AP 1000 yards south
Merville Franceville II	Heavy day bombers 06.55–07.20		AP 1000 yards south
Molineaux Battery (WN28A)	Heavy day bombers 06.55–07.20		
Tailleville Bn HQ (II/736)	Heavy day bombers 06.55–07.28		
St Julien Div (HQ 716 Div)	Heavy day bombers 07.25–07.28		
Bieville Regt HQ (GR No 736)	Heavy day bombers 07.25–07.28		
St Aubin d'Aequnay Bn HQ (WN17- "Hillman")	Heavy day bombers 07.25–07.28		
Vaux sur Aure	Fighter bombers 07.45–08.00		
Rocket Installation (WN31B)	Fighter bombers 07.50–08.05		
88 mm battery (994818)	Fighter bombers 07.40–08.03		
Bridge Cabourg Dives sur Mer	Fighter bombers 12.00		
Caen centred on bridges	Day bombers 12.30 Heavy day bombers No later than 15.00		

Notes

(1) AP = Aiming point

Air Force on Call Targets

Heavy & Medium Day Bombers		Fighter Bombers	
Target	**Remarks**	**Target**	**Remarks**
Caen		Locality 857858	
Port en Bessin 7547		Locality 848853	Incl bty Arromanches
Bayeux (7879)		Port en Bessin (7587)	
Villers Bocage 8157		Le Mon bty (249779)	
Crossings over the River Orne at Amays sur Orne (983577) and St Andres Sur Orne (012610)		Gonnerville sur Mer bty (254784)	
Lisieux 5367		Bty 280807	
Cordin 2762 (and Bridge over R Dives)		Bty 407086	
Troarn area of bridge	In event bridges not blown		
Pont L'Eveque 5203		Vire (632616)	
Alencon (3505)		Caen (0368)	
Argentan (2519)		Thierry Harcourt (941460)	
Flers (8620		Lisieux (5387)	
Falaise (1336)		Flers (8620)	
Conde Sur Noireau (8832)		Argentan (2519)	
Defended localities Carpiquet airfield (9668)			
Smoke on call to screen to deny enemy observation on a ridge which runs just East of R Dives from the coast as far south as Heut D'Angoville			

Airborne landings

The landing of the 6th Airborne Division was the first time that the British had deployed an entire division by air. Besides carrying out raiding tasks on the night of 5/6 June it had to occupy key ground and then fight on indefinitely as an infantry division.

The airborne landings were made at night, drawing on surprise rather than firepower. Artillery would play a minor role in these dramatic events. Landing a 75mm battery in gliders provided an eye-catching historic moment, but the key artillery task would be to deploy their artillery observation, command and control by air. This would test the robustness of the fragile valve communications technology and artillery procedures after the chaos of landing.

2nd Army Fire plan superimposed on German defences

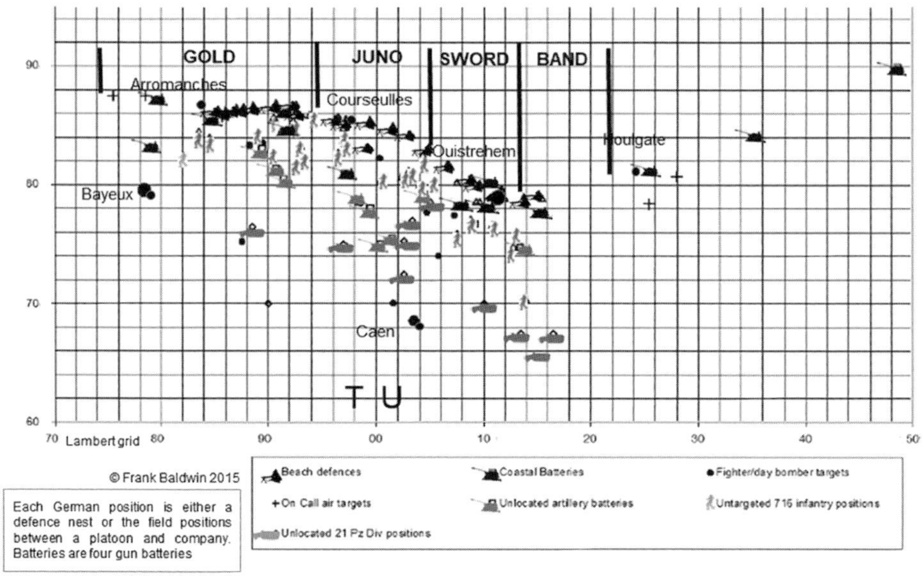

The Allies had only identified half of the defences in the Caen sector. The darker shapes mark the subjects of naval bombardment or air attacks. The Allies were unaware of any of the locations marked in grey, but if they were to achieve their D-Day objectives, they would need to locate and destroy them.

The 6th Airborne Division was tasked with seizing bridges over the Orne river and canal, neutralizing the Merville battery, destroying the bridges over the River Dives between Troarn and Varaville and occupying the high ground between the River Dives and Orne.

In addition to the 53rd Air Landing Regiment, the 6th Airborne Divisional artillery included: the 3 and 4 Air Landing Anti-Tank Batteries (sixteen 17-pounder and sixteen 6-pounder anti-tank guns), a detachment of 2 Air landing light AA battery, without guns, trained to use enemy equipment, twenty-one FOO parties and ten FOB parties.

The first troops to land were the glider-borne force that captured the Orne bridges shortly after 0016 hours. Ten minutes later, pathfinders and advance parties landed by parachute, and then the main bodies of the 3rd and 5th Parachute (Para) Brigades with some gliders. These included two FOO parties dropped by parachute and a section of two 6-pounder anti-tank guns landing by glider. The landings were badly scattered. Only a fraction of the forces landed assembled in time for each task. Carefully rehearsed plans were replaced by improvisations.

3 Para Brigade did not need artillery support to destroy Merville battery or the Dives bridges. The only artillery role was to cancel a planned bombardment of the Merville battery if the attack was successful. However, the FOB party was taken prisoner shortly after landing.

5 Para Brigade was tasked with securing the Drop Zones and Landing Zones against attack from the south. Shortly after 0335, a wave of gliders landed successfully.

Two out of four 17-pounder anti-tank guns and nine out of twelve 6-pounder anti-tank guns of 4th Air Landing Anti-tank Battery landed successfully with a selection of battery commanders FOOs and FOBs.

The BC and FOO parties from 212 Battery to support 3 Para Brigade were missing. While the BC of 210 Battery supporting 5 Para Brigade landed safely, his two FOOs crash-landed, smashing their radios. Of six FOBs, two were taken prisoner, one landed near Caen, rejoining British lines late on D-Day, and three landed safely.

The Germans reacted slowly, and an attack around dawn was beaten off easily. The Germans attacked again in mid-morning with reinforcements. No naval guns were available. The only fire support came from the anti-tank guns of 4th Air Landing Anti-tank Battery, and the attack was only beaten off with difficulty and heavy casualties.

After 3rd Division landed on Sword Beach, first a battery, then the whole of 76th Field Regiment was on call, joined in the afternoon by 7th and 33rd Field Regiments. Communications worked well, and fire from these units broke up several attacks, some supported by tanks.

At 2100 hours the final wave of airborne troops landed. These included 6 Air Landing Brigade, 211 Battery of 53rd Air Landing Light Regiment and eight 75mm howitzers in twenty-seven gliders on to LZ N, north of Ranville. The battery was

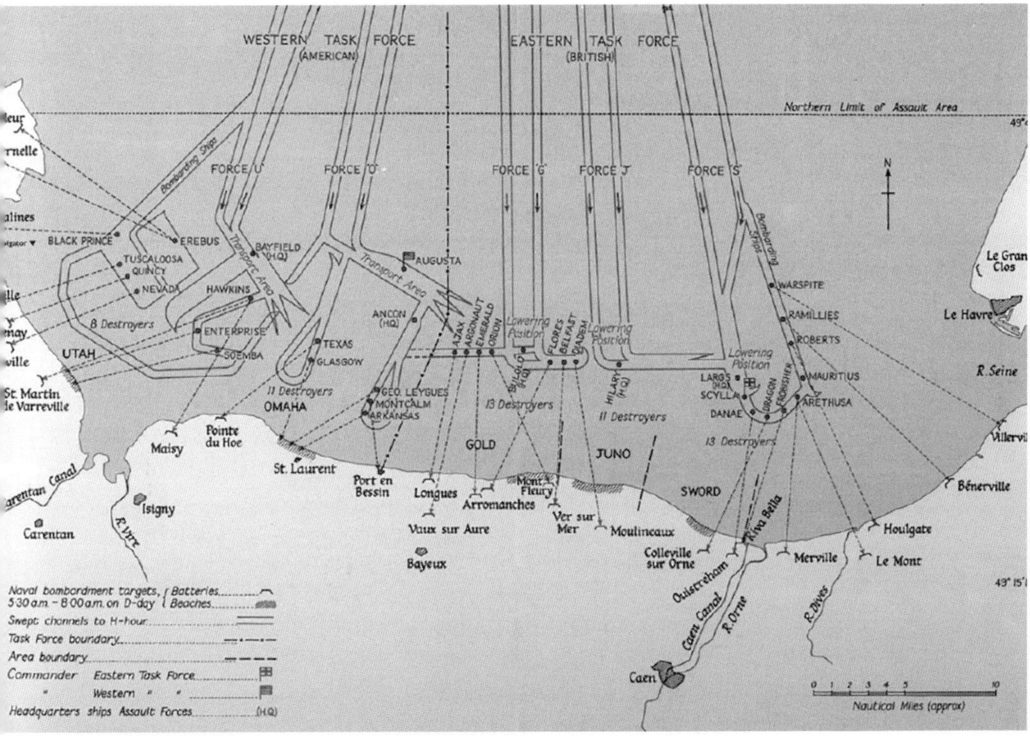

The big ships, battleships, monitors and cruisers engaged German batteries. Destroyers and smaller craft provided drenching fire on the invasion beaches to neutralize the defenders on the landing beaches.

to be in support of an ad hoc grouping tasked with creating confusion among the Germans in the direction of Caen. However, this was cancelled in the light of German opposition, and the battery was immediately deployed to support the bridgehead and came into action just north of Ranville at last light on D-Day.

Seaborne landings

The British operation was planned as an assault followed by an advance to a position on the perimeter of the beachhead. Artillery doctrine was to concentrate command at the highest level, but to decentralize control at the lowest practical level. The fire plan for the assault was an army plan. Once ashore, artillery was devolved to support brigade groups in achieving their objectives. For the first day the lack of communications would prevent the artillery from being controlled by divisional artillery cells.

Each assaulting brigade attacked a sector, with a follow-up brigade landing behind it. Each assaulting brigade kept one battalion in reserve and assaulted with two battalions, one on each beach.

The reserve battalion landed a little less than an hour later. The first wave of the assault on each beach included a squadron of tanks and close support Centaurs for fire support, flail tanks and AVREs to clear obstacles, two companies of infantry and an RE platoon to mop up all enemy opposition, and recce parties for later arrivals. The second wave consisted of two more companies of infantry, battalion HQ and more engineers. FOOs and FOBs landed with the assault waves.

How effective was the fire plan for the assault?

Each assaulting brigade was supported by a fire plan of drenching fire from destroyers, naval guns, rockets and field artillery from landing craft equivalent to around 0.1lb 25-pounder HE per sq. ft. This was in addition to bombing from heavy day bombers. It was an impressive spectacle commented on by many eyewitnesses. But was it effective?

A few days after the landings a team of scientists from the Operations Research Section visited the battlefield and inspected the German positions, recording the damage inflicted by the fighting and checking whether weapons had been fired. They noted the casualties suffered by each of the units that landed and compared them to the casualties that might have been expected.

	Weapons sited to cover landing beaches	Serviceable after bombardment	Weapons used and eventually knocked out by combat troops
Anti-tank Weapons	25	17	13
Mortars	13	12	10.6
Machine Guns	64–68	50–54	43–47

The bombardment apparently knocked out at least one tenth of the German posts and possibly as many as one fifth. The uncertainty was due to the difficulty of determining whether a weapon had been disabled by the preliminary bombardment or by a tank on

	Gold -Jig	Gold -King	Juno-Mike & Nan Green	Juno Nan Red	Sword – Queen
Assault Brigade/ Direct Support	231 Inf Bde: 147 Fd Regt (1)	69 Inf Bde: 86 Fd Regt	7th Cdn Inf Bde: 12 Cdn Fd Regt FOB67	8th Cdn Inf Bde: 19 Cdn Fd	8th Inf Bde: 76 Fd Regt
Left Assault Battalion/ Direct Support Affiliation	1 Hants: CO 90 Fd Regt & FOB 51	5 E Yorks:462 bty & F55	R Winnipeg R; 12 Cdn Fd Regt & F64	North Shore Regiment. 19 Cdn Fd	2 E Yorks: 302 bty F78
Right Assault Battalion/ Direct Support Affiliation	1 Dorset: BC 431 Bty & F52	6 Yorks:342 bty F54	Regina R, 13 Cdn Fd F65	Queens Own Rifles of C – 14 Cdn Fd	1 S Lancs:303 bty F77
Reserve Battalions/ Direct Support Affiliation	2 Devon & F53	7 Yorks: 341 Bty F56	Cdn Scot; 13 Cdn Fd Regt F66	La Regiment de la Chaudiere:19 Cdn Fd	1 Suffolk: 454 bty F79
Run in Shoot Regiments and Authorised OP	90 & 147 BC 465 bty	86 BC 431 bty	12 Cdn & 13 Cdn BC22 Cdn bty	14 Cdn & 19 Cdn BC 34 Cdn bty	7, 33 &76 BC 9 Bty
Naval support Fleet destroyers	9 × fleet destroyers 4 × escort destroyers 6 × LCG(L) 8 × LCT(R) 7 × LCF 6 × LCS(M) (FOOs) 10 × LCS(M) 4 × LCS(L)		8 × Fleet destroyers 4 × Escort destroyers 2 × LCG(L) 8 × LCT(R) 2 × LCF 6 × LCS(M) (FOOs) LCS(M) 4 × LCS(L)		4 × Fleet destroyers 2 × Escort destroyers 4 × LCF 3 × LCG LCT Concrete-Buster LCT-CB 8 × LCT(A) 321 LCT(R) 5 × LCT(R) 9 × LCA Hedgerow 2 × LCVP (Survey) 2 × LCP (Survey) 707 Assault Flotilla 12 × LCP(L)
Other Assault unit affiliations	47 RM Cdo: 431 bty(2)			48 RM Cdo:	1 Special Service Bde 41 RM Cdo

	Gold -Jig	Gold -King	Juno-Mike & Nan Green	Juno Nan Red	Sword – Queen
DD Tanks	Sherwood Rangers Yeomanry	4/7 DG	6 Cdn Armd Regt	10 Cdn Armd Regt	13/18H
Follow up Brigades in the assault divisions	56 Inf Bde: 147 Fd Regt (less 431 bty)	151 Inf Bde (6, 8 and 9 DLI) 90 Fd Regt		9th Cdn Inf Bde: 19 Cdn Fd Regt	185th Inf Bde and 7 Fd Regt 27 Armd Bde 9th Inf Bde/33 Fd Regt
Breaching teams RE	Sqn 6 Asslt Regt RE	Sqn 6 Asslt Regt RE	Sqn 6 Asslt Regt RE	Sqn 5 Asslt Regt RE	Sqn 5 Asslt Regt RE
Flail mine clearing	Sqn Westminster dragoons	Sqn Westminster Dragoons	Sqn 22 Dragoon	Sqn 22 Dragoon	Sqn 22 Dragoon
Close Support	1 Bty 1 RMASG	2 Bty 1 RMASG	3 Bty 2 RMASG	4 Bty 2 RMASG	5 Ind Bty RMASG
COBU FOB	B Tp 1 COBU	B Tp 1 COBU	A Tp 3 COBU	A Tp 3 COBU	
Anti-tank	288/102 Anti-tank Battery RA 243/73 Anti-tank Battery RA 243	99/102 Anti-tank Battery RA 198/73 Anti-tank Battery RA 107/102 Anti-tank Battery RA	52 Bty 3 Cdn A Tk Regt 247 Bty 62 ATk Regt	94 Bty 3 Cdn A Tk Regt 246 Bty 62 ATk Regt 248 Bty 62 Atk Regt	45 Atk Bty 20 Atk Regt 67 Atk Bty
Field Artillery		Recce party 74 Fd Regt			
Follow on Formations	7th Armoured Division			51 Inf Div 4th Armd Bde	
AGRA Artillery	D Day 987 FAB US Army 420th Hy By/ 52 Hy Rt , D+1 :4.5″ Btys 7 Med Regt; D+2 HQ 5 AGRA, & 64 Medium D+4 84 Med & 419 Hy Bty D+6, 121 Med Regt D+7 Remainder 52 Hy Regt		D Day 53 Med Regt D+1 HQ 4 AGRA D+1 65 Med Regt D+2 150 Fd Regt		
Survey	Det Y Svy Tp 4 Svy Regt		Det B Svy bty 9 Svy Regt	Det B Svy bty 9 Svy Regt	Det 'A', Svy Bty, 9 Svy Regt

Notes:

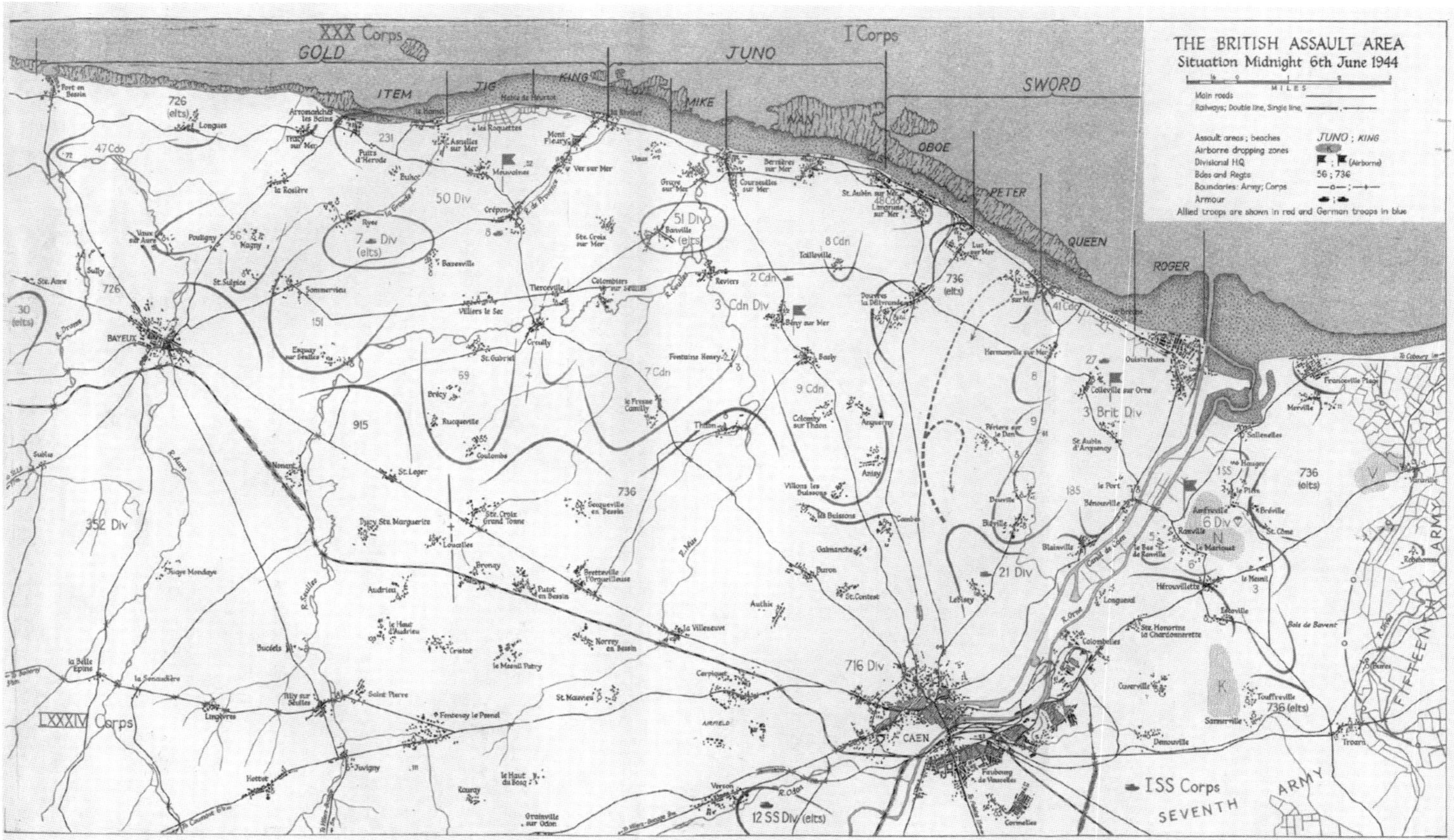

By midnight on D-Day the British and Canadians had made a firm lodgement but were short of their ambitious plans.

land. The air bombardment was responsible for knocking out 13 per cent of weapons disabled. The naval and air bombardment knocked out 8 per cent of mortars, around 21 per cent of machine guns and perhaps 32 per cent of guns from 3.7cm to 8.8cm, though this may include some guns disabled by direct fire weapons ashore. One in eight mortars, one in seven machine guns and one in five anti-tank guns were still serviceable after the bombardment but were not manned or fired. This may have been due to the psychological effect of the bombardment.

Few battles have been studied in this detail. The attackers were advancing over completely open ground compared to the undulations and cover encountered in more typical countryside. The defenders were particularly well entrenched. Most anti-tank weapons and many machine guns were sited in enfilade and under cover that protected them from bombs and shells from the front.

On each of the landing beaches, the assault battalion group landed on a frontage of 350–550 yards. At H-Hour DD tanks and Centaurs engaged the defenders from the beach. Flails and AVREs would gap obstacles, and the infantry cleared the defenders. The leading wave of two infantry companies and an engineer platoon would run the gauntlet of German weapons that could fire on to a rectangle of open ground 350–500 yards wide and 200 yards deep. The second assault wave of two companies and battalion HQ would land at H+20. With them would land the BCs and FOOs parties and artillery recce parties. At H+45 two troops of SP anti-tank guns and one or two troops of light AA SP artillery would land.

The bombardment and close support degraded the ability of the defenders to fire their weapons. The number of German weapons surviving the bombardment and manned should have inflicted 41 per cent casualties on the assaulting infantry – averaged across all beaches. crossing a 400x200 yard area. The actual casualty rates were 14 per cent.

This sounds impressive. However, weapons are generally much less effective on a two-way range. An effective barrage by the standards of the Second World War should have allowed the attackers to reach the enemy before the enemy recovered. The defenders at El Alamein recovered after around two minutes, which was the rule of thumb from mid-1943. On none of the D-Day beaches were the defenders overrun before they could recover from the bombardment. On each beach there was a fight to neutralize the defenders on the foreshore lasting between 45 minutes and 3¼ hours.

If the assault succeeded, the defenders would be too busy dealing with their immediate attackers to bring down fire on the beach. A study of the casualties suffered by each succeeding landing wave shows a sharp drop at the time when the defences were no longer bringing down effective fire. This was the time that the defences were said to be neutralized. There would still be defenders fighting in the area. The process of hunting down the surviving defenders was called 'mopping up'. At the end of this the defenders would either be prisoners, casualties or had fled.

Sword Beach

The intention at Sword Beach was to land on Queen White and Red beaches and capture Caen and a bridgehead south of the Orne. The presence of rocks to the west and sand bars to the east meant that landings were only made on a single brigade front.

It took around fifty minutes to neutralize the defences on Sword Beach and a further two hours forty minutes to mop up the defences. The 2nd East Yorkshire

(2 E Yorks) and 1st South Lancashire Regiment (1 S Lancs) landed in front of Strongpoint Cod. These two infantry battalions lost 284 men – around a quarter of the strength of the assault waves.

Flail tanks cleared the first lane through the minefields to the lateral road in 40 minutes, by 0810 hours. The first tracked exit was open at 0845, and the first wheeled exit at 1130 hours (H+80–H+4 hours). By this time it was nearly high tide, and hundreds of vehicles were waiting their turn to exit the beach.

At H-Hour eight Centaurs and two Shermans landed on Queen Red Beach, and four more Centaurs landed half an hour later. All fired during the run-in, spraying the beach and a house with fire. When ashore they provided close support, particularly on Red Beach, where the infantry was hard pressed.

Landing at 0820 hours (H+55), No 4 Commando moved along the lateral road inland from the beach to clear the coast to the River Orne. It took the rest of the day for No.4 Commando, supported by AVREs, to clear Riva Bella and Ouistreham. Around the same time, No.41 Commando RM landed on Queen Red Beach. Once off the beach they headed west for the chateau at Lion-sur-Mer and Strongpoint Trout at the far end of the village. The fight for Lion-sur-Mer lasted for the rest of the day, with losses that included the FOB dismounted party.

At 0840 hours the HQ of 1st Special Service (Commando) brigade landed with 6 Commando, followed by 3 and 45 RM Commandos. The South Lancs expanded the beachhead inland and had established their HQ in to Hermanville by 0900 hours.

The guns of the 76th Field Regiment landed at 0840 hours (H+75) and deployed in the surf. 33rd Field landed at 0910 hours (H+105). One battery dropped into action

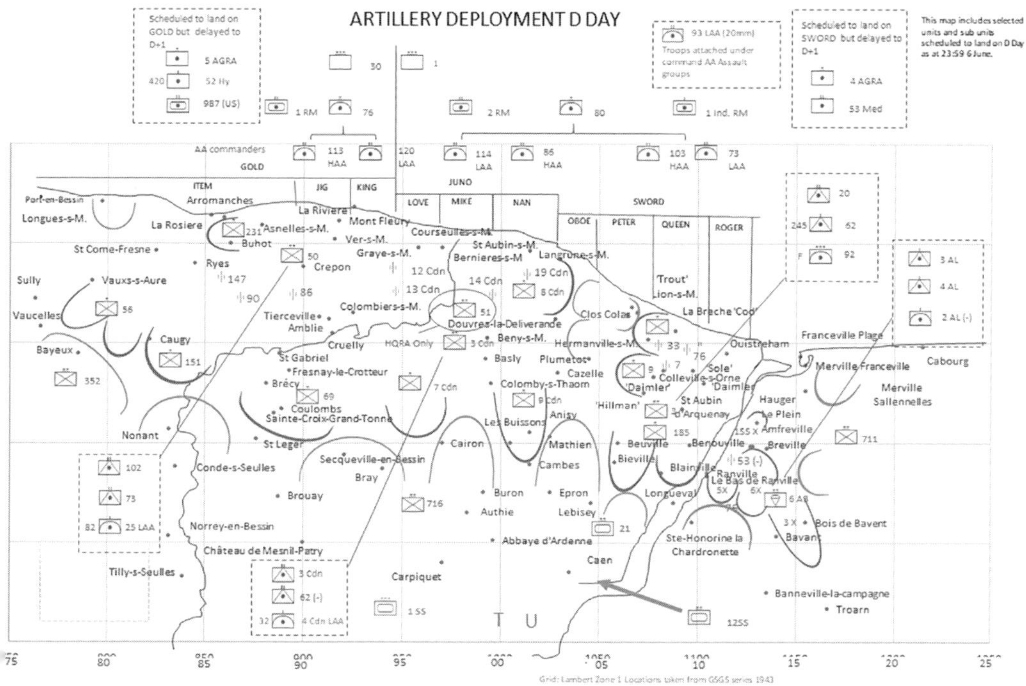

The position of British and Canadian artillery by the end of D-Day.

on the beach, while the remaining two queued for the exits and deployed after about an hour inland off the beach. 7th Field Regiment landed at 1045 hours (H+200) and deployed on the southern edge of Hermanville.

All this time, there was still fighting in the beach area. There were Germans defenders present, but they were too busy fighting their immediate attackers to interfere with subsequent waves landing. It took until 1010 hours (H+165) to mop up WN18 and WN19. During the morning, the tide came in. By mid-morning there was a considerable traffic jam on Sword Beach. Most of the delay arose from obstacles and mines rather than enemy fire.

Gold Beach

The beach assault on Gold Beach also had an H-Hour of 0725 hours. 50th (Northumbrian) Infantry division and supporting troops assaulted in Gold area on the easternmost sectors Jig and King. The actual lengths of beach to be cleared of obstacles initially were four stretches each of 350 yards on Jig Green Western, Jig Green Eastern, King Green and King Red.

The Gold Beach sector straddled the boundary between the Caen sector defended by the 716th Infantry Division, and the Bayeux sector defended by the 352nd Infantry Division, with the village of Asnelles the boundary, inclusive to the Bayeux sector. There were four anti-tank guns, one mortar and ten MGs on King beach and five anti-tank guns and thirteen or fourteen MGs on Jig Beach.

50th Division was to penetrate the beach defences between Le Hamel and La Rivière and secure by last light a line south of Bayeux and exploit towards Villers Bocage on the afternoon of D-Day.

The assault was made on a two-brigade front: on the left, 69 Brigade on King Beach and on its right, 231 Brigade to the west on Jig Beach. Each was supported by an armoured regiment, with two squadrons of DD tanks landing at D-Day and the third landing with the reserve battalion of the assault brigades. The two reserve brigades were to land behind the assault brigades at H+2 hours. One Royal Marine commando was to land about H+2 hours at Le Hamel and seize Port-en-Bessin by an attack from the south.

King Beach was one of the more lightly defended sectors, particularly on King Green opposite a small resistance nest. It took 45 minutes to neutralize the defenders and 20 minutes to clear the first tracked route off the beach.

The motor launch containing the observers for 147th Field Regiment could not contact their guns, and 90th Field Regiment passed their firing data to them. Both fired on WN36 on Jig Red, and left WN37 at Asnelles untouched. Despite this, the defenders were neutralized within 55 minutes, and the engineers had cleared a tracked route off the beach within 15 minutes.

Of sixteen LCT (A) carrying the 1st Regiment RMASG, only three beached on time, one on King and two on Jig. None engaged any targets during the run-in shoot. These had a limited effect, applying direct fire against targets of opportunity. The only Sherman to land became a casualty and burned out on the beach. In the absence of communications, none of the Centaurs fired in the indirect role from the beach.

147th Field Regiment, reduced to five troops after an LCT had engine trouble during the night, landed between H+20 and H+60. The first guns of 90th Field

Regiment landed as planned at 0825 hours (H+60). The guns came into action on the beach at the junction of Jig and King Sector. 86th Field Regiment's guns landed in two waves between H+60 and H+100, thirty minutes ahead of schedule. A, C and E Troops landed first.

Despite the speed with which the defences were neutralized on Gold Beach, it took three hours to mop up opposition from Asnelles to La Rivière. The fighting for Le Hamel lasted all day.

Juno Beach

The 3rd Canadian division had the mission of assaulting Juno Beach through Mike and Nan beaches to seize the line between Putot-en-Bessin and Bretteville l'Orgueilleuse. The HQ 4th Special Services Brigade with 48 RM Commando would land on Nan sector shortly after the assault battalions of 8th Canadian Brigade. It would then turn left and clear the village of Langrune-sur-Mer and meet No 41 RM Command, which should be attacking west from Sword Beach.

Due to rocky reefs offshore of Juno beach, H-Hour was scheduled to be 0735 hours on Mike and 0745 hours on Nan beaches. Owing to navigation problems and heavy seas, at 0630 H-Hour was put back by ten minutes to 0745 hours on Mike and 0755 hours on Nan. The fire plan from ships and landing craft was adjusted, but it was too late to reschedule aircraft, which bombed on the original times, the last bombs falling no later than 0728 hours.

On the extreme west of Mike, a company of the Canadian Scottish landed outside the main landing beaches to capture a bunker that enfiladed Mike Green beach. This bunker, containing a 7.5cm anti-tank gun, had been destroyed by the bombardment.

It is debatable whether the DD Tanks landed before or after the infantry on Mike beach. Casualties were heavy among the first wave of assault companies, one company of the Winnipeg Rifles taking 80 per cent casualties in capturing its objective.

The strongpoint west of the River Seulles was cleared by the Winnipeg Rifles, supported by tanks. It took two and a half hours to neutralize the defences. East of the river, the fighting for the main part of Courseulles-sur-Mer took all day. Neutralizing the defenders was described as 'long and arduous'.

Of the eight troops of RMASG, twenty-six Centaurs and seven Shermans landed on D-Day. One troop landed at H+10 and the remainder at H+120. The Centaurs were delayed, and smoke obscured the targets meaning they did not fire during the run-in, but they were considered to have given useful close support to the infantry against strongpoints and snipers.

On Mike Sector, 12th Field Regiment RCA landed first at H+75, 0850 hours. Unable to get off the beach, all twenty-four guns came into action at the water's edge, which by high tide consisted of a strip ten yards wide. There was no room for 13th Field Regiment, who were scheduled to land at H+120, 0935 hours. One battery landed east of Courseulles-sur-Mer to bring some guns into action.

In the Nan sector the weather was judged too rough to launch DD Tanks to swim ashore. The landing craft drew into shallow water, attracting shellfire that destroyed six tanks. It took a renewed naval bombardment to break up the defences at Bernières-sur-Mer, which was also outflanked by a penetration west of the town. The village position was neutralized by 0930 and it took a further half an hour to clear the village.

St Aubin was considered captured by 1030, though it took a further three-quarters of an hour to neutralize fire on the beach and the rest of the day to clear the village of snipers.

14th Field Regiment RCA began landing at 0925 hrs under heavy shelling and machine gun fire and had eighteen guns in action just west of Bernières-sur-Mer by 1130 hours.

19th Field Regiment RCA landed at 0945, and one troop was off the beach in ten minutes and in action on western outskirts of St Aubin-sur-Mer 200 yards from the water. It was soon followed by the other troop and a second battery. One LCT carrying was damaged and did not land until mid-afternoon. It took until 2100 hours for 19th Field Regiment to join the 14th in the gun position at Beny-sur-Mer.

Inland from the beaches

Once off the beach, the plan called for an advance to seize geographic objective inland. While the Allies anticipated vigorous armoured counter-attacks, they were not expecting to meet many Germans in defensive positions north of Caen. This would require the artillery to locate and bring fire on to targets as part of the all-arms plan. On D-Day there were no Air OPs, nor counter-battery location capabilities of the survey regiments. Furthermore, the surviving FOOs and FOBs landing on foot would need to marry up with the vehicles they would need for an inland advance.

Inland from Sword Beach

Three Commandos of the 1st Special Service Brigade headed for the Bénouville bridges 9km away across country. They reached the Orne Canal Bridge around 12.30.

After clearing Strongpoint Cod, the 2nd East Yorkshires moved off the beach to the east to clear La Brèche, which was accomplished at 1300 hours while a company captured Strongpoint Sole. This was completed at 15.45.

The 1st battalion the Suffolk Regiment (1st Suffolks), the follow-up battalion of 8 Brigade, came ashore at 08.30. An hour later, they headed for Colleville-sur-Mer. After clearing the village, B Company prepared to attack the Morris battery, which had been bombarded by the Polish cruiser *Dracka*. The FOO started to adjust his guns to support the attack, but a white flag appeared and sixty-seven disconsolate German soldiers surrendered without a fight. This took place shortly after 1200 hours.

The next objective for 1st Suffolks was Strongpoint Hillman, 500 yards further south. This contained the command post of 736th Infantry Regiment and 1st Battalion of Artillery Regiment 1716, responsible for the Orne sector – from Sword to the middle of Gold Beach. The position had been misidentified as a battalion HQ and its garrison underestimated. The Suffolks' FOB had been wounded in the landing, and the unit had no communications with the navy. The initial attack on Hillman was made by a single company at 1310 hours, but after two hours the operation was halted and the infantry pulled back, while a full battalion attack was prepared. In the late afternoon the 1st Suffolks mounted a battalion assault on Strongpoint Hillman, supported by two batteries of 76th Field Regiment. It took until 2015 hours before the operation was completed and the strongpoint taken.

Meanwhile, 185 Brigade Group landed. This had the task of capturing Caen as speedily as possible. The Brigade HQ and the infantry battalions landed around

1000 hours (H+160), and by 1130 hours the infantry of the brigade were in their assembly areas. However, the vehicles, supporting weapons and armour were held up by congestion and minefields. On the right, the 2nd battalion Kings Shropshire Light Infantry (KSLI) were to advance on the axis from Hermanville to Caen, joined by the tanks of the Staffordshire Yeomanry when they could catch up. They were joined by FOOs from 7th and 33rd Field regiments.

After reports of Germans tanks, the weight of the advance was to be on the left, via Coleville and Beuville, where anti-tank obstacles would provide some protection from German armour. The leading battalion on the left, the 1st battalion the Norfolk Regiment (1 Norfolks) was held up by the battle for Hillman and took casualties attempting to bypass the strongpoint to the east. The KSLI was harassed by artillery and mortars on the north slopes of Périers Ridge and then by machine gun fire. At about 1545 hours one company was advancing to attack guns near Périers village, while the rest of the battalion was in the Biéville area, supported by two squadrons of the Staffordshire Yeomanry and the SP troop of 41 Anti-tank battery. About 1600 Biéville was secured, and a company was told to push up to Lebisey. At about 1630 hours, a battlegroup of 21st Panzer Division attacked north from Caen into the path of 185 Brigade. This assault was stopped by the tanks and anti-tank guns, which knocked out German tanks at a cost of one SP anti-tank gun. 7th Field regiment played a part, firing concentrations on the woods where the Germans appeared to be assembling.

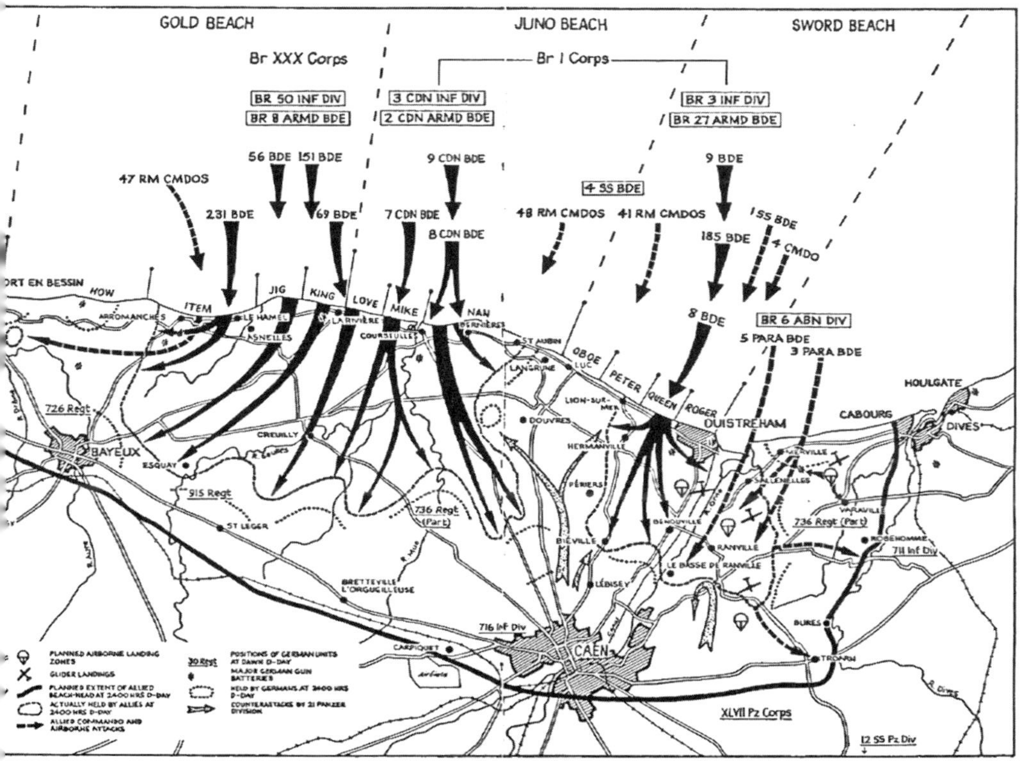

A summary of the events of D-Day in the British Sector.

Meanwhile, Y Company of 2 KSLI had reached the northern edge of Lebisey Wood but faced stiff opposition and withdrew at 1800 hours. Z Company attacked and captured a previously unidentified battery of four guns near Périers.

The infantry battalions of 9th Brigade came ashore over three hours from 1145 hours and deployed on the western flank of Sword Beach. In late afternoon, a second German armoured battlegroup from 21st Panzer Division penetrated to the sea in the corridor of German-held ground between Sword and Juno Beaches.

Inland from Juno Beach

The first German defences inland from Juno Beach were on the high ground about a mile south of the coast. There was a line of anti-tank guns and infantry positions occupied by German and *Ost* troops (Russian conscripts and volunteers).

Progress was initially faster on the western part of Juno Beach. The successful Canadian assault on Mike Green near Gray-sur-Mer and clearance of breaches on Mike Green was exploited by the 1 Canadian Scottish and the Winnipeg Rifles towards Beny-sur-Mer and St Croix. The latter was the HQ of II/726 Grenadier Regiment, the German divisional reserve, which had been ordered to counter-attack towards the beach. The battle for St Croix took several hours and resulted in the destruction of II/726 GR. The German unit lacked anti-tank weapons and was at a disadvantage against the Allied armour and infantry. Parts of the anti-tank battalion of 21st Panzer Division were lost trying to support it. A German corps artillery unit, 989 Army Artillery Battalion, was overrun in this area on D-Day as well.

14th Field Regiment RCA was caught in the congestion on the beach. The first four guns from a mix of troops were deployed in a field on the south-west corner of Bernières-sur-Mer. An anti-tank knocked out three of the guns. The remainder of the regiment deployed in a cramped gun position to the west of the church. Six gunners were killed and five wounded. At 1900 hours recce parties from 14th Canadian Field Regiment went forward, and the guns were taken to their pre-arranged gun area a mile north of Beny-sur-Mer.

A troop of 63 Battery of 19th Field Regiment RCA landed at 0945 hours and was off the beach in ten minutes and in action on western outskirts of St Aubin-sur-Mer 200 yards from the water. It was soon followed by the other troop and 99 Battery. One troop of 55 Battery did not land until mid-afternoon, and the other troop landed but became stuck in a traffic jam by a blocked beach exit. By 2100 hours the regiment had joined 14th Canadian Field Regiment in the gun position at Beny-sur-Mer.

Troops advancing south from Bernières came under machine gun fire from Tailleville. The chateau was fortified and occupied by a German battalion HQ (III/736), and clearing the position took much of the day. After the Germans had been cleared from Tailleville, Beny and St Croix, German resistance weakened. By midnight the Canadian 3rd Division's brigades had taken Line Elm but were still short of their D-Day objective of Line Oak.

Inland from Gold

The intention was to secure by last light a line south of Bayeux, with the optimistic intention of exploiting towards Villers Bocage on the afternoon of D-Day. After the assault, the aim of phase two was to enlarge the initial beachheads. 231 Brigade was to mop up Arromanches, capture Longues-sur-Mer and secure the phase line shown on the tactical map. 69 Brigade was to secure the line inland to Creully. In phase three the reserve brigades would advance and secure the line further inland.

In phase four 231 Brigade would exploit westwards and link up with 1 US Division, while 56 Brigade would capture Bayeux. 69 and 151 Brigade aligned to the 3rd Canadian Division on the East. 47 (RM) Commando was to capture Port-en-Bessin.

The 8th Armoured Brigade was tasked with providing a mobile column comprising the 8 Armoured Brigade and 61st Recce Regiment to seize the town of Villers Bocage and delay enemy reinforcements being brought against the beachhead area. This force was to assemble and be prepared to move from 1700 hours on D-Day. This plan was optimistic and would fall foul of the weather and the opposition.

By 0900 hours the high ground overlooking King sector of Gold Beach had been captured, although La Rivière had not yet been mopped up. 6th Battalion Green Howards were clearing Ver-sur-Mer and advancing toward Crépon, and 7th Battalion Green Howards were moving inland through Ver-sur-Mer toward Creully and the bridges over the River Seulles.

By late afternoon, 69 Brigade still had four miles to go to reach their objective. Many German positions had been bypassed, they had not yet linked up with the Canadians and some armoured support was still held up on the beaches. It the late afternoon they engaged elements of the German Corps Reserve KG Meyer in the area west of Creully. This battlegroup of two infantry battalions supported by ten *Sturmgeschützen* had been ordered to restore the situation in the Crépon area. Instead, it was defeated and fragmented in an encounter that lasted for the rest of the day. The indirect support from 86th Field Regiment gave the British an advantage. Naval gunfire and aircraft were a mixed blessing. The 6in gun cruiser HMS *Orion* engaged the infantry and armour in one of the most serious friendly fire incidents, causing over thirty casualties to the 6th Green Howards and 4/7th Dragoon Guards (4/7DG). To add further insult, the same units were then attacked by American fighters. 69 Brigade halted short of their D-Day objective, the Caen–Bayeux road.

The first task inland from Jig Beach was to clear the Meuvaines ridge, occupied by anti-tank guns, then to take the high ground west of Buhot, which was accomplished by 1st Battalion the Dorset Regiments (1 Dorset) with the support of 90th and 147th Field Regiments. This was followed by the advance by 1st Hampshires to Arromanches, involving a series of attacks supported by the destroyer HMS *Greville*.

Air defences of the beachhead

The story of the AA defences of the Normandy beaches is often overlooked. Air defence was given a high priority, based on the experiences at Sicily, Salerno and Anzio. The AA defence plan was thorough and sophisticated, but never fully tested. AA weapons were versatile and capable of use in the ground, anti-tank and coastal defence. Their centimetric radars could locate and engage enemy aircraft in all weathers, spot the splash from mines dropped from an aircraft 20 miles away and, somewhat temperamentally, locate mortar bombs in flight, enabling the firing mortar to be located. The secrecy surrounding radar apparatus is probably one reason why there are so few photographs of AA positions in Normandy, rendering them invisible to posterity.

Summary of AA Deployment D Day

	Gold 'Jig'	Gold -King	Juno Mike	Juno Nan	'Sword' Queen White	'Sword' Queen Red
AA HQ	**76 AA Brigade**		**80 AA Brigade**			
AA Commander	CO 113 HAA Regt	CO 120 LAA Regt	CO 114 LAA Regt	CO 86 HAA Regt	CO 103 HAA Regt	CO 73 LAA Regt
20mm LAA (1) (93 LAA Regt)	One tp 320 Bty	One tp 320 Bty	One tp 321 LAA Bty	one tp 321 LAA Bty	one tp 322Bty	322Bty (minus two troops),
40mm LAA (2)	395 Bty 120 LAA Regt	394 Bty 120 LAA Regt 82/25 LAA Battery RA (less 20mm t p) (3)	372 Bty 114 LAA Regt One Tp 32 Bty 4 Cdn LAA Regt (3)	375 Bty 114 LAA Regt One Tp 32 Bty 4 Cdn LAA Regt (3)	220 Bty 73 LAA Regt	218 Bty 73 LAA Regt 296 Bty (less two Tps 73 LAA Regt F Tp 318 Bty 92 LAA Regt (3)
3.7″ HAA	Sect 'H' Tp 395 Bty 113 HAA Two Tps 391 Bty113 HAA One Tp 366 /113 HAA	Sect of 'E' Tp 394 bty 113 HAA One tp of 362 Bty 113 HAA One Tp 362 Bty 113 HAA and one Tp 366 Bty 113 HAA.	274 Bty 86 HAA with one Tp 383 bty 86 HAA	273 Bty 86 HAA 383Bty 103 HAA Bty (- one tp),		322/103 HAA Bty with one Tp 323/103 HAA Bty
Other AA Troops landing	Det HQ 76 AA Bde RHQ 113 HAA 152 AAOR Detachment 112 PSC(4)	RHQ 120 LAA	RHQ 114 LAA Regt 474 SL Bty (- B and C Tps), 112 PSC (4) (less five Sects and three detachments).	RHQ 86 HAA 155 AAOR, detachment 112 PSC.(4)	B Tp 474 SL Bty, 324/103 HAA 160 AAOR and a detachment 112 PSC(4)	C Tp 474 SL Bty 16 FC Post, 103 COD(5) and a detachment 112 PSC (4)

Notes:

1. Each 20mm Light AA troop formed of three Crusader SP with triple 20mm each towing AA towing triple 20mm guns
2. Unless otherwise specified, each 40mm Light AA troop formed of three Crusader SP AA 40mm each towing Bofors 40mm Mk 1
3. Each troop Six Carrier, SP, 4x4 40mm, AA (Bofors) 30cwt

The leading Light AA Troops landed during the fire fight on Sword and Juno Beaches, where they brought their SP AA guns to engage German defences. With the weather and congestion on the beaches it took longer than planned to land and deploy AA guns. Several 3.7-in heavy AA guns were damaged as the axle pintles broke negotiating the sharp angle between the ramp descending from a landing craft and the upward slope of the shore. By the end of D-Day there was an air defence of sorts in place.

After D-Day

The decision to launch Operation Overlord in marginal conditions affected the tempo of events. The Germans were taken by surprise and reacted slowly. Allied operations were disrupted by the weather, which slowed landing. On D+1 the Allied plan was to continue to accomplish the objectives of D-Day. The Germans tried to co-ordinate counter-attacks by the armoured divisions in the area.

The Orne bridgehead was fought over for more than two months after D-Day. It was the Normandy battlefield contested the longest. After the initial airborne assault, the sector was the point of main effort for German attacks. There were bitter battles between 6 and 12 June as the Germans attacked west from Bréville-les-Monts and north towards Ranville. This ended with the capture of Bréville on 12 June which broke the German will. Over the next two months the fighting in the Orne bridgehead was static, redolent of the trench warfare of the First World War. The infantry patrolled and the artillery carried out counter-mortar operations. On 15 August the Germans pulled back, and 1 British Corps advanced towards the River Seine.

On 7 June, the British I Corps made a second attempt to take Caen. An attack by 185 Brigade failed with heavy casualties at Lebisey. The same day, 8 and 9 Brigades troops attacked west to pinch out the salient between Sword and Juno Beaches and mop up pockets of Germans left behind on D-Day. At the end of 7 June Sword and Juno beaches were linked, apart from the radar station at Douvres-la-Delivrande, which held out for a week. The 3rd British Division made limited attacks on Cambes and La Londe but could make no headway. The emphasis of Allied effort shifted west of Caen for the rest of June. The attack which finally captured Caen was Operation Charnwood, mounted on 7 July and supported by the heavy bombers of RAF Bomber Command.

On D+1 the 3rd Canadian Division attempted to complete its D-Day tasks, advancing to occupy the positions identified as their defensive beachhead. The 9th Canadian Brigade advanced towards Carpiquet airfield but ran into an ambush by a battlegroup from the 12th SS Panzer Division at Buron. Over the following week the 12th SS attempted to drive the Allies into the sea. The fighting centred on the 7th Canadian Brigade Fortress around the villages of Bretteville-l'Orgueilleuse and Putot-en-Bessin. The German efforts failed against a robust anti-tank defence. This area became the start line for Operation Epsom mounted by 8th Corps in late June towards the River Odon and Hill 112 to outflank Caen from the south-west. The 3rd Canadian Division launched an attack on Carpiquet airfield on 4 July, Operation Windsor, and took part in the attack on Caen on 7 July 1944.

XXX Corps had made good progress by the end of D-Day, but their lead troops were still north of Bayeux and a long way from the optimistic objectives of Villers

Bocage. On 7 June 231 Brigade advanced west to the Longues-sur-Mer battery and Port-en-Bessin, and 56 Brigade occupied Bayeux. The next moves were south of Bayeux and out of the D-Day beach area.

After D-Day the beaches and ports became the beachhead for logistic support of the British and Canadian forces. There was an organization assigned to each beach to manage the operations of the beach. The prefabricated sections of the Mulberry Harbour set sail on the afternoon of D-Day, and the first caisson was sunk at Arromanches on Gold Sector at dawn on 9 June. The artificial harbour, named Port Winston, became fully operational around 20 June. Despite being designed to last only three months, in the ten months after D-Day it was used to land over 2.5 million men, 500,000 vehicles and 4 million tonnes of supplies.

Block ships were sunk as breakwaters off Juno and Sword sectors, and stores were landed over the open beaches. The whole beachhead was protected by elaborate air defences that included AA guns, day and night fighter aircraft, barrage balloons and smoke.

Chapter 6

Orne Bridgehead, D-Day

Airborne Bridgehead D Day Walk – Visit Route

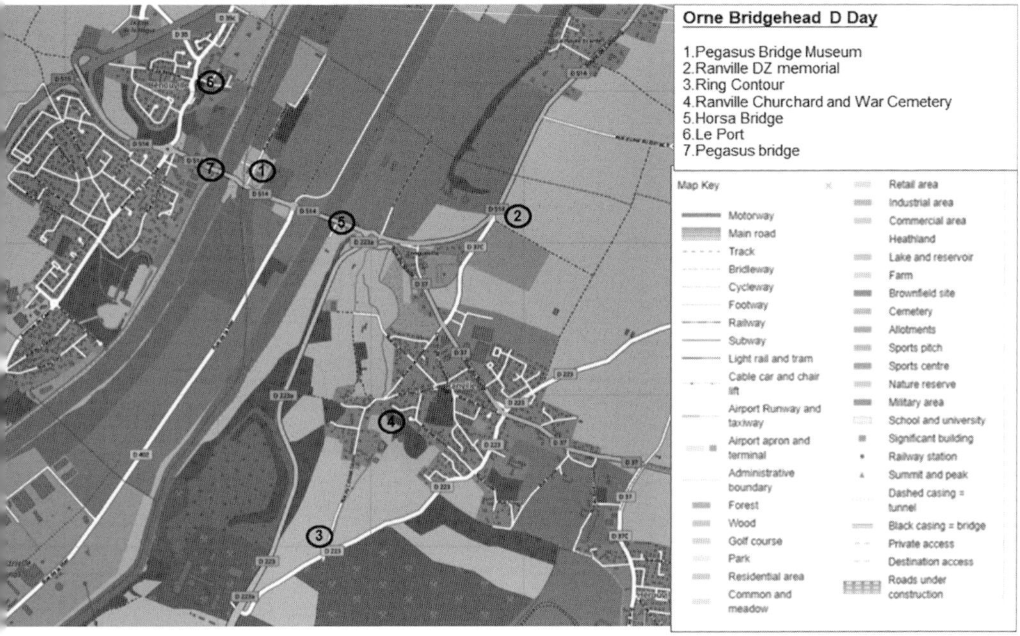

I recognized the land we were approaching, a river mouth and a canal; just what I had expected to see. The flak looked bigger and I could hear the heavy thuds of our bombing … Then from a clear night we flew into haze; the pilots were obviously worried; they could see neither the tow rope nor the light of the tug. Then suddenly it happened, there was a sickening crash. To this day we don't know what it was. I think our own tug or another aircraft hit us from below; it certainly wasn't flak … The pilots' feet were hanging over a gaping hole where there should have been a plywood floor. Things happened quickly. No.1 Pilot said, 'I'm casting off.' No.2 shouted, 'I can't get rid of the wheels.' We were flying smoothly downwards. The pilot turned the glider into the wind and out to sea. 'Stand by to ditch', came the warning and then 'Ditching now'.

It was a perfect water landing; there was a rush and a roar of water and I stood up to my arms in it. The pilots were strapped in below the waterline, but we got them clear; the glider was floating well. The seven of us got into the rubber dinghy. We tied up alongside and waited for the seaborne attack.

Major Gubbins, BC 212 Battery

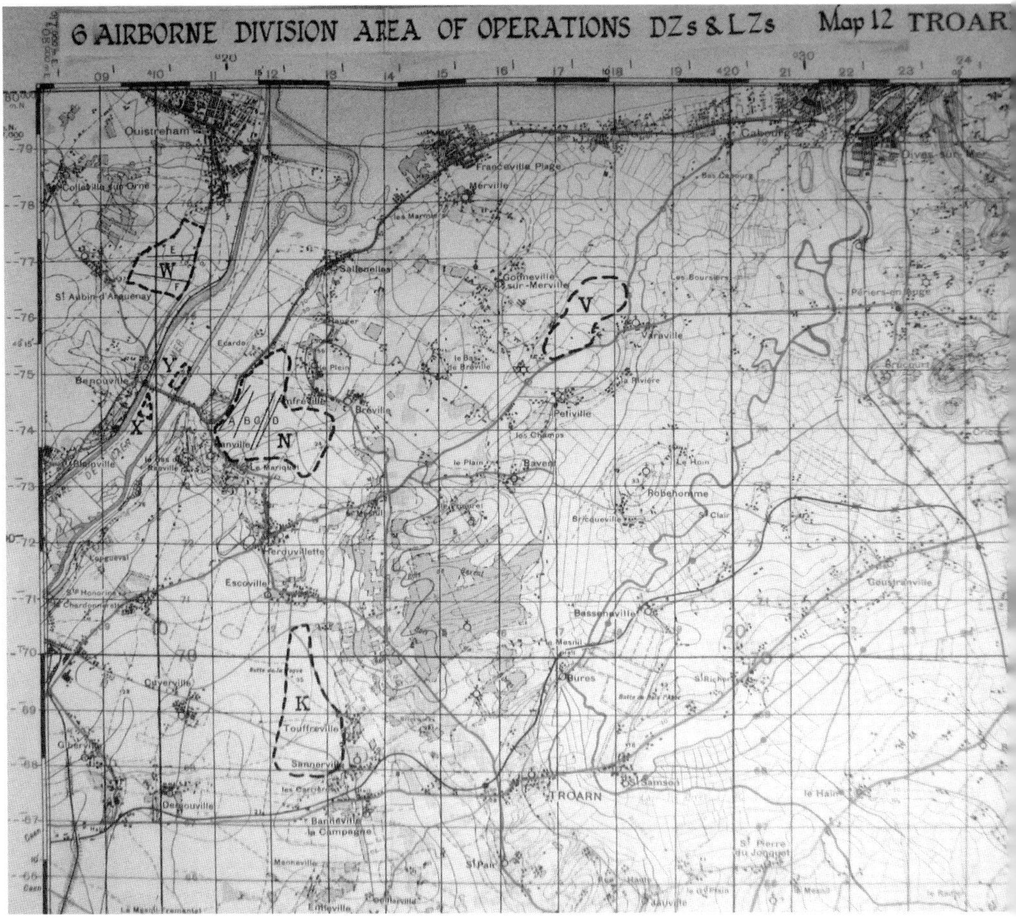

Extract from a 1:50,000 map of the Orne bridgehead.

Major Gubbins was to be the fire-controller for 3 Parachute Brigade HQ. After watching the landings on Sword Beach and failing to attract the attention of passing ships, Gubbins and his party tried to paddle ashore but were unable to overcome the wind and tide, which took them to the German-occupied coast, where they were taken prisoner. Gubbins and his men were lucky. Many who landed in the sea or in inundations inland did not survive the landing or exposure to the elements.

The 19,600 yards (17,900m) of coastline between the mouth of the River Orne at Ouistreham and the River Dives at Villers-sur-Mer was given the codename Band Beach, but is better known as the Orne or Airborne bridgehead. The German 716th Infantry Division was responsible for the sector. Two companies of the Grenadier Regiment 736 held the Franceville strongpoint covering the east bank of the Orne Canal. Most of 642 Eastern (*Ost*) Battalion was deployed south of the coast between Varaville and Bréville. The 2nd battalion of 125th Panzer Grenadier Regiment from 21st Panzer Division was billeted in the villages of Coulombs, Cuverville, Sannerville and Troarn, unknown to the Allies.

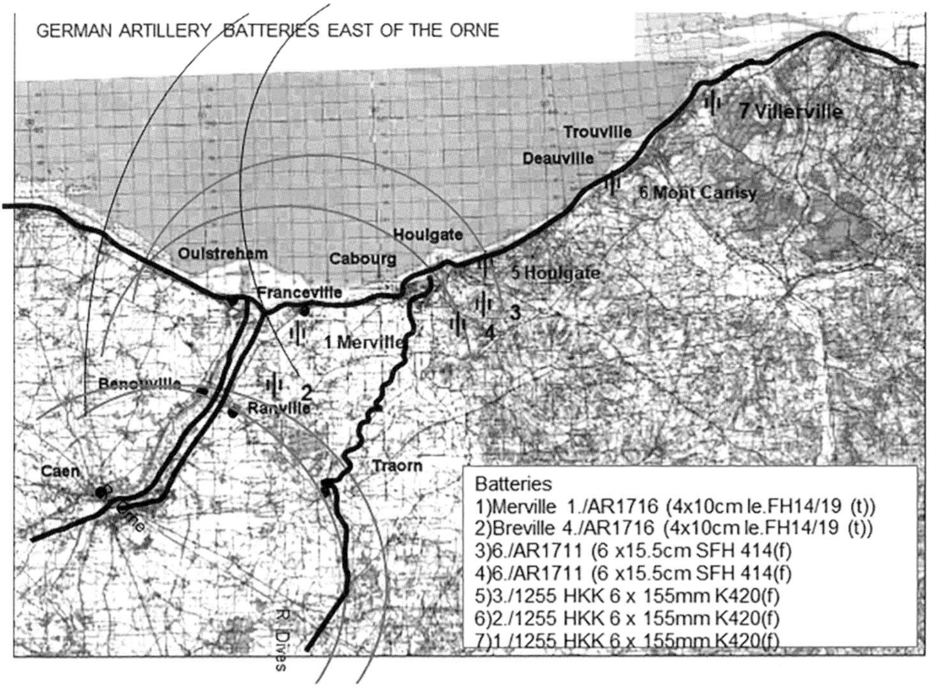

German artillery east of the Orne canal.

Two artillery batteries were in the area, each equipped with four ex-Czech 105mm howitzers, designated by the Germans as 10cm leFH 14/19(t). The 1st battery of Artillery Regiment 1716 (1/1716) was emplaced in the Merville battery, while the 3rd battery was in field positions north of Bréville, undetected by the Allies. Two 15.5cm batteries east of the Dives, in the 711th Division area, could engage troops between the Orne river and canal. The 15.5 cm guns of the coastal artillery batteries at Houlgate, Bernerville and Villerville of 1255 Army Costal Defence (HKK) Battalion could reach the Eastern Bombardment station off Sword Beach.

6th Airborne Division plan

The 6th Airborne Division was to cover the left flank of 21 Army Group. It was to capture the bridges over the Caen Canal and River Orne, seize and silence the Merville battery and destroy the bridges over the River Dives between Troarn and Varaville, to delay enemy reinforcements coming from the east. As soon as resources permitted, the Division was to secure the area between the Rivers Orne and Dives, north of the Troarn–Sannerville–Colombelles road and delay any enemy reserves attempting to move towards the area from the east.

The 3 Para Brigade Group comprised 8 and 9 Para and the 1st Canadian Para Battalion together with one section of 4th Airborne Anti-Tank Battery, supporting engineers and medics. Its tasks included capturing the enemy battery at Merville by 0450 hours and destroying its equipment; demolishing the bridges across the River Dives between Varaville, Robehomme, Bures and Troarn; and denying the enemy the use of the roads across the high ground between the Orne and the Dives.

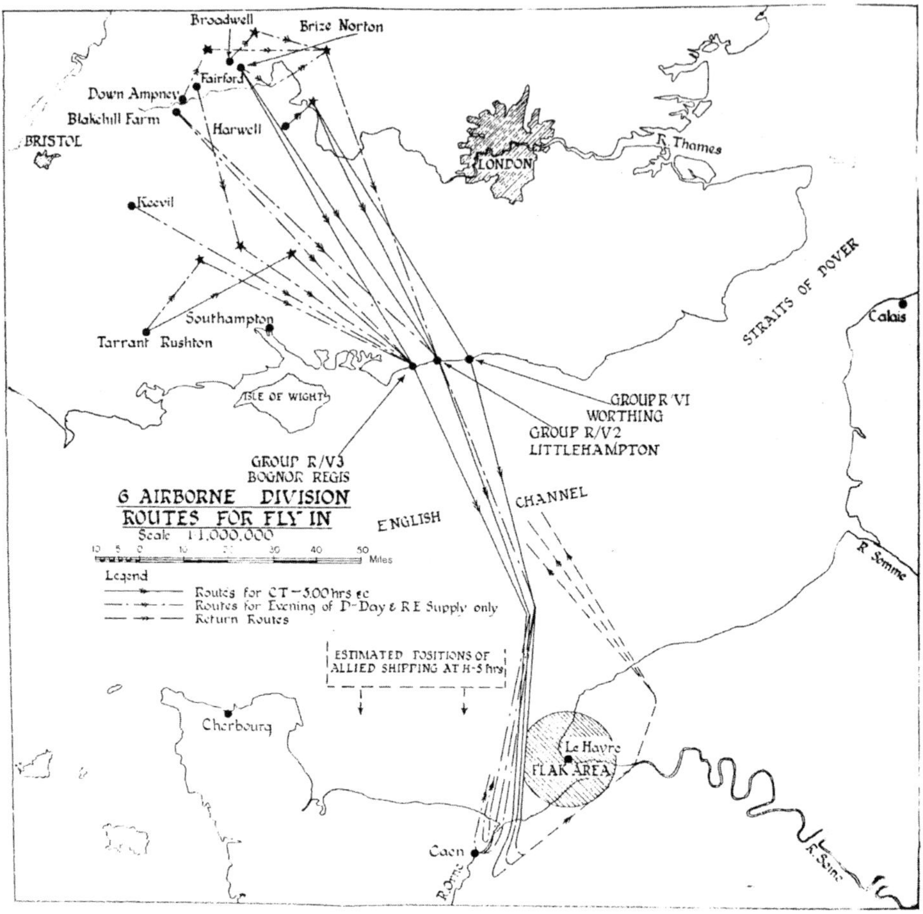

The fly in routes for the 6th Airborne Division.

The 5th Parachute Brigade consisted of the 7th, 12th and 13th Battalions of the Parachute Regiment, D Company Group of 2nd Oxford and Buckinghamshire Light infantry, (Ox & Bucks) 4th Anti-tank battery, less one section, and supporting engineers and medical services. It was to seize the crossings over the Orne river and canal at Bénouville and Ranville; secure and hold the area between Bénouville, Ranville and Le Bas de Ranville; capture an AA Battery on the canal bank east of St Aubin d'Arquenay; and clear and protect LZ N. After the arrival of 6th Air Landing Brigade, it would protect the south-eastern corner of the divisional area.

On landing, 6 Air Landing Brigade would comprise 2 Ox and Bucks (less one company group), 1 Royal Ulster Rifles (RUR), one battalion from 5 Para Brigade, 3rd and 4th Anti-tank batteries, taking over the latter from 5 Para Brigade. Its task was to occupy and hold the area Longeuval–St Honorine la Chardonorette–Escoville–Le Bas de Ranville. This brigade had the bulk of the firepower of the Division. Its infantry battalion would arrive intact as platoons. It would block the open southern approach to the landing zone.

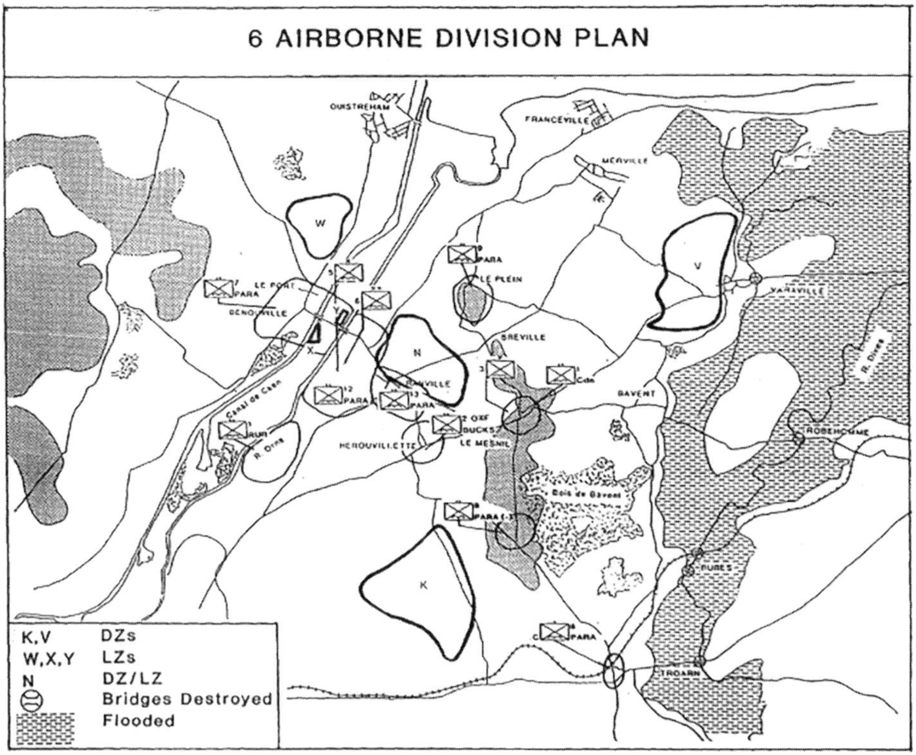

6th Airborne Division tasks.

1st Special Service (Commando) Brigade, with No 3, 4 and 6 Army and No 45 Royal Marine Commandos had the task of mopping up the coastal area Franceville–Cabourg–Varaville and patrolling the west of the River Dives roughly 6 km from the coast.

The Divisional Armoured Reconnaissance Regiment, reinforced with 211 Light Battery RA, a troop of anti-tank guns, a company of infantry, engineers and medical services, was given a task of exploiting any German weakness. It was to establish a firm base outside the divisional area, making deep reconnaissance, and impede and delay enemy troop movements south-east and east of Caen.

6th Airborne Division Artillery plan

Three factors influenced the 6th Airborne Division Artillery plan. Firstly, the divisional artillery alone was inadequate to support the 6th Airborne Division operations; secondly, should the support from flanking formations be available, there were insufficient OP officers within the division to control the fire; and thirdly, owing to its uneconomical airlift, the majority of the 6th Airborne Division artillery could not be flown in but would have to arrive by sea.

The 6th Airborne Divisional artillery consisted of:

- HQRA 6th Airborne Division
- 53 Air landing regiment of three air landing light batteries (210, 211 and 212)

- 3rd Air landing anti-tank battery (sixteen 17-pounder anti-tank guns)
- 4th Air landing anti-tank battery (sixteen 6-pounder anti-tank guns)
- Detachment 2 Air landing light AA battery, trained to use enemy equipment
- Twenty-one FOO parties (including twelve from 53 Air landing Regiment). The nine additional OP parties were mainly found from field regiments scheduled to land by sea after D-Day.
- Ten FOB parties.

6th Airborne Division could call for the support of the artillery of 3rd British Division from approximately H+2 and from 4 AGRA from pm D-Day. 76th Field Regiment was in direct support of 5 Para Brigade if needed for the capture of the Orne bridges, and 65th Medium Regiment was in direct support of 6th Airborne Division from its scheduled landing on pm D-Day.

Each parachute brigade had a cruiser and a destroyer in support from dawn D-Day. The cruisers were *Arethusa* for 3 Para Brigade and *Mauritius* for 5 Para Brigade.

Each Para brigade was assigned four parachute FOOs, and two FOOs and three FOB landing by glider. One air-landed FOO and four FOB parties would support 1st Special Service Brigade, and air-landed FOO parties would be under control of divisional HQ.

One further problem was artillery communications. Having been allocated additional FOOs, the question was how to arrange that their calls for fire could best be received by the supporting artillery. It was not practical to issue large heavy No.22 sets, which had a range of 10–15 miles in close country, to airborne FOOs. Instead, FOOs were equipped with No.68R man pack sets, with a 5-mile range. FOOs would be placed in support of battalions, under command of the battery commanders who remained at brigade HQ. Calls for fire were sent by FOOs to their controlling battery commander, who would assess the task and forward the demand to HQRA. In turn, HQRA 6th Airborne Division would forward the demand on to the HQRAs of supporting formations and any regiments placed in support. This exposed a key weakness in the firepower of British Airborne divisions. The battery commanders were liaising at brigade rather than battalion level, and there were several links between the observer and the units providing the fire. FOBs had their own communications direct to warships allotted in support. Like the FOOs, they were placed under the control of the battery commanders of 53 Air Landing Regiment.

The artillery was stationed with the rest of 6th Airborne Division in Bulford. The airlift was in four waves:

- First wave dropped 0020 hours. This did not include any artillery.
- Second wave dropped 0045 to 0103 hours. This included Para FOOs dropped with the HQ of the battalions in whose support they had been placed.
- Third wave landing 0300 hours. This included HQRA, the battery commanders and FOO parties to be air-landed, as well as the 6-pounders of 4th Air landing Anti-tank Battery.
- Fourth wave landing 2100 hours. 211 Air Landing Battery and a troop of 17-pounders of 3rd Air Landing Anti-Tank Battery.
- The residue of the units landed by sea between D+1 and D+7.

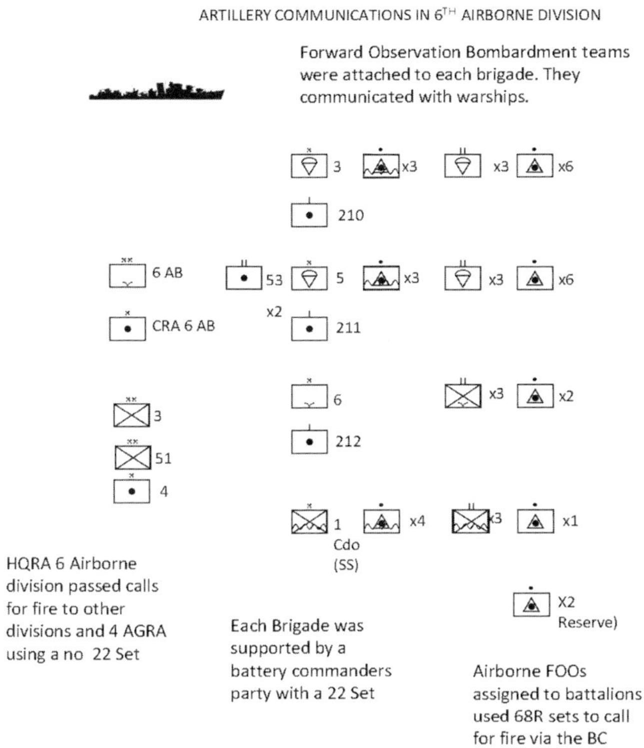

The artillery communications within 6th Airborne Division were constrained by the limitations of the performance of radios suitable for air landing.

The parachute landings were badly scattered. The wind conditions were at the 'high end of acceptable', and smoke and dust from the aerial bombing of Merville is likely to have been a factor in the scatter of units landing at DZ V. Several pilots reported their vision obscured in the critical half-minute before the drop.

Some of the airborne troops found themselves away from the correct DZ. The scattered parachute landings and unfortunate chance played havoc with the liaison and observation plan.

HQRA 6 Airborne Division landed safely, less one glider containing a No.19 Set. None of the parachute or air-landing FOOs allocated to 3 Para Brigade had arrived. 5 Para Brigade were a little more fortunate. Their parachute FOOs had turned up, but the gliders carrying both air-landing FOOs had crashed on landing and wireless sets were damaged. Three of sixteen of 4 Anti-Tank Battery's 6-pounders were missing, as were three out of four 17-pounders from the troop from 3 Anti-tank Battery, though one was later located in the UK, having been forced to return.

Merville battery was assaulted because of the threat its guns posed to the troops that would land on Sword Beach. After only a fraction of the troops could be assembled, a well-rehearsed plan was abandoned. An improvised attack by 9 Para overran the bunkers containing the guns at the cost of over 50 per cent of the attacking force. 9 Para then marched off to occupy Le Plein. Merville battery did not interfere with the landings on Sword beach, even though the Germans were able to bring guns back into action on the afternoon of D-Day.

The 1 Canadian Para assaulted the chateau at Varaville and other German positions nearby and blew the bridge. It took until 1030 hours before the last Germans in a pillbox at the chateau surrendered. Troops from No.6 Commando relieved a company at Varaville, and by 1700 hours the battalion was concentrated at Le Mesnil. German artillery east of the Dives shelled their positions during the day.

8th Para was the most widely scattered of the parachute battalions, split between DZs K and N. By 0350 hours eleven officers and 145 other ranks set out for the two bridges over the Dives at Bures and one at Troarn. Unknown to Allied intelligence, the villages Cuverville and Troarn were the billets of two companies of 125 Panzer Grenadier Regiment. Despite difficulties and adventures, the bridge at Troarn was blown before dawn and those at Bures by 0930 hours. During the day, the main part of the battalion deployed around the road junction on the high ground east of the Bois de Bures.

The commanding high ground between Troarn and Le Mesnil was occupied by 8th and 1st Canadian Para. The Le Plein feature was occupied by the weak 9th Para.

Of the 5 Para Brigade battalions, 7th Para took over the Orne bridges at 0140 hours, with the companies occupying positions by 0210 hours – about an hour later than had been hoped. Fighting was almost immediate, with 7th Para engaging elements of 716th Division, 192 Panzer Grenadier Regiment and the Panzerjäger Company of 716th Division. By dawn they had secured the southern half of Le Port, while Bénouville was contested.

By 0400 12th Para had assembled two companies in their appointed positions at La Bas Ranville and on the rising ground to the south. 13th Para cleared Ranville by 0300 hours. Few Germans were encountered at this time.

There was a lot of reorganization taking place within 6 Airborne Division's artillery, trying to contact the scattered FOOs and FOBs. Even when isolated, these lost FOOs were not entirely helpless. One of them, wandering in search of his allotted station, fell in with a naval telegraphist who had lost his FOB. Teaming up, they shot a cruiser at the village of Bréville, which was strongly held by the enemy. Having observed the first salvo land to the south of the target, the FOO ordered North 400. He had not learned that HM ships accept observations of the fall of shot and do not take orders. The next salvo landed on his toes. Indignantly he tapped out, 'For ——'s sake shoot at Bréville.' The navy understood, and Bréville disappeared under a cloud of dust.

Bombardier Clegg was part of an FOB team dropped miles behind German lines along with Leading Telegrapher Cutler, who was killed shortly after the landing. Clegg managed to join up with other paratroopers in the same predicament and made his way back to Allied lines. On the way he captured two Germans prisoner and had spent one night in a German mortar position, concealed in long grass, but got away before dawn. The citation for his Military Medal records that he returned to Allied lines on 10 July, but other records suggest that he evaded the Germans for four days rather than four weeks! The aggressive response of the little groups of airborne troops scattered across Lower Normandy is one reason why the Germans found it hard to identify the focus of the Allied airborne landings.

On D-Day the artillery support of 3 British Infantry became available after H Hour on D-Day:

- H+3 – 76th Field Regiment
- H+6 – 76th and 33rd Field Regiments
- H+9 – RA 3rd Infantry Division complete
- 1400 hours D+1 – One battery 65th Medium Regiment
- 1800 hours D+1 – 65th Medium Regiment

The support offered by the artillery of 3rd Infantry Division was regarded by 6th Airborne Division as 'extremely generous', given the other calls by that division's own assaulting troops. Warships were in continuous support.

Touring the Orne Bridgehead

This tour is intended as a walking or cycling tour of the artillery aspects of the airborne landing grounds. It covers 5km, with an optional 6km detour to Bréville-les-Monts to overlook the battlefield.

The No.61 bus service from Caen runs to Bénouville at irregular times. Check the timetable for details. If travelling by car, the Pegasus Bridge Museum has a car park. There is overflow parking opposite the museum. It is usually easy to find a parking space near Ranville Cemetery. The two cafés near Pegasus Bridge are good lunch spots, and there is a restaurant in Ranville. There are small supermarkets on Rue du Stade Ranville and Avenue de Caen, 14970 Bénouville, to pick up water or the makings of a picnic.

Pegasus Bridge Museum

Avenue du Major Howard, 14860 Ranville, France (GPS 49.242221, -0.272372)

The bridges over the Orne canal and river were captured by a glider force on one of those rare occasions in military history when an operation went almost entirely to plan.

At 0016 hours the first of three of the gliders assigned to capture the canal bridge at Bénouville landed within 50 yards of the objective, followed by the remaining two. The bridge was stormed and the defences on each side of the canal cleared with few casualties.

This bridge would become known as 'Pegasus'. Two out of three gliders landed close to the Orne River bridge, which would become known as 'Horsa'. The third landed five miles to the east.

Pegasus Bridge Museum was built to house the original Pegasus bridge after the road was widened and a new bridge needed over the Orne canal to accommodate a wider roadway. It now houses a substantial collection of artefacts associated with the capture of the bridges over the Orne river and canal, as well as interpretation, a shop and lavatories. Exhibits and information boards inside the museum cover the fighting in the area on D-Day and afterwards.

The main exhibit in the enclosure museums grounds is the original Pegasus Bridge itself. This still carries the damage sustained from German air attacks, including holes from cannon fire and bomb splinters.

There is a replica Horsa glider and a section of an original one. This type of glider was used to land the 6-pounder anti-tank guns of the independent air landing batteries, the 75mm guns of 211 Air Landing Battery and many FOU teams, as well as infantry.

After D-Day the Centaurs surviving and still running were deployed to the Orne bridgehead in the counter-mortar role.

Around the enclosure are some examples of artillery equipment used by the Royal Artillery in Normandy and described in Chapter 2.

The 5.5-in gun was the main equipment used by the medium artillery regiments, which formed the bulk of the Army Groups Royal Artillery. Note the size of the equipment.

Next to the 5.5-in gun is a Centaur tank in the markings of the 5th Independent Battery of the Royal Marines Armoured Support Group. RMASG Centaurs were fitted with dial sights which allowed them to be laid indirectly like other artillery equipment. This is not visible on the vehicle on display in the museum. The graduations around the turret are to help ensure that all guns on the troop were aligned in parallel. This ingenious improvisation increased the number of AFVs landing around H Hour by 50 per cent, making the defenders' job more difficult. On D-Day itself the rough weather conditions meant that only a portion of the unit landed, and communications difficulties and lack of training with the field regiments of the assault formations meant that they were not fully used. One troop formed an additional battery for 86 Field Regiment, and the RMASG played a part in supporting the attack by the RM Commandos into Langrune-sur-Mer as tanks. After a fortnight, the RM and RAC personnel of the RMASG were returned to the reinforcement pool. However, twelve tanks/ SP guns were retained and reorganized into two six-gun batteries, G and V, with OP parties and a B echelon, manned by British and then Canadian artillery reinforcements. They were deployed in support of the 6th Airborne Division for the duration of the campaign. The 95mm CS gun had a flat trajectory and was not ideal as an artillery piece. The advance to the Seine exposed the Centaurs' mechanical

This 17-pounder is painted in the colours of 6th Airborne Division. Their detachments included glider pilots. These guns, extra to the establishment, helped to defeat German armour on and after D-Day.

weakness. After 48 hours only two out of twelve were still running, which may explain why two examples of this relatively rare AFV remained in Normandy for 70 years.

The 17-pounder anti-tank gun was the most powerful Allied anti-tank gun used in Normandy. Its shot could penetrate any German tank. Imagine trying to manhandle it into position and digging a hole big enough to hide it.

The 25-pounder gun/howitzer was the standard equipment for field artillery. It was towed by a four-wheel drive field artillery tractor, and was less suitable than self-propelled guns for fighting on the beaches themselves. When in action, the guns were held on the turntable platform with cables. This provided a stable platform and allowed one man to pick up the trail, with a hand spike, to make a large switch between targets.

The 40mm L60 Bofors Gun was the main light anti-aircraft equipment used by the British Army. The version on display was usually towed by a Morris Gun Tractor. On D-Day these were towed behind tracked Crusader SP AA guns. The guns were usually deployed alongside radars which gave early warning of air attacks.

The M3 half-track on display is one of the most numerous armoured half-track vehicles. They were used within artillery regiments, as battery commanders' vehicles, battery command posts, gun tractors for 17-pounder guns in some units and by the forward observer and the bombardment parties which controlled the fire of warships.

The quad 0.5in gun mounting was not used by the British Army in Normandy. A version of the M3 half-track which mounted quad 0.5 guns was known as the M16 and was widely used by the US Army to protect its troops from very low-level air attacks. The British deployed 20mm AA guns in single and triple mountings for the same purpose.

There is also a section of Bailey bridge. Two sets of these bridges were built across each of the Orne canal and river to supplement the bridges captured on D-Day.

Horsa gliders, like this reconstruction at Pegasus Bridge Museum, transported 211 Battery to Normandy, the first British artillery battery to deploy by air. Each glider could carry a gun, a jeep, and the gun detachment.

On leaving the museum, turn left into Rue John Howard and left again on to the D514. Cross Horsa Bridge over the Orne. At the roundabout take the turning to Franceville and Cabourg. After 600m take the turning to the right on Rue de la Côte Fleurie, leading past a small industrial estate. The Ranville memorial is at the end of this road.

Ranville Drop Zone Nan Ranville Marker
Rue de la Côte Fleurie, 14860 Ranville (GPS 49.240142, -0.254961)

The fields to the east are the Landing Zone where the bulk of the gliders landing on D-Day morning landed. The marker stone is located where a Horsa glider landed.

At 0020 hours two sticks of pathfinders with markers and radar beacons were dropped by parachute on each drop zone and had set out lights on all three drop zones and radar beacons on DZs N and K between 0035 and 0040 hours.

Twenty-five minutes later, at 0050 hours, a force of a hundred Lancaster bombers dropped 600 tons of bombs on the Merville battery, 5.3km north-west of here. Most bombs missed the battery, hitting and setting fire to the village of Merville, creating a pillar of dust and smoke. This had not dispersed by the time transport aircraft flew over the village en route for DZ V. Aircrew reported being disoriented by the dust cloud a few second before the drop between 0050 and 0115 hours. Less than half of 3 Para Brigade's parachutists landed on the landing zone or within a mile of it. Most of the rest were dropped in the flooded Dives valley and some east of that river. Of eleven 3 Para Brigade gliders landing at 0050, three were lost in cloud off the French coast. None of the remaining eight landed on the landing zone and only one within a mile of it.

Just over half of 5 Brigade's paratroopers were dropped within a mile of their drop zone, but others were widely scattered, some well to the east. The gliders landing on LZ N included the GOC 6th Airborne Division, some FOOs and about half of the anti-tank guns – two 17-pounder and nine 6-pounder guns. As soon as enough troops had been assembled across the landing zones, units set off to carry out their appointed tasks.

Major Russell, BC 210 battery was in a glider:

> Coming over, the flak floated lazy and remote, until a bright little explosion in the middle of the glider was followed by a sharp rap on the sole of my left boot. I had the defenceless feeling of a man on a single-bar latrine, and the idea of landing had lost its terrors. A heavy jarring bounce as we touched down, a pause and then blackout. We had run into an unloading glider and everything had gone for six. Dusty moonlight showed through jagged edges and I crawled out. Nothing of the two Horsa gliders stood higher than six feet. Two killed, three with broken arms or legs; jeep trailer, motor bicycles and wireless all 'written off' and 500 cigarettes in the debris. The officer commanding the FOO and FOB parties had arrived with his party to liberate Europe and did not feel confident of success.

Russell made his way to HQRA in Ranville, hoping to find a duplicate jeep load with his 2IC, but his glider had landed 100km away north of the Seine.

211 Battery of 53 Air Landing Regiment deployed near here on the western edge of the Ranville DZ. It landed on LZ N on D-Day. Initially the battery deployed north of Ranville, at 0130 on 7 June, 'cleverly tucked away on the top edge of a slope falling away steeply behind the guns, the sort of position where only a mortar or 75mm could be deployed'. During the morning, the battery fired in support of 1 Royal Ulster Rifles moving south to Longueval. At about 1500 hours it redeployed into the Bas de Ranville to lengthen the range. Here it was mortared, losing two casualties and a jeep. The battery then moved back to its original position, where one troop engaged enemy infantry over open sights. From the morning of the 8th the battery supported the 1st Special Service Brigade defending Hauger from infantry attacks, with a 'zero line' of 060 degrees, firing no fewer than two thousand rounds that day. From the 9th to the 12th it was fully engaged in the battle for Bréville. At 0800 hours on the 10th C Troop was heavily shelled and Lieutenant G. H. N. Blower, the Gun Position Officer, was killed, Second Lieutenant A. Barrass was fatally wounded, and two other ranks were wounded, before the troop could be moved to an alternative position.

Walk south along the Rue de la Côte Fleurie towards the centre of Ranville, go straight across the roundabout into the Rue de la Vallée. After 30m turn left into the Chemin de Longueville. Walk to the church. If driving, drive south to the first roundabout. Turn left into the D37. At the third turning turn right into the D223A Rue Général Leclerc. At the first junction turn right into the Rue du Comté Louis de Rohan Chabot, then turn right into the Rue de la Brigade Piron and park.

Ranville cemetery photographed in 1944. The cemetery was started by the 6th Airborne Division.

Ranville Churchyard and War Cemetery
1 Rue du Comté Louis de Rohan Chabot, 14860 Ranville (GPS 49.231172, -0.257676)

Ranville church tower was used as an observation post. Two South Notts Hussars officers, Captain Sharman, who landed as an FOB on Juno Beach, met with Lieutenant Hastings in the church tower. One wore a red beret and the other a green one.

The churchyard contains the bodies of the first forty-seven Commonwealth war dead to be buried after D-Day in the area. Ranville War Cemetery contains 2,236 Commonwealth burials and 323 German graves. Among them are the graves of 222 Royal Artillerymen.

Seven gunners who died on D-Day are buried in the cemetery. Captain Hunter (4A.K20), the Senior Officer Bombardment with 6 Airborne Division, Bombardier Sydney (5A.E5) and Gunner Taylor (9C.15) from 4 Air Landing Anti-tank Battery and Gunner Sherrat from 3 Air Landing Battery. Captain Pyman (4A.O12) and Gunner Collins (4A.23) were members of No.6 Commando. Sergeant Mitchley (2E.35) and Bombardier Langton (2F.17) of 20 Anti-tank Regiment were killed in the tank battle at Périers on the afternoon of D-Day. (See Chapter 7)

Captain Bannerman of 126 Field Regiment (1A.C6) was fatally wounded in the fighting for Bréville on 12 June.

Lieutenants Johnson (1A.B12) and Archer (1A.B12) died on 11 and 13 June respectively. However, their parent regiments 81 Field and 116 Field had not arrived in Normandy by then. They were probably some of the additional FOOs assigned to support the airborne landings – the Forward Observation Units FOU. Brigadier D. C. M. Sanders AFC TD (2A.L11) commanded the Royal Marines Armoured Support Group. He and Majors Dickson (2A.L12) and Milliken (2A.M11) were killed on 20 June when their jeep was hit by a shell near Ranville. Sanders was an unusual, accidental, artillery officer. His Air Force Cross was awarded for service in the First World War with the Royal Air Force, and he then became a Territorial officer in the Leicestershire Yeomanry, a mounted cavalry unit which became field artillery in 1940, making Sanders a Gunner. He became the Commander Royal Artillery of the Royal Marine Division and then Commander of the Royal Marines Armoured Support Group. Very few officers served in all three arms, and few reservists reached the rank of brigadier general.

Major Jarmain, (3A.L9) BC of 193 Battery of 61st Anti-tank Regiment, died on 26 June 1944. He was a poet who wrote 'At War Grave':

No grave is rich, the dust that herein lies
Beneath this white cross mixing with the sand
Was vital once, with skill of eye and hand
And speed of brain. These will not re-arise
These riches, nor will they be replaced;
They are lost and nothing now, and here is left
Only a worthless corpse of sense bereft,
Symbol of death, and sacrifice and waste.

Leave the cemetery and turn right into the Rue du Comté Louis de Rohan Chabot. At the end of the road turn right into the D223A Rue Général Leclerc. At the first crossroads with the Rue du Colonel Fabien you have reached your destination. (1.3 km, 17 min on foot, 2 min by car)

This view is from the German positions counter-attacking towards Ranville.

Ring Contour

Rue du Colonel Fabien, 14860 Ranville (GPS 49.224463, -0.266820)

This is the point from which the Germans of 21st Panzer Division attacked towards Ranville on D-Day. The unintended scatter of the paratroops misled the Germans about Allied objectives. Although the *coup de main* attack on the Orne bridges was masked by an air raid on Caen, the Germans could not fail to notice the descent of thousands of parachutes and dozens of gliders. As soon as the landings started, the Germans were placed on high alert. German units were expected to take the initiative and counter-attack swiftly against airborne troops. As soon as reports of paratroops came in, the companies of the 2nd battalion of the 125th Panzer Grenadiers struck out from their village billets, while two sections of the 1st Panzerjäger company set off from Biéville to the Bénouville bridges. Feuchtinger, the divisional commander, tried to obtain authorization from Army Group B to launch a full-scale counter-attack, but his request was turned down.

After the naval bombardment he made a second request – also refused – but he was authorized to use the Panzer Grenadiers to capture Ranville. The 125th Panzer

The bridge over the River Orne was known as Horsa Bridge. Somewhere over the photographer's left shoulder was F6 gun.

Grenadiers would make an attack soon after dawn against the southern flank of the bridgehead. A second push was made in mid-morning, reinforced by the 21st Panzer Division's reconnaissance battalion, a battalion of tanks and the assault gun battalion. Their orders were to crush the airborne troops, recapture the Orne bridges and establish contact with the coastal units. At 0745 hours Army Group B released 21st Panzer Division to LXXXIV Corps, but the orders took two hours to reach Feuchtinger, who had assembled 120 tanks and 3,000 infantrymen to attack Ranville. However, at 10.30 Feuchtinger received orders to switch his main effort to Caen and attack west of the canal, north to the coast.

By 1000 hours on D-Day the anti-tank guns of 4 Anti-tank Battery were in their previously recced positions covering the southern approaches to the Ranville area. Gun detachments were made up with glider pilots trained as anti-tank gunners. At around 1030 hours a group of German SP guns and panzer grenadiers advanced from here towards Ranville. By 1430 one anti-tank gun had been lost, with two glider pilots and one gunner killed and two wounded.

Walk along the Rue du Colonel Fabien, the left of the two roads leading north from the ring contour. At the end of the road turn left into Rue du Moulin d'Eau. Turn right into Chemin du Bar de Ranville au Marais and at the end of the road turn left. Negotiate the roundabout using the pedestrian crossings, take the second exit along the D514 and continue to the bridge over the river Orne. (2.1km, 25 min on foot)

If driving, drive south-west along the D223A. Take the first right into the D223, at the roundabout take the third exit into the D514 towards Bénouville. Park where you can, close to the bridge over the River Orne.

Horsa Bridge

Pont de Ranville, 14860 Ranville, France (GPS 49.240182, -0.266204)

The bridges over the Orne river and canal were initially the only route between the 6th Airborne Division and the beachheads. These were vital points. Close to the east side of the beachhead, they could be attacked by the Luftwaffe with minimum exposure to Allied air defences. The high ground east of the River Dives allowed low-flying aircraft a route that would avoid detection by Allied radar until the last minute.

The Orne River Bridge was a swing bridge designed by Gustav Eiffel which at one time carried a light railway over the river. F troop of 92 (7th Loyals) LAA Regiment landed on Sword Beach on D-Day with the task of establishing a Vital Point defence for Pegasus and Horsa Bridges. Two self-propelled guns deployed near here, one on the east bank south of the Bridge and one on the west bank north of it.

Walk or drive towards Bénouville. Cross Pegasus Bridge, and when you reach the Mairie turn right into Avenue de la Côte de Nacre/D35.When you reach the church, halt. (1.3km, 17 min walking, 3 min driving)

A modern view of the Le Port church.

The hole in the church tower was either caused by a PIAT or a clip of 40mm rounds from a Bofors gun. F Troop took twelve prisoners as they cleared the village.

Le Port: Église Notre-Dame du Port
Place du Commando N 4, 14970 Bénouville, France (GPS 49.246955, -0.276284)

F Troop of 318th Battery of 92th (7th Loyals) Light AA Regiment was to provide air defence cover to the Bénouville bridges. The troop landed on schedule at 1400 hours (H+6½), but was held up by congestion, small arms and mortar fire and the arrival of 6 Air Landing Brigade. The troop commander, Captain Reid, took twelve prisoners on his recce through Le Port. Ken Holder Vale had a narrow escape:

> I heard this thump beside my head. I knew instantly that it was a bullet that had missed me. I moved like greased lightning to the other side of the truck and the shout went up from somewhere, 'Sniper in the Church Tower!' All hell broke loose. At the suggestion of a Parachute Regiment officer, Sergeant Clements' F1 gun was brought into action and opened fire. This resulted in a young German surrendering.

Now return to Pegasus Bridge.

Pegasus Bridge
Pegasus Bridge, Rue du Domaine de Camilly, 14970 Bénouville, (GPS 49.242601, -0.274912)

On the western side of the bridge, opposite the Pegasus Bridge Café, is a 40mm Bofors gun, painted a little inaccurately in the markings of F Troop of 92nd LA A Regt, which used SP equipment. However, this Light AA guns is a reminder of their

This photograph, taken in 2014, shows the modern Pegasus Bridge, with a wider roadway, built to a similar design to the original. The buildings to the left are the Café Gondree and the Trois Planeurs.

The bridge at Benouville from the east on 8 June. The 40mm guns of F Troop, 92 Regiment LAA, defended this key point, shooting down fourteen aircraft in ten days.

This 40mm Bofors gun, painted in the markings of 92 Light AA, is similar to those of the Light AA units that took over from 92.

F Troop were equipped with 40mm Bofors SP guns like these.

key role defending the Orne bridges. By 21 June twenty-four 40mm AA guns like this, and sixteen 20mm AA guns, protected six bridges across the canal and River Orne.

F Troop arrived in Bénouville at last light on D-Day. By first light on 7 June 1944, its six self-propelled 40mm guns were deployed between Pegasus Bridge and Horsa Bridge. The troop headquarters was deployed in two slit trenches on the edge of a field on the road between Le Port and Bénouville, where in 1944 there was a good view of Pegasus Bridge and the Orne Canal.

On 8 June around forty-five enemy aircraft made cannon and machine gun attacks on the bridges. F troop shot down three Fw190s. On 9 June groups of fifty or more aircraft attacked in successive waves. That day, the AA defences shot down three Me109s and six Fw190s. The attacks on the bridges continued until 10 June, costing the Germans two more Me109s, another Fw190 and a Ju88. During the first four days F Troop's four guns fired 5,000 rounds. Captain Reid, the troop commander, was awarded the MC, and Sergeant Clements an MID for courage in tackling a fire on F3 gun while under mortar fire. However, the ship carrying the remainder of 318 Battery was sunk in the Channel by German coastal guns, with the loss of eight gunners and all the remaining guns.

This tour now ends.

Aerial photograph showing the positions of the guns of F Troops F1-F6.

Layout of troop position on a 1:25,000 map.

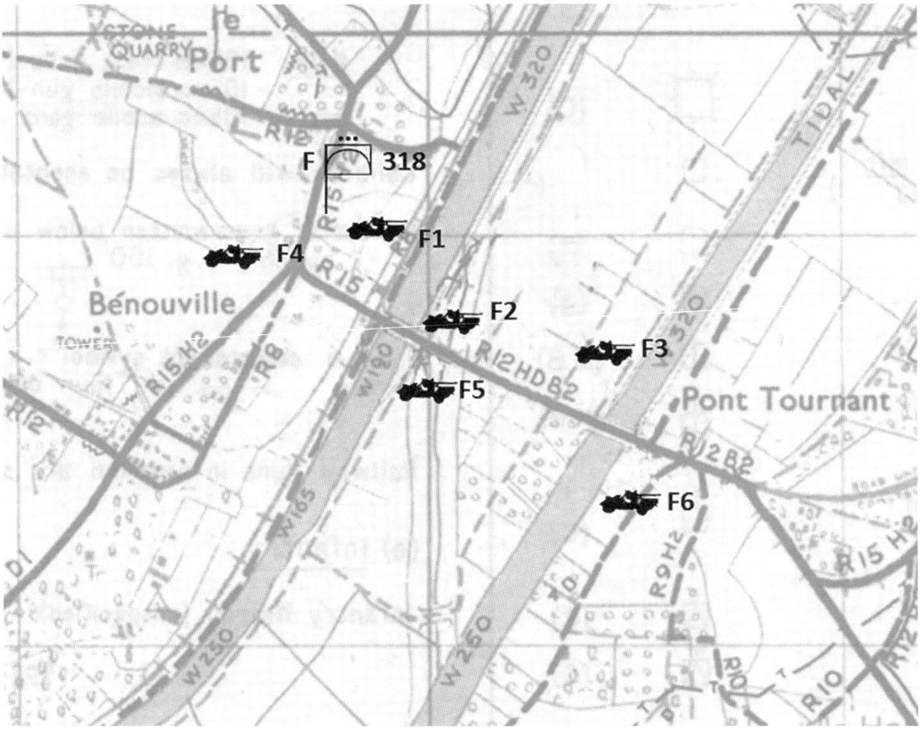

Chapter 7

Sword Beach

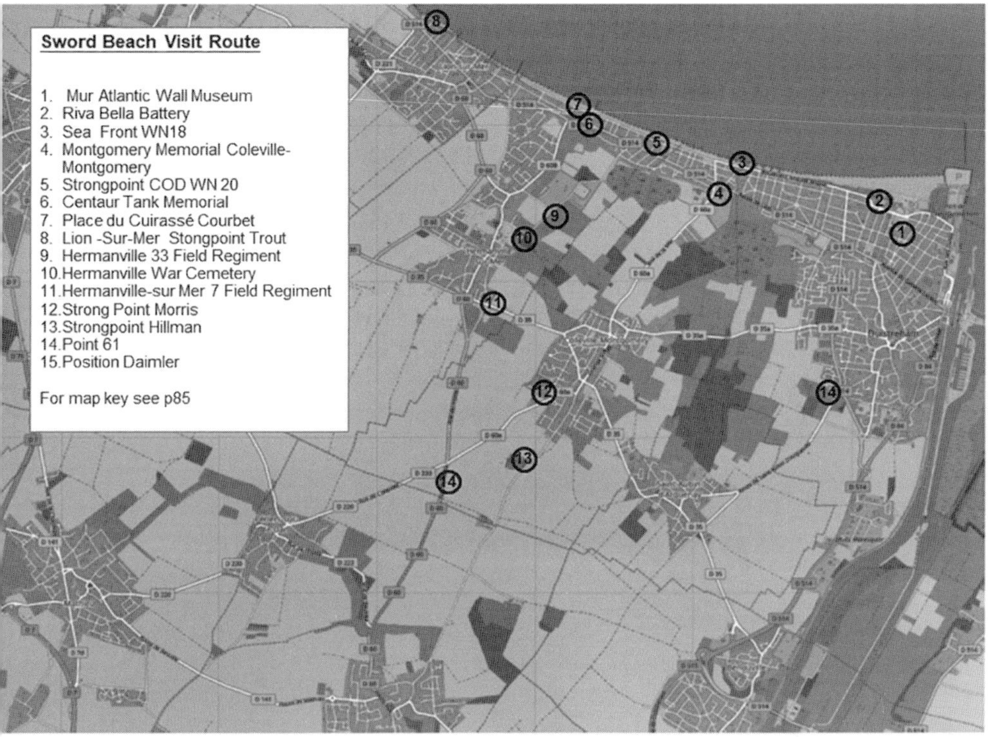

Wake at 3.30 and to my surprise ate a hearty breakfast. By that time, we were slipping along the French coast, and in the darkness could see the flashes of our bombs, and intermittent fires that they had started along the coast. At 5 am we joined the men below; stood for a moment while the ship's padre addressed us, a simple and very impressive ceremony; and then on to the assault craft. We had not been attacked or interfered with the whole time. At 6 am my flight was lowered into the water – I was with the reserve company of the left- hand assault battalion (2 E Yorks) and therefore twenty minutes behind the first flight. By that time it was light. We crept towards the coast – the assault wave and various RE craft were just visible ahead and the warships closing in on either side, and the aircraft, fighters and bombers, swirling about above our heads.

Captain Featherstone 302 Battery, 76 (Highland) Field Regiment

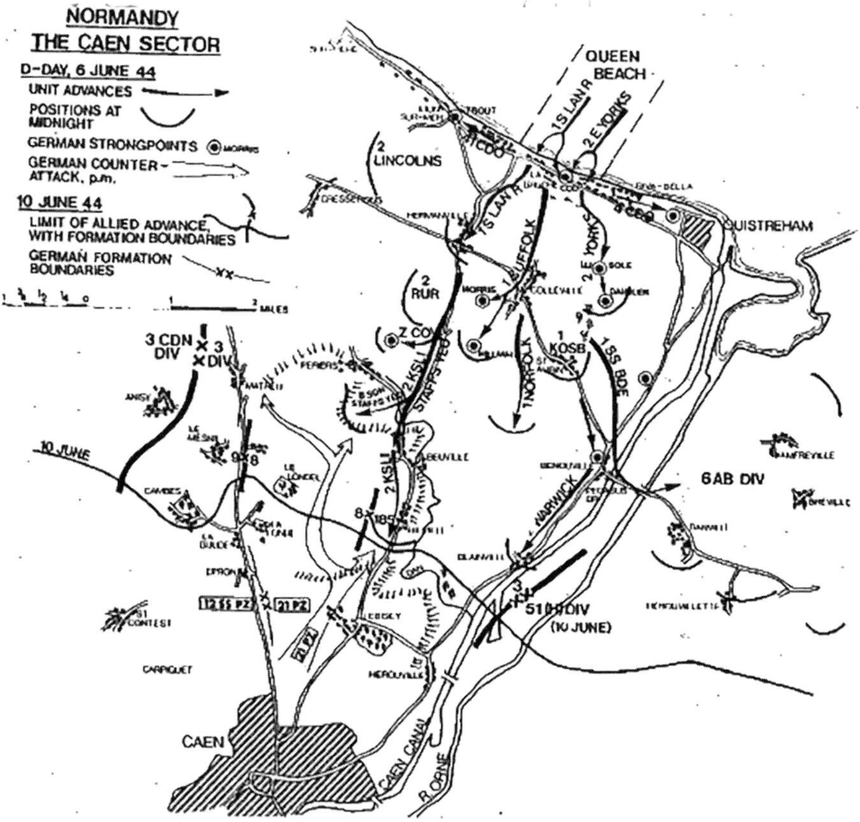

Summary of operations in Caen sector.

Sword Beach was 12,800 yards (11,700m) long between St Aubin and Ouistreham. The coastline included seven defensive positions manned by three companies from GR736 of 716 Infantry Division. The tenth company (10/GR 736) occupied the three defence posts that would be assaulted from the sea: WN18, with one 7.5cm and one 5cm anti-tank gun; WN20, Strongpoint Cod, with one 8.8cm and three 5cm; and WN21, Strongpoint Trout, with one 7.5cm and two 5cm anti-tank guns. Within these positions were sixteen machine guns, two 5cm and two 8cm mortars. Flanking the assault beach but outside small arms range were two other companies. To the west, 9/736 in WN24, and to the east, defending the Riva Bella strongpoint at Ouistreham, 2/736 in WN08 and WN10.

Behind them were four infantry companies from Infantry Division 716, and the divisional pioneer company:

- 3./Ost 642 *Ost* (10–15 MG & three Mortars) Hermanville.
- 4./GR 736 (4-12 MG, two 5cm & two 8cm Mortars) Colville.
- 11./GR 736 (12–16 MG: two 5cm & two 8cm Mortars) Cresserons.
- 12./GR 736 (16 MG: two 5cm & two 8cm Mortars) WN21a WN22 La Deliverande.
- 1/Pi 716 Herouvillette.

Six defensive positions manned by artillery batteries and unit and formation headquarters also provided some depth. Most of the positions had been identified and located by the Allies:

- 2/AR 1716 (four 15.5 cm) WN12 Strongpoint Morris.
- 4/AR 1716(four 10 cm) WN15 Strongpoint Daimler.
- 11(sf)/AR 1716 six self-propelled 10.5cm howitzers Plumetot (unlocated).
- 1/HKK 1260 (Six 15.5 cm) St Aubin d'Arquenay. Redeployed to field positions from the Riva Bella emplacements (unlocated).
- HQ I/GR 736Strongpoint Sole.
- HQ GR 736 WN17Strongpoint Hillman.

Elements of 21 Panzer Division in field positions much further north than had been identified by Allied intelligence, which positioned the division between Caen and Falaise:

- II/192 PGR, with 91 MG, three 7.5cm SP anti-tank guns and three SP 2cm flak guns, in the area between Blainville, point 61 and Périers-sur-Dan.
- Panzerjäger Battalion 200 with twenty-four 8.8cm towed anti-tank guns was deployed north-west of Caen.
- Two batteries of towed 122mm field guns and one of 100mm K 18 guns of I/155 PzArtl Regiment (twelve guns) were deployed in the Périers-sur-Dan area. The field positions of one of these had been located by Allied intelligence and was included in the D-Day fire plan.
- One flak battery of Flak battalion 305 was deployed on the high ground North of Caen (four guns).
- The armour of the 21st Panzer Division and the remainder of the division were one hour's drive south of Caen.

3rd Division plan

The intention was to assault through Queen Red and White beaches to capture the city of Caen by a rapid advance and then establish a bridgehead south of the city. The division was also assigned a series of additional tasks: secure landing areas and capture the high ground of the Périers Ridge inland; advance east to link up with the 6th Airborne Division and secure river crossings over the Orne River and Caen canal; and advance west to link up with the 3rd Canadian Division.

3rd Infantry Division and its supporting troops attacked on a front of one brigade, on the 1,600-yard stretch of Queen White and Red beaches. Rocks to the west and sand bars to the east precluded a second assault beach in the sector.

The Assault Brigade

The assault was to be mounted by 8th Infantry Brigade group, commanded by Brigadier W. N. R. Case with, under command, 13/18 Hussars, 5 Assault Regiment RE (less two squadrons) and 4th and 41st Commandos. The brigade group was to secure a beachhead from the high ground at Périers-sur-Dan to St Aubin d'Arquenay. Its detailed tasks included:

1. Assault and clear the beaches of aimed fire to enable the engineers to construct vehicle exits and clear beach obstacles.
2. Relieve the 6th Airborne Division at Bénouville and Ranville Bridge as soon as possible, or attack and capture them, if in enemy hands. Not less than a company of infantry and a squadron of tanks were to be used for this.
3. Destroy the battery known as Daimler.
4. Capture the high ground near Périers and capture the defensive positions of Morris and Hillman.
5. Destroy the coastal battery at Ouistreham battery, for which No 4 Commando was specifically allocated.
6. Mop up the coastal area to Luc-sur-Mer, for which No 41 Commando was allocated.

The 1st Special Service Brigade was to land under the command of 8th Infantry Brigade, between H+75 and H+105 on Queen Beaches and move as quickly as possible to cross the River Orne in the vicinity of the Bénouville Bridge. No 4 Commando would revert to the command of 1 Special Service Brigade after clearing Ouistreham, and No 41 Commando would revert to command of 4th Special Service Brigade once they had made contact with 4th Special Service Brigade, which landed on Juno beach.

The Intermediate Brigade

The 185th Infantry Brigade Group, under the command of Brigadier K. P. Smith, with the Staffordshire Yeomanry in support, was to land at approximately H+2½ hours. Its task was to capture Caen and secure a bridgehead south of the River Orne at Caen. The advance was to be carried out with speed and boldness to overcome the enemy's local reserves quickly and establish the brigade on its objective ready to meet counter-attacks which might develop towards the evening of D-Day. After securing the city of Caen, the Brigade was to push forwards a company of infantry and a squadron of tanks to the high ground on the Caen–Falaise road.

The Reserve Brigade

The 9th Infantry Brigade group commanded by Brigadier J. C. Cunningham MC, with East Riding Yeomanry in support, was to land at H+5½ hours. After assembling south of the beach, it was then to move to Plumetot into divisional reserve. It was to be prepared to move forwards to a forward concentration area north-west of Caen to protect the right flank of 185 Infantry Brigade. It was also to be prepared to attack Caen from the west if 185 Brigade failed to penetrate the northern defences. If the 3rd Canadian Division was held up, it was to be prepared to attack west.

The 27th Armoured Brigade was to be prepared to concentrate its units as a reserve, or to be prepared to investigate the enemy along the Caen–Falaise road to exploit sudden success.

Artillery Plan

The artillery plan reflected the size and scale of the tasks.

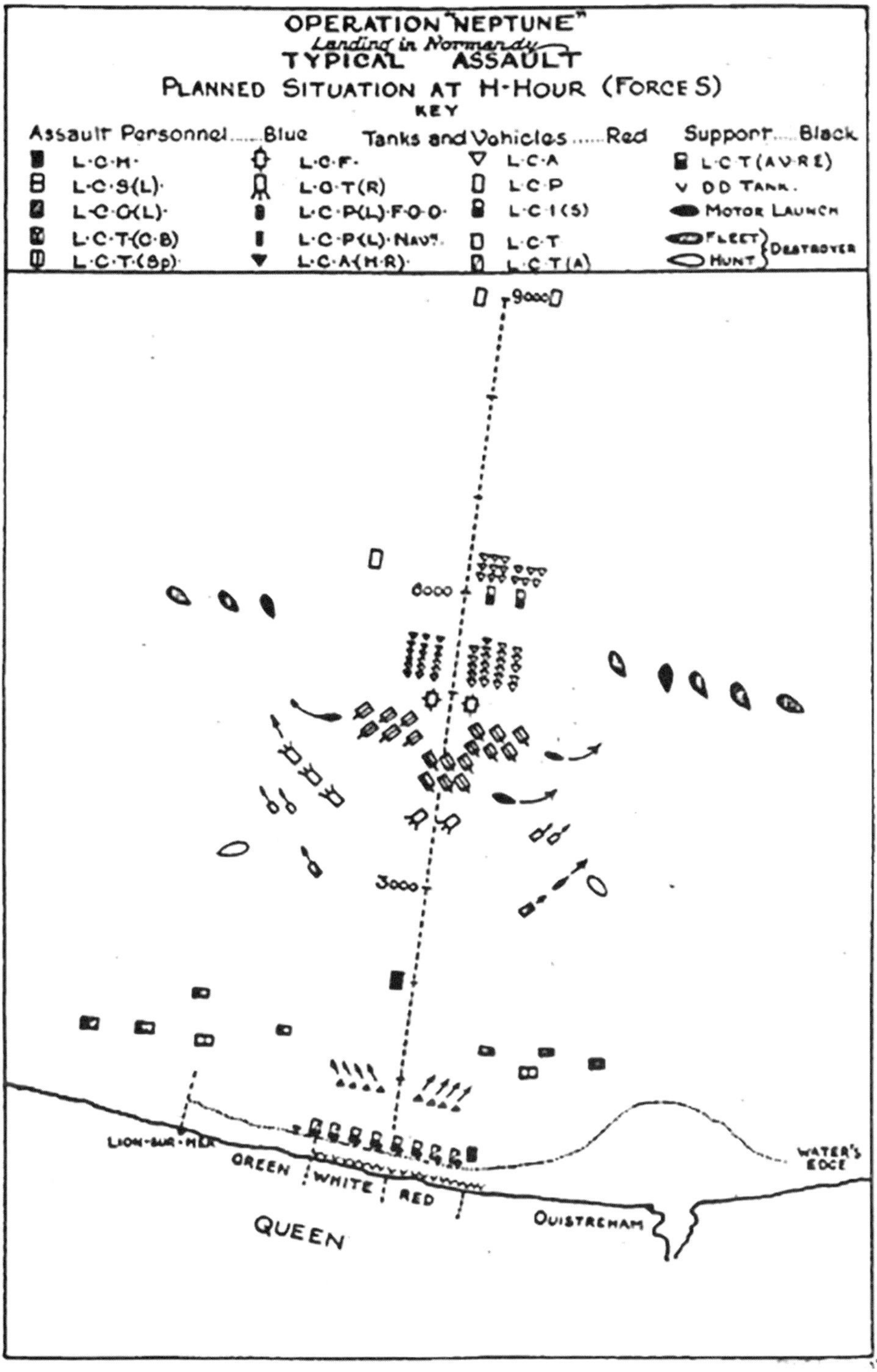

Sketch map showing the planned situation at H-20 for Sword Beach.

The Fire plan

The fire plan for the assault was a variant of the plan adopted on all beaches. The fire plan for the assault on Sword Beach is shown in the following table.

The key to applying the firepower of the warships were the seven Forward Observers Bombardment (FOB) from A Bombardment Troop of 1 Combined Operations Bombardment Unit (COBU). One was assigned to each of the battalions 8 and 185 Brigades, and one was in reserve. Air support could be obtained from RAF liaison officers with HQ 1 Corps, 3 Infantry & 6 Airborne Divisions, 8 & 185 Infantry, 1 Special Service Brigades and HMS *Largs*.

The artillery was provided by 3 Division:

- 7 Field Regiment
- 33 Field Regiment
- 76 (Highland) Field Regiment
- 20 Anti-tank Regiment
- 92 (Loyals) Light AA Regiment

Under command:

- 53 Medium Regiment (4 AGRA).
- 245 (SP17-pounder) Battery 62 Anti-Tank Regiment.
- MAA Assault Group (80 AA Brigade).
- NAA Assault Group (80 AA Brigade).
- A Survey Battery 9 Survey Regiment (I CorpsTroops).
- B Flight 652 Air OP Squadron RAF.
- A Bombardment troop COBU.
- 5 (Independent) RM Battery RM Armoured Support Group).
- Assistant Counter Bombardment Officer I Corps.
- Division Meteorology Section.

And in support 3 Division:

- 4 RHA (Army troops) (landing D+1).
- 150 Field Regiment (4 AGRA) (landing D+1).

In support 6 AB Division

- 65 Medium Regiment (4 AGRA) landing on Second tide.

On D-Day the CRA 3rd Infantry had a considerably expanded command – nine units and five sub-units. Many of these were under temporary command until their parent HQs landed. However, for a day or two HQ RA 3rd Division commanded about the same number of units that might form an entire division. This would be too many to command practically under normal circumstances. However, most of these units would be implementing pre-written orders.

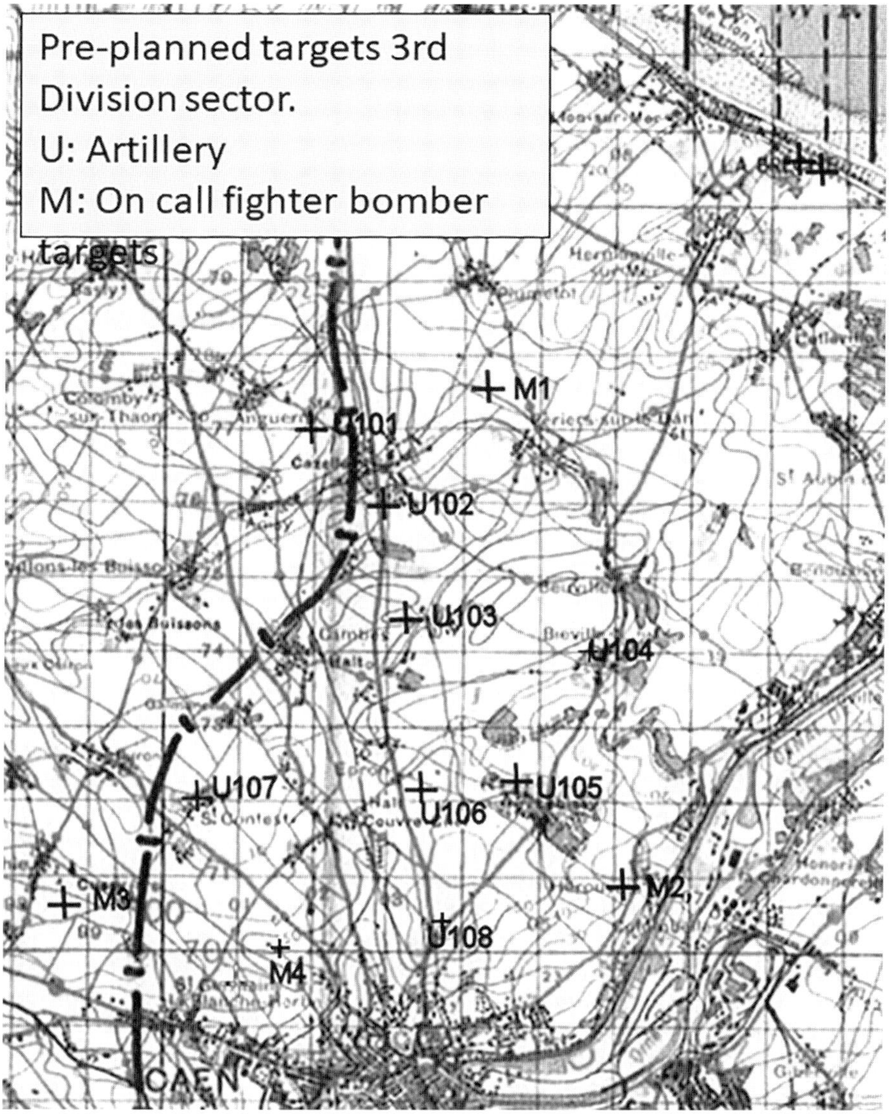

Pre-planned targets in the 3rd Division's sector.

Field Artillery

Once ashore, the field artillery of the division was to support the main task of capturing Caen as well as other conflicting and subsidiary tasks. The Germans might have assigned artillery under command of the different battlegroups. The British had some subtle distinctions in how artillery was commanded.

The order to support a formation meant that the unit had to be able to engage relevant targets and be ready to support its operations. The artillery unit could still respond to calls for fire from other formations. An order specifying that an artillery unit was 'at priority call' meant that it was reserved for that formation.

3 Division Artillery orders were intended to provide direction and flexibility. 33 and 76 Field Regiments would land in support of 8th infantry brigade. 76 Field would also support 6 Airborne Division and 1 Special Service Brigade until 8 Infantry Brigade relieved it on the Orne bridges. 7 Field Regiment would land in support of 185 Infantry Brigade Group which was to have the support of both 7 and 33 Field Regiments on passing through 8th Infantry Brigade. 185 Brigade Group would also have the first call on 76 Field Regiment less one battery. 4 RHA and

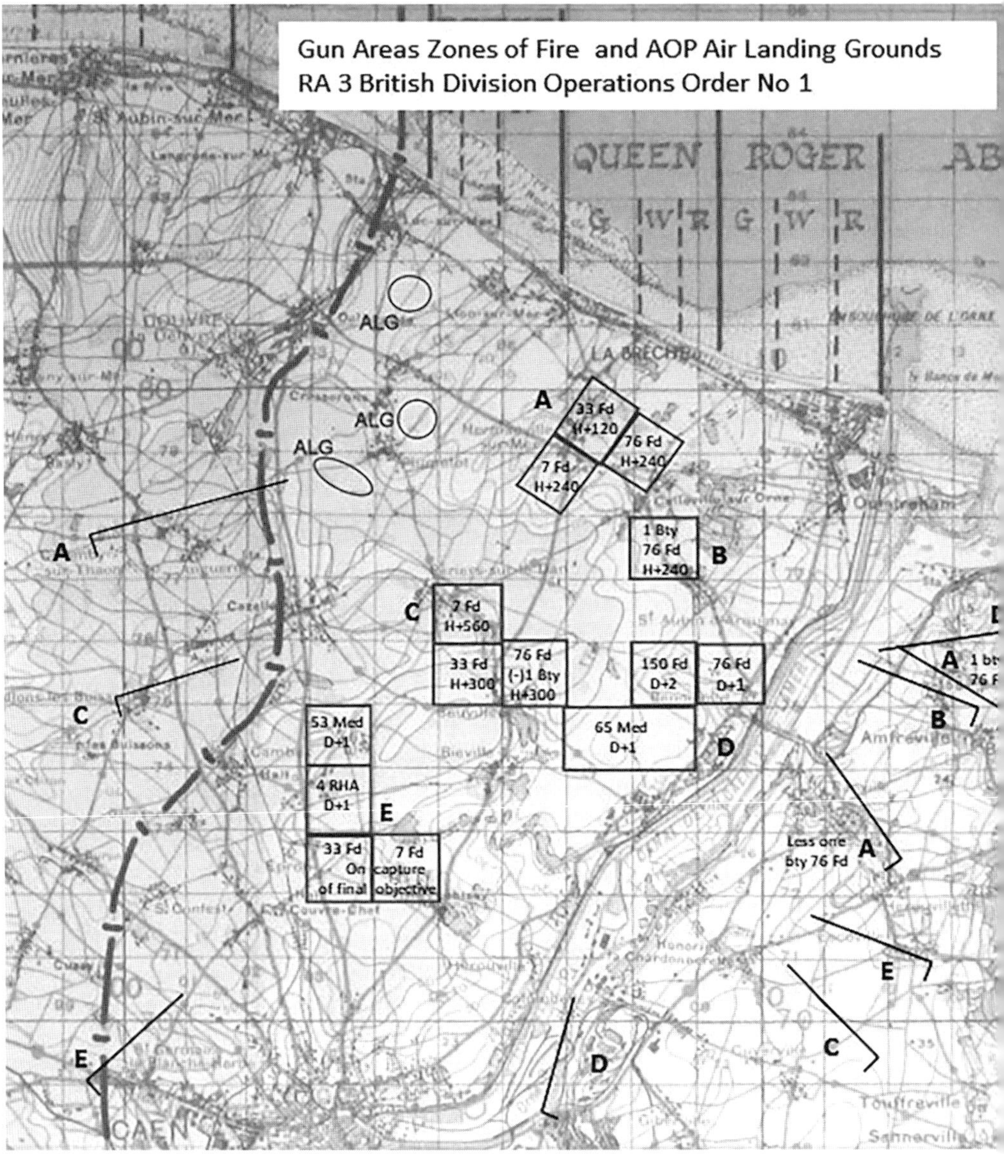

Planned 3rd Division artillery areas and air landing grounds and the zones they were expected to engage.

150 Field Regiment would remain under command of the CRA, who would control the Divisional artillery as soon as possible after he landed.

Direct support affiliation meant that artillery liaison and observation parties would be assigned to the formation, and with them the communications to make a direct link between the guns and the supported arm, 76 Field with 8 Brigade, 33 Field with 9 Brigade and 7 Field with 185 Brigade. The addition of the regiments of 27 Armoured Brigade meant that there would be some shuffling of affiliations as the operation evolved.

One third of FOOs were to be kept in reserve as far as possible. 4 RHA and 53 Medium Regiment provided an FOO each for No 4 Commando, while 33 and 150 Field Regiment each provided an FOO for No 41 Commando and an LO from 65 Medium Regiment would be at HQ 1 Special Service Brigade to call for fire from 76 Field Regiment when required.

Artillery orders also needed to specify how the guns moved. These movements were directed by the CRA or CCRA, not the infantry or armour. Orders specified a location, a centre of arc or zero line as well as timings. In the advance, artillery needed to step forwards, keeping some guns available to fire while the others moved. This mattered on D-Day, when the final perimeter was beyond artillery range of the beaches. Reconnaissance parties were to move well forward, landing early on the beaches, and one battery per regiment should be ordered forwards at the first opportunity.

5 Independent (RM) Battery would support 8 Infantry Brigade on landing. Subsequently, two troops each would support Nos.4 & 41 Cdo. When these tasks were finished, the batteries were to return to control of CRA, for counter-mortar operations under the command of 7 and 33 Field Regiments.

53 Medium Regiment would be responsible for counter-battery tasks in conjunction with the ACBO and harassing fire tasks.

A survey troop from 9 Survey Regiment was to establish a divisional grid as soon as possible on D-Day. This would accurately position batteries from different regiments making it easier for them to fire on the same target. The plan was to put all guns in the Corps grid at 1800 hours on D+2, 8 June. Meteor telegrams were to be circulated every four hours starting from D+1. The technical work of the survey units enabled field artillery to fire accurately on targets which they had not shot at before.

Anti-tank

The task of artillery in the attack was to provide continuous anti-tank defence during and after the attack. The batteries were to land as follows:

- Under Command 8 Brit Infantry Brigade. 67 A/Tk Battery (less 6-pounder Troops); SP Troop 45 A/Tk Battery.
- Under Command 185 Infantry Brigade. 41 A/Tk Battery; SP Troop 45 A/Tk Battery as 185 Brigade passed through 8 Infantry Brigade.
- Under Command 9 Brit Infantry Brigade 101 A/Tk Battery.

The 6-pounder troops 67 A/Tk Battery were to join its battery on landing. 245 (17-pounder SP) of 62 A/Tk Regiment was to come under command of 20 A/Tk

Regiment on landing. 45 A/Tk Battery (less the SP Troop) was to remain in reserve under command 20 A/Tk Regiment.

The co-ordination of the divisional anti-tank layout of the anti-tank defences was the responsibility of CO 20 A/Tk Regiment, who was also concerned with the minefield layout.

Anti-Aircraft

The task of Light AA was to provide protection from low-flying aircraft and dive-bombers. Cover from seawards for ships and craft beaching and unloading was to be provided by four LCF (each with six 20mm Oerlikons and four 2 pounder pom poms). Other 20mm and 40mm guns were not to open fire during the final approach unless specifically ordered to.

One troop of 318 Battery of 92 Lt AA Regiment landed on the first tide for the priority task of the bridges at Bénouville and Ranville. Two troops were to land on the third tide to protect the divisional gun areas.

AA Assault groups M and N were to be in support of 101 beach maintenance areas.

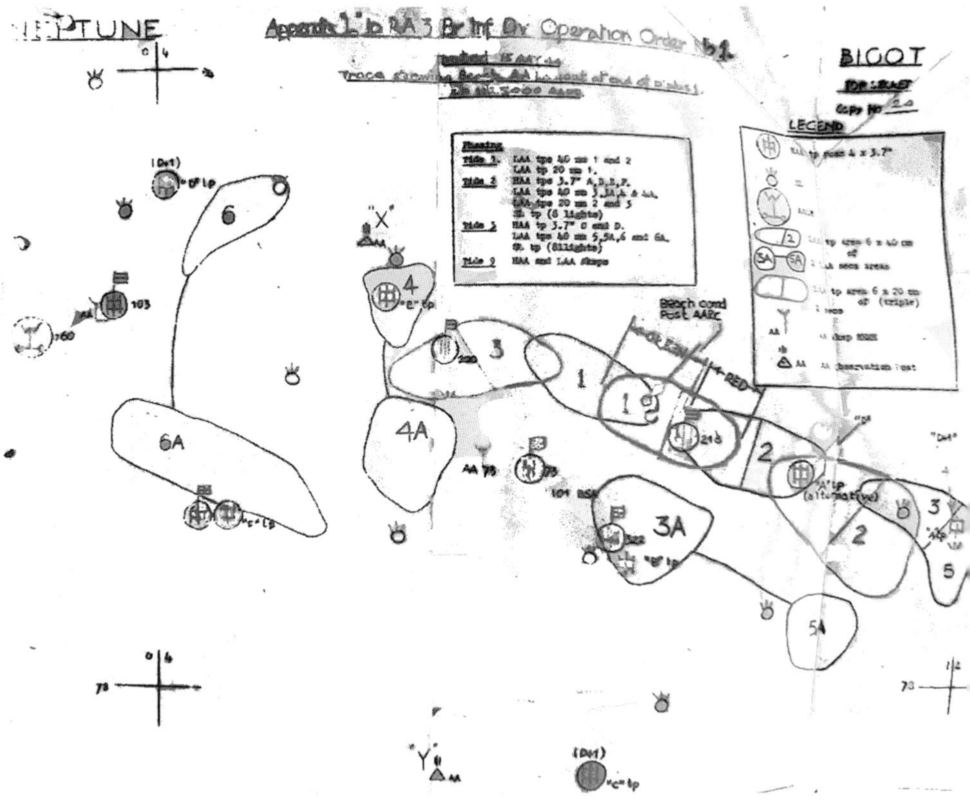

Trace showing planned positions for air defences of Sword Beach by D+1.

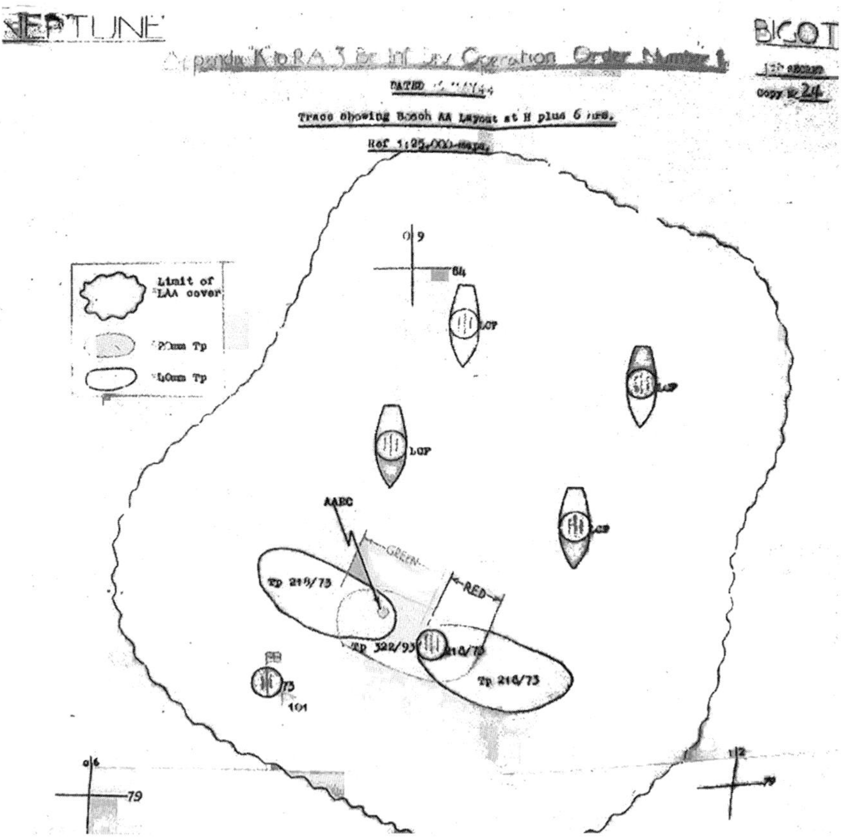

Planned Light AA positions and Landing Craft Flak for Sword Beach.

Touring Sword Beach

This 23.7km tour is designed to be undertaken on foot, by cycle or by car. There is a limited bus service from Caen to Ouistreham (Line 61) and along the beach. Buses are most frequent during the beginning and end of the school day. The area is a seaside resort and there are plenty of cafés and restaurants along the seafront. There are supermarkets near the Montgomery statue and at Lion-sur-Mer. The inland settlements of Colleville Montgomery and Hermanville-sur-Mer are residential villages. There is a restaurant in Colleville- Montgomery, 'La Ferme Saint-Hubert'.

Mur Atlantic Museum
Avenue du 6 Juin, 14150 Ouistreham (GPS 49.287213, -0.252407)

This museum offers a place to orient the visitor and see some of the artillery equipment used. The bunker was the command and observation tower for the Riva Bella battery. Between here and the sea is where 1st battery of Army Coastal Artillery

Battalion (HKK) 1260 with six 155mm K 418 (f) guns was sited.155mm guns had been deployed since 1942.

Captain Pat Porteous VC RA of No 4 Commando was among the captors of the battery:

> When we got to the battery, we discovered the 'guns' were telegraph poles. We learned afterwards that the battery had been withdrawn about three or four days before D-Day and had been re-sited some three kilometres inland, and as we got into the position, they started bringing fire down on their old position. We lost a lot of chaps there … the observers in the medieval tower were communicating with the gunners at the inland battery. There was a single staircase up the middle of the tower and these Germans were on top. They were as safe as could be. The walls were ten feet thick. One of my men tried to climb the staircase, but the Germans dropped a grenade on him. Another fired the PIAT at the tower, but it failed to penetrate – it was useless. We tried to give the Germans a squirt with the flame-thrower, but they were too high; we could not get enough pressure from those little backpack flame-throwers that we had. We couldn't touch the observers and were starting to take casualties from rifle fire from the tower, so I decided to leave it for someone else.

The German garrison of the tower did not surrender until 8 June.

In the gardens is an M7 Priest SP Gun, as used by the field artillery of the 3rd British and 3rd Canadian Divisions. It was popular with the gunners who served it, but the gun had limited traverse. To make large switches of targets would require the gun to be reoriented by tracking it left or right.

Nearby is an 8.8cm Gun flak 36/37, probably the most famous German artillery piece. By 1944 '88s' had become a generic term for German anti-tank guns. It was

Major Pat Porteus VC RA led a command force.

designed as an anti-aircraft gun, but with the sights and ammunition for engaging ground targets and tanks. The flak 8.8cm guns deployed in Normandy in 1944 were mainly used to engage aircraft rather than tanks. III Flak Corps, the Luftwaffe formation which had over a hundred 8.8cm guns, claimed 4,712 aircraft shot down compared to ninety-two tanks destroyed, of which twelve were knocked out using close-range anti-tank weapons.

The 8.8cm armour-piercing round could penetrate the armour of any Allied tank except the 150mm (6″) frontal armour of the Churchill VII. The flak version was not an ideal anti-tank gun. It was too high to easily conceal or to protect the crew and unarmoured tractor from artillery fire. The 8.8 cm Pak 41/43 fitted on a two-wheeled artillery carriage was used by anti-tank units. Some of these were used by the anti-tank batteries of 21st Panzer Division and 716 Division. There are examples of these in the D-Day Museum at Vierville and in the bunker on Omaha Beach at Vierville.

The flak 88's main ground role in Normandy was as field artillery. In the ground role its maximum range of 14,860m (16,250 yards) was 2,500m (3,000 yards) further than the 25-pounder. The Luftwaffe's flak arm was better supplied with ammunition supply than the army.

The British valued captured 8.8cm guns. No.16 Fire Control post, a troop-sized organization, deployed captured 8.8cm and 2cm guns in the coastal defence role in the Ouistreham area, engaging German craft as well as conducting a duel against the Germans across the Orne estuary. 113 Heavy AA Regiment deployed one or two on the tank approaches to Gold Beach.

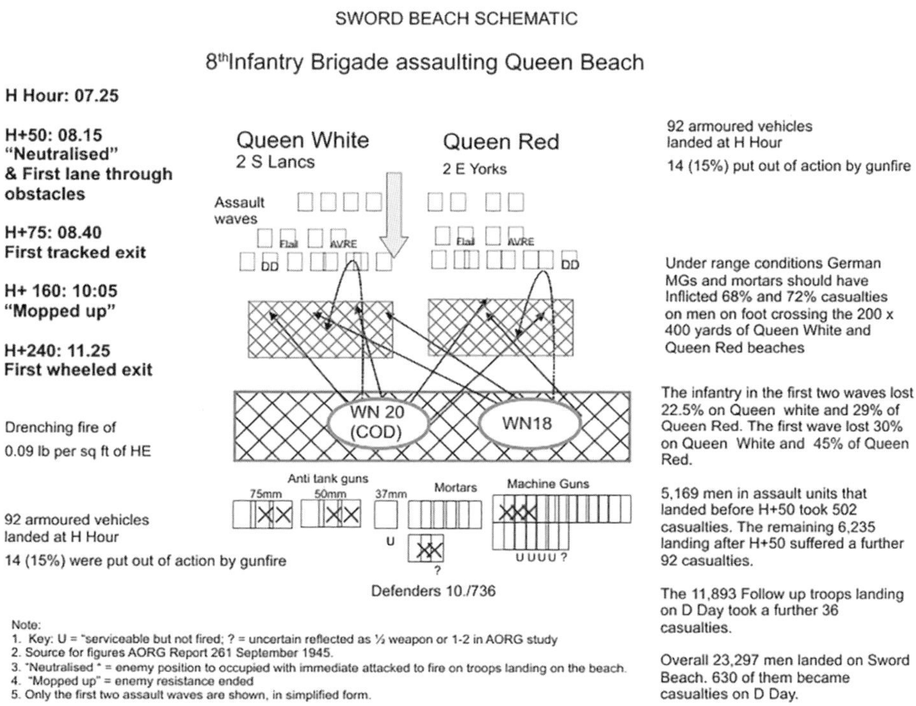

Summary of the events on Sword Beach.

The V1 missile on display is relevant, even though none were flown from the Normandy battlefield. Hitler hoped that these 'revenge' weapons would inflict such casualties on London that the British would sue for peace. The V1 was an unmanned aircraft powered by a pulse jet engine, using a gyrocompass and a simple set of automatic controls. The V1 offensive started on 13 June, and at its height a hundred were launched each day. The defences against the V1 offensive included over 50,000 male gunners and female Auxiliary Territorial Services (ATS) soldiers throughout the Normandy campaign, and this placed pressure on the Allies to capture the launch sites on the channel coast.

Leave the museum and turn left into the Avenue de la Plage. At the end of the road turn left. Between this point and the sea was the site of the Riva Bella gun position. One of these can be seen in the 'Karting' go-kart racetrack on your right.

Riva Bella Battery

Avenue Andry14150 Ouistreham (GPS 49.288942, -0.259790)

Continue west along the Boulevard Maritime and take the first exit, i.e. straight across. In front of you on the right side of the road is the Casino, built on the foundations of the Casino that formed part of the strongpoint captured by French commandos on D-Day. On your left is a large car park and behind it a large white observation platform. This is a German flak tower built to mount Light AA guns to protect the Casino and Riva Bella battery position. German 2cm and 3.7cm flak guns are less well known than the 8.8cm gun. However, these were even more numerous and an important part of the air defences. Allied air forces had substantial losses from flak when attacking ground targets. The beach north of the casino contains the remains of the defences of

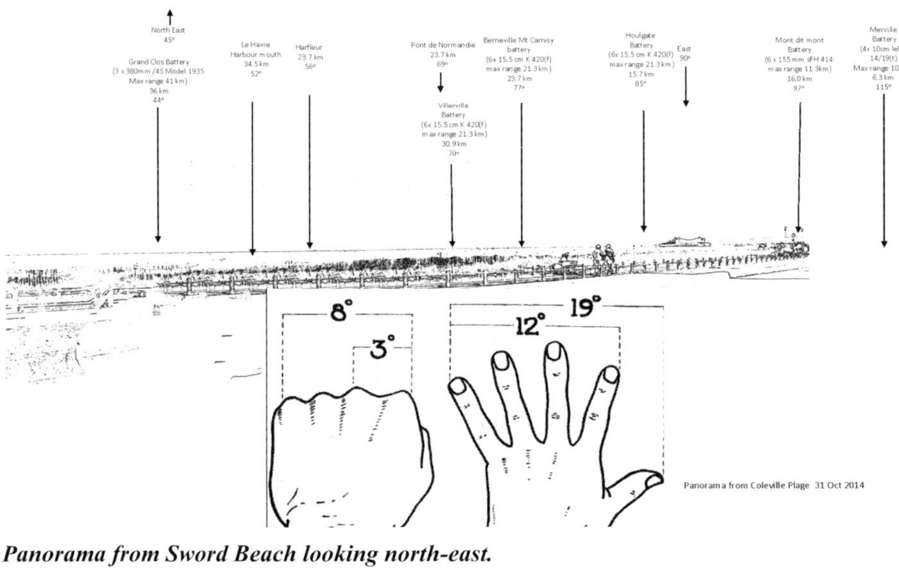

Panorama from Sword Beach looking north-east.

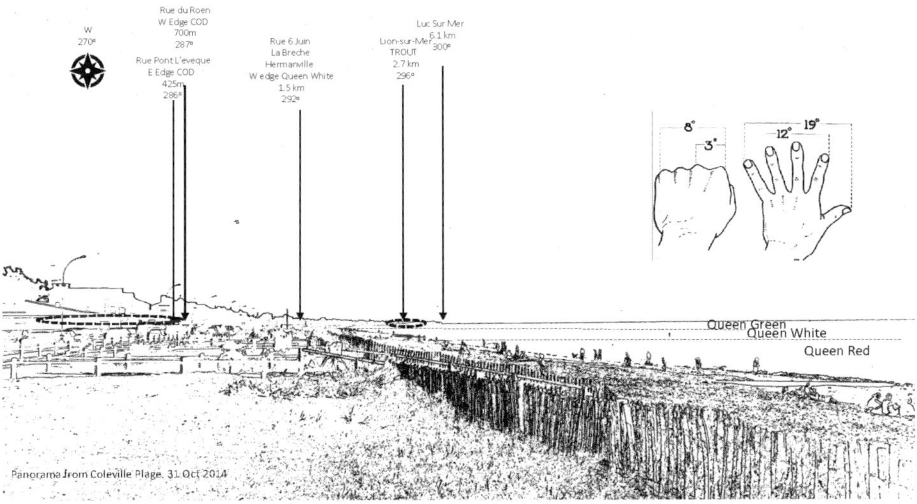

Panorama of Sword Beach looking west.

WN10. To visit them, park and walk along the Avenue Andrey and then between the two lines of beach huts. You can see 'dragons' teeth' anti-tank obstacles in the sand. The dunes contain various German concrete defences. Walk west for 150m to reach a memorial garden with a Commando memorial built on top of a German machine gun bunker. This marks the western edge of the defence nest. This strong position was not attacked from the sea but from the rear via the inland road, the D514.

Continue along the coast road for1,300m, leaving Ouistreham and entering Colleville-Montgomery Plage. You will see a memorial on your right and a German bunker on the left. The bunker is a type 677 anti-tank bunker which housed a 7.5cm gun on D-Day. If you are driving, stop and park.

WN18

Junction Rue Vauban Boulevard Maritime, 14880 Colleville-Montgomery (GPS 49.292936, -0.281115)

You are on the extreme east edge of Queen Red beach. To the east the coast sweeps around to Riva Bella and the port of Ouistreham. Beyond is the high ground east of the River Dives, and the mouth of the River Seine. On an exceptionally clear day it is possible to see Le Havre and the headland north of the Seine estuary, 35km away. This area, known as the Bay of the Seine, was the site of a naval action between the Allied navies and German coastal guns, patrol craft and ships and submarines. On 6 June it was where the easternmost of the Allied armadas would land. Colonel Nigel Tapp commanded 7th Field Regiment:

> We were up at 0400 hrs on 6 June getting ready to open up the wireless. H Hour was 0725 hrs DBST. We were to start shooting at 0655 hrs and wireless was to open at 0625 hrs. In the (ship) *Dacres* I had one ships set on the Regimental

command net and in reserve two 68 portable crystal sets. The wireless worked perfectly and by 0600hrs all Regimental nets were working and through. As the sky and sea lightened, I saw a sight that I shall never forget. The sea was a dark glossy blue flecked with white horses; it was covered with craft as far as one could see. Far away to the south I could see the smoke of the RAF bombing of the French coast. At 0644 hrs ranging of the regimental guns began and by 0655 hrs the guns opened up at 10,000 yards. It was a great relief to me that after all the years of training, all the communications were perfect, and the guns opened up at the correct range. This was much better than any of our exercises. Generally, we found on exercises that either communications were bad or that the gun LCTs were at the wrong range.

As they approached the beach, the launches carrying the observers of 33 and 76 Field Regiments were hit and sunk; Captain Daniel of 76 Field was killed, but Major Wise, the observer for 33 Field, was picked up by Captain Hendrie Bruce, the observer for 7 Field Regiment, and the whole shoot was controlled from his launch:

The big LSIs had hove-to at the lowering position and had launched the thirty-odd LCAs carrying the assault companies of the East Yorkshires and the South Lancashires. These small craft were making their way, pitching and rolling, towards the distant shore which was now clearly visible in the light of a grey stormy day and appeared absolutely deserted. We could see the long row of villas and boarding houses on the sea front and identified the mouth of the River Orne by the lighthouse at Ouistreham but had not positively identified strongpoint Cod as yet.

Meanwhile the LCTs carrying the DD tanks of the 13th/18th Royal Hussars and the AVREs of 5th Assault Regiment Royal Engineers kept steaming steadily on. It was planned that the former should heave to at 7,000 yards and launch the DDs but owing to the heavy sea running they closed to 5,000 yards. We were quite close when sometime after 0600 hours we saw them swing round with their bows downwind and lower their ramps, allowing their extraordinary amphibious tanks with high, inflated bulwarks to crawl down into the water and set off for the shore looking like a lot of rubber dinghies. We were content to cruise along in their wake, scanning the coastline constantly with our special issue naval binoculars until we were satisfied we had identified Cod.

We had now closed the shore to about 3,000 yards. Further out to sea came the group of 18 LCTs carrying the Divisional Artillery and at about 0630 hours, when they were about 15,000 yards from the shore, they began to change formation ready for the 'run-in-shoot', as it was called. Led by LCT 331 (A Troop, 7 Field Regiment aboard) the craft adopted an arrowhead formation of three groups of six each with 7th Field Regiment in the centre, and 33rd and 76th (Highland) Field Regiments slightly to left and right rear respectively. In close attendance was a motor launch equipped with a radar to calculate the opening range. The radio links were working perfectly, and all was now ready for ranging to begin at H-42. At 0644 hours (one minute late) the first ranging rounds were fired by A Troop, 7th Field Regiment, a section salvo of smoke.

To my great satisfaction I saw the third salvo hit the foreshore about 400 yards to the right of the target. I gave a correction and the range, confirmed by the radar Motor Launch, was passed to the three adjutants at the control sets of the leading craft of their regiments. Monitors, cruisers and destroyers had already begun. Promptly at H-35 (0650 hours) the seventy-two 105mm self-propelled guns of the 3rd Divisional Artillery opened fire at just over 10,000 yards range, firing HE, Rate 3.

The guns had been embarked side by side in sections with two guns forward, two aft and the other vehicles in between. Over 100 rounds per gun had been stacked on the tank decks to be expended solely on the run-in, mostly HE but some smoke also if required. At Rate 3 over 200 rounds per minute were arriving on the target which was soon seen to be well covered with burst both on the foreshore and among the buildings behind and by the end of the bombardment over 6,500 rounds, all HE, had been fired. The steady rate of decrease in the range was calculated by an instrument called the Coventry Clock with which each Gun Position Officer, standing on the bridge of his craft, was equipped. A stream of range corrections, dropping 100 yards at a time, was given out over the Tannoy loudspeakers.

The din down in the tank decks was deafening and not only the gunners but all personnel, drivers, signallers, cooks and the like were kept busy passing the ammunition and throwing the empty cartridge cases overboard. The 105mm ammunition came packed in large cardboard cylinders, and these, floating in their thousands in the wake of the LCTs laid a clear trail to the beach for those who followed.

The enemy had now woken up with a vengeance and the sea around the leading craft was peppered with splashes. Several LCTs took evasive action, causing confusion in general and some casualties … and although many of the splashes could be attributed to enemy fire, some of our rounds appeared to be falling short. We were particularly concerned at the fact that the pitching of the Divisional Artillery LCTs in the unusually rough sea might be lengthening the zone of the guns, so, as the first assault wave was nearing the beach, I gave the correction of 'add 600'. The trouble persisted on the right of the target so I stopped the 76th to try and sort things out, but it was immediately apparent that the culprit was an LCT(R) whose salvoes of rockets were falling short, so I immediately gave 'go on' and the 76th resumed at an increased rate to catch up. It was now H-5 when all the guns lifted 400 yards. The assault then went in at 0725 hours, on time. The run-in shoot terminated, and my first task of the day was over.

Turn right and look south at the concrete bunker. This position was WN18, an intermediate defence nest in-between WN08, east of the Orne, Riva Bella and WN20 Cod. The anti-tank gun was placed to cover the front of WN20. The reinforced concrete wing on the north side of the bunker protects the occupants of the bunker from splinters as a result of munitions fired from the sea. In 1944 a bunker like this was almost impregnable from the sea.

Walk south down the Rue Vauban. At the end of the road cross over and look south. You will see the brick wall of a redoubt, built 300 years ago against the

This concrete casemate, seen here in 2014, on the east end of WN 18 housed a 75mm gun which enfiladed Sword Beach.

threat of English invasion. The Germans mounted machine guns on this ancient fortification and incorporated it into their defences. The position consisted of a section of infantry and the detachments for a 7.5cm and a 5cm anti-tank gun.

WN18 was neutralized by 0815 hours (H+50) but not mopped up until 1005 hours (H+160). The anti-tank gun in the bunker may have been responsible for some of the AFVs knocked out on Sword Beach. 76 Field Regiment of 3rd Infantry Division landed in this area of Sword Beach at 0835 hours (H+70) and deployed on the beach.

Return to the seafront. The memorial on the seafront is to the 1st Special Service Brigade and the Norfolk Regiment. The actual landings took place a little further west.

Continue west until opposite the car park. This was the site of a holiday camp before the Second World War. The statue of Bill Millin, the piper of Brigadier Lord Lovat, commander of 1st Special Service Brigade, is on the east side of the car park.

The 1st Special Service Brigade landed on the beach close to this point. Pat Porteous again:

> I lost a quarter of the Troop getting over the seawall, to mines, mortars or machine-guns. We got off that beach as fast as we could. We put down smoke grenades that gave us quite a bit of cover to get across the beach. The pillbox was protected by concrete and they were safe as could be, but the smoke let us get over the beach.

Turn south along the Rue du Bruxelles inland and cross the D514, Rue Riva Bella. Make your way to the statue in the car park on the left side of the road.

Montgomery Memorial, Colleville- Montgomery

General Montgomery Statue, D60A, 14880 Colleville-Montgomery (GPS 49.290419, -0.282324)

Montgomery was an infantryman, but artillery played a big part in his success. Part of his re-invigoration of the Eighth Army involved restoring the practice of centralizing artillery fire. His defensive battles at Alam el Halfa and Medennine used an integrated framework of anti-tank guns to defeat the panzers. In attack he used concentrated artillery firepower to win a battle of attrition. Monty was the protégé of the most influential Gunner in the war, Field Marshal Alan Brooke, the Chief of the Imperial General Staff.

Walk west to the Rue de la Mer, D60a, and turn left. Travel 270m to a bridge over a stream. Stop and look at the field on the right side of the road. 76th (Highland) Field Regiment deployed into this area after moving off the beach – twenty-four Priest SP guns, in six troops, with six M4 Sherman tanks for the GPOs and three half-tracks for the battery command posts. It was from this position that they supported the Suffolks in their evening attack on the Hillman Bunker complex.

Make your way north and turn right into the D514 Rue de Lion. After 550m turn right into Rue de Pont l'Évêque.

Strongpoint Cod

Rue de Pont l'Évêque, 14880 Hermanville-sur-Mer, (GPS 49.294614, -0.288542)

Strongpoint Cod WN20 was bounded by the Rue de Pont L'Évêque and just west of the Rue De Rouen between the sea front and the lateral coast road the D514. Conveniently, the Boulevard de la Mer swings inland between these roads, leaving a wide verge between the road and pedestrian promenade. The area between the beach road and the sea contained defensive works including an anti-tank emplacement, a large concrete casemate containing an 8.8cm anti-tank gun and several 'Tobruck' machine gun posts. The central part of WN20 was inland from the coast road and contained other concrete emplacements, personnel bunkers, more wire machine guns and minefields and a network of trenches. The defenders were from the 10th Company of Grenadier Regiment 736. One 'Tobruck' is still visible as a garden shed in No 6 Rue de Pont L'Eveque.

Captain Featherstone (302 battery 76th Field Regiment) was the FOO with the reserve company of 2 E Yorks:

> At H+25 minutes we touched down; the atmosphere of cool confidence and determination was absolutely terrific. I felt in good form, I simply couldn't believe myself. As soon as the front doors dropped we jumped knee height into the water, and the sight before us was ghastly, a machine gun was sweeping our part of the beach with a hail of fire; wounded and dead lay all over the shop. Well, we ran like stink to the top of the beach; fortunately we hit no mines, and I and my party reached the dunes unscathed. We had a bit of a job getting away

A B26 Marauder Medium bomber from the Ninth US Air Force over Sword Beach on D-Day. It is easy to see the outline of Strongpoint COD. (US National Archives)

from the general muddle up there; they were still machine-gunning, sniping and dropping the odd mortar bomb.

However, we sorted ourselves out, and moved through the rubble and ruin of bombed houses into the open plain beyond. I saw the Major and Sandy as I went through, both pretty cheerful, and I was feeling pretty good myself, damned glad to be off that beach.

The Major was Halyburton Berkeley Pirie, his battery commander, and Sandy was Captain Lyall, his fellow troop commander and FOO. Pirie would be wounded on D-Day, while Lyall would command the battery through the campaign. Both were awarded the Military Cross.

At H+45, 0810 hours, eight M10 SP anti-tank guns of I Troop 45 Anti-Tank Battery and E Troop and Battery HQ 67 Anti-tank Battery landed near here, along with the two 40mm Bofors guns on Crusader tanks from 218th Battery, each towing a 40mm Bofors Gun. These were the first artillery equipment to land on D-Day. At this time Strongpoint Cod was anything but neutralized. 218's battery commander, Major Tiarks, and the troop commander were wounded by mortar bomb fragments deploying the guns, and both were awarded the Military Cross for their courage under fire. Five minutes later, the fire from Cod subsided, possibly influenced by the appearance of a phalanx of SP Guns.

If on foot, walk west along the sea front as far as the Rue de Rouen. If driving, return to your car, turn around and drive south to the D514. Turn right and continue to the traffic lights. Turn right into the car park in Place de la 3ème D.I.B (3rd British Infantry Division), park and walk to the beach road, turn

An aerial view of the western half of Strongpoint COD taken on 3 June and showing the zigzag trenches.

right and walk to the next road junction, the Rue de Rouen. The villa on the corner of the Rue re Rouen is called Les Fronts de Bassen and has a road sign outside marked Boulevard de la Mer. This and its adjacent neighbour existed in 1944 and are prominent in contemporary photographs.

The boundary between Queen Red and Queen White beaches is between the Rue de Boulevard de la 3ème Division and Rue du Cherbourg. 1st Battalion South Lancashire landed on this part of the beach and almost immediately lost

Medics treating wounded on Queen Beach in the shelter of a knocked-out AVRE. To the right is an M10 of 20 Anti-tank Regiment RA.

their CO and several other officers. The first two companies moved to the west and began to clear the houses on the sea front. The follow-up companies landed a little further east in front of the west of Strongpoint Cod and became involved in the battle to take it.

If on foot, continue along the sea front to the Avenue Felix Faure. If driving, return south to the coast road. Turn right on to the D415 at the main road. Drive for 300m until the road begins to swing left. Take the next right before the Centaur Tank and the follow the road to the left. Park and return to the tank.

Centaur Tank and Naval Memorial

Junction Rue du Dr Turgis and Avenue Felix Faure 14880 Hermanville-sur-Mer. (GPS 49.296640, -0.300136)

The Centaur tank was used by the Royal Marine Armoured Support group. It is a memorial to the men of 5 Independent Battery RMASG which supported the landings on Sword beach.

At the sea end of the Avenue Felix Faure is a memorial to the men of the Royal and Merchant Navies. The largest regiments in the Royal Artillery in the Second World War were the Maritime Regiments. These provided detachments for the 3-in and 40mm guns mounted on Defensively Equipped Merchant Ships (DEMS), alongside sailors from the Royal Navy.

If on foot, walk along the seafront to the Place du Cuirassé Courbet. If driving, drive west along the Rue du Dr Turgis for about 150m and park on the road. Walk a little further and turn right into the Place du Cuirassé Courbet. Walk across the square to the seafront.

Seawolf ***landed near here on D-Day. Battle damage is visible on the turret. The markings are to help the gun be aligned for indirect fire.***

Place du Cuirassé Courbet

Junction Place du Cuirassé Courbet and Avenue du 6 Juin, 14880 Hermanville-sur-Mer, (GPS 49.297451, -0.302843)

This was one of the main exits from the beaches leading to the road to Hermanville-sur-Mer. The 1 S Lancs and 41 RM Commando exited the beach close to here. Looking to the west, the houses at the top of the beach merge with those of Lion-sur-Mer, the next village. The German Strongpoint WN21 'Trout' is at the western end of Lion-sur-Mer, just before the caravan site. Further west are the cliffs between Lion-sur-Mer and Luc-sur-Mer.

Now return to the square, where memorials to the midget submarines commemorate the boats which acted as navigation marks and to the 3rd British Infantry Division. On the seaward side is a plinth commemorating the ships sunk to create the Gooseberry artificial breakwater offshore of this point after D-Day. Half of the British stores landed in Normandy were landed on open beaches rather than the Mulberry Harbour.

The square is named after the old French battleship *Courbet*, which was scuttled as part of the Gooseberry offshore. She seems to have attracted disproportionate attention from the Germans. She was attacked by a German one-man Niger submarine on 15/16 August and possibly by a Mistrel air-to-ground missile. This was a combination aircraft with an Me109 fighter fitted above the Ju88 fuselage and the fighter pilot operating both aircraft's controls until the flying bomb was released. It is an example of the German air threat and of their technical ingenuity.

A self-propelled 40mm Bofors gun on a Crusader tank. Three of these guns landed on Queen beach around 0810 on D-Day, each towing a 40mm Bofors gun.

There is a memorial to the Norwegian destroyer *Svenner*, sunk on D-Day by a torpedo from a German torpedo boat. It is a reminder of the importance of coastal artillery and the coastal defence role of the AA units after D-Day.

80 AA Brigade was responsible for providing the AA defences for the Sword and Juno Beaches. The most effective of the German weapons was a modified version of acoustic mines fitted with pressure switches, which only armed the mine after a large vessel passed over the mine, making them harder to detect and disarm. Mines could be dropped by air from outside the range of AA guns. The radars of AA gunners tracked mine-laying aircraft and spotted the splashes made by the release of the mines. This speeded up the clearance of the mines the following morning.

There is a memorial on the west side of the square to the Royal Artillery in the 3rd Division. These were 7th, 33rd and 76th (Highland) Field Regiments, the 20th Anti-tank Regiment and the 92nd Light AA Regiment. Set in the ground is a red triangle inside a large black triangle, the symbol of the 3rd Divisional sign.

The guns arrived between 0835 and 0845 hours. The deployment was not without problems for 76 Regiment. One of 302 Battery's LCTs grounded and the other was hit, burning out a gun and trapping two half-tracks on board. By 0840 five guns of 302 Battery were in action on beach and were receiving fire from enemy shelling. 303 Battery had fewer problems. One LCT was hit by a shell, two guns became waterlogged, and another was hit by a beaching LCT.

E Troop of 454th Battery landed without incident, but because of the congestion on the beach the guns deployed 200 yards further west, where Sergeant Allen's A Sub put five rounds into a house containing snipers.

Soldiers sheltering behind universal carriers on a congested Sword Beach. A towed 40mm Bofors gun is visible on the right and an M10 on the left of the photograph.

33rd Field Regiment landed on Queen Red and Queen White at H+105, 0910 hours, 400 yards west of their planned position. Rob Hinton GPO C Troop 109 Battery recalled:

> The skippers rammed the beaches at full speed ahead. I remember how tense we were, wondering, hoping, that we should not meet the mines or underwater obstacles which we had worried about so much in planning. But we got there, the ramps went down and our leading tanks went through five feet of water to the sandy beach. Mortars, shells and small arms were coming from all directions, but we as a regiment were lucky and few casualties were had.
>
> I well remember the confidence Lieutenant Colonel Hussey, gave us as we saw him striding up and down the beaches. An exit was found and through the minefield gap we went to a gun area about 500 yards inland. This was the same area which had been picked off aerial photographs during the planning and this alone reminds one of the finer points considered before the assault took place.
>
> The first thing which vividly stands out in my mind was some very nasty oil bombs which dropped close. The heat from them was terrific. We fired the odd target and dug out slit trenches at great speed. The noise was terrific. Odd snipers still remained in the houses on the beach and altogether everyone kept low but on constant lookout.

Walk away from the beach to the junction with the Rue du Dr Turgis, which was the main lateral road during the Second World War. The current D514 was built post-war. The buildings around the crossroads existed in 1944 and can be seen in some contemporary photographs.

Just past this junction is 41 RM Commando's first HQ, where the commandos re-organized. Captain Dixon was the FOB with the commando and was assigned Royal Marine signallers to replace his naval telegraphers, all of whom had become casualties crossing the beach. Dixon had been wounded at the same time. Captain Peter Cory Dixon was twenty-nine years old and the oldest son of Alderman Michael Dixon, the Lord Mayor of Liverpool 1938/39. The commandos had no assigned field artillery or FOOs. The FOB was the sole conduit to the firepower of naval guns that the lightly armed Commandos would need.

If on foot, return to your car and continue west into Lion-sur-Mer, to the first set of lights is in the centre of town with a pedestrian street to the church on the left.

Lion -sur-Mer (Stongpoint Trout)
Rue de la Heve, 14780 Lion-sur-Mer (GPS 49.303417, -0.320364)

This route was taken by the group of commandos attacking Trout. The strongpoint is at the top of the rise. The commandos advanced under heavy mortar and machine gun fire from houses on either side of the road and from the strongpoint itself. The advance was stopped a few hundred metres from the strongpoint, roughly opposite the small supermarket. Three AVRE's were brought up, but all were knocked out by an anti-tank gun and the attack halted. Lance Bombardier Berryman was Lieutenant Dixon's OP Assistant. He landed with the party's half-track and found Lieutenant Dixon up the church tower directing artillery fire.

A view of Strongpoint Trout from the beach. Note the house with the porch on the left of the picture, seen from a different angle on the next page.

Another creation from Major Becker's workshop. German gunners loading a self-propelled multiple rocket launcher for a demonstration at Lion-Sur-Mer on 30 May 1944. The building in the background is the one at the end of the Rue de la Heve.

Continue along the D514 and stop before Camping Normandie-sur-Mer Oasis Park and walk along the Rue de la Heve to the seafront. This was within the Trout fortified position. It stretched from the seafront through the camp site and across the road. The defences included trenches and barbed wire and an anti-tank gun which knocked out the Churchill AVREs.

Note the view of Sword Beach from the west. The building on the west side of the street overlooking the beach can be seen in several photographs from 1944. In May Rommel witnessed a shoot by one of Major Becker's multiple rocket launchers into the sea, but these do not seem to have been used on 6 June. The Germans had lots of indirect firepower but did not use it effectively. Either the rockets were not deployed close enough to the beaches or there was some confusion about their use.

If on foot, continue along the path on the seafront to the end of the built-up area, then follow the path left to the tank and memorial. If driving, return to your car. Drive to the roundabout and take the second exit. Park in the bus and coach park. The AVRE is a specialist armoured engineering version of the Churchill tank. The Eisenhower memorial contains a quotation from President Franklin D. Roosevelt about the four freedoms: of Speech and Worship, and from Want and Fear. The next town 3.5km to the west is Luc-sur-Mer. No 41 and No 48 RM Commandos were expected to meet at the far side of Luc-sur-Mer and link Sword and Juno beaches. The No 41 RM Commando Memorial lists the names of the commandos who fell on 6/7 June. Among them is Captain Dixon RA.

Return to your car. Take the southern exit from the roundabout towards Cresserons, D221. Continue along the road and across the traffic lights to pass beside a stone wall on the right. Take the next turning on the right and go on about 200m to view the Château of Lion-sur-Mer on the right. This was the D-Day objective for the second commando group. In 1944 this was a defensive position. In May 1944 Rommel visited here for lunch and a demonstration of some of 21st Panzer Divisions multiple mortar carriers on the day he witnessed the multiple rocket shoot.

Carry on, turn right and head north. The open area to the left is where the Kampfgruppe from 21st Panzer Division reached the sea on the evening of D-Day. At the next road junction turn right and head east. Cross the road at the traffic lights and head towards Lion-sur-Mer.

This troop of four 105mm Priest SP guns is probably B Troop of 109 Battery of 33th Field Regiment. The guns look very warlike, backed tactically into the wood line. However, they may be in this position so that shells can clear the trees at the front of the field.

This superimposed image shows the fit between the historic image and the view from the corner of the field.

This was the furthest point that the second group from 41 RM Commando reached on D-Day. The leading commandos were halted by fire from the chateau. A little later the Germans counter-attacked from the Commandos' left across the fields from Plumetot. At the same time German infantry supported by SP guns attacked the rear troop in the flank from further left. The Commandos pulled back to a new line in the centre of Lion-sur-Mer.

On 7 June 41 Commando advanced towards Plumetot, but the Germans counter-attacked. Dixon succumbed to his wounds at noon on 7 June. Lance Bombardier Berryman carried on, on his own, as the officer and wireless operator supporting No 41 Commando. For his actions Berryman was awarded the Military Medal.

Continue through Lion-sur-Mer along the D60 towards Hermanville until the T Junction. Turn left into the D60B and take the first turning right. At the end of the road turn right and stop on the verge. The field on your right was occupied by 101 Battery of 33rd Field Regiment on 6 June 1944.

Hermanville 33 Field Regiment Gun Position

Junction Chemin des Hautes Sentes and Chemin du Douet14880 Hermanville-sur-Mer (GPS 49.288610, -0.305386)

This is probably the location of a widely published photograph of 33rd Field Regiment Priest SP Guns on D-Day. The landscape has changed much over the past seventy years. The villages are larger, and the road network has improved. Many of the orchards have disappeared, as have many of the small fields and the *bocage* of thick hedgerows. But this corner of the field remains.

Small fields and orchards posed problems for gun position officers. Crests such as trees imposed a minimum range. Although backing the guns into the treeline

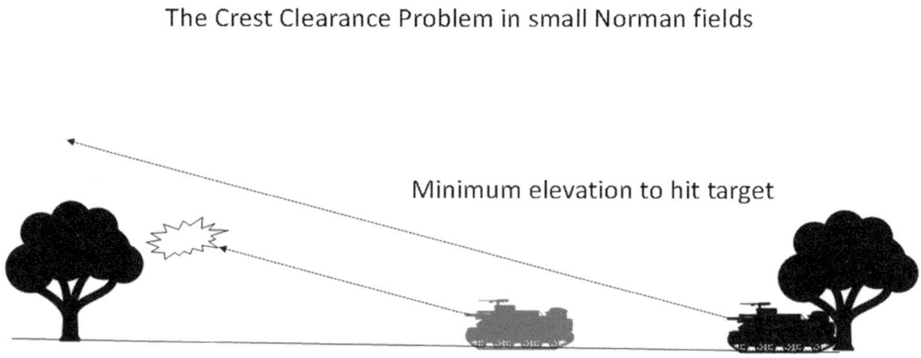

The reason the SP guns are backed into the tree line is probably due to crest clearance problems.

This is probably the Gun Position Officers' group of B Troop 109 Battery. This photograph was obviously taken on D-Day. Once they had been under mortar or shell fire, soldiers slept in slit trenches rather than on the surface.

may appear to offer good camouflage, this is not ideal. Field gun platforms were the workstations of industrialized twentieth century warfare. Gun detachments need to manhandle heavy ammunition. Priest guns needed space to track left and right to switch targets beyond the narrow traverse on the gun. This position may have been the best way for the guns to engage targets a kilometre or so away. Backing the guns through the treeline so ammunition could be loaded from the track behind the hedge may have mitigated the problem of ammunition handling.

Hermanville War Cemetery

6129 Rue du Cimetière Anglais, 14880 Hermanville-sur-Mer. (GPS 49.286375, -0.308772)

Return to your car and drive south along the road beside the field. At the end of the road park in the Hermanville War Cemetery car park.

Notice the red and black triangle motif of the 3rd Divisional sign in the paving outside the cemetery. Hermanville CWC contains 900 war dead. Sixty-seven Gunners are buried in the cemetery. Of these, twenty-seven are anti-tank gunners. During the Normandy campaign 2,000 extra anti-tank gunner reinforcements were sent to replace the higher-than-expected numbers lost in the intense battle against tanks. Three Captains from 76th Field Regiment are buried in the cemetery. Joseph Daniel (1F.21) was killed when his motor launch was sunk on the run-in shoot. Ian Bell (3A.3), 303 Battery was killed in the attack on Cod as FOO to the S Lancs. The third, Captain J. M. Nickerson, was killed with his party when his tank was knocked out on 28 June. The attrition rate among forward observer parties was high.

Return to your car. Turn left and drive to the end of the Road. At the T Junction by Hermanville Church turn left and drive south though the village. At the end of the village turn left on the D35 towards Colleville. After 300m stop on the verge or in a field entrance.

Aircraft and gliders overflying the guns of 7th Field Regiment as the evening wave of 6th Airborne Division comes over.

Hermanville-sur-Mer and 7 Field Regiment
248-586 D35, 14880 Hermanville-sur-Mer (GPS 49.279634, -0.312757)

At 11.30 on D-Day the guns of 7th Field Regiment followed this route. The CO, Nigel Tapp:

> I remained concerned that the Regiment would get bottled up on the beaches and I was delighted to see the Regimental gun column led by BC 16 Battery, Major Dunn, in his carrier race through Hermanville with the inhabitants showering them with flowers at 1130 hours to come into action on the southern edge of the village just ahead of the leading infantry. At 1200 hours I was able with some pride to report to the Brigade Commander that 7th Field Regiment was in action in France with all its guns ready to support the Brigade.

This was still a battle area, and Driver Quemby became the Battery's first casualty when, while driving Q2, a stores 3-ton truck, he was shot through the mouth:

> In front of the battery position lies a large open expanse of cultivated ground rising gradually to a crest. Tanks and infantry are dotted all over ground and the sounds of battle are heard from over the ridge. An 88mm concealed near Plumetot suddenly opens fire and two of our tanks brew up. Five mins later, an M14 [half-track] and another tank catch fire. Staffs Yeomanry send troop of tanks round to destroy 88 mm.

This is the area occupied by 7th Field Regiment on the afternoon of D-Day. This open area is large enough to accommodate twenty-four guns in six troops with a frontage of around 600m. The position is on a reverse slope screening the guns and their muzzle flashes from enemy view. After the German armoured columns passed west of Hermanville, 7th Field Regiment moved to a new position 1,000m east on the eastern slope of the ridge around the water-tower.

> *Continue along the Rue du Bac du Port D35 for 920m. Turn right into Rue du Crespley and continue for 400m. Turn right into Rue du Sapin Bleu. After 100m you will see a bunker on your left.*

Strongpoint Morris
Rue du Sapin Bleu, 14880 Colleville-Montgomery. (GPS 49.272355, -0.306460)

> *This is within the fortified area of the WN16 Morris. The area was open fields in 1944. This was a fortified position for a field artillery battery. The defenders of this position surrendered as the FOO began adjusting fire before the Suffolks launched an attack. On the right is a footpath that leads to a circular gun emplacement. Park where you can if you want to explore on foot.*
>
> *Return along the Rue du Sapin Bleu to Rue du Crespley and go straight across into the Rue Porte Morinto. At the T Junction turn right into Rue du Tour de Ville. Follow this as it bends left. At the T Junction turn right into Rue*

The Hillman Bunker site is open all year round, but until Covid it was manned every Tuesday from 1 July to 30 September by the Friends of the Suffolk Regiment, who operate 2-hour guided tours at 3.00 pm.

du Suffolk Regiment, this will become a sunken lane with high banks. Look out for a sign on the right-hand side of the road to the Hillman Blockhouses. Park in the car park on the right side of the road.

Hillman Bunker

Site fortifié Hillman, France, Rue Suffolk Régiment, Colleville-Montgomery (GPS 49.264617, -0.309608)

The Hillman bunkers and part of the fortified position have been preserved as a memorial to the Suffolk Regiment. There is an orientation table above the large supply bunker close to the road. There is a good view to the east over the fields through which the 1st Battalion the Norfolk Regiment advanced toward Biéville. During this move, the OP tank of Captain Handford, the troop commander of F Troop 16 battery, was hit by two shots from a 47mm anti-tank gun, knocking out his tank. On this occasion the tank crew all survived uninjured, and the only loss was personal kit. The Norfolks suffered many casualties, including some fatalities caused by fire from Hillman.

The Hillman command bunker through the hedge contains exhibits that recreate the appearance of the regimental command bunker of Colonel Krug, the commander of 736 Grenadier regiment responsible for the defence of the Orne sector.

Hillman contained several machine guns and at least one anti-tank gun with arcs to the east. The position does not appear on the fire plan as a target for naval gunfire but was bombed at 0730 hours by two squadrons of heavy day bombers. Any neutralizing effect produced by this bombardment had long worn off by the time the position was attacked.

While B Company of the Suffolks were clearing Morris, C Company had cleared Colleville and A Company prepared their attack on WN17, Strongpoint Hillman. The BC, Major Waring, registered the guns and mortars, and by 1300 hours all was ready. H-Hour was given as 1310 hours, and the HE came down, laid on by artillery, mortars and tanks exactly on time. As soon as the HE lifted, the guns changed to smoke, under the cover of which a platoon of D Company crawled forward to make the breach, followed by A Company, the assaulting company. This first attack failed in the face of heavy machine gun fire from the dug-in positions which killed the company commander, and A Company withdrew. More fire support was required. As there appeared to be no anti-tank guns on the position, tanks of A Squadron of the Staffordshire Yeomanry came up to the wire and engaged the bunkers with their main armament, but the 17-pounder AP shot merely bounced off the cupolas that seemed to be causing most of the trouble – although as you can see, these were merely observation bunkers. The BC, whose tank with its more reliable 19 set had arrived, went off to observe from a flank; he returned twenty minutes later, his tank having been wrecked on a mine and burnt out. As soon as the gap had been widened to take tanks, CO 1 Suffolks ordered a preliminary bombardment for five minutes from the tanks and two batteries at Rate 4. When this lifted, the tanks went through the gap, followed by the infantry who started winkling out a determined enemy, a task that went on till 2015 hours; even so, the Commander of 736 Regiment and his staff remained in their bunker and did not surrender until the following morning. The

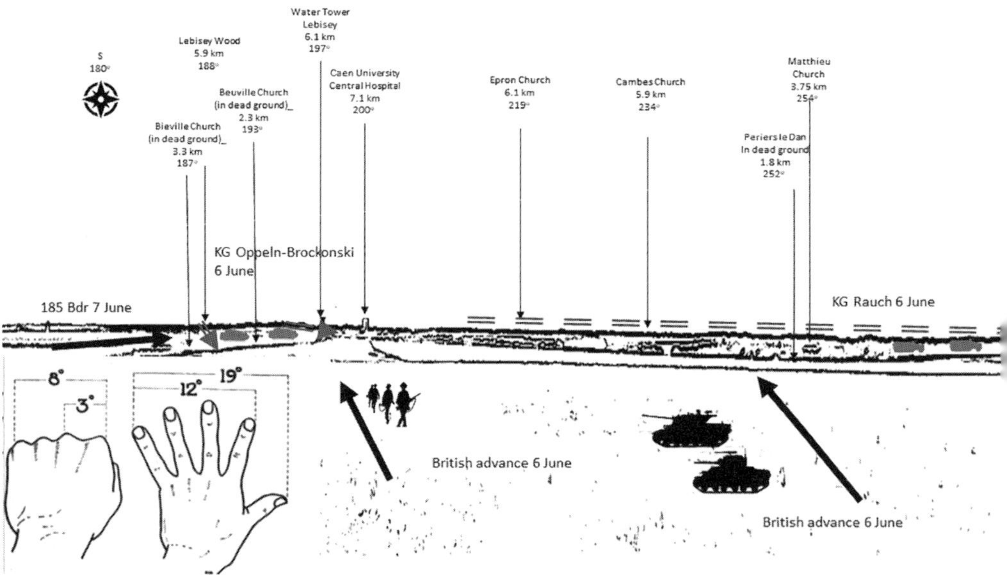

Point 61 offers a good view to the south to the ridge north of Caen.

battalion then moved on to its final objectives and dug in during what little remained of daylight.

If walking or cycling, continue south west along the Rue du Suffolk Regiment for 640m. You will see a farm on your right. Turn right and follow the track to the right of the farm buildings for 600m then turn right onto the D60A. After 190m turn right into the road to a water tank.

Drive back into Colleville along the Rue du Suffolk Regiment and then turn left into the Rue De Caen (D60A), follow the road around to the left and continue for 2km. You will see a bunker, part of the Hillman fortifications, in the fields to your left and the trees on the Hillman position. At the top of the hill is a crossroads with a sign straight across D225 to Périers-sur-Dan and left to Biéville and Caen. Turn left and drive to the summit, just past a reservoir on your left. This is point 61, the highest point on Périers Ridge.

Point 61
(GPS 49.263765, -0.320508)

The skyline is the ridge just north of Caen. The massive square hospital building is 1,000m beyond the village of Lebisey, the high ground on which the Germans defended Caen for the next month.

The village of Périers is in the valley half right south-east. There is a memorial in Périers-sur-Dan to the Allied soldiers who died and were initially buried in their commune, including members of 7 and 33 Field Regiments.

While 1st Suffolks were engaging the Hillman fortifications, 185 Brigade had been carrying out their mission. At 1200 hours the commander of 185 Brigade decided not to wait any longer for the tanks and sent 2 KSLI off on the route to Caen through Beuville, Biéville and Lebisey on foot, leaving the tanks to catch up, accompanied by Major Rae, BC 17/43 Battery, his FOOs, Captains Tooth and Ashman, and the FOB, Captain Gower. The advance up Périers Ridge was dogged by small arms and mortar fire, and on reaching the crest the Battalion was engaged by a German howitzer battery near Périers and an 88-mm gun that knocked out five tanks of B Squadron the Staffordshire Yeomanry, which had now caught up. Among these was the OP tank of Captain Gower, the FOO from 33rd Field Regiment with the Yeomanry who, along with his driver, was killed, and his OP Ack seriously wounded; Captain Gower was replaced by Captain Dawson. The Battalion detached Z Company to deal with the battery, supported by a FOO. Observation was difficult owing to the flatness of the crest; the battery was finally silenced after a number of regimental concentrations had been fired at it and the infantry had broken in through the wire at back of the position, which was secured by 2100 hours.

The German artillery was from the batteries of I/155 Artillery Regiment, and from Panzerjäger Battalion 200 from the 21st Panzer Division, which had been deployed forwards to support the 716th Division. The regimental artillery concentrations must have been effective, as Feuchtinger reported that the division had lost two howitzer batteries and most of its divisional anti-tank regiment on D-Day.

B Troop, 41 Anti-tank Battery (M10 SP troop) and B Squadron of the Yeomanry were left to secure Périers Ridge, and A Squadron to assist 1 Suffolks at Hillman, while the remainder of the KSLI Battalion and the Yeomanry continued the advance. By 1600 hours Biéville was secure and the lead platoon was approaching Lebisey Wood, on the ridge ahead.

At 1615 hours the Recce Troop of the Staffordshire Yeomanry reported a company of panzers advancing rapidly from Caen, reports of their numbers steadily increasing to about forty. The CO of the Staffordshire Yeomanry immediately called for the return of A Squadron, and they and the KSLI deployed to meet the threat: the anti-tank platoon, B Troop 41 Anti-Tank Battery and A Squadron north of Biéville and B Squadron, the reserve squadron, at Périers. The Germans made a detour to avoid their own anti-tank obstacle around Lebisey, and Kampfgruppe von Oppeln hit the British anti-tank screen head-on, losing two tanks to A Squadron and two to the anti-tank platoon of the KSLI.

The Kampfgruppe then swung to the west and lost four more panzers to A Squadron and two to No 4 Gun, B Troop, 41 Battery, which had spotted two Mk IVs about 2,000 yards away:

> Accordingly, the guns laid on the tanks and waited for them to approach. Simultaneously with this, other tanks must have been working their way forward in dead ground and two more tanks suddenly appeared in hull down positions about half a mile away. They immediately opened fire on No 1 Gun and got two or three rounds away before the slow traverse of the M10 allowed the Troop to reply. A slogging match now followed with the tanks rushing to join in. The No 1 Gun was hit very early on by a round that struck it at the join of the turret ring just above the drivers head. Sergeant Mitchley was killed and the two gunners wounded, one dying ten days later in England. The driver and wireless operator were unhurt, and the SP was immediately backed off the position with the gun hanging helplessly over the front with both trunnions shattered.

The panzers then ran into B Squadron at Périers-sur-Dan. At the same time the Garmans lost six tanks, a total of sixteen tanks in a matter of minutes. The 21st Panzer Division history describes the events:

> The British positions were tactically well chosen and their fire both heavy and accurate. The first Mark IV was blazing before a single tank had had a chance to fire a shot. The remainder moved forward firing to where the enemy were thought to be; but the English weapons were well concealed and within a few minutes we had lost six tanks … The fire of the English from their outstandingly well-sited defensive positions was murderous.

Thus ended the only armoured counter-attack mounted by a panzer division on D-Day. The German armour attacked without the support of its artillery or anti-tank guns, which had been deployed separately. They were stopped on Périers Ridge.

Allied tank crews felt at a disadvantage taking on heavier German tanks with the M4 Sherman. Spare a thought for the detachments of the SP Anti-tank guns which duelled with tanks from thinly armoured M10 SP anti-tank guns, and for Sergeant Mitchley, the first fatality from a duel with a tank in Normandy.

Walk, cycle or drive north on D60 towards D220 for 190m, then take a slight right on to Rue de Caen/D60A for 1.5km. Stay on the D60A. Turn left on to Rue du Tour de Ville for 640 m. Turn left on to Grande Rue for 140m. Turn right on to D35A/Rue des Écoles/Rue du Château d'Eau. Continue to follow Rue des Écoles for 260 m then turn right on to Rue de Ouistreham/D35A for 1.2km. When you reach the entrance to Ferme Vergy, continue to the edge of the next field to your right.

Position Sole WN14
Rue de Ouistreham/D35A (GPS 49.274478, -0.267480)

Look at the far corner of the field half right. The remains of a bunker are just visible. This was part of WN14, nicknamed Sole. The position held at least one 7.5cm anti-tank gun. C Company of 2 E Yorks advanced towards this position from La Brèche, 2km north-north-west of here, supported by B Squadron 13/18H and Captain Featherstone of 302 Battery:

> At last I had word that the guns were ashore, and I therefore tried to do a bit of indirect shooting into some of the known strongholds which I could see. It was whilst doing this that a mortar bomb landed close by, and I felt a pang as if someone had tried to hit me as hard as he could with a stick on the shoulder. I also felt a feeling of intense fury, because it was obvious that I was not badly hit, but I was bleeding pretty hard, and had lost the use of my left arm completely, but I got myself bandaged, and we went forward. Despite the inconvenience of my wound, I thoroughly enjoyed the day. We managed to make ourselves quite useful to the infantry, although later the country became rather closer and wooded (yielding plenty of snipers of mixed breeds).

M10 3-inch SP Gun from 20 Anti-Tank Regiment supporting infantry from 2nd East Yorks in their secondary role as assault guns.

What Featherstone did not say was that he could not see the bunkers clearly and that, despite his wounds, he climbed on to a tank which advanced into sight of the position to adjust fire. This is mentioned in the citation for the Military Cross he was awarded. C Company took 30–40 prisoners around 1545 hours.

If walking, you have the option to take a short cut. Walk back to Ferme Vergy, turn left and walk to the end of the track. Turn left in front of the last two barns. Look to your right. You should see the edge of a wood 100m away. A few hundred metres into this wood is where the Germans hid the guns that had been emplaced at Riva Bella. They were overrun by Commandos around noon on D-Day. Look left to spot WN14. Follow the footpath for 1km to Rue du Petit Bonheur. Stop in front of the entrance to the sports club.

If driving, continue to the roundabout. Take the first exit into the D514 Route de Liberté, at the first turning turn right into Rue du Petit Bonheur and halt in front of the sports club.

Position Daimler WN12
Rue du Petit Bonheur (GPS 49.274478, -0.267480)

Look south across the field. You should see two of the casemates that held the guns of 4th battery of Artillery Regiment 1716, Strongpoint Daimler, if they are not obscured by tall crops. The position was taken by 2 East Yorks in a set-piece attack supported by the guns of 76th Field Regiment and the tanks of B Squadron 13/18 Hussars and the SP troop of 67 Anti-Tank Battery and fell without a shot being fired. Captain Featherstone again:

> We had a good fight towards the end of the day whilst clearing up an area north of Ouistreham and just before dark I had the satisfaction of doing a successful Regimental Concentration to support the final attack for which my company commander was well pleased.
>
> The Battalion had a pretty bad time with casualties, the CO was wounded, one company commander, the MO and several subalterns were killed and wounded as well, but they put up a damned good show, moving almost mechanically from objective to objective; and the number of prisoners was fantastic, three or four hundred I would say, which is not bad for a severely depleted battalion.

Captain Featherstone was evacuated with a broken collarbone and was awarded the Military Cross for his actions on D-Day.

The tour ends here.

Chapter 8

Juno Beach

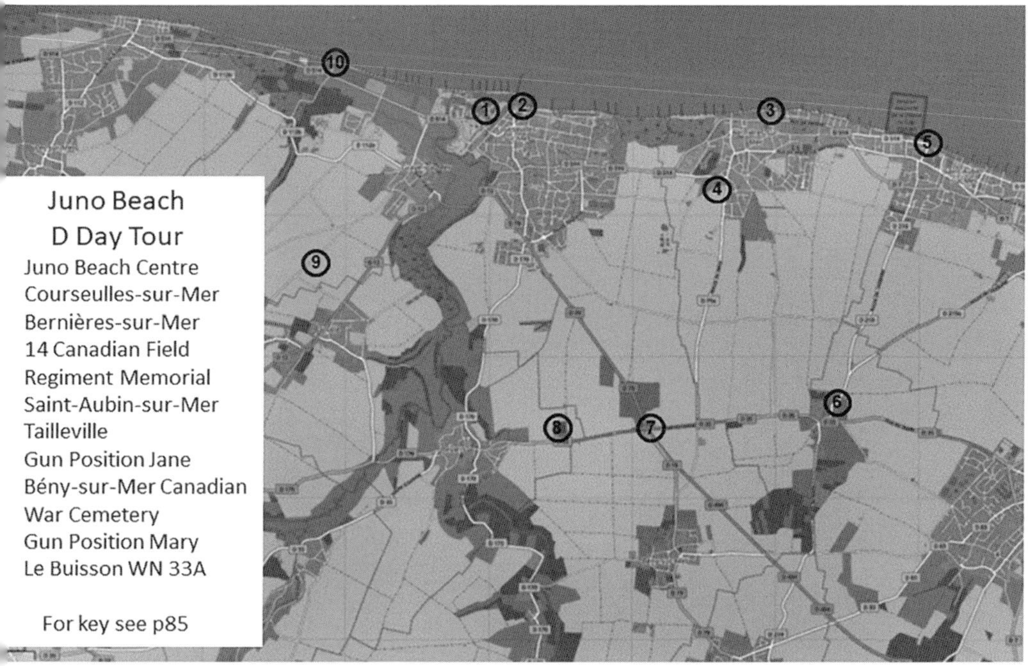

> In those last tense moments, as we loaded and fired and loaded and fired like automatons, the shore of France was fully visible, rent and torn with violent explosions and with a dense pall of smoke … And then the beach itself became visible with a few figures scattered across it, some running, some standing and some lying motionless on the sand. There was no difficulty in carrying out this operation. With our guns fixed facing forward as they were on the craft … we were aimed directly toward the shore. As the beach got closer, the crews adjusted the guns, raining round after round down on the German defences … breakfast was a self-heating can of cocoa and oxtail soup.
>
> Sergeant Wes Alkenbrack 14 Canadian Field Regiment

Juno beach was 9,800 yards long from Rue de Provence to St Aubin-sur-Mer. The beaches to be assaulted were Mike Green, Nan Green, Nan White and Nan Red. Wooden groynes built to prevent erosion stopped vehicles from moving from one sector to the next. The built-up areas of the seaside towns of Courseulles-sur-Mer, Bernières-sur-Mer and St Aubin-sur-Mer extended to the seafront. The assault troops would need to engage in street fighting shortly after landing.

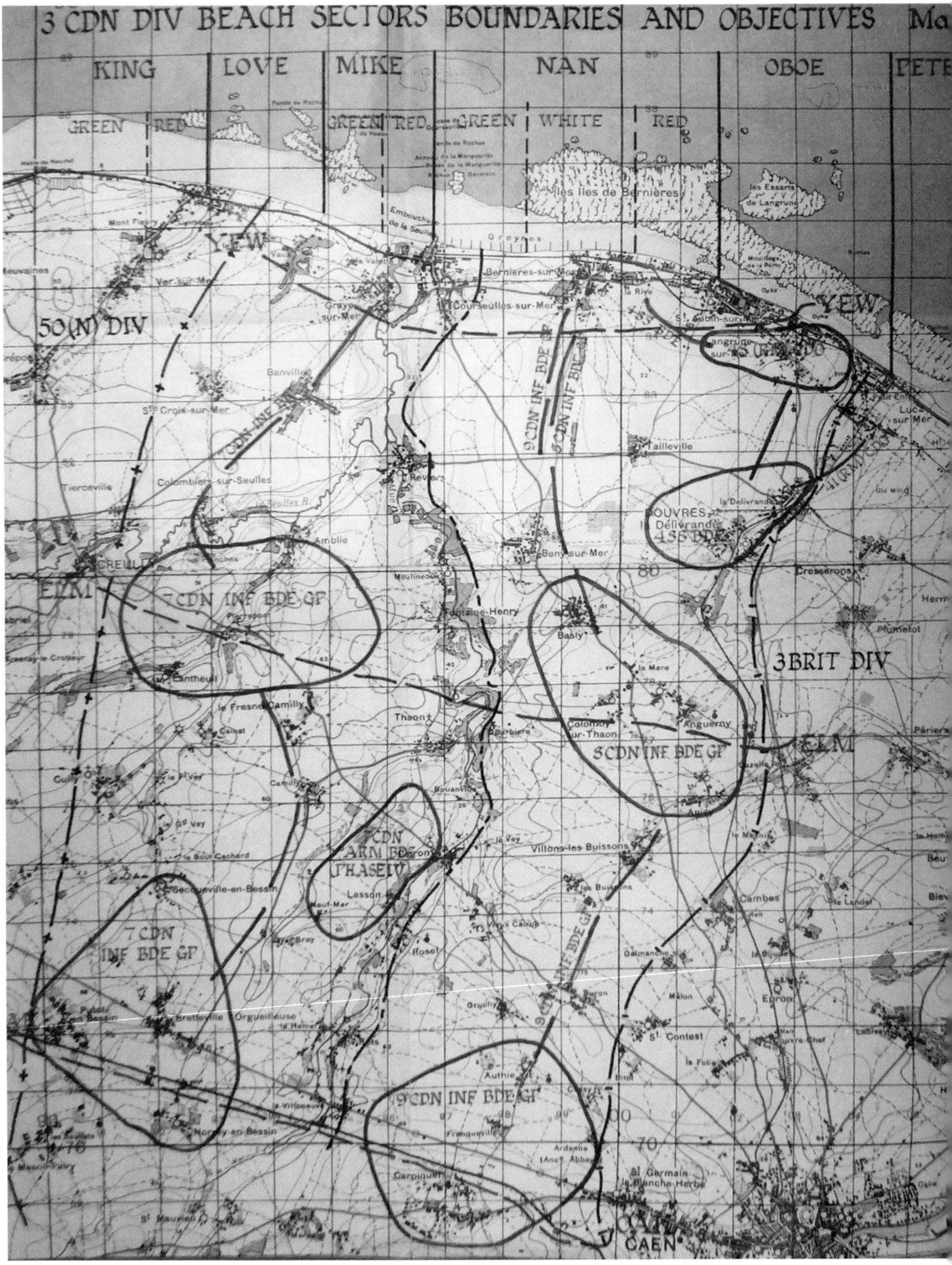

Juno Sector showing report lines and planned moves.

The coastline included six defensive positions manned by elements of three companies from GR736 of 716 Infantry Division. The fifth company occupied two defence posts that would be assaulted from the sea on Nan Beach, WN27 (St Aubin) and WN28 (Bernières), each with one 5cm anti-tank gun. The positions included 14–18 machine guns and three mortars. The ninth company occupied WN22, 25 and 26 around Langrune and Petit-Enfer between Juno and Sword beaches but was outside small-arms range.

The sixth company defended three positions that made up Strongpoint Courseulles. To the east of the river WN29 had one 8.8cm, one 7.5cm and one 5cm anti-tank gun, and to the west WN31 had one 7.5cm and one 5cm anti-tank gun. The third, WN30, was in depth at the rear of the village. Within these positions were twenty-three machine guns and two 5cm mortars. A 7.5cm and 5cm were sited 1,500m west to provide flanking fire on to tanks landing on Mike Green in front of Courseulles.

Behind them were seven infantry companies from Infantry Division 716:

- 2./441 *Ost* (10-15 MG & three Mortars) Reviers.
- 8./GR 736 (4-12 MG) West of Tailleville.
- II/716 was headquartered in St Croix-sur-Mer, with its four companies billeted between Crépon and Banville (forty-eight MG, nine 5cm and six 8cm mortars). It was the divisional reserve.
- Twelve anti-tank guns from the divisional anti-tank battalion were deployed on the ridge overlooking the exits from Courseulles and Bernières.

Six defensive positions manned by artillery batteries and unit and formation headquarters also provided some depth. Most of the positions had been identified and located by the Allies:

- The Douvres strongpoint was a radar site known to the Germans as *Distelfink* (Goldfinch). It consisted of two fortified positions with a garrison of around 200 men from the eighth company of Luftwaffe Signals Regiment 53. Their weapons included one 7.5cm field gun, five 5cm anti-tank guns and a 5cm mortar.
- 7/AR 1716 (four 10 cm) WN15 Beny-sur-Mer.
- Army artillery battalion 989 with twelve 12.2cm guns had its headquarters in Reviers (unlocated by the Allies).
- HQ II/GR 736 WN23 Taillville.
- Panzerjäger Battalion 200 with twenty-four 8.8cm towed anti-tank guns was north of the Bayeux–Caen road south of Creully (unlocated by the Allies).

The 3rd Canadian Division had the mission of assaulting Juno Beach through Mike and Nan beaches to seize the line between Putot-en-Bessin and Bretteville-L'Orgueilleuse. 3rd Canadian Division's operation was to be undertaken in four phases.

Phase 1 would be the assault and capture of the beachhead objective known as Yew, with 7th Brigade group assaulting Mike Beach, while the 8th Infantry Brigade Group assaulted Nan Beach.

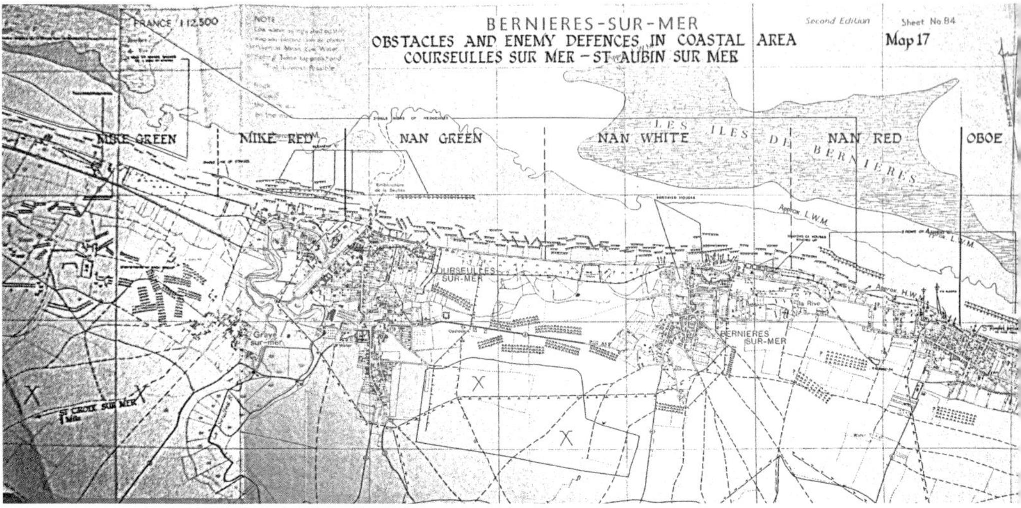

The defences on Juno Beach.

In phase 2 the right-hand brigade group was to secure crossings over the River Seulles and establish itself on the southern bank. At the same time, the left-hand brigade group was to establish a firm base on the high ground, as shown on the map on p.152, in order to integrate the advance of 3 Canadian Division with the 3rd British Division to its east. This intermediate objective was known as Elm.

In phase 3 the reserve brigade 9 Infantry Brigade would advance as fast as possible to secure the area Athie–Ardenne–Carpiquet, and in conformity the right-hand brigade would advance to its final objective of Putot-en-Bessin – Bretteville-L'Orgueilleuse.

The HQ 4th Special Services Brigade with 48 RM Commando would land on Nan Beach shortly after the assault battalions of 8th Canadian Brigade. It would then turn left and clear the village of Langrune-sur-Mer as far as the divisional boundary and contact No 41 RM Command, which should be attacking west from Sword Beach. In phase 2 the two commandos were to clear the village of Douvres-la-Delivrande, after which they would redeploy to the west of the 3 Canadian division to relieve 7 Canadian Brigade on the crossings.

Field Artillery

The first artillery to land would be the thirty-two Centaurs of the 2nd Regiment RMASG which would provide artillery support until the field artillery landed. Thereafter, this unit would be attached to the field artillery regiments.

Five FOOs would land with each assaulting battalion plus a COs representative and one spare. The Reserve battalion would land with one FOO and one would land with Brigade HQ.

The 7th Brigade would be supported by the 12th Canadian Field Regiment Artillery Group commanded by Lieutenant Colonel R. H. Webb with 12th and 13th Field Regiments. Preceded by their recce parties, the guns of 12th Field would land at H+75, while the 13th would land at H+105.

The 8th Brigade would be supported by the 14th Canadian Field Regiment Artillery Group commanded by Lieutenant Colonel H. S. Griffin, consisting of the 14th and 19th Canadian Field Regiments. Both of these were due to land at H+75.

The 12 Canadian Field Regiment artillery group consisted of:

- 3 Battery 2 (RM) Armoured Support Regiment.
- 12 Canadian Field Regiment (SP).
- 13 Canadian Field Regiment (SP).
- 94 Battery 3 Canadian Anti-Tank Regiment.
- 246 Battery 62 Anti-Tank Regiment.
- 248 Battery 62 Anti-Tank Regiment.
- 32 Battery less one troop 4 Canadian LAA Regiment.
- Detachment B Survey Battery 9 Survey Regiment.
- Four FOB Detachments A Troop 3 CO Bombardment Unit RN.

The artillery in support of 8th Canadian Infantry Brigade landing on Nan beach was as follows:

- 14 Canadian Field Artillery Regiment (SP).
- 19 Canadian Field Artillery Regiment (SP).
- 52 Battery 3 Canadian Anti-Tank Regiment.
- 247 Battery 62 Anti-Tank Regiment.
- 32 Battery 4 Canadian Light AA Regiment.
- Four FOB Detachments A Troop 3 CO Bombardment Unit.

The artillery would be regrouped to support the advance by 9th infantry Brigade in their advance to the phase 3 objectives:

- 14 Canadian Field Artillery Regiment.
- 19 Canadian Field Artillery Regiment (SP).
- 52 Battery 3 Canadian Anti-Tank Regiment.
- 105 Battery 3 Canadian Anti-Tank Regiment.
- 247 Battery 62 Anti-Tank Regiment.
- 32 Battery 4 Canadian Light AA Regiment.
- Four FOB Detachments A Troop No 3 CO Bombardment Unit RN.

105th Battery was a composite battery formed from the four troops of M10 SP anti-tank guns.

Anti-Aircraft artillery

These British units of the 80 AA Brigade were each formed into an AA Assault group based on the RHQ of an AA Regiment. The AA guns would also provide the last line of anti-tank defences for the beaches, and gun positions were selected with this as a factor. 3.7-in HAA guns were also expected to be able to support ground operations. The AA defences included the Pioneers, who would operate the smoke generators providing passive air defences for the beaches. The AA guns would initially deploy under the command of CRA 3 Canadian Division and revert to I Corps via 80 AA Brigade on D+1 or D+2:

- O AA Assault group.
  - RHQ 114th LAA Regiment RA.
  - 372 Battery (Less one Troop) 114th LAA Regiment RA.
  - 321 Battery (less one Troop) 93rd LAA Regiment RA.
  - 274 HAA Battery 86 (HAC) HAA Regiment RA 12 × 3.7-in Guns.
  - 114 LAA Regiment Workshop.
  - 2½ Sections 112 Pioneer company (smoke).
  - Three LBF (Landing Barge Flak) with 40mm guns.
- 'P' AA Assault group.
  - RHQ HAA 86 (HAC) Regiment RA.
  - 375 Battery 114 LAA Regiment RA.
  - 321 Battery (less one Troop) 93 LAA Regiment RA.
  - 273 HAA Battery 86 (HAC) HAA Regiment RA 12 × 3.7-in Guns.
  - 383 HAA Battery 86 (HAC) HAA Regiment RA 12 × 3.7-in Guns.
  - One Troop 474 Searchlight Battery RA.
  - 112 Pioneer company (smoke) (less 2½ Sections).
  - Two LBF (Landing Barge Flak) with 40mm guns.

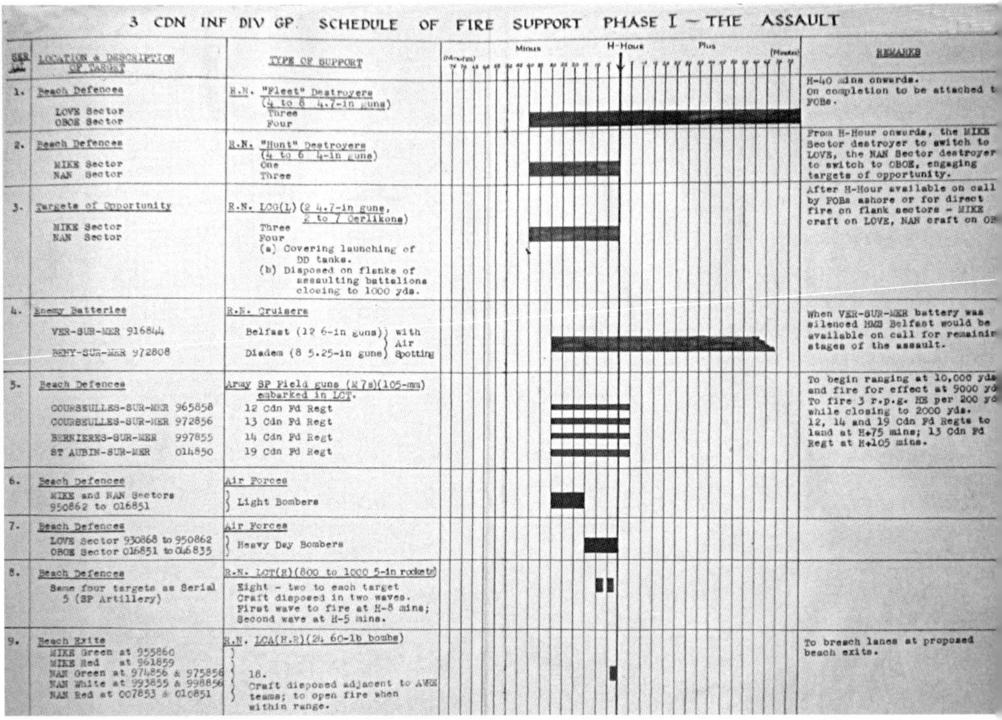

3 CDN INF DIV GP. SCHEDULE OF FIRE SUPPORT PHASE I – THE ASSAULT

SER No	LOCATION & DESCRIPTION OF TARGET	TYPE OF SUPPORT	(Minutes) Minus – H-Hour – Plus (Minutes)	REMARKS
1.	Beach Defences LOVE Sector OBOE Sector	R.N. "Fleet" Destroyers (4 to 6 4.7-in guns) Three Four		H-40 mins onwards. On completion to be attached t FOBs.
2.	Beach Defences MIKE Sector NAN Sector	R.N. "Hunt" Destroyers (4 to 6 4-in guns) One Three		From H-Hour onwards, the MIKE Sector destroyer to switch to LOVE, the NAN Sector destroyer to switch to OBOE, engaging targets of opportunity.
3.	Targets of Opportunity MIKE Sector NAN Sector	R.N. LCG(L) (2 4.7-in guns, 2 to 7 Oerlikons) Three Four (a) Covering launching of DD tanks. (b) Disposed on flanks of assaulting battalions closing to 1000 yds.		After H-Hour available on call by FOBs ashore or for direct fire on flank sectors – MIKE craft on LOVE, NAN craft on OB
4.	Enemy Batteries VER-SUR-MER 916844 BENY-SUR-MER 972808	R.N. Cruisers Belfast (12 6-in guns) } with Air Diadem (8 5.25-in guns) } Spotting		When VER-SUR-MER battery was silenced HMS Belfast would be available on call for remainir stages of the assault.
5.	Beach Defences COURSEULLES-SUR-MER 965858 COURSEULLES-SUR-MER 972856 BERNIERES-SUR-MER 997855 ST AUBIN-SUR-MER 014850	Army SP Field guns (M 7s)(105-mm) embarked in LCT. 12 Cdn Fd Regt 13 Cdn Fd Regt 14 Cdn Fd Regt 19 Cdn Fd Regt		To begin ranging at 10,000 yds and fire for effect at 9000 yd To fire 3 r.p.g. HE per 200 yd while closing to 2000 yds. 12, 14 and 19 Cdn Fd Regts to land at H+75 mins; 13 Cdn Fd Regt at H+105 mins.
6.	Beach Defences MIKE and NAN Sectors 950862 to 016851	Air Forces Light Bombers		
7.	Beach Defences LOVE Sector 930868 to 950862 OBOE Sector 016851 to 046835	Air Forces Heavy Day Bombers		
8.	Beach Defences Same four targets as Serial 5 (SP Artillery)	R.N. LCT(R)(800 to 1000 5-in rockets) Eight – two to each target Craft disposed in two waves. First wave to fire at H-8 mins; Second wave at H-5 mins.		
9.	Beach Exits MIKE Green at 955860 MIKE Red at 961859 NAN Green at 974856 & 975856 NAN White at 993855 & 998856 NAN Red at 007853 & 010851	R.N. LCA(H.R)(24 60-lb bombs) 18. Craft disposed adjacent to AVRE teams; to open fire when within range.		To breach lanes at proposed beach exits.

The schedule of fire support for the assault on Juno Beach.

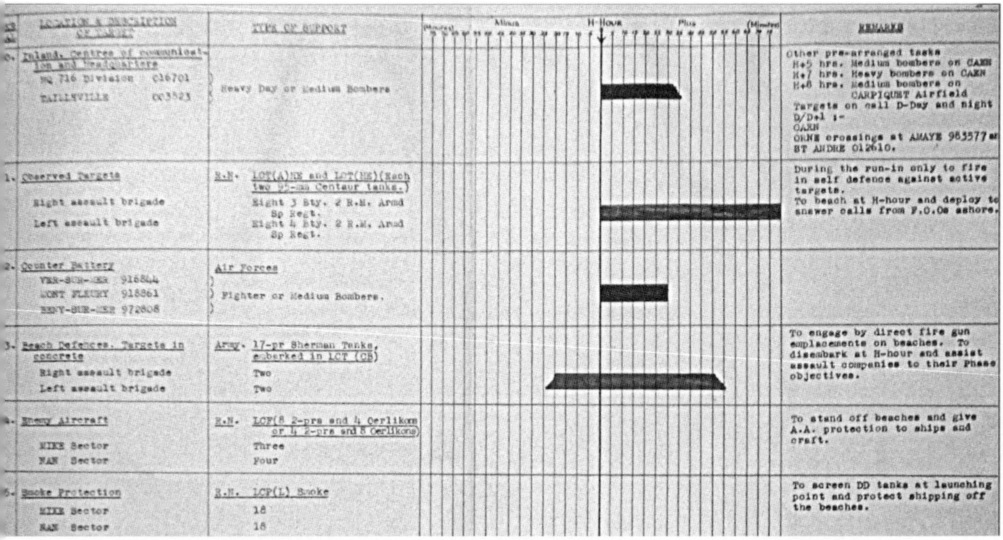

Ser No	Location & Description of Target	Type of Support	Minus – H-Hour – Plus	Remarks
6.	Inland. Centres of communication and Headquarters HQ 716 Division 016701 TAILLEVILLE 003523	Heavy Day or Medium Bombers		Other pre-arranged tasks H+5 hrs. Medium bombers on CAEN H+7 hrs. Heavy bombers on CAEN H+8 hrs. Medium bombers on CARPIQUET Airfield Targets on call D-Day and night D/D+1 :- CAEN ORNE crossings at AMAYE 983577 and ST ANDRE 012610.
1.	Observed Targets Right assault brigade Left assault brigade	R.N. LCT(A)HE and LCT(HE)(Each two 95-mm Centaur tanks.) Right 3 Bty. 2 R.M. Armd Sp Regt. Right 4 Bty. 2 R.M. Armd Sp Regt.		During the run-in only to fire in self defence against active targets. To beach at H-hour and deploy to answer calls from F.O.Os ashore.
2.	Counter Battery VER-SUR-MER 916844 MONT FLEURY 918861 BENY-SUR-MER 972808	Air Forces Fighter or Medium Bombers.		
3.	Beach Defences. Targets in concrete Right assault brigade Left assault brigade	Army. 17-pr Sherman Tanks, embarked in LCT (CB) Two Two		To engage by direct fire gun emplacements on beaches. To disembark at H-hour and assist assault companies to their Phase objectives.
4.	Enemy Aircraft MIKE Sector NAN Sector	R.N. LCF(8 2-prs and 4 Oerlikons or 4 2-prs and 8 Oerlikons) Three Four		To stand off beaches and give A.A. protection to ships and craft.
5.	Smoke Protection MIKE Sector NAN Sector	R.N. LCP(L) Smoke 18 18		To screen DD tanks at launching point and protect shipping off the beaches.

The schedule of fire support, continued.

Miscellaneous:

- Survey Troop B Battery 9 Survey Regiment.
- Detachment 652 Squadron AOP RAF.

In phase one the field artillery would be expected to deploy on the beaches, in the surf if necessary.

In phase two, 12th and 13th Canadian Field Regiments would deploy to the areas of St Croix-sur-Mer to Banville, known as 'Mary', with 3 Battery 2nd RMASG on Mike and Nan Green. 14th and 19th Canadian Field Regiments would deploy astride the road from Courseulles to Beny-sur-Mer to the area known as 'Jane'. 4 Battery 2nd RMASG Regiment would deploy on Nan White and Nan Red.

In phase three, batteries would be leapfrogged to areas 'Nora' for the 12th and 13th Canadian Field Regiments and 'Dorothy' for the 14th and 19th Canadian Field Regiments, the Regimental COs ensuring that at least two batteries per regiment were in action at all times. In phase three 2 RMASG was to deploy just north of Jane and Mary.

Anti-tank guns were tasked with the immediate support of the brigades against armour and with neutralizing enemy strongpoints. The anti-tank batteries were due to come ashore from H+4 hours onwards and support each assault brigade until 9 Canadian Infantry Brigade had passed through 8 Canadian Infantry Brigade, when it would pick up the batteries supporting 8th Canadian Infantry Brigade for its advance.

The consolidation of the beachhead would be supported by the landing of two field regiments and a medium regiment. 6th Field Regiment were due to land on 8 June and deploy to Nora, with 191st Field Regiment landing two batteries on 9 June and one on 11 June and deploying in Dorothy, and 79th Medium Regiment landing on

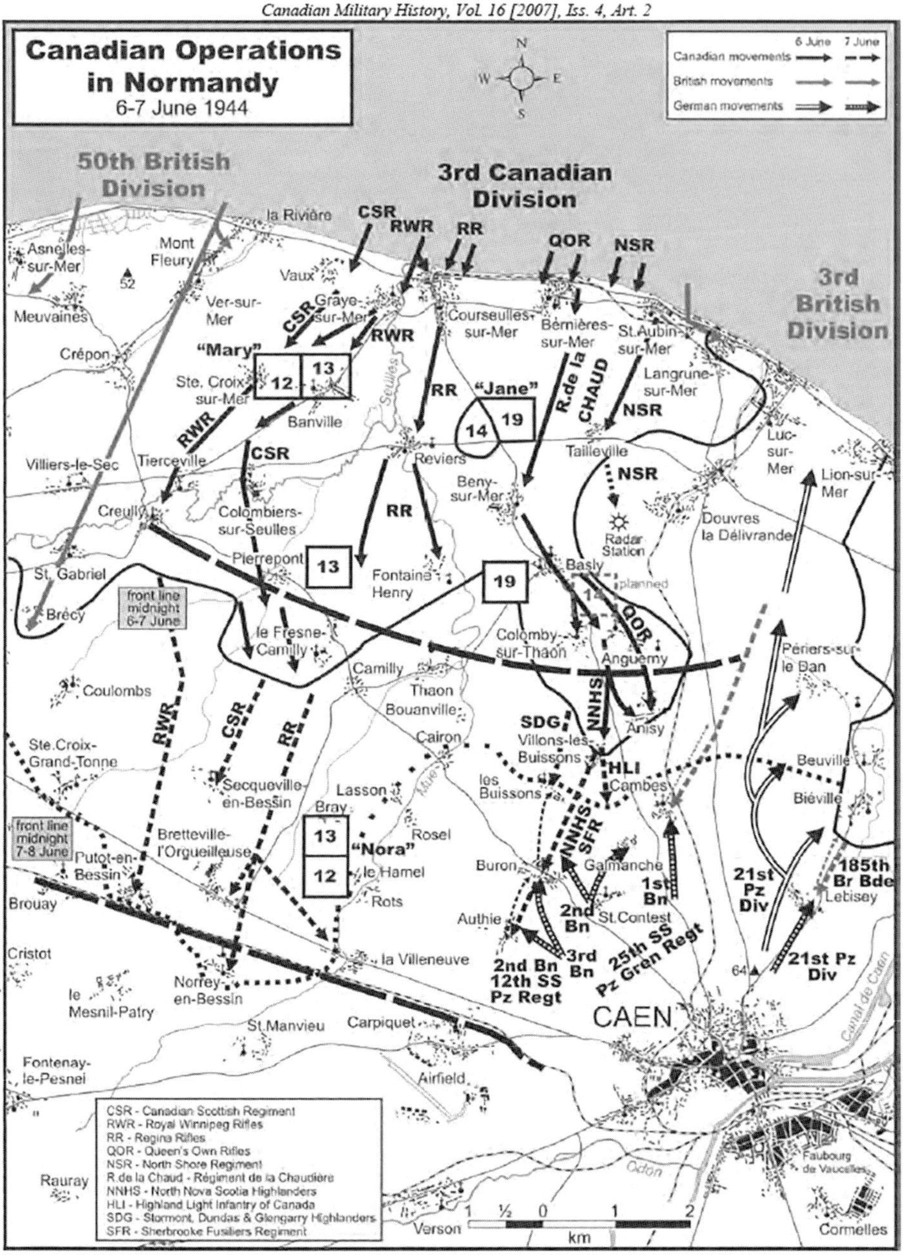

Canadian operations 6-7 June 1944. (Marc Milner)

7 June and deploying to Dorothy with the main task of counter-battery. HQ 4 AGRA was to land on 9 June to take over responsibility for counter-battery fire.

Due to reefs off Juno beach, H-Hour was scheduled to be 0735 on Mike Beach and 0745 on Nan. Owing to heavy seas, the advanced parties could not find the correct swept channels in the minefields. Four groups, including the one carrying the

AVREs for the 7 Canadian Brigade, found their way into the wrong swept channels, heading for the wrong beach. It took a while to reposition the errant craft, and at 0630 hours H-Hour was put back by ten minutes to 0745 hours on Mike and 0755 hours on Nan. While the supporting fire plan from ships and landing craft was adjusted accordingly, it was too late to reschedule aircraft, which bombed on the original times, the last bombs falling no later than 0728 hours.

Touring Juno Beach

The tour is around 25km and probably better done as a drive or cycle ride. For less than a full day's walk, consider walking along the length of the assault beaches and timing the tour to take a convenient bus. It is possible to reach Courseulles with bus line No.3 from Caen railway station, the Côte de Nacre tram stop or from Bayeux on Line 74. The bus service is infrequent, and you should check the timetable. Courseulles, Bernières and St Aubin are all seaside resorts with cafes, restaurants and shops.

Juno Beach Centre

Centre Juno Beach, Voie des Français Libres, BP 104 14470 Courseulles-sur-Mer. (GPS 49.336470, -0.460886)

The Juno Beach Centre is the main Canadian memorial in Normandy. The centre tells the story of Canada's involvement in the Second World War and in Normandy. Outside are several surviving bunkers. On the east side of the river the bunkers were removed during the redevelopment of the town. The westernmost bunker has settled at an angle. This was captured by B Company the Winnipeg Regiment despite high casualties.

Nearby are memorials to the Canadian Scottish Regiment and the Regina Rifles, while 100m further east is a memorial to the Royal Winnipeg Regiment in the form of a crusader sword. A few hundred metres to the west is a memorial to the arrival of General de Gaulle.

The Juno sector was the site of the only scientific investigation into the effectiveness of the D-Day fire plan. Some of the evidence can still be seen, and the results raise some interesting questions about the effects of artillery fire.

A few weeks after D-Day, the 21st Army Group's Operational Research Section carried out an exhaustive investigation into the effectiveness of the D-Day fire plan. The heavy bombers of the Eighth US Air Force were unable to hit any targets closer than 1,000m from the coast to avoid the risk of bombing the troops landing, and thus no bombs fell on Juno beach on D-Day. The Typhoon fighter squadrons assigned to attack targets found the wind and overcast conditions difficult. There was no evidence that fighter-bombers played any part in destroying the Atlantic Wall. It was easy to find the craters left by aircraft bombs and the shallow elongated marks left by rocket projectiles, but none could be found in the resistance nests on the beaches. Major John Fairlie, a Canadian Artillery officer, conducted an exhaustive investigation and concluded that naval gunfire had

> caused no significant damage to the defences … The effects claimed for naval gunfire were difficult to assess because the Germans sited guns to enfilade the beach area only. As few guns could fire seaward, it was hard to say whether the delay in the enemy opening fire was due to the neutralization or the fact that the guns could not bear. In any event the defences were substantially intact when the infantry touched down and the enemy were able to deliver lethal fire in great quantity against our troops.

The German account of the defence of Juno beach was a little different. The Commander of the 716th Division, General Richter, in a post-war interview said that 'The Strongpoint of Courseulles was greatly impeded in its effectiveness before and during the landing because of very heavy fire from ships and bombers and of smoke screens.'

The decision to shift the aiming point of the day bombers 1,000 yards south was fatal for Germans in the supporting positions on the ridge south of Juno beach. At 0510 hours an erroneous report of airborne landings south of Bernières led to No 8 Company of 736 GR undertaking a fruitless search. 8 Company was returning to its positions near Tailleville after a fruitless search for parachutists. A German historian claimed that 'They were caught in the fire of the heavy naval bombardment and annihilated. There were no eye-witness reports and no survivors returned from any of the units taking part.' Eighth Company's position was not one of the targets for the naval bombardment, but it was for two squadrons of US four-engine heavy bombers.

Although the bombardment caused extensive collateral damage, it missed most of the defended positions.

However effective the bombardment was in disrupting the Germans inland, the assaulting infantry were most concerned with the effect of fire on the defences on the coast itself. The Canadian infantry were disappointed by the effects of the naval gunfire. ('The majority of infantry war diaries and reports make bitter reference to the ineffectiveness of the preparatory bombardment and the close support.') Operations Research could not find any damage caused to anti-tank guns or mortars and considered that at the most three of the twenty or so MGs had been neutralized by the preparatory bombardment. The observers did find one mortar and one MG which, though serviceable, had not been manned during the attack. It took about three and half hours to suppress the Germans on Nan Red and half a day to mop up the defenders of St Aubin-sur-Mer. Four lanes ashore had been cleared within an hour, three of which were cleared within thirty minutes, and the first wheeled exit from the beach was cleared within four and a half hours.

The artillery support on Mike Red was by 12th Canadian Field Regiment (SP) under the command of Major Young, 2IC of 12 Field Regiment, and targeted on a strongpoint thought to contain four 75mm guns, Ranging commenced at H-35 and 10,600yards. The mean point of impact was reported on the target by the FOO, and fire for effect was opened at H-32 with one correction. One hundred rounds per gun were fired, then the craft circled around. The FOO reported that a 75mm gun and a machine gun were considered silenced. The unit considered that the rounds fell in an area 400–600 yards wide by 600 yards in depth.

The results on the ground were less impressive. None of the concrete fortifications were damaged by shellfire, though some of the communications trenches had been collapsed. The maximum crater density was estimated to have been approximately 200 yards plus of the targets and 100–200 yards east.

The overwhelming success of the fire support was in support of the flanking operation by Canadian Scottish. The gun in the bunker WN33A was found to have been put out of action by naval gunfire.

Operational researchers could find no evidence of damage to any other guns or mortars, and most machine guns were manned after the assault. The Winnipeg Regiment took two and a half hours to neutralize the defenders of WN30 to the west of the River Seulles, and the Reginas all day to neutralize and deal with WN 29 and clear the town of Courseulles-sur-Mer. Fighting through a built-up area immediately after an amphibious assault was one of the more difficult tasks on D-Day, only overshadowed by the US losses on Omaha beach.

Seven out of the sixty-eight Allied AFVs landing around H-Hour were knocked out on the beach, Most AFV casualties were in the eastern sector. The 6th Canadian Armoured Regiment (1st Hussars) suffered relatively few casualties, possibly because of the destruction of the gun at WN 33A which would otherwise have enfiladed them. This also helped the company of the Canadian Scottish who landed at H-Hour to the west of the main assault on Mike Beach. The infantry suffered 303 casualties on Mike Beach, of which 288 were assault troops and fifteen follow-on troops.

P and Q Troops of 2 RMASG were delayed at sea and did not land until 0900–0930. They claim to have landed six Centaurs and two Shermans with 12th Field Regiment. Two of Q Troop's Centaurs had been lost at sea. Three of P Troop's Centaurs became immobilized on the beach after shingle damaged their tracks, and

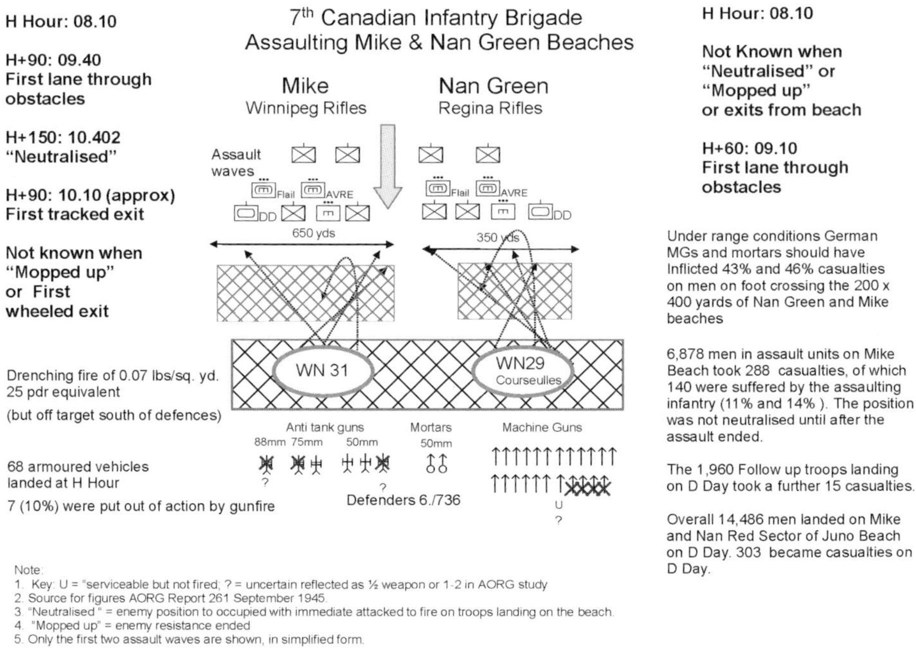

Summary of the assault on Nan Green and Mike beaches.

Rhino Ferries were used to transfer vehicles from ship to shore. One of these caught fire after striking a mine. Two George Medals were awarded to AA gunners who rescued the men aboard.

the battery remained deployed on the beach. No calls for fire were received during D-Day. The battery occupied its time sniping and rounding up prisoners. They claim to have knocked out one machine gun nest and collected twenty-one prisoners.

12th Field Regiment OP and recce parties landed with the infantry. The recce parties deployed on Mike Beach and engaged targets over open sites, despite losing casualties to small arms fire. By the end of the day, they had deployed to position Mary.

I Corps AA Assault Groups landed on Juno Beach, but only two German aircraft overflew the beachhead that day.

If driving, leave the Juno Beach centre car park and turn right into Voie des Français Libres, left into Rue de Marine Dunkerque and at the T Junction turn left on to the D514. If walking or cycling, take the shorter route. Turn left into Voie des Français Libres at the end of the road, right into Quai des Frères Labreques and left into the D514. Cross the bridge over the River Seulles and turn left into Quai des Alliés. Car park close to the sea front.

Courseulles-sur-Mer

Rue Léo Gariepy, 14470 Courseulles-sur-Mer, (GPS9.335675, -0.458477)

There is a prominent Canadian memorial in the form of a DD Tank from the 1st Canadian Hussars recovered in 1970. Named 'Bold', it carries plaques from the different Canadian units which landed on D-Day. This is the only DD tank on display on the British beaches. The metal flange around the hull was to attach the canvas screen. To the left, on the quay, is a 5cm gun damaged in the attack.

Walk out on to the pier east of the mouth of the River Seulles. From east of the river you get some idea of the perspective of the troops who landed there on D-Day. This was a murderous location.

On Nan Green 13 Canadian Field Regiment SP engaged the seafront of Courseulles-sur-Mer, also identified as a strongpoint with four 75mm guns. With Major Goldie, the 2IC, as the FOO, fire was opened with troops smoke salvos at 9,700, 10,000 and 10,600 yards. Rounds at 10,000 yards landed ashore at H-35. Approximately 100 rounds per gun were fired until within 1,800 yards of the beach, when the navy stopped fire in order to circle about. The mean point of impact was assessed to be a little plus of the target. The shoot was considered the best conducted by the Regiment. One 7.5cm gun was thought to have been put out of action. After the battle, the OR team found 90 per cent of the buildings along the sea wall were destroyed and the remainder of the town seriously damaged to a depth of 600 yards, with 30–40 per cent of buildings affected. The outer bearing walls, 18–24″ thick, offered little resistance to shells, while the internal lath and plaster offered virtually none and the internal fabric had mainly collapsed. Many buildings were hit high up by SP rounds. The mean point of impact was estimated to be '200 yards plus but on for line'. The gun claimed to have been put out of action was apparently damaged by a DD tank, since the shell was an AP round fired from the shore.

13th Regiment lost five officers and seven soldiers. Captain Else and his assistant Gunner Robinson were wounded. His signaller, Gunner Holzmann, carried on,

Panorama from the pier at Courseulles looking west.

Panorama from the pier at Courseulles looking east.

German bunker on Strongpoint Courseulles East with an 88mm gun after capture. A triple 20mm cannon from 93 Light AA Regiment is mounted on the roof of the bunker.

contacted S Troop No 2 RMASG and used them to engage a pillbox which was holding the infantry up. Holzmann was awarded the Military Medal.

The time that the guns of 13 Field Regiment landed is likely to have been around 0930 hours on Nan Green. 44 Battery were the first ashore and took up a position just south of Courseulles, before deploying to the regimental gun area Mary at around 1800 hours.

If walking or cycling, travel east along the seafront path to the memorial on the seafront at Bernières-sur-Mer, 2.5 km. If driving, drive east along the Avenue de la Combattante. At the end of the road turn right into Avenue de la Libération and at the second junction turn sharp left on to Route de Bernières/ D514. Continue into Bernières. You will see a car park on the left side of the road with a prominent monument on the seafront. Turn left into the Place du 6 Juin and park. If you pass the tourist office, the old station building with 'Bernières s/Mer' on the side, you have missed the turning. Walk to the memorial on the seafront.

Bernières-sur-Mer

This is Nan White beach, one of the major exit routes from the beach on D-Day. The series of photographs in the Place du 6 Juin shows the area on D-Day and afterwards. Note the photograph showing German prisoners standing on the railway station. The building on the east side, which is now the Museum of the Queen's Own, is a prominent landmark in many contemporary photographs.

The 8th Canadian Infantry Brigade had the task of assaulting Nan Beach and capturing Bernières-sur Mer and St Aubin-sur-Mer. Fire support was from the 14th and 19th Canadian Field Regiments respectively. When the run-in shoot started it was reported that Bernières and St Aubin received 'a terrific pounding, though the main effect seems to be more inland and not on the immediate beach defences'. During the run-in little opposition was evident.

The run-in shoot was provided by 14th Canadian Field Regiment, whose fire was controlled by Major Dogood against WN28 at Bernières. Ranging began at 10,000 yards at H-40 and was directed at the junction of the sea wall and the beach. Two salvos were observed as minus and one as plus. Fire for effect was begun at H-35. The tide carried the craft to the left, eastwards, which required a change of course. After eighty rounds per gun had been fired, the fire was stopped at a range of 4,000 yards due to notification of the postponement of H-Hour not being received. When it was received, it was too late to reform.

Thus, for the final ten minutes of the run-in, no SP artillery fire fell on Bernières-sur-Mer. The mean point of impact was assessed to be 100–200 yards to the left and just plus, an assessment agreed by the OR team inspecting the battlefield a week or

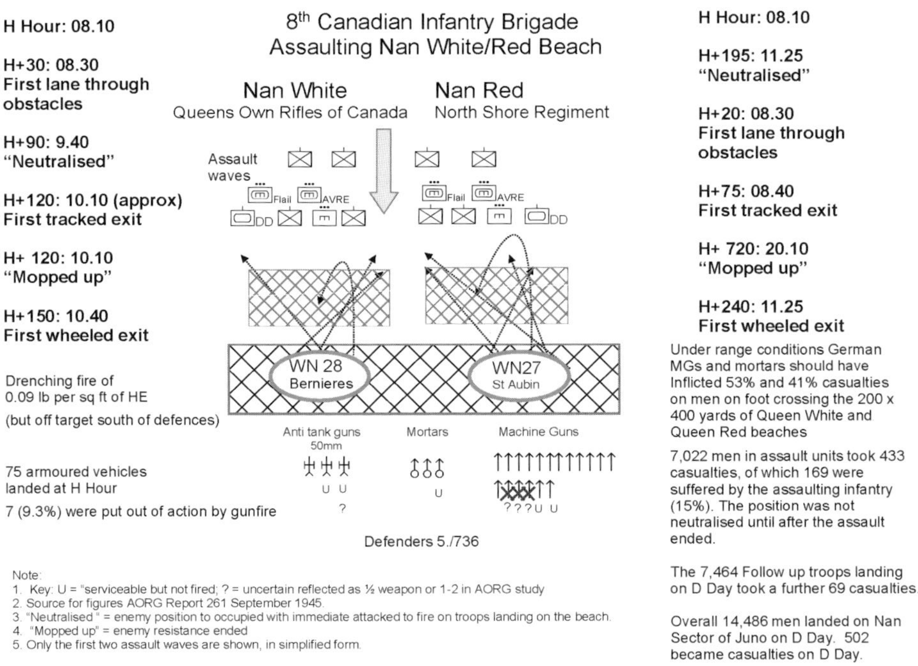

Summary of the assault on Nan White and Nan Red beaches.

so later, which estimated the area in which rounds fell to be 700 yards wide by 500 yards deep. The OR Team found that 90 per cent of the buildings on the sea wall were destroyed, with the remainder of the town severely damaged and 30–40 per cent of the buildings hit to a depth of 400 yards. There was no evidence that the Germans had reinforced any of the buildings, or that the bombardment had damaged any of the defences, since the fire landed plus with limited effect in the defended area.

The Queen's Own Rifles of Canada were to land on Nan White Beach opposite Bernières-sur-Mer. A and B Companies were the assault companies. They should have been accompanied by the DD Tanks of C Squadron of the Fort Garry Horse and W and X Troops of No 4 Battery 2 RMARG. W Troop could not contact their FOO, who had been killed. As no targets were offered, the troop moved off the beaches to a gun area about a mile inland, and later obtained orders to move forwards with the infantry of 8 Canadian Infantry Brigade. X Troop landed about 300 yards east of its correct position but could not find the pillbox which had been given it as a special target. Groynes and other obstacles and prevented lateral movement along the beach. About 0900 contact was made with their FOO, but the troop was not called on to fire and remained on the beach until midday, when it was able to take up a position west of Bernières.

In front of WN28 the Queen's Own Regiment landed without any armoured support against defences undamaged by naval gunfire or artillery. The AVREs landed 300m too far east and were unable to take part in the fight. The Queen's Own Rifles suffered the heaviest casualties of any Canadian unit on D-Day, losing sixty-one dead and seventy-six wounded. The FOB responsible for naval gunfire was Captain Sharman from the South Notts Hussars, who survived despite his exposed radio set attracting enemy fire. He controlled the fire of the Canadian destroyer *Algonquin*. It took 90 minutes for the German positions to be neutralized, and it was a further 30 minutes before resistance ceased. The first lanes through the obstacles were clear within 30 minutes; the first tracked exit from the beach was open within two hours and the first wheeled exit within two and a half.

After the run-in shoot, 14 Canadian Field Regiment turned away and beached at 0925. Meanwhile, the FOOs and recce parties landed with the infantry. Owing to the congestion on the beach the regiment did not get off the beach for an hour. No guns were lost and only two other vehicles were drowned, but subsequently recovered. The Regiment's first gun position was in the fields west of Bernières about 200 yards behind the beach, after a disastrous attempt to deploy in the fields south-west of the village. At 1130 hours eighteen guns were in action but were hampered by a lack of crest clearance. Some support was given during the late morning and afternoon.

Walk east along the seawall for 150m. You will see a Tobruck which contained an MG08 in 1944 and beyond it a concrete emplacement which housed a 5cm anti-tank gun on D-Day. 100m further east is a Tobruck which housed a mortar. A little beyond it was another Tobruck which housed the turret of an obsolete French FT17 tank with a machine gun. The position stretched from the machine gun Tobruck on the western edge for 250m, as far east as the Voie du Debarquement. The position extended 150m from the seafront, with an anti-tank ditch south of the D514. The Operational Research teams later identified nine concrete positions containing two 5cm guns and seven machine guns.

View east from the machine gun bunker Bernieres sur Mer.

View West from Bernieres anti-tank bunker.

Gunners Donald Harper, Dalton Keyes, George Lindop (Ganonoque, ON) and Andrew Fairhurst (Englehart, ON), 14th Field Regiment, RCA, sitting on a Priest self-propelled gun in Normandy, 20 June 1944. (Wes Alkenbrack)

Return to your car and drive south to the crossroads. Cross over and down the Rue du Regiment de la Chaudière. Turn right into the Rue du General Leclerc and follow the road to the roundabout, then take the first exit signed D79A to Beny-sur-Mer. After 100m there is a Memorial. Walk along the lane beside the memorial marked 'authorized vehicles only' to a spot where you can see into the field.

14 Canadian Field Regiment Memorial

Junction Route du Beny and Chemin Dit de Reviers, 14990 Bernières-sur-Mer, (GPS 49.328079, -0.425102)

The first SP guns of 14th Canadian Field Regiment left the south-west corner of Bernières with the leading elements of the Regiment de la Chaudière. In these fields the GPO, Lieutenant Webb, had reconnoitred a gun position, the first with no obstacles such as trees or bushes for crest clearance. Webb identified aiming points and had set up a director to pass the angles to the guns so that they would fire in parallel. The first gun was commanded by Sergeant Art Evans, followed by those of

Ed Crockett, Bob Sciberas and Wes Alkenbrack. Each gun was towing a Porpoise sledge full of ammunition and had additional small arms ammunition and mines stowed on the back decks. Evans' gun was approaching its gun platform when it was hit by an AP round. Wes Alkenbrack, the No 1 of Dog 4, recalled:

> Above the sound of our labouring engines and clanking tracks came the grinding screech of an armour piercing shell meeting steel at high velocity. As smoke and dust billowed up from the stricken vehicle and the gun crew leapt from the deck to hit the ground with incredible swiftness, the second gun, Crockett's, was struck and similarly abandoned.

Several hundred metres along the ridge line was an 8.8cm anti-tank gun sited to cover the exits from Bernières. Alkenbrack pressed on to his firing position, but the Porpoise made it hard to manoeuvre. The third shell from the 88 struck Sciberas' gun and must have detonated some of the explosives.

> There was a flame and the next moment revealed the stark and utter disintegration of what had been 30 tons of moving steel, now strewn on the

Gun B 2 detachment with (front left to right) Bombardier L.A. Boyle, Gunner H.W. Embree, Gunner H.D Armstrong. (Mid-left to right) Lance Bombardier W. J. Pelrine, Sergeant D. Mills, L.T Groves. (Top left to right) Gunners J. R Robinson and C.F. (B. Embrey)

ground like scattered garbage, the gun barrel and bits and pieces of steel plate and the remnants of tracks and heavy castings blown here and there, and not the slightest evidence that six men had stood on the deck of that SP when sudden destruction came.

Alkenbrack managed to extricate his SP with difficulty, under machine gun fire, only after Lance Bombardier Buck McDonald crawled under the gun to unhook the Porpoise. The only occupant of the GPOs tank was the signaller, Ken Darling. Acutely anxious about the vulnerability of the tank, he slipped into the driving position and moved the tank out of the line of fire. The Chaudière infantrymen located and overran the gun. Six artillerymen had died and five were wounded.

There was a weakness in pre-D-Day artillery training. Gun end training concentrated on the technical aspects of gunnery. They were not taught the survival skills needed in forward battle areas, which were admittedly hard to teach. Soldiers needed to learn to spot danger, especially when they might be under enemy observation. At Bernières the 14th Canadian learned a sharp lesson about the lethality of German weapons and their own vulnerability. Although the orders were to push on with all speed, after D-Day it would be rare to order guns to deploy in advance of their own infantry.

This well-preserved bunker containing a 50mm anti-tank demonstrates the cunning design that covers access from the beaches and down several streets inland, while remaining invulnerable from the sea.

The view west from the anti-tank bunker.

Return to your car if you have one. Turn round and drive north back along the D79A to the roundabout and take the first exit on to the D7 heading north. Note the church on your right. 14 Field Regiments guns deployed in what were open fields on the left, western side of the road after the loss of the three guns. The war diary mentions local crest problems, which could have been either the buildings of the villages or trees in the field. These would have made it difficult to engage targets at close range, such as Tailleville, a mere 2,000m away. A contemporary map shows the southern half of the field as an orchard. 14 Canadian Field Regiment occupied this position until 1900 hours.

Follow the road round to the right and continue along the Rue du General Le Clerc and across the roundabout, when it becomes the Rue Maréchal Montgomery. Following the signs to St Aubin-sur-Mer, go straight across two roundabouts to join the D7B Rue Charles de Gaulle. When you reach the sign marking the entrance to St Aubin-sur-Mer turn left into the Avenue de la Libération. At the end of the road turn right into the D514 Rue de Verdun. Park your vehicle and walk to the plaza with the memorial at the east end of the car parking.

The view east from the anti-tank bunker.

St Aubin

Rue Pasteur, 14750 Saint-Aubin-sur-Mer (GPS 49.332274, -0.394029)

There is an anti-tank gun in a German bunker on the plaza. The bunker is sited facing south, the seaward wall protected by thick reinforced concrete. The anti-tank gun inside the bunker has an arc of about 270°, allowing the gun to engage targets on the beach to the left and to the right as well as anything approaching from inland down the roads into the plaza. The gun itself has been damaged by fire from the south and south-west, caused by three tanks from the Fort Garry Horse, which approached from inland. This 5cm gun had fired seventy rounds on D-Day, sunk one LCT and damaged a second.

Walk down to the beach using the steps beside the bunker. On the seaward side of the bunker you can see dozens of marks made by the fire from warships on D-Day. Bunkers constructed and sited like this could only be taken by groups of infantry, armour and engineers working together. Even after the 5cm gun had been knocked out, resistance continued for some time until eventually four officers and seventy-five men were taken prisoner. It took even longer to clear the village as far east as the railway station.

There was a second bunker on the cliffs 100m to the west of the plaza, and the resistance nest extended into the buildings on the seafront for 150m. In 1944 St Aubin was a seaside resort and the sea wall was lined with villas offering a good view of the beach and some protection for the defenders.

19th Canadian Field Regiment supported the assault on Nan Red beach, with the target identified as the two bunkers, each erroneously thought to contain a 7.5cm gun, and the strongpoint between the two. Fire was controlled by Major Preene, 2IC of 19th Field Regiment, and Major Stronach as the FOO. Fire was opened at H-35 at 1,000 yards east of the target due to the course being set on the steeple at Langrune rather than St Aubin. Approximately thirty rounds per gun were fired before the error was noticed. The course was altered, and after dropping range twice, the fire was reported to be on target by the FOO. Approximately 100 rounds per gun were fired from twenty-four guns and fire was stopped at 2,500 yards, apparently due to congestion on the beach and the risk of friendly fire. The MPI was estimated to have been 200 yards plus of the target, with rounds falling in an area 600 yards wide by 300–400 yards deep.

The FOO reported that the hedgehog rockets landed 500 yards west of the town; two thirds of the aircraft bombs landed in the area, while one third landed well concentrated in the target area.

The artillery rounds were seen to be falling on St Aubin, and then smoke obscured the target area. The OR teams reported similar results to elsewhere on Juno. Some 90 per cent of the buildings along the sea wall were destroyed. These had been prepared for defence with sandbags placed inside and holes for snipers cut below the window boxes. No damage was seen on the defensive system as the fire landed well plus and its main effects were outside the target area.

Y troop No 4 Battery 2nd Regiment RMASG landed on the beach at about 0755 hours but could not contact the FOO for some time. The troop came into action at about 0930 hours with 19th Canadian Field Regiment and engaged targets in St Aubin with indirect fire. The troop was joined by two Centaurs of Z Troop of the same battery, and all six guns fired fifteen rounds per gun at nearby houses at a range of 650 yards. Later they moved to St Aubin and supported 48 RM Commando in street-fighting. The second craft of Z Troop with the troop commander, a Sherman and two Centaurs did not arrive until D+1.

48 Royal Marine Commando landed on Nan Red Beach after the North Nova Scotia Highlanders. Their task was to advance east of Juno and contact the commandos advancing from Sword. They were carried in unarmoured small LCIs, which were vulnerable to fire. Less than half of the unit landed and joined the North Shores clearing the village of St Aubin. They moved off east on 6 June supported by the RMASG Centaurs that landed on this beach and took Langrune-sur-Mer later that day.

The officers and recce parties of 19th Canadian Field Regiment landed with the loss of one officer wounded and one OR killed. D Troop touched down at 0910 hours. It was heavily mortared getting off the beach, but its first gun was in action at 0920 hours. Three more troops followed quickly, making the equivalent of two batteries ashore. The LCT carrying one troop suffered a damaged propeller and did not land the troop it carried until 1500 hours. A troop had one SP gun and a half-track set on fire by direct hits. Two more SP equipment and a half-track caught fire. The remaining vehicles got away to a safe distance. RHQ beached under heavy mortar fire and sustained several casualties.

19th Field Regiment reported that due to the type of fighting and the intermingling of friend and foe there were few calls for fire, but 63 battery brought down fire on call at 1030 hours against 'tanks heading towards the beach' – apparently dispersing them. It is not known what German armoured vehicles could have been in that area. 19 Field Regiment seem to have spent the day on or near the beaches until recce parties moved forward at 1700 hours to a new gun position half a mile south of Bernières. There were no calls for fire for three hours after landing.

Even after the fighting on the beach itself died down, Juno Beach was still a dangerous place. The obstacles, enemy fire and sea conditions off Juno Beach caused difficulties throughout the day. At 2200 hrs, as it was getting dark, a Rhino ferry and an LCP ran into mines on underwater obstacles, despite efforts to divert them by voice and the use of red lamps. As soon as the mine exploded, the Rhino ferry burst into flames about 100 yards away from the beach. Four three-tonners laden with petrol caught fire, and the flames stretched over the beach. Some men on the Rhino were doubtful about coming ashore because of the danger of mines. Sergeant James Finlay and Lance Bombardier Frederick Harrison of 114 Light AA Regiment waded out to the craft and succeeded in getting fifteen men ashore. A first aid party was organized on shore which attended to the wounded, giving artificial respiration for nearly two hours. Four men survived out of the five given artificial respiration. Throughout the period, petrol was exploding, and it was known that there were ten three-tonners at the rear of the Rhino loaded with ammunition, which posed a constant danger. Fortunately, the wind carried the flames away from the craft, and the three-tonners were saved. Findley and Harrison were both awarded the George Medal.

Return to your car and drive away from the bunker south along the Rue Carnet. Turn right into the Rue Maréchal Foch and then immediately left into Rue Abbé Bossard, following this road to a roundabout where the road becomes the D219 Route de Tailleville. At the junction north of Tailleville stop by the farm buildings.

Tailleville

Route de St Aubin, Tailleville, (GPS 49.307139, -0.407157)

The first German defences inland from Juno Beach were on the high ground about 2–3km south of the coast. There was a line of anti-tank guns and infantry positions occupied by German and Russian *Ost* troops. The village of Tailleville was the headquarters of the 2nd Battalion of 736th Grenadier Regiment. The chateau, now a youth hostel, was fortified and its ground entrenched, and there is a Tobruck in the grounds.

A Company of the North Shore Regiment reached as far as here on the morning of D-Day. However, it took until early evening before a co-ordinated infantry and armoured attack eliminated German resistance in the village.

Look north towards Bernières and St Aubin. This is the view that the German anti-tank and field gunners would have had on D-Day when the Queen's Own Rifles and the Chaudières began to move south from Bernières, and it may help you to appreciate why the 8th Brigade advance was so slow and why the decision to land the reserve brigade at Bernières caused such a pile-up.

Continue into the village on the Rue de St Aubin. At the end of the road turn right on the D35 towards Bayeux.

In the fields to your right after you leave Tailleville were the positions of 8/726. The decision to shift the aiming point of the day bombers 1,000 yards south may have been fatal for the 8th company. At 0510 hours, after a mistaken report of airborne landings south of Bernières, the battalion HQ launched 8th company against this enemy. As No.8 Company of GR 736 were returning to their positions near Tailleville after a fruitless search for parachutists they were caught in a heavy bombardment and annihilated. Although some accounts attribute the losses to naval gunfire, 8/716's position was not one of the targets for the naval bombardment but was bombed by two squadrons of US four-engine heavy bombers around the same time.

Travel west 2km on the D35 'Delle de Tombette' to the roundabout junction with the D79, Rue de Caen. You are on the centre of the southern edge of gun position Jane.

Gun Position Jane
D35 junction with D79 (GPS 49.303590, -0.435421)

Look north. The gun area extended approximately 1,000m to the east and the west of the D79 and approximately 1000m north, with an extension south of the road to the west. The area to the west was reserved for 14th Canadian Field Regiment, and to the east for the 19th Canadian Field Regiment. The open ground meant there were few crest problems.

German maps show one or two 88 mm anti-tank guns in this area covering the southern exits from Bernières. If you look north, you can see the field where the three Priest SP guns of 14 Field Regiment were knocked out.

Continue west on the D35 until you reach the Bény-sur-Mer Canadian War Cemetery on the north side of the road. This is roughly the western edge of gun area Jane.

Bény-sur-Mer Canadian War Cemetery
This contains 2,032 graves, of which 181 are those of Canadian Gunners. Twenty-one Canadian gunners died on 6 June. Twelve are buried here and one in Portsmouth. Ten have no known graves and are commemorated on the Bayeux Memorial to the Missing. The bulk of the fatalities were from two regiments. 14 Field Regiment suffered ten fatal casualties on D-Day, five of whom have no known grave, including men lost in the three SP guns burned out. Major G. E. Purcell (1H.10) commanded 81 Battery and was the Unit Deployment Officer. Captain J. M. Barclay (1B.9) was a 14 Regiment FOO who landed with the assault companies on Nan White Beach at Bernières.

Major G. F. Rainnie (2H.11) was the 2IC of 13 Field Regiment. He and Gunner Higgs (5E.12) died when their landing craft struck a mine on Mike Red Beach. Captain Dirks (1F.12) drowned when his landing craft struck a mine on Nan Green

An M7 from 13 Regiment on gun position Mary on D-Day.

Beach. Lance Corporal Swan of the Royal Canadian Corps of Signals (5E.13) was part of the 13 Canadian Field Regiment's regimental reconnaissance party. Gunner Robinson, Captain Elze's assistant, is buried in 10C.4.

Travel west on the D35 through Reviers. At the junction at the end of the village turn right on to the D176 signed Bayeux, cross the River Seulles and turn right into the road signed to Banville. Bear left on the metalled road which will become Rue du Camp Romain in Banville. At the T junction, turn right into Avenue des Chasses/D12. You will see a crucifix. Turn left on to a metalled road across the fields. At the junction with the 'no motor vehicle access' sign, halt.

Mary Gun Positions RCA
14480 Banville (GPS 49.318899, -0.491196)

This is the northern, rear edge of gun position 'Mary', roughly in the centre of where 13th Field Regiment RCA deployed on the afternoon of D-Day. 12th Regiment RCA were further west, north of St Croix. This is almost a School of Artillery gun position as found on Salisbury Plain. The shallow valleys east and west of the ridgeline offer good gun positions for the two regiments. They are on the reverse slope with no close crests. Any armour approaching over the crest would also be exposed to anti-tank fire from the guns at a range at which their anti-tank shot could be effective.

Somewhere between Courseulles and here, 13 Regiment RCA's first vehicle casualty was GA, a GPO's tank. This had thrown a track on the beach and was making its way to the gun position, when it was destroyed by a hidden 8.8cm gun, without any personnel casualties.

13th Field Regiment RCA suffered one famous casualty in this position. Lieutenant J. Doohan, CPO of 22 Battery, having landed with the reconnaissance parties on Mike Green beach at H+20, survived the German fire on Juno beach. Late at night, he was accidentally shot by a trigger-happy sentry with a burst of machine gun fire which hit him six times and removed a finger. Doohan recovered from his wounds to become an Air OP pilot and, after the war, an actor best known for his portrayal of Chief Engineer Scott in the TV series *Star Trek*. In this area 44 Battery captured four snipers, a German NCO and three Russians.13 Regiment's war diary entry for the day ends: 'Fatigue was noticeable due to 24 hr packs, the rough voyage over, lack of sleep and the natural tension of a combined operation against a prepared enemy.'

Turn right and drive back to Graye-sur-Mer, joining the Rue Saint Croix. At the T junction turn left on to the Rue Grande/D112B, then immediately right into the D112C. At the T junction with the coast road, turn left on to the D514 and then take the first right along the D112C, the Avenue de General de Gaulle – named for the general's route inland after he landed in August 1944. When you reach the crossroads with the D514 coast road, turn left on to the D514 Route d'Arromanches. If driving or cycling, take the third track on the right – after travelling 1.89km you should see the bunker among the dunes. This leads to a sandy parking area. Walk forwards to the beach and turn right. About 50m away is a bunker. If walking, when you reach the D514, cross over and walk to the seashore. Turn left and walk along the beach or through one of the paths in the dunes until you reach the bunker.

This bunker containing a 75mm or 88mm took a direct hit on D-Day. A rare visible success for the preliminary bombardment.

Le Buisson WN 33A
Bunker WN33a, 14470 Graye-sur-Mer (GPS 49.342160, -0.493805)

This bunker was built to house anti-tank guns that could fire obliquely, in enfilade across Juno Beach to the east and the eastern side of Gold Beach to the west. You have a good view across Mike Beach from here, well within range of an 8.8cm anti-tank gun. This bunker was the site of one of the successes of the D-Day fire plan. It was struck by a bomb or naval shell on D-Day before the landings took place, and its destruction is one reason why the attacks on Mike Green and Red and King Red did not have more vehicle casualties.

This is the end of the tour. You can return to the Juno Beach centre by returning to the D514 and turn left. Alternatively, walk along the beach.

Chapter 9

Gold Beach

At 5.30 the cruiser *Belfast* 'opens the party' by firing star shells at the Ver-sur-Mer Battery, the RAF bombers come in at that time too, and we break wireless silence. The other cruisers join in as we continue shore wards. Nothing from the shore at all, all the way from Arromanches to Courseulles it is extraordinarily peaceful, with just a whomp of shells or bombs now and again. At 06.30 the destroyers open fire from the left.

At 06.50 off go our own SP guns on the run-in shoot. By now our LCH is only 2,000 yards offshore and taking up station to control the landing. I have a perfect view of our shells falling on their target of La Rivière, and over the wireless I can hear George Loveday and Ted Hall on the air observing and correcting the firing from their speedboats in front of us. Wireless perfect, weather bloody, no DD tanks launched.

The whole coastline is now under bombardment from the sea, and above the smoke and flashes of the explosions we can see now and then our aircraft flying low inland. By this time their bombing of the beaches has ceased. The bombardment from the sea is quite superb. The cruisers and destroyers are bombarding the higher ground at Le Hamel all the way round this half circle of low hills to Mont Fleury, with each cruiser or destroyer having its own target to neutralise.

Captain Robert Kiln 432 Battery, 86 Regiment Hertfordshire Yeomanry

Gold Beach was 19,400 yards long from Port-en-Bessin to the mouth of the River de Provence, the stream between Mont Fleury and La Rivière that flows into the sea at the east end of Boulevard de la Plage. This was the official boundary between Gold and Juno beaches. East of St-Côme-de-Fresné the land inshore was low-lying. The seashore was lined with sand dunes, behind which there was a stretch of marsh up to 1,000m wide and then the Meuvaines Ridge, broken by the valley of the River Gronde. The coastline to the west consisted of rocky cliffs, except for the coves in which nestled Arromanches and Port-en-Bessin.

The coastline of the King Beach sector included three defence posts manned by the seventh company from GR736 of 716 Infantry Division. WN33 at La Rivière was armed with one 8.8cm and one 5cm anti-tank gun, WN34 at the Mont Fleury lighthouse had one 7.5cm and one 5cm anti-tank gun, and WN 35 had one 5cm anti-tank gun. The defences included five machine guns and a mortar.

The boundary between the 716th and 352nd Infantry divisions ran east of Asnelles, straddled by the Jig assault sector. WN36 mounted a 5cm and a 3.7cm anti-tank gun

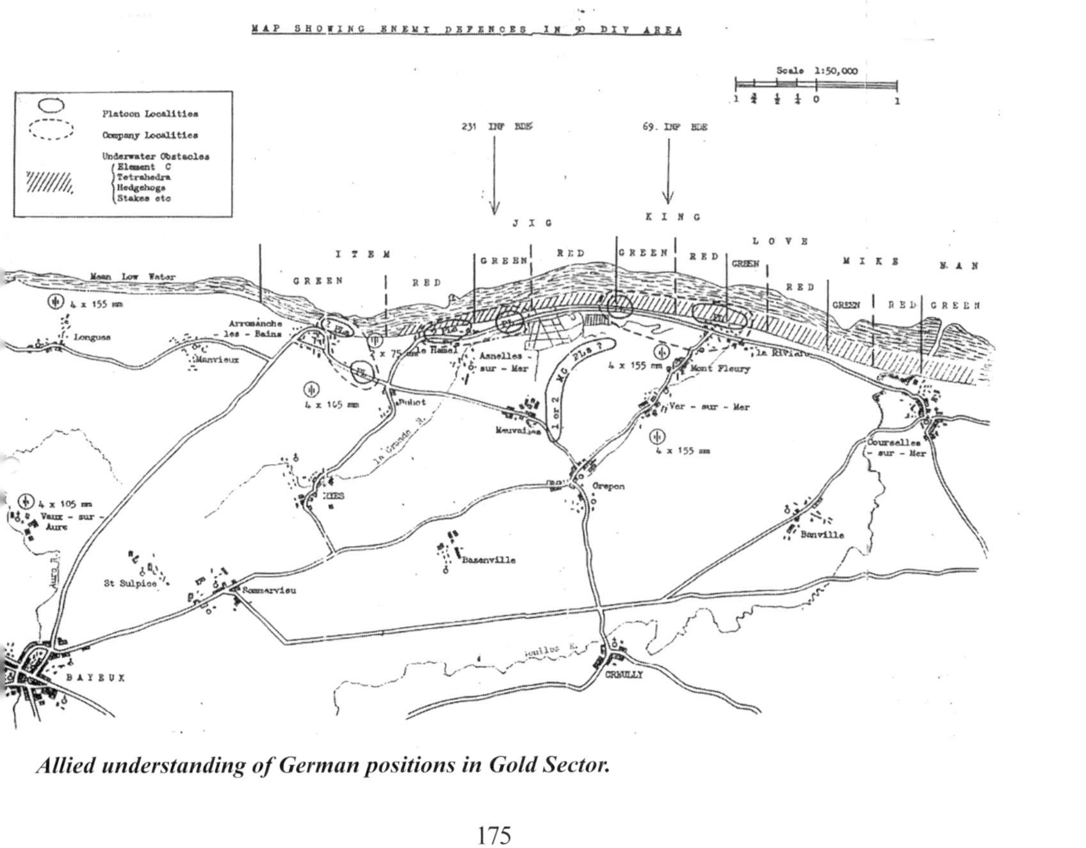

Allied understanding of German positions in Gold Sector.

manned by troops from 441 *Ost* Battalion. WN37 at the east end of Le Hamel had one 7.5cm and one 5cm anti-tank gun. At the west end of the village WN38 mounted a single 5cm anti-tank gun. The defences included 13–14 machine guns. Four other defence posts along the coastline to Arromanches were garrisoned by the first two companies of I/926, but outside small-arms range.

Behind the coastal defences were the following positions:

- Two companies from 441 *Ost* battalion in field positions on the Meuvaines Ridge.
- Two companies from I/916, and the battalion headquarters in reserve near Ryes.

Defensive positions manned by artillery batteries and unit headquarters also provided some depth:

- 2/ HKAA 1260 (four 12.2 15.5 cm) 'Mont Fleury battery'.
- 6/AR 1716 (four 10 cm) WN32 'Ver-sur-Mer battery'.
- 5/AR 1716 (four 10 cm) WN36A (unlocated).
- Two batteries of 10.5 cm artillery from AR 352 (unlocated).

69 Brigade was to land on Gold Beach, King sector. Their task was to seize the area of St Leger on the Caen–Bayeux road and link up with 3 Canadian Infantry Division on their left. This was to take place in three phases.

Phase 1 was to secure the beach and the high ground overlooking it. 6 Green Howards on King Green were to capture the Mont Fleury battery and secure Point 52. 5 East Yorks on King Red were to mask La Rivière, capture the lighthouse position, then clear La Rivière. 7 Green Howards were to clear Ver-sur-Mer and capture its battery.

Phase 2 was to seize the crossings over the River Seulles at Creully. 6 Green Howards were to capture Crépon and 7 Green Howards were to bypass Crépon, capture Creully and seize the crossings.

Phase 3 was to advance to the high ground at St Leger and link up with the Canadians.

231 Brigade was, in phase 1, to secure Jig Beach and the immediate hinterland, then in phase 2 mop up Arromanches, capture the Longues battery and secure the phase 2 line.

After 151 and 56 Brigades landed, and at the conclusion of phase 2, certain supporting elements would be transferred to them from the assault brigades.

In phase 3, 69, 151 and 56 Brigades would secure the high ground north of Bayeux, with 231 Brigade protecting the right flank of the beaches.

Phase 4 was for 56 Brigade to capture Bayeux and 151 Brigade to secure the phase 4 phase line, while 231 Brigade advanced to a junction point with the US V corps.

47 Royal Marine Commando was to capture Port-en-Bessin on D-Day.

8 Armoured Brigade was to form a mobile column between H+8 and H+14 to exploit and seize Villers Bocage from D+1.

Artillery order of battle
Artillery under command 50th Division for D-Day:

- 86 Field Regiment (Herts Yeomanry)
- 90 (City of London) Field Regiment
- 147 Field Regiment (Essex Yeomanry)
- 102 Anti-Tank Regiment (Northumberland Hussars) (less 107 & 289 Batteries, plus198 & 234 (SP) Batteries, 73 Anti-Tank Regt)
- Det. 76 AA Brigade
- RHQ 120 LAA Regiment:
- A Troop 320 Battery 93 LAA Regiment
- 394 Battery, 120 LAA Regiment (less one troop)
- 362 Battery, 113 HAA Regiment (plus one troop 366 HAA Battery)
- Half of 356 Search Light Battery
- Detachment 112 Pioneer Smoke Coy
- 54 Flight RAF Balloon Coy
- RHQ 113 Heavy AA Regiment:
- B Troop 320 Battery 93 LAA Regiment
- 395 Battery, 120 LAA Regiment (less one troop)
- 391 Battery, 113 HAA Regiment (plus one troop 366 HAA Battery),
- half 356 Search Light Battery
- 152 AA Operations Room
- 55 Flight RAF Balloon Coy
- Detachment 47 Survey Battery, 4 Survey Regiment
- Assistant Counter Bombardment Officer
- A Flight, 662 Air OP Squadron
- 1 RM Armoured Support Regiment
- 82 LAA Battery 25 LAA Regiment, less one 20mm troop
- 987 Field Artillery Battalion US Army (5 AGRA)
- 420 Heavy Battery (5 AGRA)

Fire plan
The air forces were to commence a programme of bombing of the coast installations from midnight to 0530 hours, striking at the main coast batteries, the Longues and Mont Fleury batteries in the Gold Beach sector. Close air support would then be provided by Mitchells, Mosquitoes and Typhoons attacking the coast defences at La Rivière and Le Hamel, headquarters and other targets as requested, with 1,000lb bombs.

Support from the Royal Navy would come from the bombardment force as shown in the table

The weight of drenching fire on the Gold Beach defences amounted to 0.07lb/sq. yd.

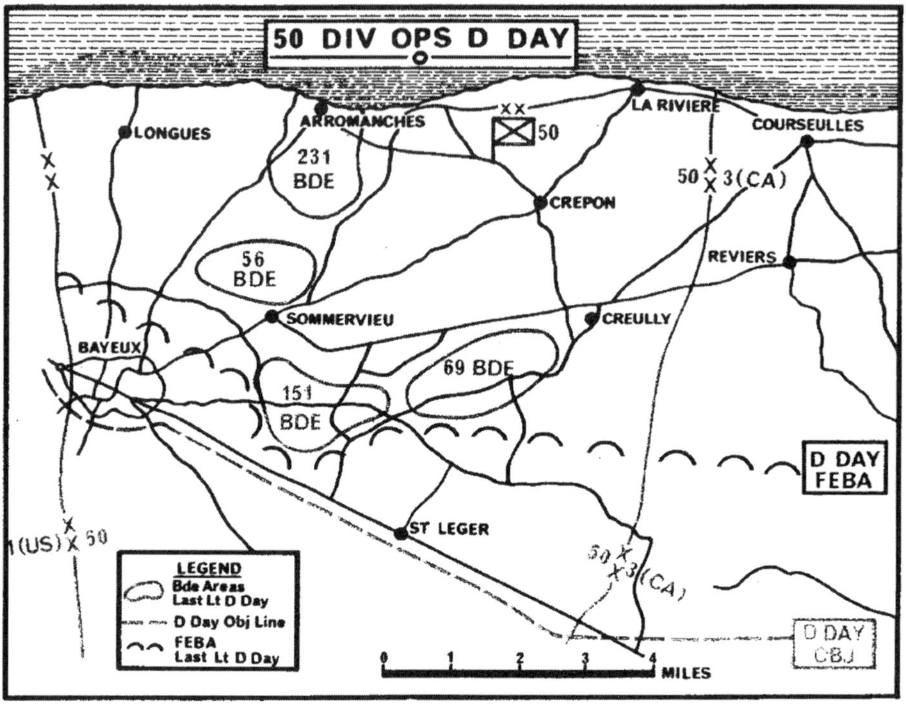

Overview of 50th Division operations on D-Day.

Field Artillery

Only one of 50th Division's three field regiments, the 90th, was an SP regiment able to take part in the run-in shoot. Two SP army field regiments joined the divisional artillery for D-Day, 86 (Hertfordshire Yeomanry) Field Regiment and 147 (Essex Yeomanry) Field Regiment. 74th and 124th Field Regiments with their towed 25-pounders would land later. With five brigades in the division, including 8 Armoured Brigade, landing on D-Day, and only three field regiments, which would rise to four on D+2 with the arrival of 74th Field Regiment, there would have to be considerable regrouping to support brigades and units as the battle progressed, starting on D-Day itself.

In phases 1 and 2, 90th and 147th Field Regiments were allocated to 231 Brigade on Jig sector as it was assessed to be the more difficult objective, and 86 Field Regiment was allocated to 69 Brigade on King Sector.

In phases 3 and 4, with the arrival of 56 and 151 Brigades and the move of the battle inland, the field regiments with 231 Brigade would regroup: 90 Field Regiment to 151 Brigade and 147 Field Regiment, less one battery, to 56 Brigade. 231 Brigade, remaining near the coast, would then rely on naval gunfire for support and the 431 battery of 147 Field Regiment. However, this battery's principal task was to support the 47 RM Commando attack on Port-en-Bessin. 86 Field Regiment remained in support of 69 Brigade.

Regrouping required those elements of the field regiment that were based with the infantry or armour to leave the units they were currently supporting and find the units they needed to join. These were the CO, the three BCs and six FOOs, scattered over the brigade area. The first step is usually to rejoin their own transport. But on D-Day, the artillery tanks and carriers landed later than the walking parties and needed to find them first. Wireless sets would need to be retuned to the new infantry or armour wireless nets, in the contemporary term to be 'netted in'.

The planned advance to Villers Bocage was beyond the range of naval guns. 987 Field Artillery Battalion (FAB) of the US Army equipped with tracked M12 155mm guns would provide medium artillery.

Anti-tank

Each assault brigade would be supported by an anti-tank battery with an M10 troop and two 6-pounder troops, followed by the two M10 SP batteries from the corps anti-tank regiment, 73 Anti-Tank Regiment. Medium artillery, survey and anti-aircraft units and an Air OP Flight would also land on D-Day to support the Division and the recce parties of the units landing on the following days.

The anti-tank defences during phases three and four were to be co-ordinated by CO 102 (Northumberland Hussars) Regiment. 234 Anti-Tank Battery, landing on Jig Beach at about H+2 hours, would concentrate in an area just south of Asnelles. Its initial role was to act as the 231 Brigade mobile reserve. 198 Anti-Tank Battery landing on King Beach at around H+6 hours would concentrate in the area of Vaux-sur-Seulles as a mobile reserve. 288 battery, less one troop under command 56 Brigade, would be prepared to move under command 8th Armoured Brigade after completion of phase four.

Anti-Aircraft

82nd Battery of 25 LAA Regiment would land on the second tide. One troop was tasked with protecting the bridges over the River Seulles at Creully. The remainder of the battery would protect the gun areas.

All other AA landing on Gold Beach in the initial stages was to protect the beaches and the Beach Maintenance Area under 76 AA Brigade. The rest of the corps and the division's own Light AA regiments would arrive later and cover XXX Corps as it advanced inland.

In phase 1, the Anti-Aircraft Defence Commander would be CO 113 HAA Regiment, Lieutenant Colonel Gilbert. The light anti-aircraft troops would land on the first tide, and the first two troops to land on each beach were to deploy on the high-water mark, then move off the beach; their task was to protect the beaches and beach exits to a depth of 500 yards out to sea and inland. On Jig Beach the third troop to land would protect the lateral road and the DUKW transhipment area, and the fourth troop was to protect the 85 Base Gp GCI, while on King the third troop was to protect the Ver-sur-Mer road junction and traffic congestion and the fourth was to protect Crépon.

The Heavy anti-aircraft troops would follow on Tides 2 and 3: on Jig, two troops of 391 Battery on Tide 2 were to deploy to positions south of Crépon and east of St Côme-de-Fresné, followed by a troop of 366 Battery on Tide 3 to Ryes. On King, on Tide 2, a troop of 362 Battery between Le Hamel and La Rivière was to be followed on Tide 3 by the second troop of 362 Battery and one of 366 Battery to the east of Asnelles, and the third at Arromanches.

These would be supported by searchlights from 356 SL Battery, 54 and 55 Flights of 980 Balloon Squadron and A Group 112 Pioneer Smoke Company providing smoke over the beach and anchorage at night.

CO 125 LAA Regiment, with 62 LAA Battery of 20 LAA Regiment under command, was in control of all LAA guns on the Mulberry Harbour. CO 120 LAA Regiment, with 320 LAA Battery of 93 LAA Regiment under command, also controlling C Group 139 LAA Regiment in the landing barges flak, was in command of the air defences on Gold Beach.

152 AA Operations Room was to set up close to the RAF GCI site at Buhot. The first LAA units to land were to set up an Anti-Aircraft Reporting Centre (AARC) on the Red and Green sectors on each beach, one on each beach to be the Main AARC with the LAA CP as close as possible; all anti-aircraft units were to report to the nearest AARC on disembarkation. Early warning would be provided by the HQ ship *Largs*, then the GCI on deployment.

Touring Gold Beach

The Gold Beach tour is 27km. Visitors seeking a shorter walk might consider routes based on King Beach and Jig Beach. There is an infrequent bus service from Caen to Ver-sur-Mer (Line 3) and from Bayeux (Line 74).

Ver-sur-Mer Museum

2 Place de l'Amiral Byrd, 14114 Ver-sur-Mer. (GPS 49.336649, -0.525359)

Follow the signs to the 'Musée'. The museum has a collection of images and artefacts connected with the landings on Gold Beach. One display concerns the 987th Field Artillery Battalion (FAB), US Army. This was the only US unit to land on the British invasion beaches and fought under British command to the end of June 1944.

This unit was a late addition to the invasion force. XXX Corps demanded medium artillery on D-Day since their D-Day objectives were beyond the range of naval artillery. The British did not have a suitable tractor to tow medium artillery on the assault beaches; the Americans did. The M12 GMC (Gun Motor Carriage) mounted a 155mm M1917 (or M1917A1/M1918) on an M3 tank chassis. When the British asked to borrow twelve guns for D-Day, the Americans generously offered a complete unit. The soldiers arrived in the UK in April, while the guns arrived in early May. Weather and congestion on the beaches meant that the 987th did not land until 7 June. The 987th FAB joined 5 AGRA.

Continue to La Rivière and Ver-sur-Mer. As you reach Ver-sur-Mer, at the traffic lights turn left into the Avenue du 6 Juin and then right into Espace Robert Kiln. Park in the car park. On D-Day Robert Kiln was battery captain of 342nd battery of the 86th Hertfordshire Yeomanry. After the Second World War he became a successful businessman and funded the park and memorial dedicated to the 86th Hertfordshire Yeomanry.

Walk or cycle NE along the Rue de la 8ème Armée, continuing into the Avenue du 6 Juin. As you walk past the turning to the Rue du Pavillon look right and identify the lighthouse. This was the area of WN34. Continue to the end of the road and turn left into the Espace Robert Kiln.

Espace Robert Kiln

Espace Robert Kiln, 14114 Ver-sur-Mer, (GPS 49.343324, -0.516611)

The memorial is a 25-pounder Sexton self-propelled gun, painted in the markings of the 86th Field Regiment the Hertfordshire Yeomanry.

Behind the Sexton is a Porpoise ammunition sledge used on D-Day. The information boards explain more about the gun and its role. The graphic representation of the fire support delivered on King Beach shows the part played by the Hertfordshire Yeomanry. It is based on one of the pre-D-Day briefing diagrams, since the Royal Marine Armoured Support Group, a late addition, are not shown.

One information panel explains the heraldry of British military vehicles. 86th Field Regiment was not part of a division, so its formation badge was the crusader shield of the 21st Army Group and the unit number of 1147. Each vehicle in an artillery unit would have letters indicating its function from A to Z. Anyone looking at a vehicle could identify exactly its role and place in the organization. 86th Field Regiment retained their Yeomanry stag's head as their cap badge rather than that of the Royal Artillery.

Cross the road. On the north side of the D514 opposite the Sexton is the memorial to the artillery of the 50th (Tyne and Tees) Division. This division had originally been raised from Territorial soldiers in the North-East of England. Five field artillery regiments are listed. 74th and 124th (Northumbrian) Field Regiments were Territorial units raised in the North-East. The 90th (City of London) Regiment had been transferred to the 50th Division after Tunisia. 86th and 147th Field Regiments are listed because of their temporary assignment for D-Day.

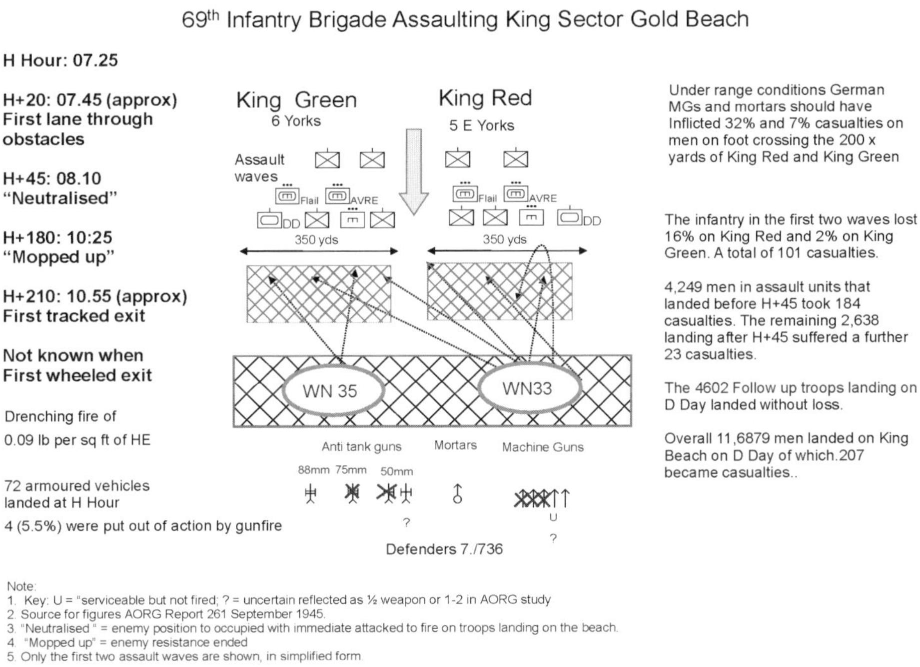

Summary of the assault on King Beach.

The 88mm bunker at La Rivière is top centre of this image. The 50mm position is off to the right of the image.

The Divisional anti-tank regiment was the 102th (Northumberland Hussars) Anti-tank Regiment, another Yeomanry regiment. They were mobilized in 1939 as mounted cavalry and converted to artillery in 1940. They had fought in Greece, Crete, North Africa and Sicily and were one of the most experienced anti-tank units in any army.

This 88mm gun emplaced in an H677 pattern bunker was invulnerable from seaward.

The divisional Light AA regiment was the 25th Light AA Regiment, a TA regiment mobilized in Liverpool. It had defended the Suez Canal before joining 50th Division.

A few metres to the east is a memorial to the 2nd Battalion the Hertfordshire Regiment. This was part of No 9 Beach Group responsible for close defence and labour for the King Red Beach. On D-Day a patrol attempted to capture the German position WN35, between Gold and Juno Beaches. However, when they came under fire from German infantry, they had no communications to artillery or warships and were forced to withdraw.

Walk or drive north along the Avenue Colonel Harper to the seafront.

La Rivière

Boulevard de la Plage, 14114 Ver-sur-Mer (GPS 49.344675, -0.515349)

There are information boards on the east side of the square telling the history of Ver-sur-Mer and of the assault by 69 Brigade. The seaside resort village at La Rivière was much smaller in 1944 and many of the buildings had been boarded up and loopholed. The seafront lifeguard station is built over a 5cm anti-tank gun emplacement. This was the north-eastern side of defensive position WN33.

Walk 250m west along the Boulevard du Plage. You will find a bunker which housed an 8.8cm gun covering Gold Beach to the west. The position also contained a second emplacement for a 5cm gun as well as several concrete shelters. You are at the eastern extremity of King Red Beach, with the defenders' view of the beach assaulted by 5th Battalion the East Yorkshire Regiment.

Major Loveday, BC 341 Battery, was the controlling OP for the run-in shoot on King Beach assisted by Captain Hall, Troop Commander of A Troop, and led the

Modern view of the 88mm position at La Rivière.

force. They would land later and join up with their battalion, 7 Green Howards, the reserve battalion in 69 Brigade. The Battery's other FOO, Captain Perry, B Troop Commander, landed with the Battalion.

Major Swann, BC 342 Battery, and his FOOs, Captains Street (C Troop) and Ash (D Troop), were to land with their battalion, 6 Green Howards. Major Scammell, BC 462 Battery, and his FOOs, Captains Turnbull (E Troop) and Pamphilon (F Troop), were to land with their battalion, 5 East Yorks, which would assault this sector.

The guns were in six LCTs at the rear of the force, behind 7 Green Howards and the Brigade priority vehicles, loaded as standard with one troop of four to an LCT. The sea being too rough to launch the DD tanks, the first units to land were the AVREs of 81 Assault Squadron RE as scheduled at H-5 (0720 hours), followed by the flails of the Westminster Dragoons, then B and C Squadrons 4/7 RDG, which had launched only a few hundred yards offshore and arrived at the same time as the leading infantry of 5 E Yorks on King Red and 6 Green Howards on King Green at H+5, 0730 hours.

Captain Robert Kiln was a liaison officer with the Royal Navy aboard a Landing Craft Headquarters:

> The fire of our SP guns is falling on the La Rivière causeway and its defences. At sea other craft are joining in. We have two Landing Craft Guns (LCGs) armed with two 4.7-inch naval guns. We are using these to bring accurate observed fire on the strongpoints at La Rivière and the two pillboxes on the beach.

The lighthouse can be seen from the sea front. This was the centre of a secondary position in Ver-sur-Mer.

> As our craft approach the beaches, German guns and Spandaus come into action, but few of their big guns are firing out to sea. Close behind the infantry landing craft are three LCT(R) packed with 60-pound rockets and when they are just behind us they open fire. The firing is not selective; all the 100 or so rockets go off together. First one craft, then the other two. They are aligned to land just behind the beach in several great clumps. I follow the rockets arching high in the air over the landing craft in front of them and crunching down on the German defences.
>
> At 0720, as the infantry are within 1,000 yards of the beach, our gunfire shifts from the beach at La Rivière to its second target which is the area of the Mont Fleury battery just behind the beach on the higher ground, which we suspect to hold guns, machine guns and enemy observation posts. This shift we can clearly see and hear on the wireless.
>
> It is now within ten minutes of the touch-down of the assaulting infantry in their LCAs, but they are going to be a few minutes late which, considering the state of the sea is really superb. Commander Haines asks me to keep our guns firing for another ten minutes. So, for the first time that day I use my wireless to contact George Loveday and arrange for the Regiment's firing to continue for the extra period, wondering whether they will have enough ammunition, and hoping that they will have enough time after they finish firing to prepare all the guns and vehicles for landing.

The bombardment was, for the most part, effective, the defenders being numbed into inactivity, especially the troops of 441 *Ost* Battalion. The Marefontaine battery, WN34, and the positions at the lighthouse were hard hit, and the Mont Fleury battery made no reply.

At 0715 hours it became apparent on King Beach that the leading assault craft with the AVREs, flails and DD tanks, which were taken right into the beach, were behind schedule, and the OP officers ordered the shoot to continue for an extra ten minutes; at 0725 hours the guns lifted on to their depth targets, and it was not until 0735 hours that the run-in shoot was completed and the OP officers and guns turned to a flank to await their turn to land.

Some 500m inland from the beach around the lighthouse was a second defensive position, WN34, containing a 5cm anti-tank gun as well as concrete shelters and field defences. WN33 and 34 were manned by 7th Company of Grenadier Regiment 736. There is little to be seen of this position today. Both positions were cleared by 5th Battalion the East Yorkshire Regiment with assistance from naval gunfire. Captain Ash was an FOB deployed afloat in support of the 5 East Yorks:

> The Navy bombard 'Desk' [the code name for the centre of La Rivière] with destroyers to help the East Yorks, and Lt Woods and I use the two LCGs to bombard the pillboxes along the sea wall. I am through on the wireless to Eric Scammell, BC 462 Battery, supporting the East Yorks. One of the problems from the sea is to locate exactly where the front line of our own troops is. We solve this problem using yellow recognition signals. I tell Eric to get his forward troops to hang out their yellow squares over the sea wall and to release yellow

The view west from the bunker showing where the assault battalions landed.

> smoke. We can now see where they are, which is the first step, and it is easier to locate the enemy strongpoints. Woods and I relay Eric's target to the LCGs which then engage the targets. We help a bit and soon after midday the East Yorks clear La Rivière of German troops, but not mines and booby-traps, at a cost of around 100 casualties.

The preliminary bombardment knocked out two of the anti-tank guns and five of the ten machine guns covering King beach. Once ashore it took 45 minutes to neutralize the defences. It still took three hours to mop up the enemy in La Rivière. While the first lane in the obstacles took twenty minutes to clear, it took three and a half hours for a tracked exit to be cleared. 11,689 soldiers landed on King Beach on D-Day, of which 7,087 were in the assault waves. There were 207 casualties, all from the assault troops.

Turn west into the Rue America and then, at the T junction turn right. Drive through the village and down to the beach. Turn around and park close to the tram shelter.

King Red Beach

Herbage des Prés 14114 Ver-sur-Mer, France, (GPS 49.345251, -0.528062)

You are on King Red Beach close to the point where the 6th Battalion the Green Howards landed.

The view looking east across King Red Beach.

Look south. Identify 'Lavatory Pan House' on the left side of the housing estate on the brow of a ridge, the Meuvaines Ridge, running roughly parallel with the coast 1,000m south. The Germans defences in this sector were based on this ridge as well as the seashore. Behind the coastal dunes was a stretch of marshland between Ver-sur-Mer and Asnelles.

86 Field Regiment's guns on King Green Beach, approximately 0945 on 6 June.

The M12s of the 987 Field Artillery Battalion, shown here landing on Gold Beach on D+1. This was the only unit of the US Army to land on a British beach.

There were two defence positions along the seashore on King sector: WN33 to the east at La Rivière which we visited earlier and WN35 1,000m to the west at what is marked on 1944 maps as Habel de Herlot, where a strip of dry land led through the marshes to the coastal road. This contained another 5cm anti-tank gun and concrete shelters.

King Beach from the air on D-Day. Note the light marks from bomb and naval gun craters, mainly inland from the beaches.

Looking towards the Mont Fleury Battery from the tram stop.

Besides the defensive position around the lighthouse, WN34, there were infantry companies manning field defences between Mont Fleury and Meuvaines 2km further west and between Ver-sur-Mer and Vaux to the east. There were three artillery battery positions nearby. An army coastal artillery battery, 3/HKKA 1260, was sited just to the west of the Lavatory Pan House. The 6th battery of Artillery Regiment 1716 was deployed in concrete emplacements WN32 south-east of Ver-sur-Mer, while the 5th battery of the same regiment was in WN36B, field defences south of Crépon.

While the defences on the seashore avoided aerial bombardment, the troops on the Meuvaines Ridge 1,000 yards from the shore were targets for the heavy bombers of the Eighth Air Force. The Germans considered the 441st *Ost* battalion as their most reliable east unit, but it did not put up much of a fight on D-Day.

This is the starting point for the route WO2 Stanley Hollis took in the actions for which he was awarded the Victoria Cross.

Travel up the Herbage des Prés to the crossroads with the D514. You will see the area of marshland behind the dunes. The fields on your right were a

This view is from the command and observation bunker looking south to the partially completed bunkers.

The one completed gun casemate at Mont Fleury.

The guns in the Mont Fleury Battery were captured Russian 122mm M1931 (A19) as 12,2 cm K.390/1(r). This particular gun is in the Finnish artillery museum.

minefield which was breached by the assault pioneers with mine detectors. The marsh prevented flail mine-clearing tanks from being used. The company of the 6th Green Howards crossing the minefield was pinned down by fire from the Mont Fleury battery. Drive straight across into the Avenue Franklin Roosevelt and park near the next crossroads with Rue Claude Debussy on the right. The property immediately south-west of the junction between is the Lavatory Pan House, a 1944 landmark. The rest of the housing estate is post-war. The company commander pointed out the bunker which was engaging the Green Howards, and Hollis launched a one-man charge.

The first German bunker and the position from where Hollis attacked are now under the housing estate. Follow Rue Claude Debussy around to the left until you reach Rue Hector Berlioz. The bunker on the south side is one of the remaining ferro-concrete embrasures, now used as a stable. The information board in front of the bunker provides an explanation of the construction of the battery. Walk to the west end of Rue Hector Berlioz.

Mont Fleury battery

Rue Hector Berlioz, 14114 Ver-sur-Mer, (GPS 49.338436, -0.528521)

On the north side there is a partially completed bunker converted into a house. Beyond it is a set of breezeblock walls erected by the Germans as shuttering, and further into the field is an embrasure at an even less completed stage. The second observation bunker is in the field 75m north of the third bunker. The field itself is uneven, bearing the weathered scars of bomb craters.

The Mont Fleury battery on the ridge 1km inland from the exits from King Red Beach was potentially a formidable position mounting four 155mm guns alongside a battalion of *Ost* troops the Germans considered particularly reliable. The Mont

The bomb and shell craters testify to the effectiveness of the D-Day bombardment of the Mont Fleury and Marefontaine batteries.

Fleury battery was incomplete on D-Day; the guns were not mounted in the embrasures but in the open ground. There is no evidence of concrete Tobrucks or the man shelters found in completed batteries. The gun detachments were ill protected. The unfinished defences are evidence of the success of commando raids and the Allied deception plan.

While there was no fire support for WO2 Hollis' attack, the battery had been hit hard by the bombers and the naval gunfire, which might have ensured that WO2 Hollis survived his attack, which might have been suicidal under other circumstances.

The British Normandy Memorial opened in 2021 and lists those who fell in the campaign in date order. It is a reminder that while D-Day may have been the first and bloodiest day, the campaign continued for three further months.

Return to the end of Rue Hector Berlioz. Turn right onto the D65. After 120 metres the British Normandy Memorial is on your right, if you wish to visit. Follow the D65 to Crépon. Pass the Green Howards memorial on your left and turn right into D112. Park close to the Manoir de Mathan. If you have permission to visit the Ferme de Papillon to see Hollis' rhubarb patch, visit the site and return. (For details of Hollis' action see the Battleground Europe inland from King). Walk along the wooded path on the right of Le Manoir de Mathan; after 100m the path turns right and left and the woods thin, revealing a field on the right. The far side of this field is the eastern edge of a German gun position.

Crépon

Le Manoir de Mathan, Route de Bayeux, Crépon (GPS 49.315063, -0.552770)

The second part of Hollis' VC citation involved the engagement of a German battery and the rescue of a section under fire. However, Hollis left the battery to be dealt with by someone better equipped to do so. The German troops were the 5th Battery of Artillery Regiment 1716, equipped with four 10cm Czech artillery pieces. This battery occupied field positions not identified or on the target list for the D-Day fire plan. Hollis' 'someone' turned out to be the gunners of 462nd Battery, 86th Field Regiment, who occupied a position across the fields south of Crépon by dark on D-Day. Nearby, a troop of flail tanks occupied a wood. These came under fire and lost a tank to gunfire at dawn on the 7th. F troop under Lieutenant Carpenter of 462 Battery supported by two crocodile tanks and the two flails captured the battery and over sixty prisoners.

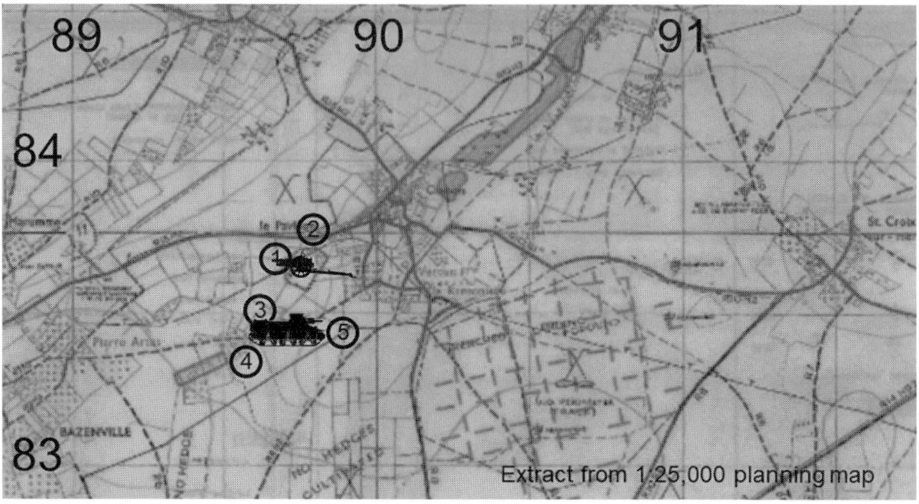

1. Battery position marked on Allied map , but not identified as an artillery battery.
2. WO2 Stan Hollis engaged the battery from the rhubarb patch of the Pappillion Farm midday D Day. Leaves battery to be dealt with by someone better equipped.
3. 462 Battery position occupied from late afternoon D Day. During the evening German sniping from wood noted as and engaged by command tanks
4. Flail tanks come inder fire when seeking a harbour area.
5. Attack by troop of Churchill Crocodiles, two flail tanks and fifteen gunners from 462 battery results in surrender of the battery and capture of four howitzers and one "88" mm gun. (but may have been misidentified 75mm gun. ..

The actions around the German battery at Crépon illustrate some of the confusion and chaos of war.

Return to your car and drive to the centre of Crépon. Turn right on to the D65 towards Creully which becomes the D22. As you approach the town you will cross a bridge over the River Seulles. After 100m pull into a parking space on the left (east) side of the road in front of a memorial.

4/7 Dragoons Memorial Creully
Rue du Maréchal Montgomery, 14480 Creully (GPS 49.286849, -0.540515)

The battle in this area is an overlooked part of the D-Day story. German LXXXIV Corps reserves Kampfgruppe Meyer, two infantry battalions and an assault gun company were committed to restore the situation on the Bayeux sector, where they had been defeated and largely dispersed. 69th Infantry brigade advanced south from Crépon. There was a series of actions from mid-afternoon as 69th Brigade forced German infantry back from Villers-le Sec to Brécy. German assault guns appeared around 1800 attacking from the south. An attack by 6th Green Howards supported by a fire plan from 86th Field Regiment and medium machine guns drove the Germans back to within 1,000m of the Caen–Bayeux Road.

This memorial commemorates the men lost by the 4/7 Dragoon Guards in North-West Europe. Their troop commanders suffered heavy casualties, none more tragic than the loss of Lieutenant Pillman killed and Aizlewood badly wounded outside their tanks by fire from the 6-in guns of HMS *Orion*. 7th Green Howards suffered several casualties.

A **Sturmgeschütz** *from 352 Division knocked out by 69 Brigade in its attack on St Gabriel on D-Day. These German AFVs may have been the origin of the request for naval gunfire.*

The incident illustrates some of the problems of applying the firepower of the Allies. Sometimes friendly fire was inevitable; on this occasion it was not. The FOB, Captain J. G. Corke RA, ordered a mission at a valid target, requested fire on tanks moving north from Rucqueville, the German StuG. However, the target was not engaged owing to no spotter aircraft being available. Meanwhile, 69 Brigade won the tank battle and advanced. After an hour's delay, an aircraft was assigned

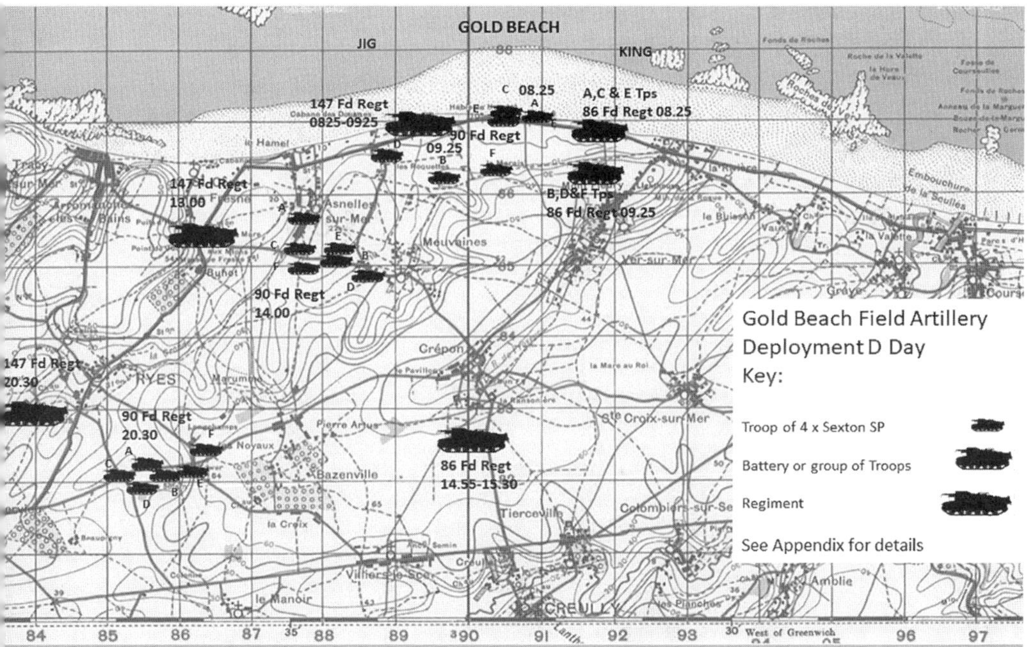

Positions of the 50th Division Field Artillery during D-Day.

to spot for HMS *Orion* and she engaged Allied tanks, with fatal results. Procedures existed to ensure that this should not happen. Either the FOB should have declared the target unsafe or, given the delay, the Army Liaison Officer on *Orion* should have checked the tactical situation before allowing the shoot to continue. There was no communication between the naval spotting aircraft and the soldiers on the ground.

To add insult to injury, the 4/7 were then attacked by American P47 Thunderbolts. Allied vehicles were at great risk of friendly fire from aircraft in mobile operations where the front lines were unclear.

The bridge over the River Seulles just north of the memorial was the vulnerable point to be protected by a troop of 82nd Battery of 25 Light AA Regiment. The buildings to the right of the road are the Chateau de Creullet, which was occupied by HQ 21st Army Group. The Chateau de Creully, overlooking the memorial, was occupied by the press corps.

Head north on Rue du Maréchal Montgomery/D22. After 800m turn left on to D12 (signs for Villiers le Sec/Bayeux). After 2km turn right on to the D87 towards Ryes. After 2.7km pull into the parking space in front of the War Cemetery on the right.

Ryes War Cemetery

Ryes War Cemetery, D87, 14480 Bazenville (GPS 49.299918, -0.601644)

Cross back over the road to where there is an information board unrelated to D-Day. Look north towards the crossroads. The ridge along the road was the position occupied by the twenty-four Sexton SP guns of 90 Field Regiment on the evening of D-Day.

The CWC at Ryes contains 652 Commonwealth burials of the Second World War, as well as one Polish and 335 German graves. Eighty-eight gunners are buried here, the earliest six being from 8 June. Four of these are from 62nd Anti-tank regiment, probably casualties from the action by 245 Anti-Tank Battery against the 12 SS (see Chapter 10). Major Lyle (3H.3) BC of 109 Battery was killed on 9 June while registering targets at the OP. The following day, the BK, Captain David Ramsey, recovered Major Lyle's body under fire. Ramsey was a descendant of Major Norman Ramsey, an RHA officer in Wellington's army. He was killed eight days later and is buried in Bayeux War Cemetery (see Chapter 10).

Drive back to the crossroads and take the turning towards Ryes. 147th (Essex Yeomanry) Field Regiment occupied gun positions in the valley south-west of Ryes at the end of D-Day and in La Gronde. In Ryes turn right on to the D205, drive through Le Buhot until the T Junction. Turn right on to the D514 coast road, then take the first left and find a place to park. One option is the customer car park of a seafood and wine bar, which sells fruits de mer *of the region. Walk to the seafront.*

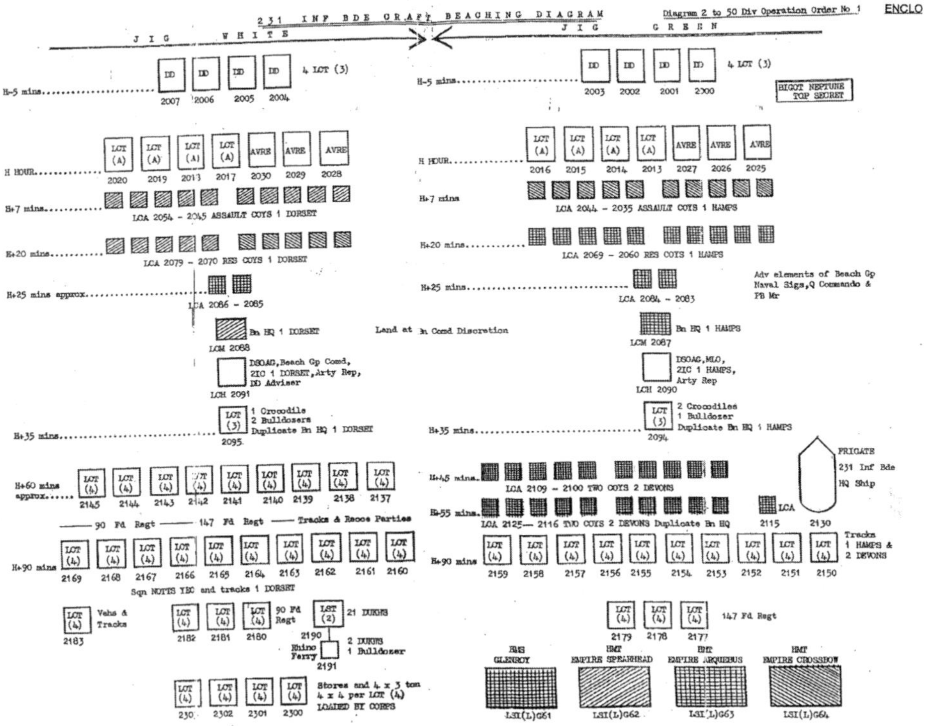

Beaching diagram, Jig Beach.

Summary of 231 Brigade's assault on Jig Beach.

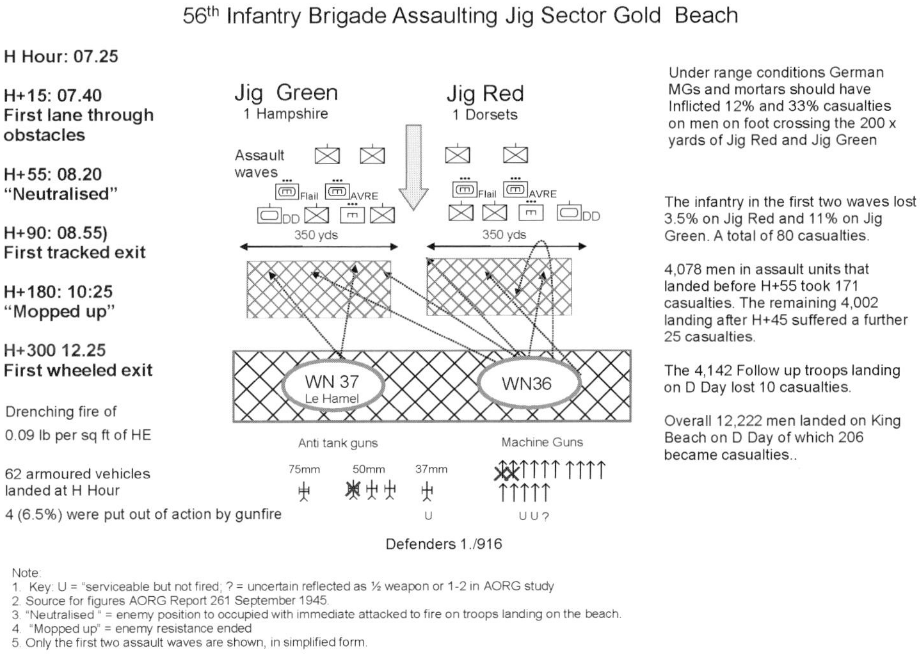

Aerial Photograph WN 35 on the junction of Jig and King beaches.

WN36
Route du Débarquement, 14960 Saint-Côme-de-Fresné (GPS 49.340451, -0.595495)

There is an anti-tank gun position on the edge of the sea wall. As at St Aubin, this offers a wide arc of fire through around 240°, giving the gunners a protected position from which to enfilade the beach to left and right or respond to an attack from inland. This was part of WN38, a defended post containing a 5cm gun. The German defenders on this position were from the 1st Company of Grenadier Regiment 916 under command of 352nd Infantry Division responsible for the Bayeux sector. This was on the flanks of the western edge of Jig Beach

Walk east along the sea front until you reach a bunker. If in a car, drive to the junction with the coast road, turn left on to the D514 coast road and follow it for about 1km. Turn left on to Rue du Débarquement, drive to the end of the road and park in the car park on your left. Walk to the big bunker on the seafront.

Asnelles WN 37
This is Jig Green Beach with the assault sector centred on German Strongpoint WN36 about 1km to the east. In 1944 the area immediately behind the beach was marshland. West of the car park it has been reclaimed and built over. However, to the east of the car park the landscape remains largely as it was in 1944. It is this area where the landings on Jig Beach took place. You are standing in front of a bunker housing a 7.5cm anti-tank gun firing across Jig Green.

WN36 contained emplacements for one 5cm and one 3.7cm gun, sited to prevent an exit from the beach via the roadway. It was garrisoned by troops from 441 *Ost* Battalion. On D-Day this was the area where 1st Battalion the Dorset Regiment and C Squadron the Sherwood Rangers would assault, supported by their assault engineers and by the fire from 90 and 147 Field Regiments.

Lieutenant Sidney Vines 90th Field Regiment was in the advanced party for his troop, with the task of clearing a path through the minefield to allow his troop to move inland:

> About an hour before dawn I clambered into one of the LCAs with a platoon of the 1st Hampshires. We were to assault a beach codenamed Jig Green, now invisible in the darkness. The side of the ship fell away and we were lowered into a dark and choppy sea. At the outset we were going through a well-rehearsed drill and it seemed like another, rather bigger exercise. I gave no thought to our enemy, but much to our Colonel, whose wrath I feared and would certainly incur if I didn't carry out my orders to the letter.

The guns were at the rear of the force, each Regiment in six LCTs sailing in two rows of three firing the run-in shoot. The guns started adjustment and set the Coventry Clocks. As 147 Field Regiment's ML could not make contact, 90th Field Regiment's observer passed the radar plot to the adjutant of 147 Field Regiment, which then joined in the bombardment of WN36 rather than their planned target, WN37. The guns opened fire at 0650 hours and fired for thirty-five minutes right up until H-Hour at 0725, as described by Sergeant Major Jack Villader Brown of 90 Field Regiment:

View across Jig Beach from the 147 Field Regiment (Essex Yeomanry) Memorial.

Centaurs approaching Jig Beach.

> Everybody opened up, the noise was horrific, it was ear-shattering. In that run-in shoot, the guns got so hot the blokes could hardly handle them. Grease was running out of the breech blocks and the empty cartridge cases were being thrown over the side. Each gun fired between 150 and 200 rounds – as soon as one's gone, you put another one in. We didn't have time to be afraid, you don't get time to think.

The bombardment was accompanied by the fire of the cruisers and destroyers, the LCTs (Gun) and LCTs (Rocket) and the last wave of bombers. The OPs and guns then turned to a flank to wait their turn to land, 90 and 147 Field Regiments on Jig in two waves at H+60 for 90th Field Regiment (A, C and E Troops) and H+120 (B, D and F Troops) and 86 Field Regiment on King at H+90 and H+105.

Sidney Vines continued:

> There was much to see, but it was never so crowded or noisy as films have made it out to be. The sea is a big place, you could talk to your neighbours without raising your voice. We were enjoying ourselves. There was so far no reaction from the Germans on the beaches ahead which were becoming steadily clearer as it grew fully light. It was a dull, damp day with low scudding clouds – a typical English summer's day.
>
> We came within small arms range of the beach, and the order was given to crouch under the gunwales. I stared at the back of the man ahead of me with his small pack and bandoliers of ammunition; then across at the row of steel-helmeted figures opposite, each clasping a rifle or Sten-gun.
>
> My mind was blank and unpleasant thoughts rushed in to fill it. For the first time I thought of the enemy ahead – real Germans, not umpires. It occurred to

me that in the next few minutes I could, quite possibly, be shot or blown up, and there was nothing at all I could do about it. My hands became clammy and I felt seasick. Then there was a bump, the LCA lurched, there was a rattle as the ramp came down and there in front of us were the beaches of Normandy. What is more, I knew where I was, for I saw the skeleton of an upturned boat that I recognized from air photographs. This was indeed Jig Green; the Royal Navy had landed us in the right place. My morale rose. Seasickness was forgotten.

My job, with three men under command, was to clear paths through the minefields at the back of the beach. I concentrated on it which was the best possible antidote to fear. We ran ashore, water round our ankles. It was low tide and we had about a hundred yards to go to reach the dunes at the back of the beach.

With WN37 scarcely touched by the bombardment, 1 Hampshires soon ran into problems in Le Hamel, where we are standing. The BC Major R. B. Gosling of 431 Battery 147 Field Regiment described it like this:

> A swarm of angry bees buzzed just above our heads; our Hampshire comrades, war-experienced, recognized German heavy machine-gun fire and ran forward. In front of us the sand furrowed and spurted from Spandaus firing down the beach in enfilade on fixed lines from Le Hamel. The Colonel shouted to us to lie down, but the wet sand was unattractive, so we sprinted for the cover of the dunes fifty yards ahead. Some mortar bombs were falling and one of the former fell beside the CO and me, smashing one of his arms and filling my leg with shell fragments. We managed to make it to the dunes and flung ourselves in a depression in the sand.

The 2IC took over command of the Hampshires, and the BK of 431 Battery took Major Gosling's place.

At 1430 the FOO with 1 Hampshires reported mopping up in Le Hamel around WN37, which consisted of several positions centred on the Sanatorium. One of the five AT Guns and two of the 13–14 MGs on Jig Beach was knocked out by bombing. One anti-tank gun and a further two machine guns were serviceable but unmanned. The scientists estimated that it took fifty-five minutes to neutralize the defences and until 1030, H+3 hours, to mop up Le Hamel. While the engineers cleared their first gap in the obstacles in fifteen minutes, it took ninety minutes to clear a tracked exit and five hours to clear a wheeled exit. On D-Day 12,222 troops landed on Jig beach of whom 8,080 were assault troops. There were 206 casualties on the beach.

The first guns of 90 Field Regiment landed as planned at H+60 (0825 hours) when the LCTs carrying A and C Troops and some RHQ vehicles landed. Underwater obstacles and a heavy swell led to congestion on the narrow beach. The guns came into action on the beach at the junction of Jig and King sectors. The remaining three troops, B, D and E, and the remainder of RHQ landed by H+120 (0925 hours) on Jig Red to the west of the other troops, deploying 500 yards inland and followed by F Troop at 0945 hours.

Lieutenant Tony Richardson was the GPO of D Troop, 431 Battery. 147 field Regiment:

> Dawn on 6 June was clear but still windy. The Regiment was reduced to five troops, the sixth having been unable to join in the run-in shoot because its LCT had had engine trouble during the night. Also missing was the ML equipped with radar whose job it was to give the Regiment the opening range and line for the run-in shoot. This was obtained by D Troop's LCT by Aldis lamp from the ML with 90 Field Regiment who were supporting the Brigade [Battalion] on our left. We started firing at about 10,000 yards and closed to about 2,000 yards by H-Hr, when the LCTs swung away and prepared to beach. Corrections were obtained from one of the battery commanders who went close inshore to observe the fire.
>
> The guns were due to beach between H+20 and H+40 [the landing plan has H+60 and H+120]. DD tanks swam in and they were to give covering fire to the infantry from H-Hr until the artillery was in action ashore. C Troop got ashore and went into action on the beach at about H+20 and D Troop followed at H+40. The tide was almost up to the sea wall, but by driving the LCT in at half ahead together, D Troop's LCT beached firmly and the troop got ashore without losing any of the vehicles. The troop was meant to go ashore about two miles inland, as the other two batteries were held up and it had been landed about a mile to the east of where it should have landed, the Troop linked up with C Troop who were in action nearby on the beach. It went into action on the coast road between the beach and a minefield. The director had to be set up in the minefield, but fortunately no one stood on a mine while passing line to the guns. The guns started firing immediately in support of 1 Hampshires, who were having difficulty in clearing Le Hamel, which was their first objective. Additional ammunition was obtained from the LCT which had not taken part in the run-in shoot but which had beached and become stranded nearby.
>
> By this time one of D Troop's SPs had was out of action as it had torn off a back-idler wheel trying to negotiate a deep bomb crater. All the ammunition was transferred to the other three SPs. Everyone was busy and had no chance to worry about the desultory shell fire that was coming the other way. The Troop suffered no casualties or damage.

102 Anti-Tank Regiment also had problems when they tried to land. The LCT carrying Tac HQ hit a mine on the bows, backed off to try again and hit another mine that damaged the engine room. Many vehicles were drowned and one M10 had a track blown off by a mine. Sergeant Thompson went out on foot to find a position from which his M10 could destroy an 88 that was covering the beach exit near Le Hamel, the first of two actions that would earn him an MM.

At 1200 hours Captain Bishop established an OP with 1 Dorsets on the high ground south of Asnelles. At 1345 hours, D Company 1 Dorsets, supported by tanks of the Sherwood Rangers, took the company position 800m west of Buhot WN40, and at 1500 hours fire was brought down on the enemy battery 300 yards further west (WN41) in support of another successful attack by 1 Dorsets. Captain J. P. Cook of 90 Field Regiment was an FOO with the Dorsets:

> The wood on the high ground west of Buhot was a pre-selected rendezvous for commanders and FOOs, and from where fire plan was observed for the attack.

However, the wood was strongly held and Spandaus sent the FOOs and infantry commanders hopping smartly into the ditch as they looked at it. Two troops of 90 Field Regiment were now in action on the beaches and the target was duly registered and plastered good and proper as tanks and infantry moved forward across open country. The objective was taken, not without some trouble, and a good bag of prisoners was collected.

A Company 1 Dorsets was given the task of taking the defended locality to the west. The attack was timed to go in at 3 o'clock and we ranged a troop on to the target and gave the area forty rounds as the attack went in. The guns were beautifully together and the infantry went right in close to the concentration and took the position without loss.

At 1500 hours the two regiments started to regroup for phases 3 and 4 as planned; 90 Field Regiment supporting 151 Brigade, newly landed on King Sector, with 357 Battery supporting 6 DLI, 358 Battery 8 DLI and 465 Battery 9 DLI and the CO joining Brigade HQ. At 1600 hours the Regiment changed to the normal four-frequency wireless layout (regimental and three battery nets) from two frequencies. At 1800 hours the 2IC ordered a recce of positions in the intermediate area south-east of Ryes, in accordance with Division Arty OO; this was complete by 1900 hours, with the guns in action in their new locations by 2030 hours. Phase 3 was complete by 2100 hours.

The Sextons of 147 Field Regiment disembark on Jig Beach.

AA guns landing on Gold Beach. On the left, 3.7inch guns followed by generators and radars. On the right, 40mm SP Crusader.

Meanwhile, the AA defences were being prepared. Major Whitten, BC 395 LAA Battery carried out a

> recce of the DUKW park inland and sited two guns there. Minefields were cleared and guns were in position by 2100, but no enemy aircraft had so far been seen. At dusk several E/A flew over and were engaged. Several other E/A flew over during the night but dropped no bombs in spite of two heath fires just behind the beaches which appeared to be good pointers. A large number of LSTs with naval escort off the beaches were also attacked but put up a considerable barrage which appeared to be effective. At dawn [7 Jun] two FW190s and several ME109s were engaged and two were shot down. We claim one.

The fire support procedures did not always work smoothly. As A Company 1st Devons approached Ryes they came under effective small arms fire. Captain Dupont, the FOB, called for fire from HMS *Jervis*, but as the infantry were within 1,000 yards of the target, the destroyer declined to engage anything closer.

At 1430 1 Hampshires were mopping up in Le Hamel around WN37, which consisted of several positions centred on the Sanatorium, behind the bunker where we are standing. An AVRE destroyed the German positions in the Sanatorium and then approached the rear of the bunker on the seafront. As you can see, this covered the approaches to Le Hamel from the east, either along the seashore or on the coastal road.

Initial Calculating Station, 4th Survey Regiment.

As this was happening, Sergeant Palmer, the No 1 of a Sexton SP gun of 511 Battery 147th Field Regiment, had been told to bring forward his Sexton SP gun:

> Six tanks passed along this track with a line of trees on their right-hand side, which meant the trees would be between them and the sea. Each time a tank passed that line of trees, 'boump', they were put out of action by that gun. A German 88mm that was, mounted in a strong, highly fortified concrete structure. After it had put out these six tanks, this officer, he wasn't from my own troop, came up to me and yelled, 'Sergeant see what is happening! You have the best gun nearest to that. It is imperative put it out of action!' I could understand what he meant, but it is one thing to say it, another thing to do it.
>
> I climbed over the side of my self-propelled gun and got down to the unmade road, walked along the road until I got level with where the line of trees was. And then I looked across with my field glasses. There was this enormous monster of a place that looked like a big, big mushroom. As far as I could see, the only bit that was likely to be of help to us was their gun aperture, where their gun came out. The rest of it you would only be bruising the concrete. So, we had to get one in the aperture.
>
> So, I said to my crew, which included our sergeant major, 'It's no good going up there like all the others have done, we shall simply be number seven.' Normally you drove up steady, looking out one side and the other.
>
> 'We got to do something different and take them by surprise.' So, I said to the driver, 'When I say "go", put your foot down and go. When I tell you to stop' – a pat on the head was the signal to stop – 'I want you to immediately turn 45 degrees to your offside.'

This is top traverse. I hit him in the back which was the signal to go. We flew across at 35mph and we took them by surprise. After about 80 yards past the trees, I tapped him on the head. He stopped and turned 45 degrees to the right. The gun layer who was going to fire the gun could see clearly what the target was, so I had instructed him to travel, which you shouldn't do, with the gun already loaded and the safety catch off, to save seconds.

The layer fired almost as soon as the tank stopped bouncing, which it does if you stop suddenly. He fired almost immediately. We hit the target and you can see where it hit, but it wasn't where we wanted it. It was a fraction high and a fraction to the left. So, I ordered him to deflect one to the right and drop 25 yards and fire again. We fired again and the shot went right in the aperture. If we had practised it all morning you could not have got it better. It exploded inside and put the gun out of action. About four people struggled out, with their hands over their head.

Sergeant Palmer from Colchester was awarded the Military Medal.

Look east along the beach. One slightly bizarre activity on Gold Beach was the action of 4th Survey Regiment who, on a battlefield where most people were trying to look inconspicuous, erected a bright orange beacon to enable ships to accurately orient and locate their position. That was an important aid for accurate naval gunfire.

The guns of 90 Field Regiment landed in two groups and found themselves scattered across Jig Green and King Green beaches.

Return to your car and rejoin the coast road D514 heading west in the direction of Arromanches.

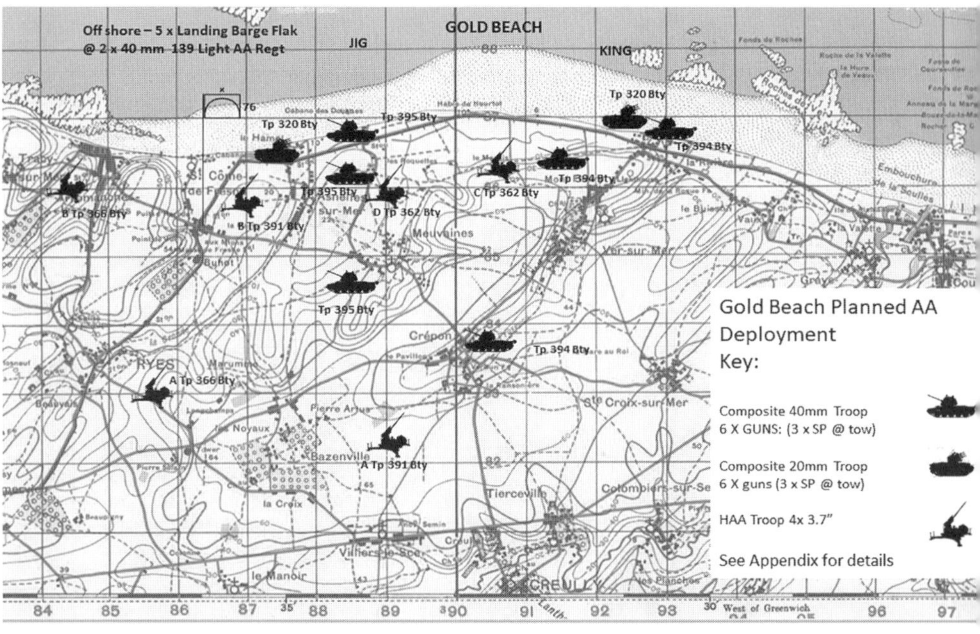

Anti-aircraft positions on Gold Beach.

As Le Hamel was being cleared, D Company 1 Hampshires bypassed the town through Asnelles and headed towards the radar station on the cliffs overlooking Arromanches. This was protected by the position at Le Cabane, WN39. Assisted by the Sherwood Rangers and HMS *Grenville*, directed by Captain Beddows, D Company captured WN39 by 1530 hours. Four hundred yards to the west was the radar station; following a 15-minute bombardment from the *Grenville* and a further 10-minute concentration from 147 Field Regiment, the radar station was captured by 1700 hours. D Company were sniped at from Arromanches until the snipers were suppressed by a few rounds from *Grenville*. Having finally cleared Le Hamel, B and C Companies joined D Company on the cliffs. After a 15-minute bombardment from the *Grenville* and a further 10-minute concentration from 147 Field Regiment, D Company was to advance on the town from the south, while B and C Companies gave covering fire from the cliffs. The attack started at 1900 and by 2000 hours the town had fallen to 1 Hampshires after little more than token resistance.

The tour ends here.

Chapter 10

After D-Day

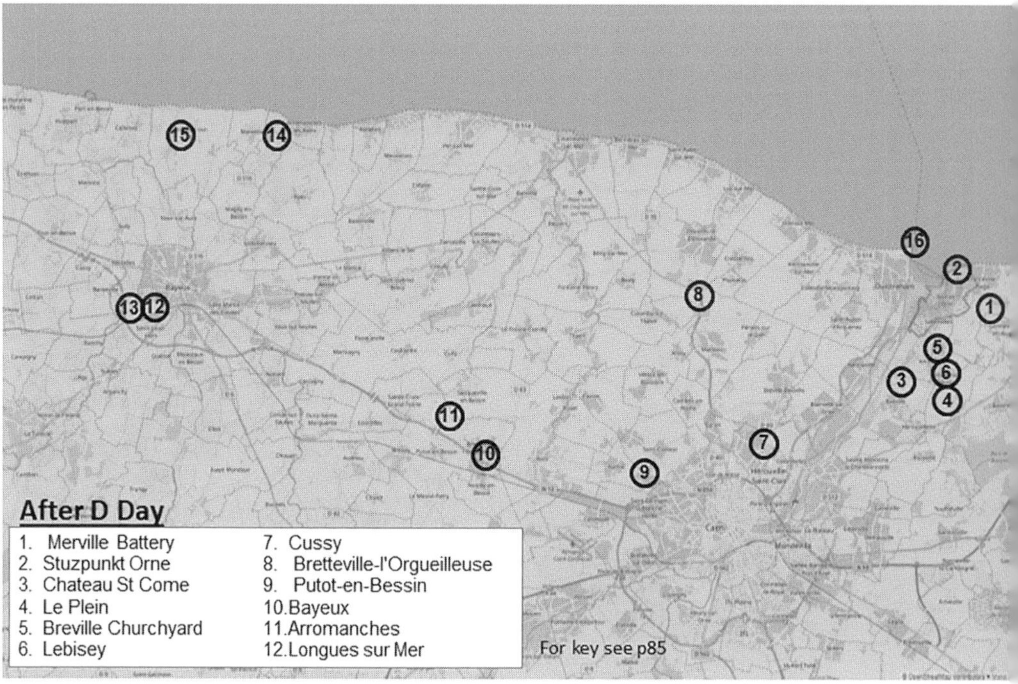

'Continuous artillery fire, together with the fighter-bombers, devours our division.'

Standartenführer Kurt Meyer, 12 SS Panzer Division

This tour covers sites that illustrate how artillery affected the battles on the beaches and landing grounds after 6 June. It starts at Merville battery and ends at Longues-sur-Mer. The total distance is 103km, a drive or a full day's tour for a fit cyclist.

The Airborne Bridgehead

For a week after D-Day the Germans attempted to eliminate the Orne bridgehead, culminating in the Battle of Bréville-le-Mont on 12 June. The fighting in the bridgehead was static until 15 August, when the Germans withdrew towards the Seine.

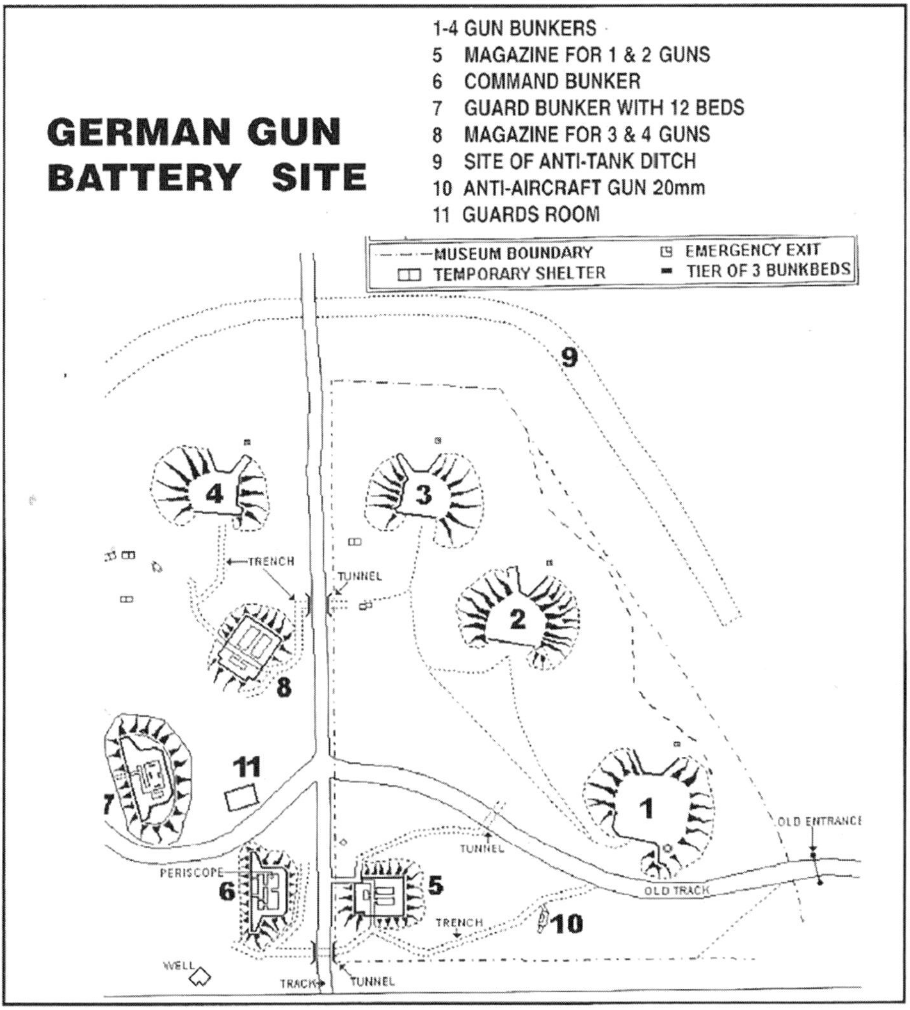

The layout of the Merville battery and the first battery Artillery Regiment 1716.

Merville Battery

The tour starts at the Musée de la Batterie de Merville, Place du 9ème Bataillon, 14810 Merville-Franceville. (GPS 49.270133, -0.196348) There is parking outside.

Merville battery was fought over from D-Day almost to the end of the Normandy campaign. The museum provides the best information on any German artillery unit in Normandy. The garrison of Merville battery was Artillerie Batterie No.1 of Artillery Regiment 1716. This unit was raised in May 1941 in Scharnhorst Kaserne, Osnabrück. It was equipped with four 7.5cm guns and was part of a static formation raised to defend the Atlantic Wall. Its establishment was five officers, 149 soldiers, 127 horses and 17 horse-drawn vehicles, plus two motor vehicles and two motorcycles. In March 1942, the battery deployed to the Caen area and then to Merville on 25 January 1943.

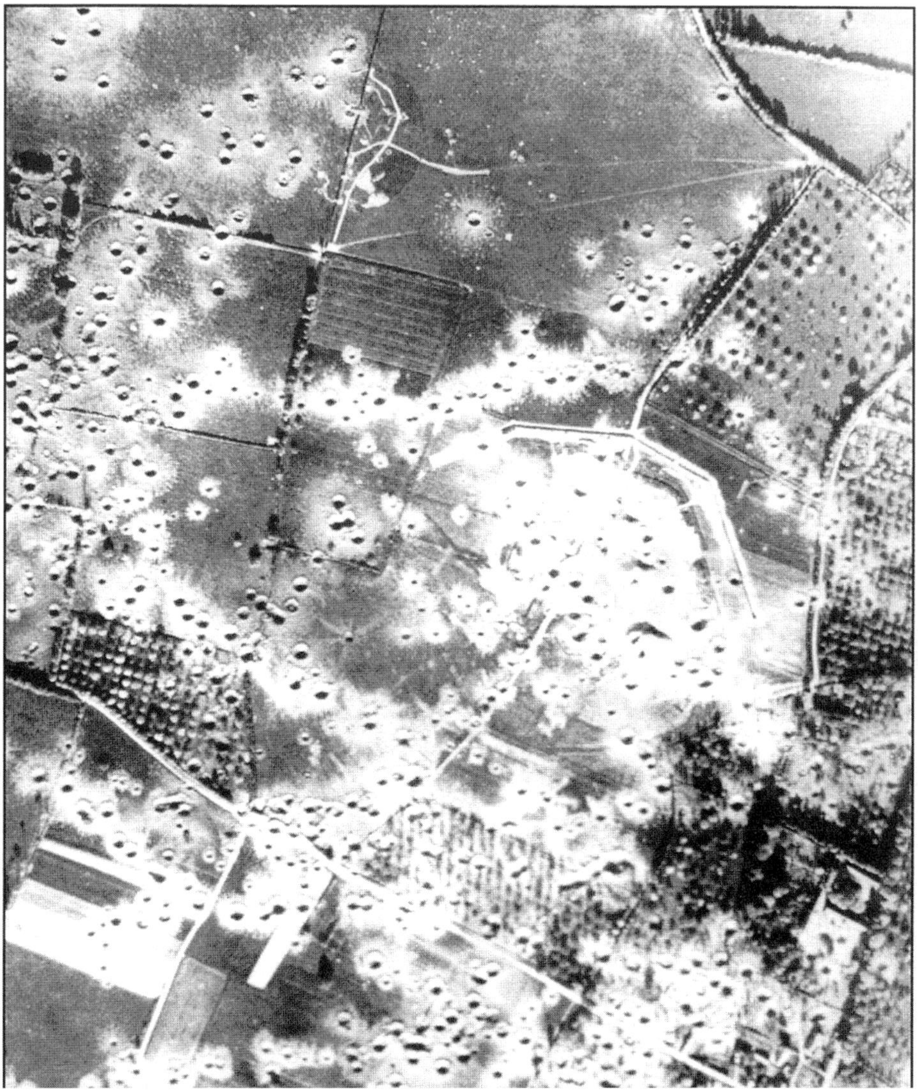

As cratered as Verdun – the Merville Battery.

It received a 2cm flak 38 AA gun on 1 March 1943 and a Ford motor tractor. Four 10cm LfK H (t) howitzers arrived in April 1943.

Initially, the guns were deployed on concrete open emplacements, allowing them to engage targets in any direction. The huge Type 611 casemates were completed in May 1944.

The battery was positioned to engage an enemy landing on the beaches. The observation post was in WN05 on the coast by Franceville Plage. 1/1716's priority defensive fire task was to engage the lock gates on the Orne Canal at Ouistreham, to deal with waterborne incursions up the canal. A gun programme with the bearing, range and altitude of various targets is on display in Casemate No.1.

A plaque commemorating the commando attack on June. The Merville Battery was occupied by a second line artillery unit, which fought off assaults by two elite British units.

The battery commander, Leutnant Raimond Steiner, was wounded twice on the Eastern Front and a recipient of the Iron Cross Class 2. He was at the OP on the night of 5/6 June. The senior officer on the gun position was Sergeant Major Buskotte. He joined the battery on its formation and spent his military service in France. Many of the soldiers were *Volksdeutsche*, Eastern Europeans with enough German ancestry to be considered German. On the night of 5/6 June, horses, wagons and about half the manpower of the battery were in the village of Merville.

The battery was attacked on D-Day by 9 Para, since the huge casemates were thought to house guns capable of hitting ships. At 0040 on D-Day a hundred heavy bombers dropped 600 tons of HE, mainly on the village rather than the battery. A force in gliders was to land on the battery at the same time as the Paras attacked from outside. However, high wind and dust and smoke from the bombing resulted in a very scattered parachute drop. An FOB party dropped to conduct a shoot by a cruiser, to neutralize the battery if the assault failed, was lost in the scattered drop. Despite only 150 men assembling, the Paras attacked through gaps in the rear face of the perimeter. They ran through the minefield surrounding the position and attacked the casemates containing the guns, attempting attempted to damage them with improvised charges, inflicting casualties and capturing twenty-three prisoners.

The battery staff barricaded themselves into their bunker, and the soldiers in the wagon lines were outside the perimeter. The Paras lacked the capability to inflict serious damage on the guns themselves. Steiner called for fire on the battery from neighbouring batteries, including from the Fifteenth Army east of the Dives. He redeployed with infantrymen to where he could correct the fall of shot on to the battery, but 9 Para withdrew from Merville under fire. The battery's spirited defence cost the attackers half their number.

During D-Day one gun was brought back into service and fire was directed on to Sword Beach on the afternoon of D-Day. No.3 Commando were ordered to make a second attack on Merville battery the following day, D+1. This was led by Major John Pooley RA, who was killed in the attack and is commemorated on a plaque.

After its losses 1/1716 was reinforced with gunners from 711th Division. Merville was the closest German battery to the British lines and threatened Sword Beach and shipping offshore. Consequently, it attracted a lot of fire, and a visiting journalist reported:

> We found crater upon crater like the moon. Not a scrap of earth was undisturbed by bomb or shell. The men of the battery continued in their work in dim emergency lighting in the bunkers and casemates. They had insufficient ammunition to fire continually at the enemy fleet. They reserved a few shells close to the guns in case of absolute emergency. They were weary, exhausted and dirty, but they were proud.

On 15 August, this horse-drawn battery withdrew along the coast. Steiner was captured in the Belgian town of Ieper after his rearguard of a single gun was ordered to attempt to stop the Polish Armoured Division. Two other guns were lost when the barge ferrying them across the River Scheldt was sunk by an air attack.

The first casemate tells the story of the German garrison. A sound and light show brings to life the experiences of the night of 5/6 June 1944. The second casemate is focused on the Parachute Regiment, while the third tells the story of the Commandos who attacked on 7 June. The bunkers for ammunition storage and command are not currently open to the public.

The 600 tons of HE dropped by bombers generated comparable energy to a tactical nuclear weapon. The small, fortified defence installations proved their worth as shelters for men and ammunition and as observation posts. The little Tobrucks were popular, but large casemates like those housing the guns at Merville were less well regarded. A detonation in front of the embrasure would create a blast wave which could kill everyone sheltering in the casemate. Guns were a small target, hard to damage, easily repaired and mobile. The Germans believed the best defence for coastal guns was camouflage and protection for the detachments.

After leaving Merville battery turn left and drive through the village of Franceville. Take the left fork at Merville village church. Continue along to the end of the Avenue de la Hogue du Moulin and turn left on to the Route de Cabourg D514. Take the first turning to the right, following the sign to the Base Nautique de Franceville. Follow the road to the car park by the beach in the Estuaire de L'Orne. Take special care not to leave valuables in your car. Walk on to the beach towards the large German bunker north-east of the car park, turn right and walk along the wide stretch of sand between brush-covered dunes. The observation bunker is 300m along the path.

This was the official observation bunker used by Leutnant Steiner. He preferred a less obvious Tobruck behind the bunker.

View from Leutnant Steiner's OP towards Sword Beach.

This is what Steiner saw. The cluster of ships mainly consists of the sunken block ships.

Stützpunkt Orne
14810 Merville-Franceville-Plage (GPS 49.284186, -0.218723)

The bunker is part of Strongpoint WN05, one of three strongpoints on the coast between the Orne and Dives rivers. The Germans thought this was where the main threat to the Caen sector would come. This position was complete by D-Day, unlike many west of the Orne.

From here we can see Ouistreham and where ships would unload at Sword Beach. This was the German front line for over ten weeks. However, Merville battery lacked the ammunition to engage more than the most important targets.

The rear entrance leads to accommodation containing three bunk beds. The observation platform was raised above the level of the bunker floor and accessed through a wooden door and a short corridor. Using a binocular periscope, the occupants could observe without exposing themselves. Leutnant Steiner did not use this bunker very often. The observation bunker was visible from Ouistreham and engaged at least once by a 3.7-in gun from 103rd Heavy AA Regiment. One of Steiner's soldiers was killed by a bullet while observing from the observation platform. Steiner preferred a Tobruck in a nearby infantry position. One of his soldiers, a *Volksdeutsch* Pole, deserted to the Allies and used a megaphone to harangue his ex-commander across the Orne with personal abuse and criticism.

This was the most advanced German post. Steiner's visitors included reporters and the Luftwaffe General Peltz making a reconnaissance before a night bombing raid.

Return to your car and retrace your route to the D 514. Turn right. After 500m you will see a bunker on the right, used as a night club at some time in the past. This is the site of the German defensive position and mounted a 5cm anti-tank gun. Continue along the D514 in the direction of Bénouville for a further 1.2km. Turn left into the Rue de Troarn/D37B and continue for 3.8km through the village of Bréville-les-Monts until you see a stature of a piper on the right side of the road. Park carefully.

Ranville Landing Zone

211 Battery of 53 Air Landing Regiment deployed near here on the western edge of the Ranville DZ. It landed on LZ N on D-Day. Initially, the battery deployed north of Ranville, at 0130 on 7 June, 'cleverly tucked away on the top edge of a slope falling away steeply behind the guns, the sort of position where only a mortar or 75mm could be deployed'. During the morning the battery fired in support of 1 Royal Ulster Rifles moving south to Longueval. About 1500 hours it redeployed into the Bas de Ranville to lengthen the range. Here it was mortared, losing two casualties and a jeep. The battery therefore moved back to its original position, where one troop engaged enemy infantry over open sights. From the morning of the 8th the battery supported the 1st Special Service Brigade defending Hauger from infantry attacks, with a 'zero line' of 060 degrees, firing no fewer than two thousand rounds that day. From the 9th to the 12th it was fully engaged in the battle for Bréville. At 0800 hours on the 10th C Troop was heavily shelled and Lieutenant G. H. N. Blower, the Gun Position Officer, was killed, Second Lieutenant A. Barrass was fatally wounded and two other ranks were wounded before the troop could be moved to an alternative position.

Drive south on the Route de la Côte Fleurie, at the roundabout take the third exit, turning left at the Rue de Stade, D37. Take the third turn to the left, on

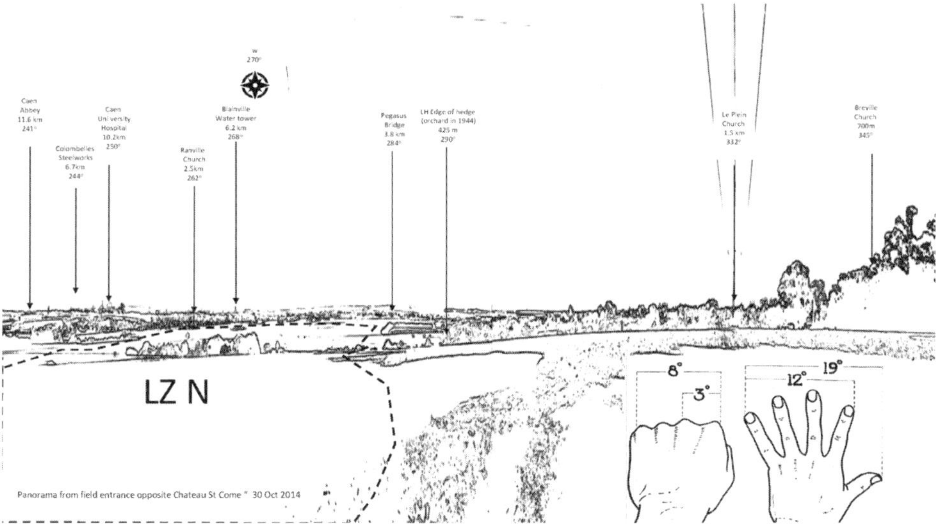

This view over the Orne valley shows why this area was heavily fought over in the week after D-Day.

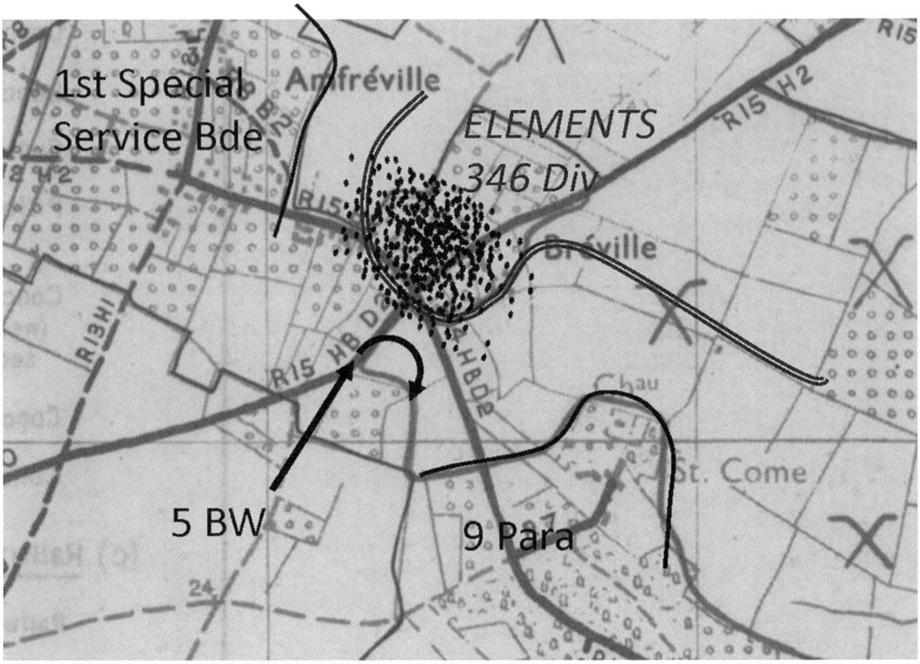

This diagram shows an impression of the pattern of artillery fire supporting the attack on 11 June.

to the junction with Rue Albert Camus, the D223, in the direction Merville, Franceville, Bréville. Drive up the hill to Bréville, at the crossroads turn right. After 500m you will see a collection of memorials at the entrance to a driveway on the left and, beyond it a stature of a piper. Park carefully.

Chateau St Come
Battle of Les Bois des Monts Stele, D37B, 14860 Bréville-les-Monts (GPS 49.234874, -0.223241)

By the entrance to the Chateau St Come are memorials commemorating 9th Battalion the Parachute Regiment and the Dutch Princess Irene Brigade which occupied the area in August 1944.The Piper commemorates the 51st Highland Division. The Division's three field artillery regiments and anti-tank regiment were also recruited from the Scottish Highlands.

Walk to the edge of the field on the south side of the road and look south-west. From here you can see the terrain between Caen and Ouistreham.

After the Allied landings, Hitler ordered the elimination of the Orne bridgehead as a prelude to rolling up the beachhead from the east. The 346th Infantry Division stationed near Le Havre was ordered to clear up the area between the Dives and Orne from the east, while a battlegroup of the 21st Panzer Division attacked from the south. The first troops of the 346 Division went into battle on 7 June, a battalion of cyclists supported by SP guns that had been ferried across the River Seine. On 10 June, the Germans recaptured Bréville. An infiltration attack across the old landing

How close do you follow the barrage? The infantryman's dilemma.

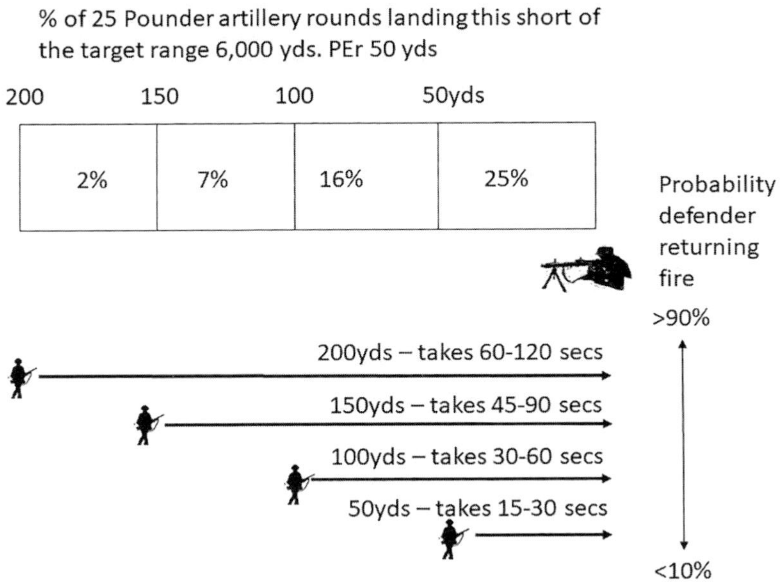

Infantry seeking to take advantage of the artillery fire are faced with a dilemma: do they remain at a safe distance from their own artillery and risk the enemy recovering from neutralization, or do they risk friendly fire to close with the enemy before they recover? The term was euphemistically known as 'leaning on the barrage'.

zone using wrecked gliders for cover nearly reached Ranville. It was only stopped by 211 Battery's guns firing over open sights.

9 Para defended this area from attacks from three directions, hanging on with the support of artillery and naval gunfire. By 10 June the British knew they needed to recapture Bréville.

5th Black Watch of the 51st Highland Division assembled south-west of 9 Para on the night of 10/11 June. The plan was simple: an advance preceded by a preliminary bombardment by five artillery regiments and the mortars of 5th Black Watch and 9 Para. However, at 0430 hours the leading company met intense fire from machine guns and mortars as it began to cross open ground 250m from the objective. The attack failed at a cost of some 200 casualties. The verdict was that the assault company was too far behind the supporting artillery barrage. By the time the fire lifted, the Germans were ready for them.

Return to your car and drive north-west back through Bréville across the crossroads along the Route de Sallenelles towards Amfreville. You will pass the churchyard on your right. Note the second turning on the right. This is the Rue de la Belle Étoile and marks the western extent of the village in 1944. You will pass a primary school on your left and a field on your right. Turn right into the Rue des Champs Saint-Martin, with the cemetery wall on your left. Drive as far as the bend to the left and park on the verge on the right. You are at the eastern end of a village known as Le Plein.

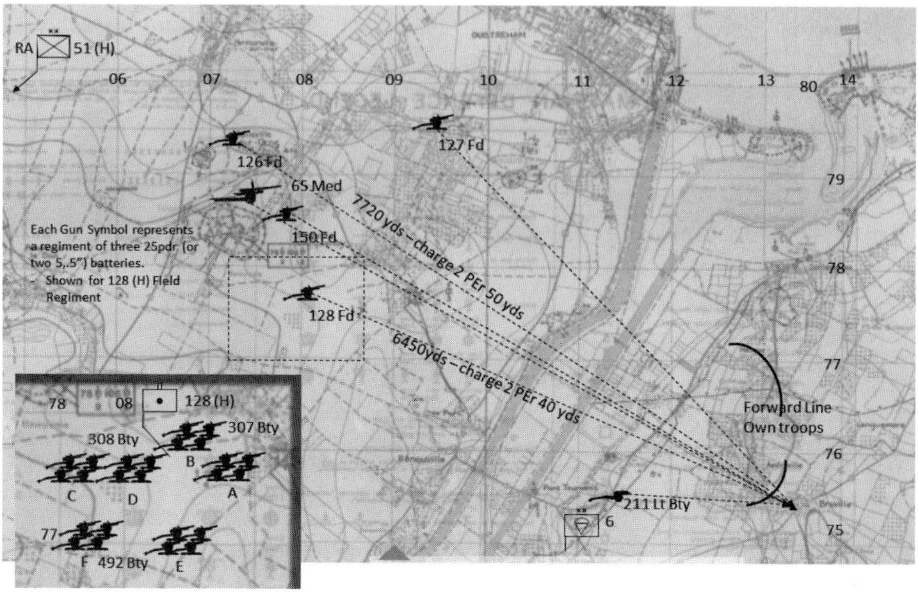

Most of the artillery support for the attacks on Bréville was from artillery deployed west of the River Orne. Artillery rounds would pass over the heads of the British troops at the target 350 yards away. Half of the rounds would land 40 or 50 yards short or beyond, but the other half might be up to 200 yards closer or beyond. This assumes that the guns' locations have been accurately surveyed and the effects of the weather are known.

The forming up place for the attack on Bréville was 350 yards from the church. No British troops in training would be allowed to be this close to artillery fire except in a tank.

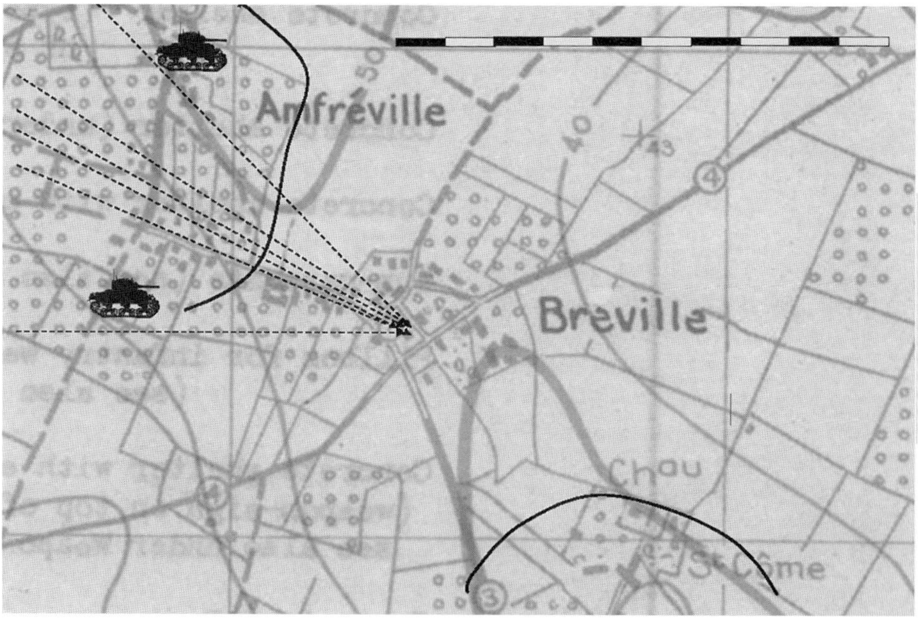

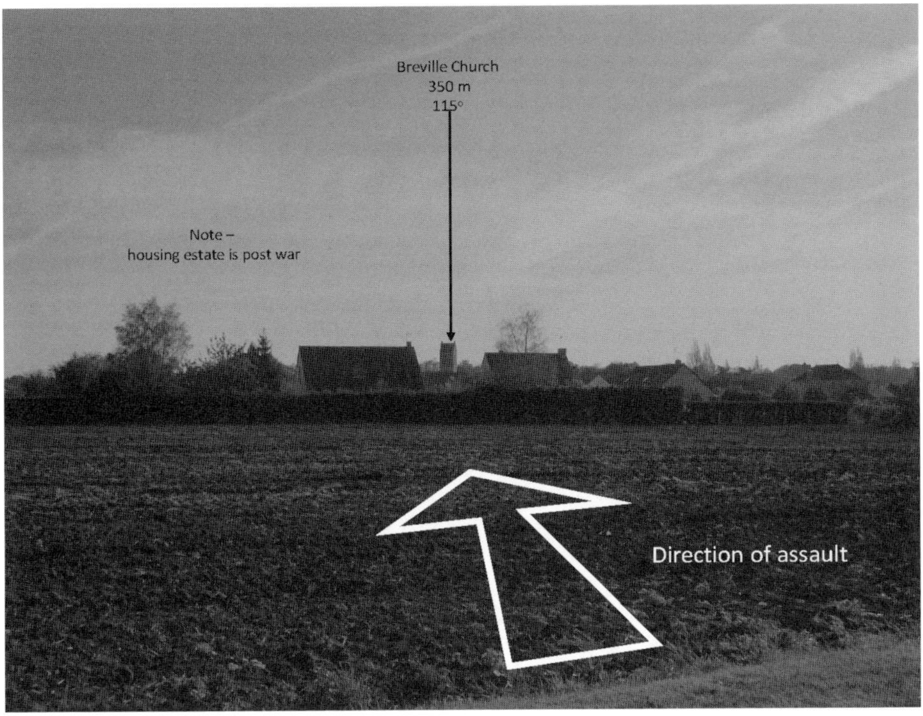

During the artillery bombardment, in theory shells would have been falling no closer than the end of the field. It would have been easy for a mistake to result in fire on the infantry waiting here. The Germans might also have fired on likely forming-up places.

The detailed records for this fire plan were not kept, but the diagram illustrates the potential for misunderstanding and miscommunication.

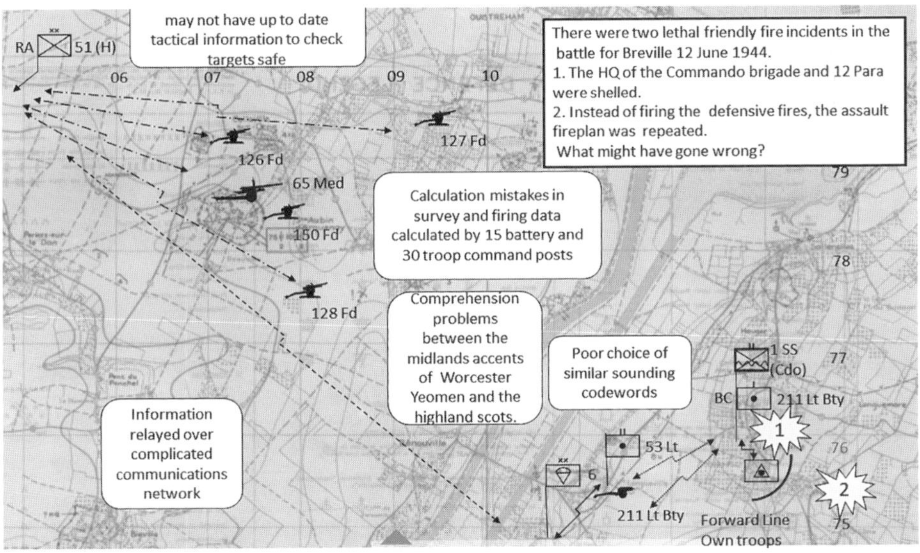

Le Plein

Rue des Champs Saint-Martin, 14860 Amfreville (GPS 49.242542, -0.230646)

In 1944 the sports pitch was an orchard. The forward edge of vegetation was the edge of the orchard. Ahead is a post-war estate. Only the older buildings to the south of the road between Amfreville and Bréville were there in 1944. On 12 June 1944 this was the start line for a desperate attack. The battlefield has been much visited by the British Army as an example of the realities of war. Amidst confusion, soldiers made a difference by doing the right thing on a difficult day.

During 11–12 June the situation deteriorated. General Gale, the commander of 6th Airborne Division, thought the Germans would be as exhausted as his men and ordered an attack starting at 2200 hours. 12th battalion Parachute regiment, reinforced by D Company 12th Devons and a squadron of 13/18 Hussars, were to mount the attack. Tanks were positioned to shoot up the left- and right-hand flanks of the objective.

Artillery support was from three regiments of the 51st Highland Division, 150th Field Regiment, 65th Medium regiment and 211 Light Battery. In total there were sixteen 5.5-in medium guns, ninety-six 25-pounder gun howitzers and eight 7.5cm howitzers, organized in thirty troops in fifteen batteries. These would fire at different targets to ensure that the area occupied by the enemy would be neutralized, along with any known mortar and artillery positions. The limited artillery assets within the Airborne Division meant that liaison with 12 Para was by Captain Ward of 211 Battery. There were other FOOs, but Ward would go into the assault with the CO 12 Para and control for fire on the ground. HQRA 51st Highland Division co-ordinated fire from the fourteen batteries outside the 6th Airborne Division.

The details of the fire plan have not survived. However, there was a single code word assigned to the concentrations to support the attack. A second code word was assigned to the defensive fire plan to protect the attackers from counter-attacks.

At 2145 hours the artillery opened fire. 12 Para and its attached company of Devons moved forwards into the orchard. There had been little time for briefing, and few except the officers knew the plan. A few minutes before zero hour, some artillery fell short and caught the troops forming here. The Germans also called their own defensive fire. Casualties were heavy. The commander of the 12 Para was killed, and Colonel R. G. Parker, the Assistant Brigade Commander of 6th Air Landing Brigade, himself wounded, took command of the battalion, assisted by Major Eddie Warren, an officer of the 12th Devonshires present by accident.

The troops crossed the start line on time and went in with great dash. The ground in front of them was pitted with shell holes, through which the men stumbled forward. There was little small arms fire directed against them; the enemy were either dead or cowed. The leading company reached the village practically unopposed, and the right-hand troop of tanks moved up in close support. A second company could then get through and establish themselves north of Bréville church.

At this point, more heavy fire fell on the village. Much of it was British. Someone, probably within 51st Highland Division, mistook the codeword for switching to defensive fire for the codeword for repeating the preparatory fire. Ward was killed, possibly by this fire, but his signaller, Gunner Allsop, took charge and quickly cancelled the fire. He was mentioned in dispatches for his calmness and initiative.

By the end of the attack, the orchard where you now stand and the fields between this point and Bréville were littered with British casualties. 12 Para lost eight officers and 133 men, and the Devons lost three officers and twenty-eight men. But the effect on the Germans was devastating. The British estimated 200 dead Germans in the area, and the battle broke the will of the 346th division, which did not mount any further attacks.

It was risky to attack Bréville from here. The church is only 350m away, very close for artillery fire. In peacetime, no one outside a tank or bunker would be allowed this close to artillery fire. Even in war, special procedures are used for targets closer than 700m. Theoretically, shot should all fall within 200 yards plus or minus of the target if every gun was carefully adjusted on to the target. However, many of the guns firing on this fire plan were probably applying a mathematical correction. Any arithmetical error might have resulted in friendly fire casualties.

French villages sometimes asked for war dead to be buried in the village cemetery. It seems poignant that they chose to look after the grave of Captain Ward, who was instrumental in the destruction of the village.

Return to your car and drive into Bréville. Turn left into the Place de l'Église and park.

Bréville Churchyard

Place de l'Église, 14860 Bréville-les-Monts (GPS 49.240476, -0.226324)

Walk to the crossroads at the far end of the churchyard. There is a memorial to the 6th Airborne Division showing the significance of the battle for Bréville. Captain Pyman RA of No 6 Commando led a patrol into Bréville on D-Day, unopposed by any enemy. While exploring the village, he was killed by a shot in the neck, and the patrol came under mortar fire and withdrew. This patrol was within 200 yards of a troop of four German 10cm howitzers, in an orchard on the northern edge of the village. These guns had not fired a single shot whilst the troop was coming up.

Re-cross the road and enter the churchyard via the gate leading from the parking spaces.

The ruins of the church destroyed in 1944 have been retained as a memorial. Church towers were obvious observation posts, and Bréville had been a target from D-Day.

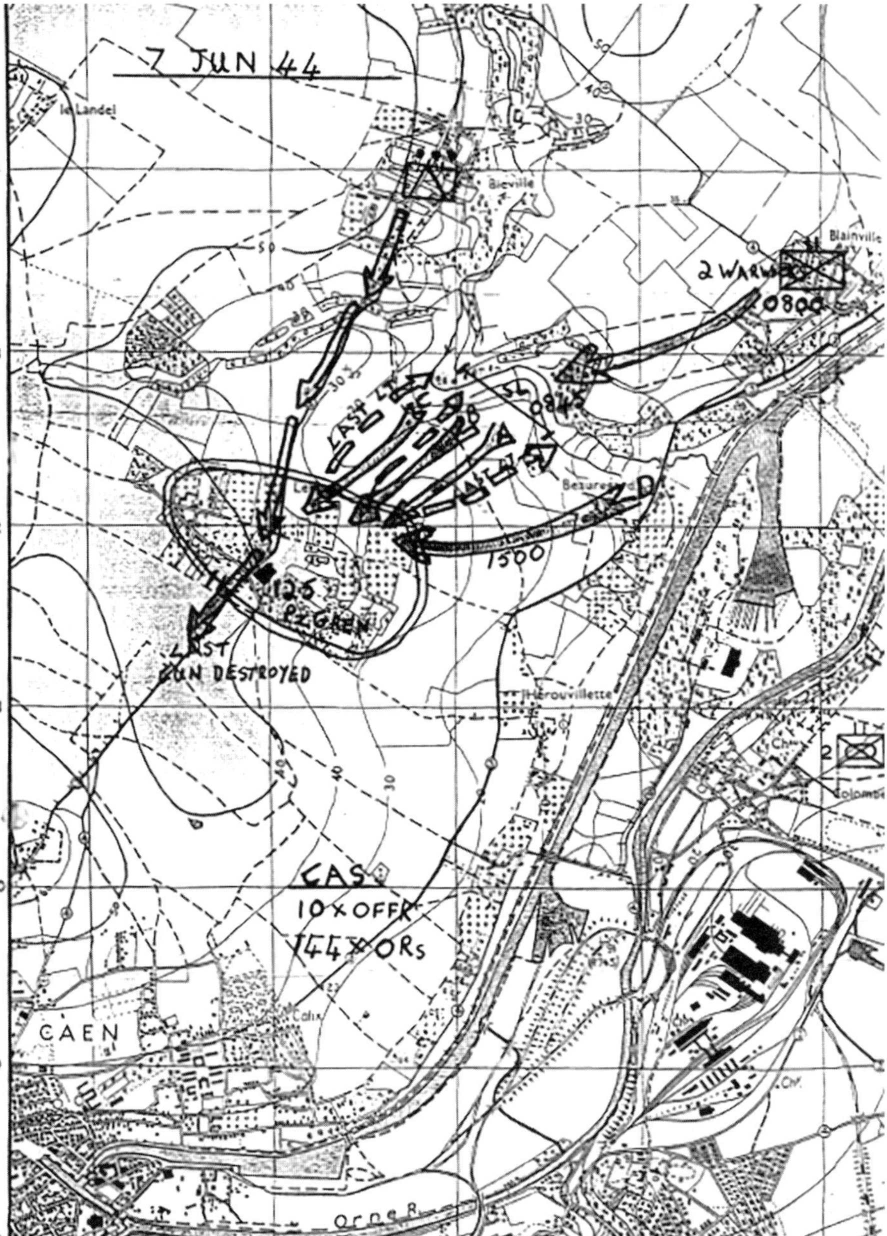

The repulse of the Warwicks at Lebisy woods illustrates the limitations of British infantry.

One of the two CWGC graves in Bréville Churchyard is Captain Ward of 53 Air Landing Regiment, an FOO who fell in the attack on 12 June. This appears to have been the choice of the inhabitants of Bréville. The graves and the ruined church are reminders of the cost of defending liberty.

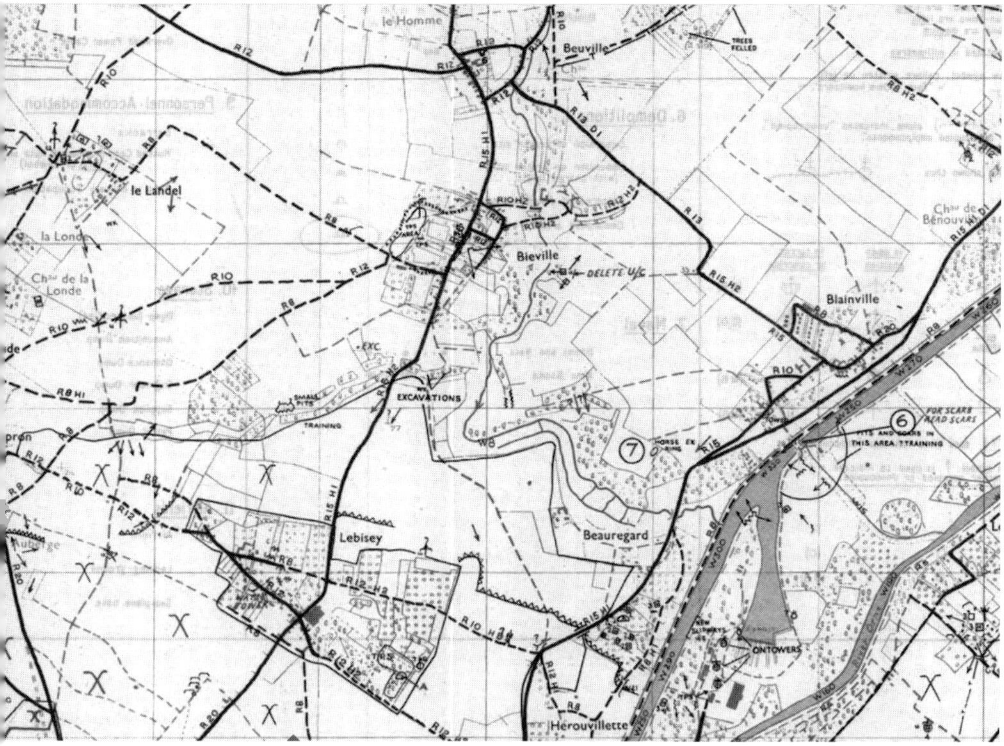

This extract from an Allied 1:25,000 engineering map is marked with fortifications and obstacles. Note the anti-tank ditch preventing Allied vehicles from accompanying the Warwicks' advance.

Return to your car and drive towards the crossroads. Turn right on to the D37, drive through Ranville, take the second exit at the roundabout and cross Horsa and Pegasus bridges. Drive through Bénouville and join the D515 – the dual-carriageway in the direction of Caen. After 5.1km take the D226 exit in the direction Hérouville-Saint-Clair, Lebisey-le Bourg Montmorency. Look out for the mosque on the left – it's a two-storey white building surmounted with a crescent. Drive to the junction with the D60. Park and walk carefully across the crossroads to the north side of the road.

Lebisey Wood

Route de Colombelles, 14200 Hérouville-Saint-Clair (GPS 49.215678, -0.339216)

One piece of unfinished business on D+1 was for 185 Brigade Group to attack towards Caen, its D-Day objective.

Look north. From here, imagine Lebisey Wood is still a large wood about 1300m × 800m rather than a suburb of Caen. The only remaining woods are in the park south-east of the crossroads. To the right of the road, the field boundaries follow the historic blocks of trees. The mosque 750m east of you marks roughly the eastern extent of the woods in 1944.

Look left. The treeline on the left-hand hand side of the D60 road currently screens a housing estate. In 1944 it was the edge of a wood extending 300m north and 900m west. One third of the wood extended north of the D226, the road to your back, and two thirds extended south of it.

Overnight of 6/7 June, 2nd Battalion the Warwickshire Regiment was given orders to attack German positions in Lebisey Wood and the village itself first thing on 7 June. As a preliminary, they cleared the village of Blainville at first light and reconnoitred routes forwards.

The attack was supported by three field regiments, less one battery, and one cruiser. When the leading infantry were within 200 yards of the wood the field guns would lift to the west end of the wood and the cruiser to the 60m ring contour, 1,000 yards south-south-west of Lebisey. The battalion was to attack with two companies forward to the east end of the wood. When this was secured, a third company was to clear the western half. The fourth company was to follow up the attack. H-Hour was 0845 hours.

The leading companies set off for the start line at 0800 hours but came under fire from Beauregarde. The CO obtained permission to delay H-Hour by an hour. However, this news never reached the right leading or follow-up company, which advanced at the original time without the postponed fire plan. The two companies penetrated the northern edge of the wood but were pinned down by fire from further inside the wood. The CO, seeing two of his companies advance, followed with the third company and headquarters. After reaching the wood, the CO was killed and the 2IC took command. The infantry could make no progress on their own. No one knew where the leading troops were, which prevented artillery fire from helping them.

9 (Irish) Battery of 7th Field Regiment was in direct support. The Battery Commander Major Lister and Troop Commander FOO Captain Appleby were joined by Captain Talbot of 16 Battery as a replacement for Captain Gregory, who had been wounded on D-Day. They walked forwards carrying short-range No.18 sets, re-broadcasted through the No.22 set in Talbot's tank manned by the driver and signaller from near Biéville. The three companies of Warwicks were pinned down in the northern edge of the wood under machine gun and mortar fire from noon to 1500 hours. The fourth Warwicks company launched a flanking attack that improved matters, until the Germans counter-attacked with tanks.

During the afternoon, under the mistaken impression that the battalion had secured its position, the battalion headquarters, carriers platoon, mortars, anti-tank guns and the attached FOB attempted to join the battalion via the D60 road, which runs up to Lebisey between high banks. The Germans held their fire and then ambushed them with infantry and tanks further south along the road where we stand. The COBU unit reported:

> Some vehicles broke through to the open country beyond where they were hit by anti-tank gun fire including Captain Lee, the FOB controlling the cruiser who was last seen standing in the back of his half-track firing his Bren gun in support of the infantry. He was killed, and support from the naval gunfire ceased. By evening the Battalion was surrounded, under tank attack and almost out of ammunition.

The 1st Battalion the Norfolks were sent into the wood at 1830 hours to restore the situation. Their leading elements may have reached the line of the D226 – at that time, the first lateral track – before becoming pinned down. Both the Norfolks and Warwicks were ordered to withdraw around 2200 hours – just before a heavy German barrage hit the recently vacated positions. Captain Handford 16 Battery 7th Field Regiment was awarded the Military Cross for keeping communications open and bringing down fire to cover the Norfolks' withdrawal under heavy and accurate shell fire.

The British did not attempt to attack Caen via this route again until 8 July, and then with a full corps attack of three divisions supported by hundreds of guns and the heavy bombers of the RAF. Where you are standing is on the German side of a no-man's-land reminiscent of the static conditions of the First World War Western Front.

The British Army in Normandy has been criticised as ponderous, predictable and over-reliant on indirect firepower. However, the Warwicks' CO had taken advantage of the unhindered advance into the wood to exploit apparent success. An infantry battalion lacked the firepower to capture and hold ground held by Germans in modest numbers. Firepower from artillery and warships was useless without communications and knowledge. This action illustrates the limitations of the British infantry when fighting a chaotic battle, and the preference of its commanders for a tidy battlefield.

Visit the memorial to the 2nd Battalion Shropshire Light Infantry, and others from the 3rd British Infantry Division, 50m south, then return to your car. Head south-west on Avenue du Général de Gaulle, D60. Turn right into Avenue

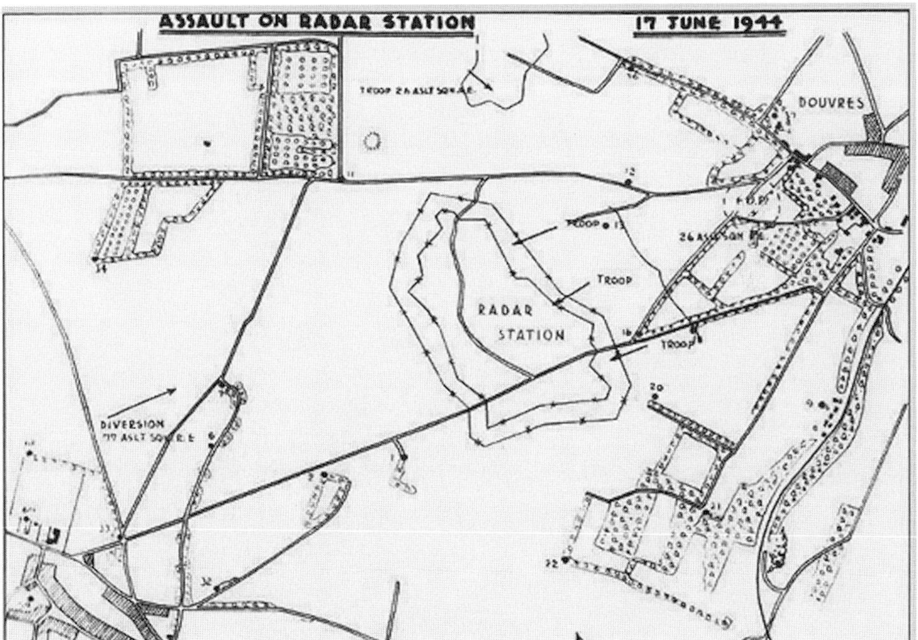

The southern site of the Douvres-la-Delivrande radar station had resisted several assaults before 17 June.

The radar site.

The 7.2-inch Howitzer, with a range of about a mile, supported the attack on the radar station.

de Garbsen. At the roundabout, take the second exit and stay on Avenue de Garbsen. At the roundabout, take the first exit into Rue d'Epron, which becomes the Rue de Lebisey, D226B. Continue to follow Rue de Lebisey to the junction with the D7 in Epron. It is not well signed, but there is a large trattoria/ pizzeria on the left. Turn right into the D7 to the roundabout signed to the left Courseulles, Bernières and Musée Radar du Douvres. Take the third exit to the D404. At the first roundabout take the first exit signed to the museum, D83. Follow the signs to the museum.

Douvres-la-Delivrande Radar Station

Radar Museum 1944, Rue de Basly, 14440 Douvres-la-Délivrande (GPS 49.285491, -0.402831)

At the end of D-Day, the situation on the beaches was far messier than portrayed by tactical maps showing a neat front line. The reality was that there were hundreds if not thousands of armed Germans who had been bypassed by the Allied advance inland. The Douvres radar station was the largest strongpoint that remained after a few days. It contained a garrison of 200 Luftwaffe troops and was reinforced by the parts of two companies of GR 736 and PGR 192. It was surrounded by wire and minefields, and its defences included five 5cm anti-tank guns, a 7.5cm field gun and a mortar. On 7 June mortar or artillery fire from this position prevented 14 Field Regiment RCA from occupying a preferred gun position. It was too strong for the single battalions that the 3rd Canadian and 51st Highland Divisions could spare when tasked with dealing with the position. It was only on 17 June that the British had the resources to mount an attack, which would be supported by 33 Field Regiment, 245 Anti-tank Regiment and Centaurs of the RMASG, and six 7.2-in heavy guns of 51st Heavy Regiment RA deployed scarcely 1,500m away on the southern edge of the town of Douvres. These heavy howitzers were updated versions of the 8-in howitzers used to smash German bunkers in the First World War.

* * *

We are now going to look at the actions of the 9th Canadian Brigade on 7 June. This, too, was to complete unfinished business from D-Day. Its objective was Carpiquet airfield. The brigade consisted of three battalions, with the leading battalion the North Nova Scotia Highlanders riding on the tanks of the 27th Armoured Regiment (the Sherbrooke Fusiliers). Anti-tank support was from A Troop of M-10 tank destroyers of the 3rd Anti-Tank Regiment, RCA. The direct support regiment was 14th Canadian Field Regiment, and 14th and 19th Field Regiment's guns were to support the advance. The cruiser HMS *Belfas*t was assigned to support the advance, and an FOB travelled with the brigade.

The advance of the brigade group skirted the Douvres strongpoint, which was well armed and in German hands.

Leave the museum and turn right into the D83, then follow it to the outskirts of Basly. Turn left into the D219 signed Caen. At the T Junction turn left on to the

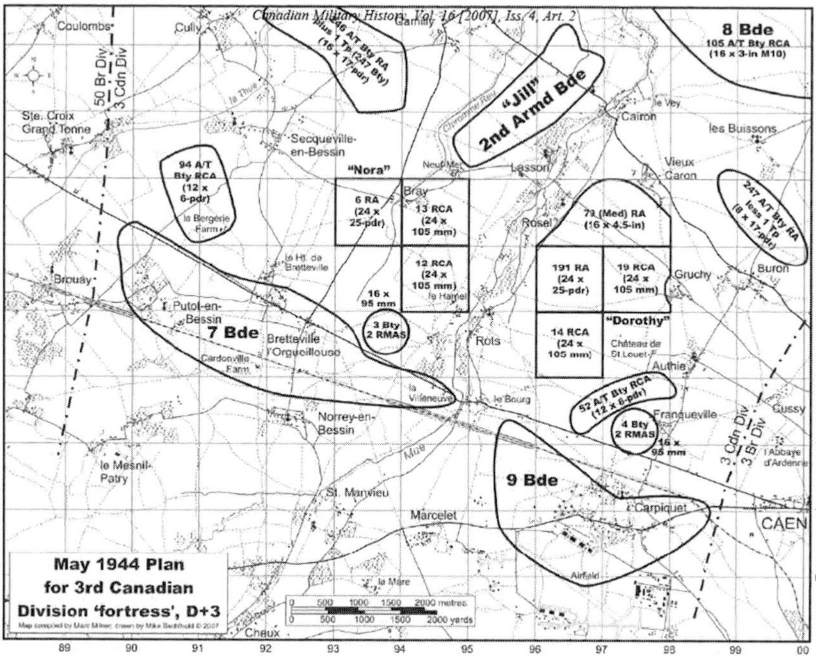

The Canadians planned to deploy in a strong position to defeat expected counter-attacks.

This is an example of the kind of defensive fire plans made for all formations. The firing data would be calculated for each of these and held ready to respond to calls for fire.

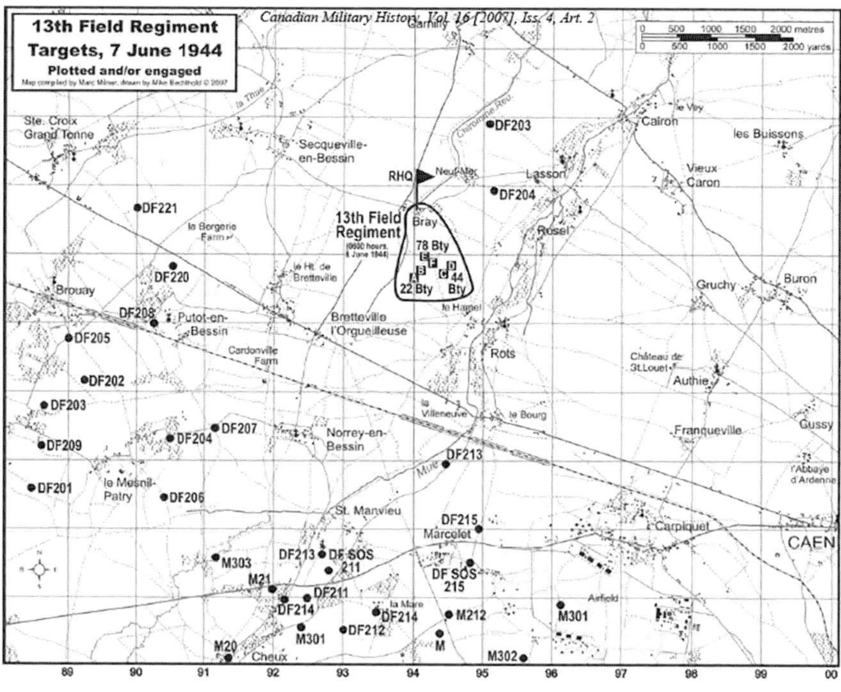

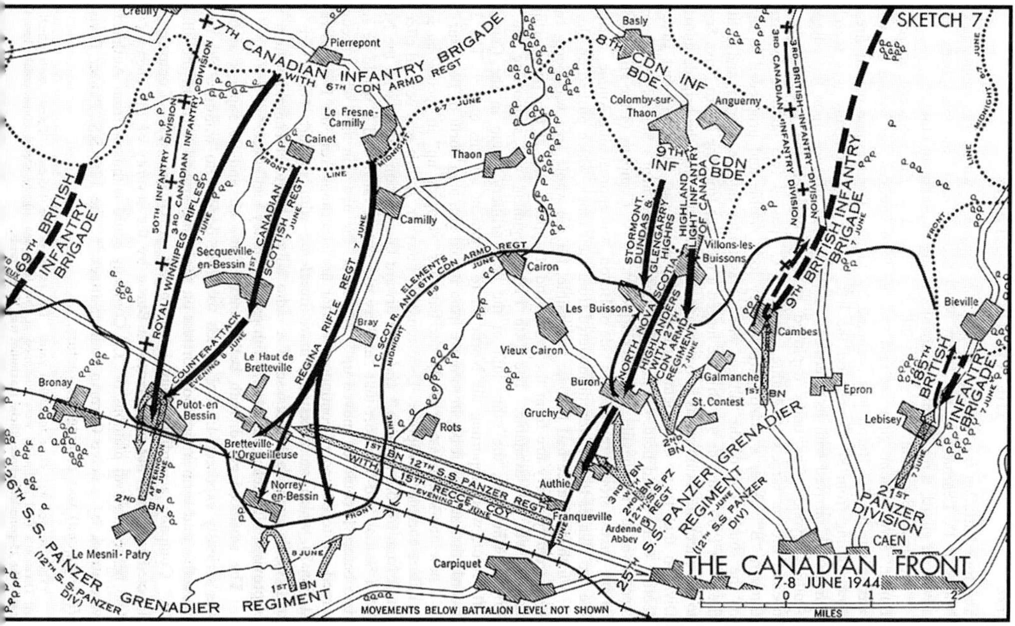

This map from the Canadian official history shows the operations of 7-8 June 1944.

D79. Follow the D79 for 2.2km, then turn right on to the D220 signed Villons-les-Buissons. Stay on the D220 for 3.6km through Buron. There is a memorial to the 27th Cavalry Regiment (Sherbrooke Fusiliers) in the Place des Canadiens, on the left side of the road. When you reach the Mairie in Authie turn left into the Rue de l'Abbaye and drive 1km to the edge of the next built-up area.

Cussy – O Canada!

Rue de l'Abbaye, 14280 Authie (GPS 49.202384, -0.418900)

You are at the forward edge of Cussy. You have driven from Authie, roughly west-north-west. Look half right and identify the village of Buron, with its centre 1.8km away. Beyond it is a patch of high ground. The villages of Les Buissons and Villons-les-Buissons are beyond the ridge to the right of Buron. Now turn 90 degrees to the left, roughly west-south-west, and 1.2km away is the village of Franqueville. It is on the right-hand edge of a hedge line a few hundred metres away. Look to the left-hand edge of the hedge line. A fist's width to the left is a village in the distance. That is Carpiquet. Turn a little under 90 degrees further left, look south-west and identify the Ardenne Abbey 700m away through the treeline.

After D-Day, three panzer divisions, the 21st Panzer, 12th SS and Panzer Lehr Divisions under the command of the I SS Panzer Corps, were committed to the area between Caen and Bayeux. The 12th SS Panzer Division was raised in 1943 from 20,000 politically motivated teenagers under a cadre of experienced officers. It was strong in infantry and armour, with sixty Mk V Panther and sixty Mk IV tanks. Based near Lisieux, it had been ready to deploy since the first airborne landings.

However, confusion and indecision in the German High Command delayed its deployment until the evening of D-Day, and air attacks delayed its move. Its orders were to drive the Allies into the sea.

The first battlegroup of three battalions of Panzer grenadiers, a battalion of Mk IV tanks and battalion of 15cm artillery arrived north-west of Caen in the early hours of 7 June. Its commander, Kurt Meyer, climbed the abbey to make a personal reconnaissance. His troops deployed in an arc some 8km from the village of La Folie, 3km in our right rear, to the Caen–Bayeux road 1.5 km to our left. His infantry had left their vehicles south of the road, and an artillery observer occupied one of the towers of the abbey. They waited to start an attack co-ordinated with 21st Panzer Division and scheduled to start at 1600.

Around 1400 Meyer saw the 9th Canadian Brigade Group advancing from right to left towards Carpiquet. Meyer identified the opportunity to counter-attack and told his men to hold fire until ordered. The German fire discipline was good. When a panzer platoon reconnoitring towards Franqueville became engaged with the leading Canadian armour, Meyer sprang the trap. They hit the exposed Sherbrooke Fusiliers in Franqueville and swept on to Authie. They overran C Company of the North Nova Scotia Highlanders and pressed on out of the village to Buron. More panzer grenadiers advanced from Cussy, where you are, to Authie and Buron. For about two hours there was a tank battle in the fields in front of you, while panzer grenadiers advanced on foot. The Canadians were forced out of Buron, back to Les Buissons.

The Germans should have presented an ideal target for defensive fire by field artillery and a cruiser, which could create a lethal barrier to infantry. However, when Meyer sprang his trap, the Canadians found themselves without artillery support. 9 Brigade had moved beyond the range of the two field regiments supporting the advance to Carpiquet. Worse still, the FOB lost radio communications with the cruiser HMS *Belfast*.

On 7 June, 14th and 19th Canadian Field Regiments started the day near Beny-sur-Mer. 19th Field Regiment remained to support an attack by the North Shore Regiment. At noon, 14th Field Regiment started to move forwards to Anguerny, which was in range of Carpiquet. However, they came under fire from the German radar site at Douvres, and the 14th Regiment redeployed to Basly, over 9,500m from Authie and beyond the effective maximum range of the M7. The first rounds fired by 14 Regiment in support of 9 Brigade seem to have been around 1800 hours, four hours after the start of the battle. Nor does there seem to have been any support from 12th and 13th Canadian Field Regiments, which appear to have been in range.

The guns of 3rd Canadian Division were decentralized until the division had occupied its defensive perimeters. Therefore, at this time the CRA had not assumed command of the guns. However, even if the guns were assigned elsewhere, the artillery cell should have monitored the situation, and the CRA should have prepared to exercise positive control if the circumstances demanded. The CRA on whose staff the author served would have regarded this as a soggy performance.

This battle was one of several in Normandy which demonstrated that the Germans could and would punish tactical errors.

Once the Canadians had fallen back to Les Buissons and brought their artillery into play, the Germans suffered heavily. The Canadians recaptured Buron during

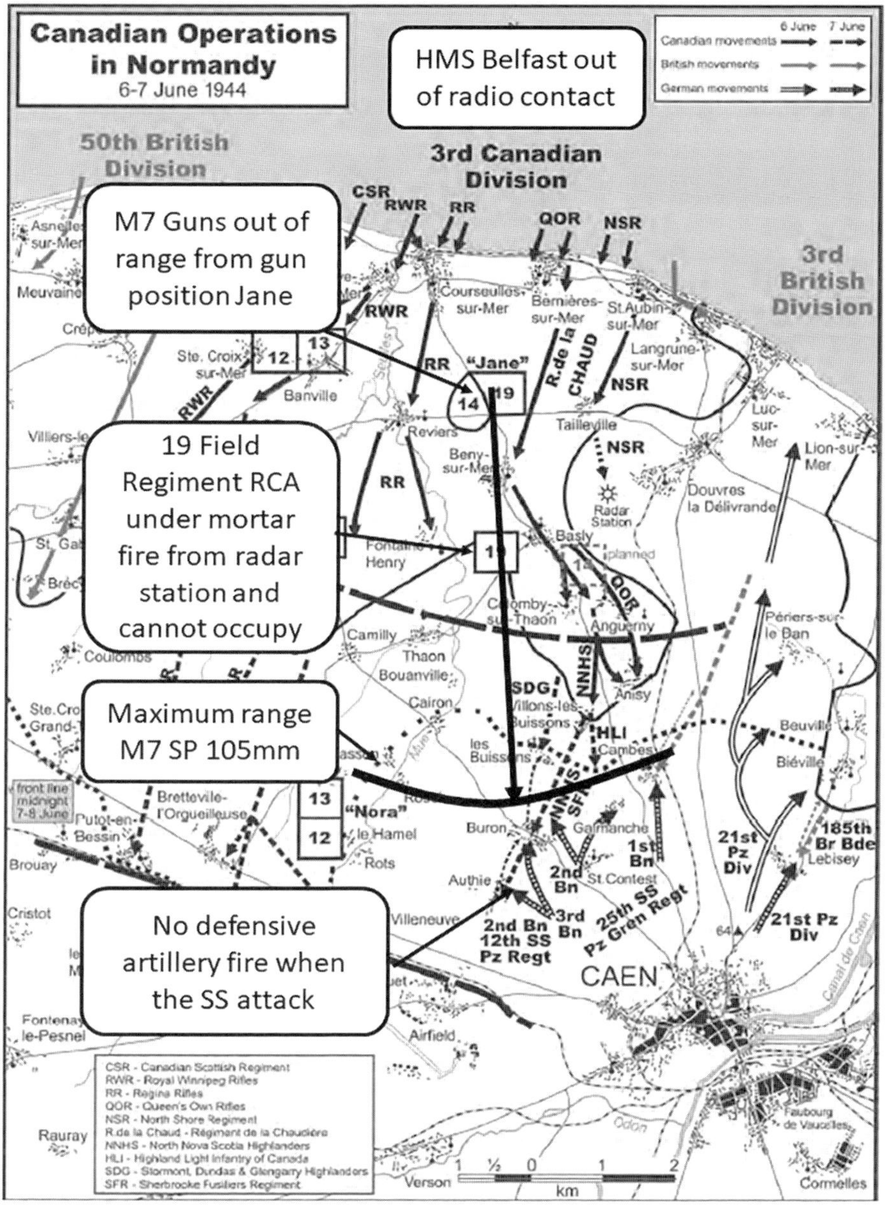

A recipe for disaster: the events that led to 9th Canadian Brigade to have no artillery support when attacked.

the evening of 7 June, but later withdrew. The Allies suffered over 300 casualties, including 128 taken prisoner, and twenty-one tanks knocked out. 12 SS also took over 300 casualties, with nine tanks a total loss and a higher number damaged. One of the 14th Canadian Regiment Forward Observers, Captain Norman Buchanan, MC*, was awarded a second bar to his Military Cross for his three days service manning an OP

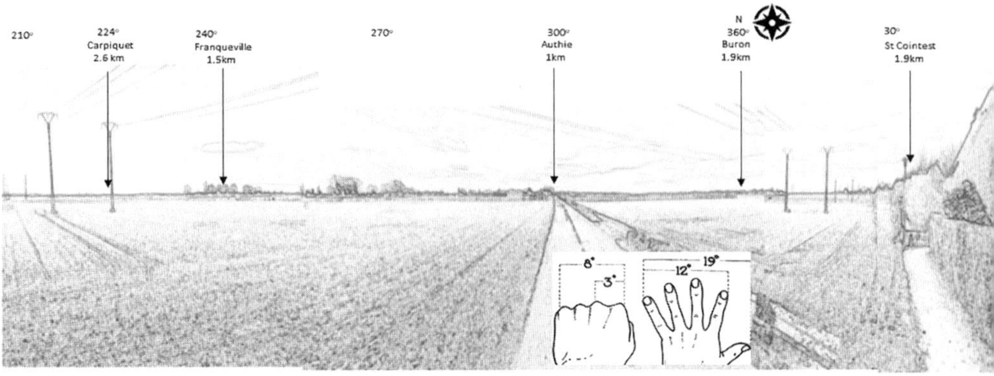

The view from the German positions in the counter-attack on the 9th Canadian Brigade.

at Les Buissons, 7–10 June. He was one of only twenty-three officers to be awarded this decoration three times.

Drive to view the Abbey. Check if it is open to the public, but you can see the building through the gaps in the walls. There is a memorial to eighteen Canadian prisoners murdered by the SS in the Abbey grounds.

Turn around and drive on the D220C to Authie. Look out for the memorial to the North Nova Scotia Regiment at the crossroads with the D220. Drive south towards the N13. At the roundabout take the third exit signed to St Lo Cherbourg, Rots, Bayeux. Drive for 1.3km and take the first exit signed D613, Rots, Bretteville-l'Orgueilleuse. As you leave the dual carriageway, take the second exit at the roundabout and the minor road parallel with the N13. At the next small roundabout take the second exit on to the road between Bayeux and Caen that existed in 1944. Drive through Villeneuve towards Bretteville-l'Orgueilleuse. Note the field on the right just before you reach the village of Bretteville-l'Orgueilleuse. Stop just before the church at the crossroads.

Bretteville-l'Orgueilleuse

72-74 Rue de Caen, 14740 Thue et Mue (GPS 49.209731, -0.509882)

The house with the white railings was the headquarters of the Regina Rifles from 7 to 11 June. They were the left forward battalion in the 7th Canadian Brigade. The Winnipeg Rifles were the right forward battalion, based on Putot-en-Bessin. The third battalion of the brigade, the Canadian Scottish, were near Secqueville-en-Bessin. The field artillery support for the Reginas was to be provided by 13 Canadian Field Regiment. Unusually, each of the forward battalions was assigned a regiment in direct support. The CO of the 13th Canadian Field Regiment, Colonel Clifford, deployed alongside the Reginas.

C Company was in Norrey-en-Bessin 2km south, with Captain Steele as the forward observer. B Company of the Reginas was deployed in the Mue valley near Rots, with Lieutenant O'Brennan as the FOO. What remained of D Company after D-Day near Villeneuve with Captain Macdonald and A Company in the village of

Bretteville-l'Orgueilleuse could call on the gunners at battalion HQ. Some anti-tank guns were deployed in the field just outside the village, the field you passed on the way in. Each of the OP parties had a Sherman tank. The officer, the assistant and a signaller would deploy forwards with a radio, leaving the tank with a signaller and driver to relay messages.

The guns of 12th and 13th Canadian Field Regiments were deployed in the Mue valley about 2km north in gun area Nora. The day of 7 June was spent preparing defences. Telephone lines were laid forwards to the OPs. 13 Canadian Field Regiment prepared a target list which included the most likely enemy concentration and approach routes. SOS fire tasks were arranged with the rifle companies to cover forward defence lines and areas immediately to the front which could not be swept by infantry weapons.

In the early hours of 8 June three companies of the 1st Battalion, 26 SS Panzer Grenadier Regiment (I/26th), moved north from St Manvieu to push the Reginas out of Norrey and Bretteville. The I/26th's third company moved straight on Norrey in the dark, driving into C Company's advanced positions; but their attack was repelled by artillery fire on a pre-arranged DF task. Meanwhile, the I/26th's first company tried to slip around Norrey to the east, where they too were stopped by artillery fire. This company eventually occupied the Mue valley as far as Rots – directly opposite the gun positions. The second company of I/26th attacked west of Norrey but stopped at Cardonville farm, south of the railway line.

13th Canadian Field Regiment fired 976 rounds between 1800 hours on 7 June and 0600 hours the next day. The perimeter was maintained by a series of DF and 'Mike targets' regimental shoots. One concentration on the road leading south-east from Norrey at 0500 hours on 8 June was fired at 'scale 5' from both regiments at Bray – 240 shells on a single grid reference in a few short minutes. Two other Mike targets were fired in that area over the next few hours.

While the I/26th was pounded by fire, the main effort of the rest of 26 Panzer Grenadiers on 8 June, supported by artillery and assault guns, took place against the Winnipegs at Putot-en-Bessin. 12th and 13th Canadian Field Regiments fired, almost continuously, on targets over an arc of 240°. The Reginas concentrated their defences. B Company pulled back to the east edge of Bretteville – to the area of the field pointed out at the start. D Company were redeployed to Cardonville farm to cover the south-west approach to Bretteville. One measure of the confusion is that at noon on the 8th a German officer drove up in a *Kubelwagen* (light military car) to the Reginas' headquarters – where you are standing. He stepped out and was shot.

During the evening of 8 June, the Germans mounted a second attack on the Reginas from the east with two companies of Panther tanks – about thirty, together with a company of motorcyclists and a battery of self-propelled guns. The Germans crossed River Mue, then shook out for the attack. Meyer expected the panzer grenadiers to the south to join the attack, but the newly arrived 79th Medium Regiment firing from Thaon kept these in their slit trenches. Few German infantry reached the village. Three Panther tanks were knocked out by 6-pounder anti-tank guns of the 3rd Canadian 3rd Anti-Tank Regiment, from the area of the field at the east end of the village. Two Panthers that made it into Bretteville were knocked out by infantry. One reached as far as the Reginas' HQ.

The German tank attack also threatened the 12th and 13th Canadian Field Regiment's gun position, which engaged at least one tank over open sights. During 9 June, up to 216 guns within I Corps were firing at targets on a 180° arc from in front of Caen to south of Bayeux. 13 Canadian Field Regiment engaged targets in one direction at 8,000 yards range – and then came back to the tanks in front, 1,600 yards away.

During the night of 8/9 June, D Company in Cardonville farm south of the railway line was attacked by infantry and tanks. The line connection from D Company's FOO, Captain Macdonald, was cut. The line party sent to restore it was not heard of again. Macdonald was killed, and the remaining forty-five men of D Company only survived after the company commander called for artillery fire from the battalion HQ. It arrived within a minute, the rounds skimming over the roof of the farm and landing among the Germans.

The last major attack on the Reginas in this position came at 1300, when a company of Panther tanks passed under the railway bridge at Villeneuve and attacked across the open fields to Norry-en-Bessin from the north-east. They were hit from the flank by fire from Canadian tanks to their north and lost seven Panther tanks in a matter of minutes. Few if any German infantry joined this attack, being pinned in their trenches by artillery fire. The fighting did not end on the 9th, but diminished in intensity.

A battalion of troops who had already taken part in a bloody assault on D-Day had fought off the worst that the Germans could do. 12th SS were fresh, well trained and equipped, highly motivated troops, led by experienced commanders. Artillery fire helped to defeat infantry attacks and separate the armour from infantry. If 9 Brigade's action on 7 June showed how dangerous the Germans could be in an encounter without artillery support, the 7 Brigade battle showed the difference made by the support of the field artillery of an army corps.

Return to your car. Continue for a block to the west to the Mairie. There is a memorial to the Regina Regiment in the Place des Canadiens. Continue west along the Rue de Bayeux until you reach the roundabout at the west end of Bretteville. Take the third exit towards Putot-en-Bessin on the D94. Drive under the N13 dual carriageway, and at the next roundabout take the second exit to Putot-en-Bessin. Drive through the village on the D94. This village was defended by the Winnipeg Rifles. Their companies were in line along the railway line south of the village. Before you reach the railway turn sharp right on to the D217. At the roundabout before the N13 take the third exit towards Secqueville-en-Bessin over the dual-carriageway. At the next roundabout, on the north side of the N13 dual carriageway, take the second exit to continue along the D217. After 500m stop at the first strip of wood on the left.

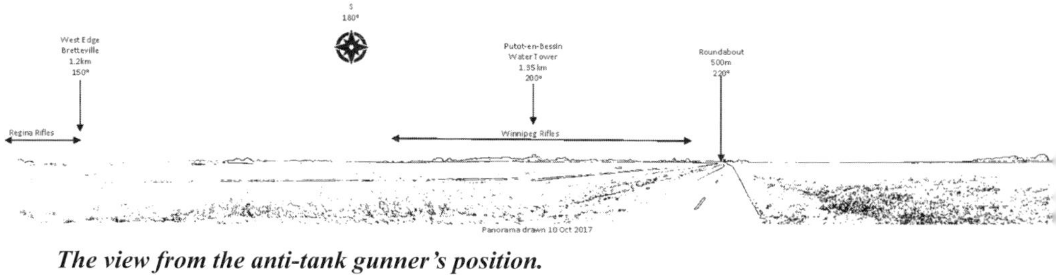

The view from the anti-tank gunner's position.

Putot-en-Bessin
D217, 14740 Thue et Mue (GPS 49.224824, -0.534583)

Look south down the road. One hand-spread to the left you should see the water tower of Putot-en-Bessin, occupied by the Winnipeg Rifles. Three hand-spreads further to the left is the village of Bretteville-l'Orgueilleuse.

On 8 June 1944 this was a backstop anti-tank position, occupied by a troop of four 17-pounder anti-tank guns from 246 Battery of 62nd Anti-tank Regiment under Lieutenant Blanchard, four 6-pounder guns from 94th Battery of 3rd Canadian Anti-Tank Regiment RCA under Lieutenant May and some medium machine guns. They had been positioned to cover any penetrations of the right flank of 7th Canadian Brigade. Any tank crossing the ridgeline would be vulnerable at a range in which an anti-tank gun was lethal.

On the night of 7/8 June an attack by 12th SS overran the positions of the Winnipeg Rifles in Putot-en-Bessin. At about 0945 hours on 8 June an enemy force of about nine tanks accompanied by infantry appeared. The enemy held back from the wood and engaged the Winnipegs with heavy machine gun and mortar fire. Lieutenant Blanchard's troop knocked out four tanks and, in turn, had two of its own guns knocked out. Despite intense small arms and mortar fire, Lieutenant Blanchard reorganized his troops, brought two new guns into action, re-allotted men to 6-pounder gun and infantry positions to replace casualties and attended to the wounded. The Germans kept the position under fire until 1630 hours. Blanchard was awarded a Military Cross for his part in this action.

At 2000 hours the Canadian Scottish Regiment, in reserve at Secqueville, retook Putot, supported by the fire of five field regiments. Artillery fire neutralized the Germans, isolated the battlefield with a smoke barrage, provided a creeping barrage to allow the Canadian Scottish to walk on to the objective and then maintained defensive fire to the south and west until the position was consolidated.

Drive south to the N13 and take the first exit towards Bayeux. Take exit 37 towards Bayeux/Balleroy/Saint-Lô. After 200m, at the roundabout, take the 2nd exit on to the D572. After 2km, at the roundabout, take the 3rd exit on to Boulevard Maréchal Leclerc, D5. The Museum of the Battle of Normandy will be on the right.

Bayeux War Museum
Boulevard Fabian Ware, 14400 Bayeux (GPS 49.272405, -0.711050)

The Bayeux War Museum is dedicated to the Battle of Normandy rather than just D-Day.

On the edge of the car park, next to the museum is a German *Jagdpanzer* 38t (Sd.Kfz138/2) *Hetzer.* This mounted a 7.5 cm Pak 39 L/48 anti-tank gun in an enclosed fighting compartment on a version of the Czech Panzer 38(t) Chassis. The German anti-tank guns on light tank chassis provided mobile anti-tank defence for their infantry divisions. The *Jagdpanzer* 38(t) was not in service on the Western Front on D-Day but would eventually replace the open-topped SP Anti-tank guns

Bayeux War Cemetery.

in 716th and 352nd Infantry Divisions used on D-Day. These were supplemented by *Sturmgeschutz* or assault guns, which mounted 7.5cm and 10.5cm guns on Pz III and IV chassis.

In front of the Museum are three green-painted AFVs. The closest to the car park is an M4 Sherman, a 75mm variant painted in US Army markings. The white star was an Allied rather than an American national symbol. Metal patches have been crudely welded on in an attempt to provide extra protection for the petrol tanks.

The next vehicle across is an M10 self-propelled anti-tank gun as described in Chapter 2, the standard British SP Anti-tank gun. This mounts the US 3-in gun. A minority on D-Day mounted the much more powerful British 17-pounder.

The Churchill tank is the Crocodile variant. The Churchill was the most heavily armoured tank of the Western Allies. It was slow and armed with either the 75mm or 6-pounder gun. The Crocodile variant mounted a flame thrower in the hull front in place of the co-driver's machine gun. This had a range of 100–150m. The fuel was carried in an armoured trailer towed behind the tank, and the armoured pipe is visible under the belly of the tank. Crocodile tanks were effective; even their appearance could induce surrender. Two of these tanks helped 86 Field Regiment to capture the 4/AR 1716 on D+1. (See Chapter 9)

Behind the Crocodile are memorials to the Essex Regiment and the capture of Bayeux.

Walk back to the footpath and turn right, crossing the road. Stay on the north side of the Boulevard Fabian Ware and walk to the grassy area opposite the entrance to the Bayeux War Cemetery.

Bayeux War Cemetery

The Bayeux Memorial bears the names of more than 1,800 men of the Commonwealth land forces who died in the early stages of the campaign and have no known grave. They died during the landings in Normandy, during the intense fighting in Normandy itself, and during the advance to the River Seine in August.

The memorial contains the names of 118 gunners: eighty-five from the Royal Artillery, ten Royal Horse Artillerymen and twenty-three Canadians. Twenty-five died on 6 June. These include seven or eight men lost in the airborne landings. Gunner J. E. Woolmore is listed on the memorial, but his unit, 107 Medium Regiment, did not land until July. He may have been a member of one of the Forward Observation Unit parties dropped with the 6th Airborne Division. Six soldiers from 92 Light AA Regiment are listed who died when their ship SS *Sambut* was sunk off Calais. Captain J. Lee from 14 Medium Regiment was the FOB officer with 2nd Battalion the Warwickshire Regiment. Ten members of 127 Light AA Regiment died on 12 June when the Mulberry Harbour caisson they were on was sunk by a torpedo from an E-Boat on the passage to Normandy.

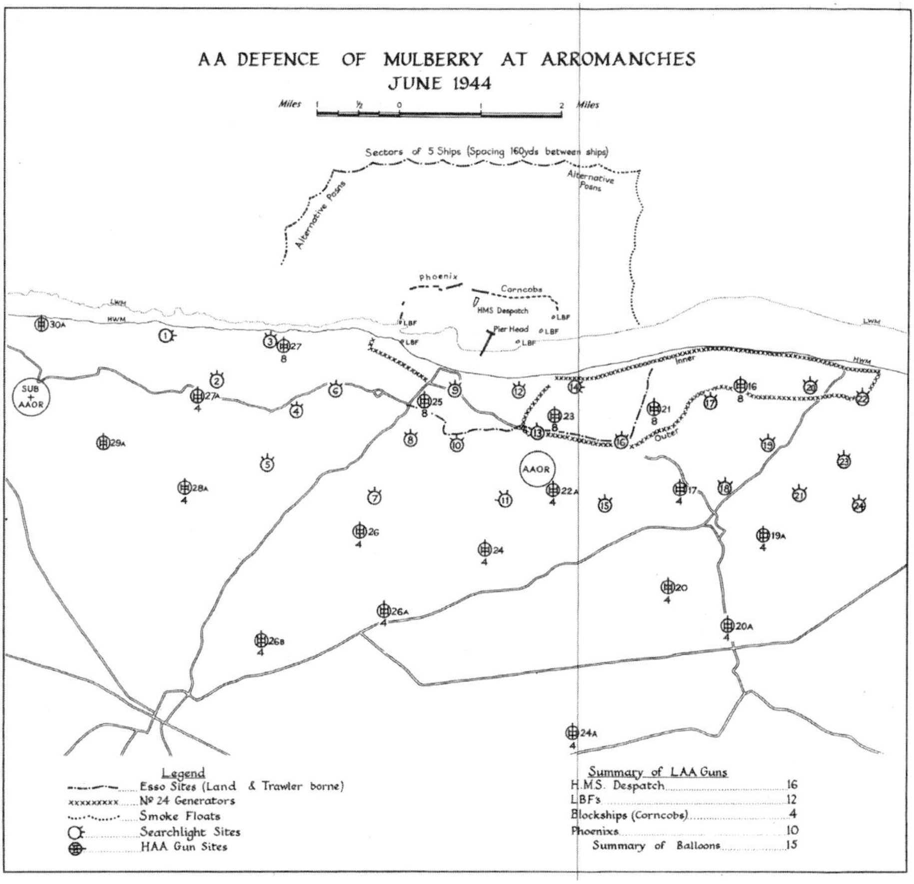

The Heavy AA defences of Mulberry Harbour, described by one experienced Luftwaffe pilot as the heaviest he faced – worse than London or Malta.

This phoenix caisson still has the remains of the platform for the 40mm AA gun that was once mounted on it.

The Bayeux War Cemetery is opposite the Bayeux War Memorial. It contains the graves of 4,144 Commonwealth soldiers, including 268 artillerymen. Sixteen Gunners who died on 6 June are buried in Bayeux. These include Major Onions, BC 101 Battery of 20 Anti-tank Regiment (10G.24). There are six soldiers from 90th Field Regiment, including Lieutenant Calkin (10F.5), killed by a sniper while bringing the COs tank ashore. There are two soldiers from 86 Hertfordshire Yeomanry, although Captain Platt (14L.10) was the FOB from No3 COBU, not one of their officers.

Major John Pooley of No.3 Commando, killed at Merville battery on 7 June, was reburied in plot 24F2. Brigadier John Currie DSO and two Bars, MC (15G.12) was killed by enemy shelling while commanding 4th Armoured Brigade on 26 June 1944. He had commanded a battery, then 4th Regiment RHA and then 9th Armoured Brigade at El Alamein.

Lieutenant Colonel P. R. C. Manser (2F.14), CO 25 Field Regiment, was fatally wounded by shellfire on 1 August and died the following day. Lieutenant Colonel O. W. R. Dent TD (19A.10), the CO of 110 Light AA Regiment, was killed by a mine on 18 August 1944. The 110th Light AA Regiment suffered the highest number of fatalities of any Royal Artillery AA unit in the Normandy campaign.

Return to your car. Take D572 and D613 to Route de Courseulles/D12 in Saint-Vigor-le-Grand. Continue along the D12. Take D205 to D514 in Arromanches-les-Bains. As you approach you will see the very conspicuous statue of the Virgin Mary and a car park. Park in Parking 360.

Arromanches

Parking 360, D514, 14117 Arromanches-les-Bains (GPS 49.339016, -0.615261)

The 360 Degree Museum offers the visitor a way to experience some of the sights and sounds of 1944. It is sited on the cliffs overlooking Arromanches, and the concrete foundations are the remains of the German radar station there. The hexagonal base was the mounting for a giant Wurzburg radar dish, and the site was designated WN43.

The cliff top and the viewing platform are the best places from which to appreciate the size of the Mulberry Harbour, the artificial Port Winston. Take care near the cliff edge, which is only bounded by a low wooden fence.

The Allies needed the port capacity to bring in sufficient troops, ammunition, fuel and other supplies to defeat the defenders. The Germans strongly defended points with the capacity to sustain large armies, but they did not suspect the existence of the Mulberry Harbour and underestimated the size of the Allied landings and build-up after D-Day. There was a second Mulberry Harbour at Omaha Beach. Fuel tankers could unload near Port-en-Bessin via a pipeline.

These were vulnerable points for the Allies. 76th AA Brigade was responsible for providing AA guns for the integrated air defence of Arromanches, Port-en-Bessin and Gold Beach, while 80th Brigade was responsible for Sword and Juno Beaches. By 24 June, the AA defences provided an Inner Artillery Zone that stretched over the beaches from Port-en-Bessin to Ouistreham and the River Orne. The land-based defences included 136 Heavy AA guns, 180 40mm and 34 20mm AA guns.

There were additional AA defences afloat. On 24 June there were ten 40mm Bofors guns mounted on Phoenix caissons, four on blockships and sixteen on the HQ Ship HMS *Dispatch*, manned by 127th Light AA Regiment. Some of the caissons off Arromanches still have the supports for the Bofors guns' platforms. Off the beaches were ten Landing Barge Flak. These were Thames barges or lighters mounting two Bofors guns, manned by 139th Light AA Regiment. In addition, there were thirty-six 20mm guns at the end of the piers to be manned by 969 Port Floating Equipment Company RE when necessary. What's more, five Landing Craft Flak were off Gold Beach, as were six Landing Craft Flak manned by the Royal Navy.

The gunners joined their ships and prefabricated caissons in the UK and travelled to France in the exposed caissons under tow. This was not without risk. On 12 June, a Phoenix caisson was sunk and many of the detachment from 127 LAA lost.

These were part of an integrated air defence system that could draw on early warning radar controlled by No.83 group RAF. Besides AA guns, there were sixty barrage balloons manned by the RAF to hamper low-flying enemy aircraft. It was also possible to cover the harbour with a smokescreen from lines of smoke generators ashore behind the beaches. Offshore, thirty trawlers with smoke generators were ready to lay a smokescreen north or west of the harbour, while a line of smoke floats protected the eastern side.

This formidable air defence system was never fully tested. By D-Day the Luftwaffe had few night bombers available, having expended its strength in costly retaliatory raids on London. The Luftwaffe considered that the anti-aircraft fire over the Normandy beachhead was some of the most intense they had experienced. After heavy losses, the Germans switched to mine laying beyond the range of AA guns.

The living conditions on the Phoenix caissons were basic. Food was composite rations or came from a Landing Barge Kitchen. The storm on the night of 19/20 June destroyed Mulberry A on Omaha beach and caused much damage to Mulberry B. Phoenix units and the decks of blockships were swamped, and six AA barges were driven ashore. There had been no local warning. The unhappy gun detachments, drenched even in their raised towers, were in danger of being lost altogether. The naval commander's opinion was that no boat could get alongside. Evacuation of the worst affected was achieved, at considerable hazard, by the efforts of Royal Army Service Corps launches. Several guns suffered damage, and 13,000 rounds were washed overboard or ruined by flooding.

Drive down to Arromanches town. Park in the car park on the front. The museum has some excellent models and dioramas showing the full extent of the components of the Mulberry Harbour and how they worked. Arromanches is a popular tourist destination and well supplied with cafés, restaurants and shops.

Arromanches is situated in a narrow valley. The Germans constructed defences on the east and west sides of the valley. A Sherman tank is sited on the top of a concrete

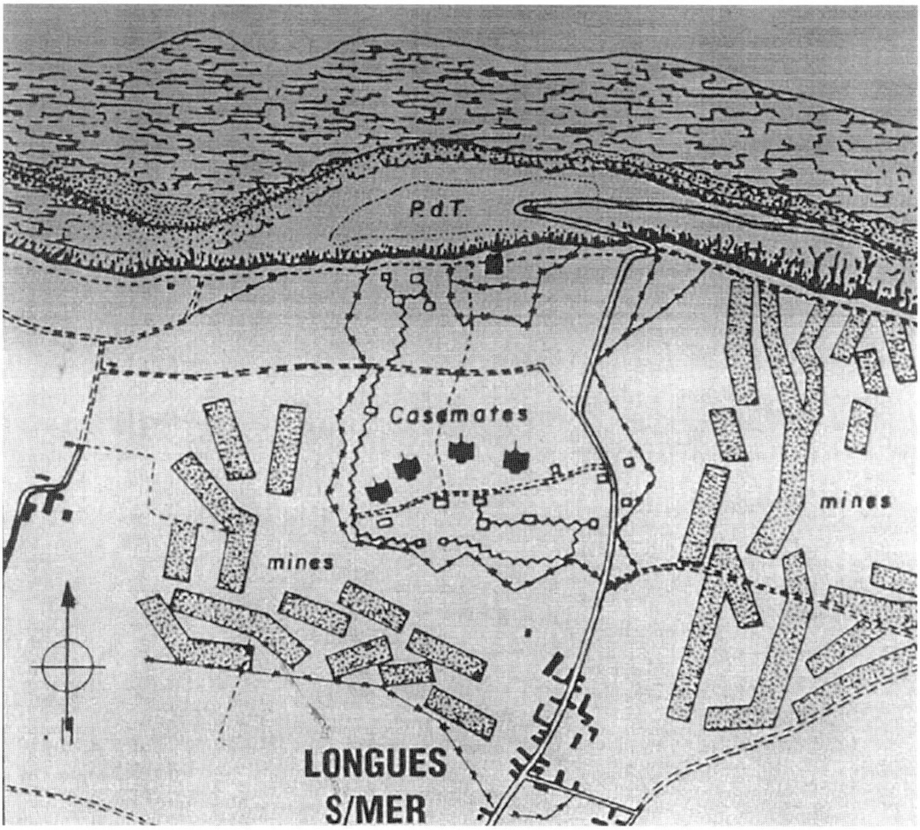

This battery was one of the few that replied to the Allied bombardment.

bunker which housed a field gun on D-Day. This can be reached via steps from the seafront.

On the west side of the seafront car park there is a German flak 88mm gun. On the east side flanking the museum is a 25-pounder gun howitzer. On the east side of the museum is a Bofors gun of the type that formed the basis of the Light AA defences, as well as a section of the type of causeway that linked the beach to the pier head.

Depart Arromanches via the D514 in the direction of Omaha Beach and Grandcamp-Maisy. In the village of Longues-sur-Mer turn right at the traffic lights following the signs for the Batteries de Longues. Park at the entrance to the battery. Entrance is free.

Longues-sur-Mer Battery

This battery was manned by 184 Kriegsmarine sailors, under the command of Army Coastal Artillery Battalion 1260. The battery covers an area approximately 500m by 500m.

The four embrasures each hold a 15cm TbtsK C/36 150 mm (5.9″) naval gun. On the edge of the cliff is a well-preserved Type 262 command and observation bunker. A path leads to it from the western edge of the battery. The large concrete fire control bunker has rooms on two floors. Calculating the azimuth and elevation to engage a moving ship was a challenge in the pre-computer age. The emplacements for coastal artillery were more elaborate than for the field artillery, such as the observation bunker in WN05. The upper section has an observation slit, originally intended to be protected by shutters. The fire control and observation centre would have an optical range finder to estimate the range and a protected environment for the technicians to carry out their manual calculations. The battery was protected by barbed wire and mines, and fourteen bunkers provided positions for local defence as well as shelter for the garrison. A 2cm AA gun was provided for local AA defence.

This was only coastal battery to engage ships off the British beaches on D-Day. First it fired at the battleship USS *Arkansas* off Omaha beach, but then switched to HMS *Bulolo*, the HQ Ship for Gold Beach, and straddled the ship with its opening salvo. The return fire of 114 rounds from HMS *Ajax* was devastating, scoring direct hits on the westernmost two embrasures, Nos.3 and 4, and near-misses on the other two. No.1 gun opened fire on the afternoon of D-Day but was silenced by 1800 by return fire from the French cruiser *Georges Leygues*.

A coastal battery would normally expect to fire on data based on calculations made in the fire control and observation centre, but 1,500 tons of bombs were dropped on the battery in two air raids on 28 May and 3 June 1944. By D-Day the telephone lines that connected the fire control centre and the guns were cut, despite their being buried underground. Nor had the construction been completed; the observation slits were obscured by an earth wall that had not been removed. On 6 June fire control was undertaken by individual guns.

After the war was over, the earth was removed from the vision slits for the film 'The Longest Day', which showed Major Pusket of Artillery Regiment 352 gaining the first sight of the D-Day invasion fleet from the bunker.

Optional extension to an Omaha Beach visit – Laurent-sur-Mer churchyard
If you are visiting Omaha Beach, consider making a diversion to Laurent-sur-Mer churchyard. Major Gustavus Henry March-Phillipps DSO, MBE was one of the first allied soldiers to die on what would be called Omaha Beach. A soldier, master of fox hounds and novelist, he was a larger-than-life figure. Disgusted by allied failure in 1940, he formed a 'private army' called No 62 Commando to support the Special Operations Executive. In January 1942 his unit seized three Axis ships from a neutral Spanish harbour in an exploit worthy of James Bond, and he may have been an inspiration for Ian Fleming, who took part in the same operation. In September his force made a navigation error and landed in front of the alert defences rather than unoccupied cliffs. March-Phillipps' poem 'If I Should Die' is engraved on a memorial in the graveyard. He is buried alongside two of his soldiers, one of whom was a middle aged Jewish Sudeten German communist, a reminder of the political and ethical dimension to the war.

The view from the sea
Ouistreham Ferry Port (GPS 49.288570, -0.247701)

If you are travelling to or from Normandy via Brittany Ferries' Portsmouth–Caen service, you have a chance to observe the D-Day beaches from the water.

There is usually plenty of time to take a look while the ferry is alongside the dock, as passengers are embarked well before departure and it takes a while to tie up on arrival. The ferry will dock with the stern facing inland. The café/bar sun deck on the highest passenger deck offers the best view. Looking to the right you can see Sword Beach, then a little left, the observation tower for the Riva Bella battery and Ouistreham church. Looking past the stern of the ferry you will see the Caen Canal. On the left bank you will see the lighthouse. If you look carefully, you should be able to make out the hexagonal markings where a 5cm KwK had been mounted, and to the left and closer, a metal observation bunker. This area was captured on D-Day by Commandos. After D-Day it was occupied by an unusual British unit, the 16th Fire Control Unit (16 FCU) with two Coastal Observation Detachments under command. These were Coastal Artillerymen who took over German equipment to defend the port of Ouistreham, including two 5cm KwK, two 2cm Flak and an 8.8cm anti-tank gun. They used radar to monitor the sea in the Bay of the Seine. 103 Heavy AA Regiment had some of its 3.7-in guns in the area. A flash-spotting team used the lighthouse as an OP. The Germans used motor patrol boats and midget submarines against the shipping off Sword Beach. 16 FCU took a midget submarine sailor prisoner after his submarine sank.

Looking further to the left you will see the mouth of the River Orne, and further left the bunkers of WN05, where 1/AR 1716 had its OP. This was no-man's-land in the ten weeks of static war between mid-June and mid-August on this sector. 16 FCU and 103 Heavy AA exchanged shots with the Germans in WN05 and Merville battery. Further left, you can see the wooded hills to the east of the River Dives.

After the ferry sails, see if you can identify the invasion beaches to the west. Looking to the east, you may be able to make out the mouth of the Seine and the port of Le Havre. At sea you can see how close this port is to the shipping offshore.

Chapter 11

Touring the D-Day Beaches

This section of the book is intended as a practical guide for visitors to the D-Day battlefields.

Planning a visit

How much time do you have? There is a lot to see on the D-Day beaches and Normandy battlefields, far more than can be covered in one day.

When do you want to travel? The first week of June is always busy, and accommodation can be more expensive then. Visiting during major anniversaries can be an intense experience, sharing Remembrance with other visitors and pilgrims, but traffic can be heavy and travel curtailed to accommodate the big crowds and presence of VIPs. In the winter months there will be fewer hours of day light, and many museums close during December and January.

Guidebooks

These tours are intended to focus on the artillery aspects of the D-Day beaches. There are several guides which give an all-arms perspective and should be considered alongside this book. Other Pen & Sword titles covering the D-Day beaches include:

- *Pegasus Bridge and Horsa Bridge* (paperback), Carl Shilleto ISBN: 9781848843097
- *Sword Beach: British 3rd Infantry Division/27th Armoured Brigade* (paperback), Tim Kilvert-Jones ISBN: 9780850526738
- *Juno Beach: Canadian 3rd Infantry Division* (paperback), Major Tim Saunders ISBN: 9781844150281
- *Gold Beach: Jig Sector and West, June 1944* (paperback), Major Tim Saunders ISBN: 9780850528664
- *Gold Beach Inland from King, June 1944* (paperback), Christopher Dunphie and Garry Johnson ISBN: 9780850526615

Maps

A satnav or a good road map is useful. To recreate the landscape of 1944, some reproduction maps are available. IGN publish a 1:100,000 map with a 1944 overprint of the dispositions on D-Day.

Accommodation

Normandy is a holiday destination. There is a wide range of accommodation, from hotels to holiday rentals, caravans and camp sites. Bayeux and Caen are the largest cities in the area behind the British beaches. Arromanches, Port-en-Bessin, Ouistreham and Houlgate are smaller towns with holiday accommodation.

Dress

The weather in Normandy is similar to that of south-west Britain. It can be changeable, and it is prudent to take rainwear. Take sun cream and clothing providing protection from the sun in summer – coastal breezes keep the visitor cool but do not protect from the sun's rays. Take shoes or boots suitable for walking over fields and the beach. Take swimwear for the beach if you want to wade ashore.

Driving

Most people will have travelled to Normandy by car and will have some experience of driving in France. Caen is a busy university town and commercial centre. The ring road, the *Boulevard périphérique de Caen*, can be busy at rush hours 8–9 am and 5–7 pm. Be careful when sightseeing on the minor roads. Park and walk rather than dawdle on the road. Busy commuters and farmers may not expect to find your car around a blind bend.

Water

It is easy to become dehydrated in sunny weather and with sea breezes. Take water with you, especially if you are in a hurry. French tap water is safe to drink, unless marked '*non potable*'. Bottled water and other drinks can be obtained from the many supermarkets.

Refreshment

There are plenty of cafés and restaurants in the tourist destinations. However, many smaller villages have lost their shops, and there is no guarantee that a quaint village will contain anywhere to buy a drink.

Accessibility

Battlefields vary in their accessibility. The major memorials are regularly visited by an ageing corps of veterans, and many of the beaches were pre-war holiday resorts. Preserved fortifications are likely to include stairs and may preclude full participation by those with mobility difficulties.

Safety

There are many hazards on the Second World War battlefields. In France landowners have a legal obligation to protect visitors on their land. However, France has a different attitude to health and safety, and a different legal system. Visitors should not expect safety signage to protect them from foolish acts.

Some battlefield sites are overgrown. Beware sudden drops into bunkers, craters or trenches. There are some obvious waterside hazards. Be careful of cliff edges and river or canal banks. Do not venture beyond any wire or fencing. Check the local advice before venturing into the sea.

Be careful on the roads, whether driving, cycling or walking.

While France is generally a law-abiding country, thieves and criminals can be found everywhere. Look after your possessions. Be mindful of personal security.

Battlefield souvenirs

It is illegal, and potentially dangerous, to remove relics from battlefields in France. Be mindful of the differences between UK and French regulations regarding offensive weapons and the rules about prohibited items on ferries, the Channel Tunnel, or aircraft.

Museums

Caen Memorial Museum

The Mémorial de Caen Museum in Caen is a 'Centre for History and Peace'. The aim of the museum is to put D-Day and the Battle of Normandy in the context of the conflicts of the twentieth century, with a focus on reconciliation.

The museum is situated on the site of the quarry which held the headquarters of the 716th Infantry Division. General Richter's headquarters are recreated as part of the permanent exhibition.

Outside the museum are commemorative gardens, which have been planted over the past forty years. The British garden includes memorials to each of the formations which took part in the campaign. The Canadian garden was designed by a team of architecture students and is designed to encourage reflection. The American garden is based around a fountain symbolizing Life.

Rots

The D-Day Academy at Rots offers a series of D-Day experiences ranging from travelling in the area in historic vehicles to handling weapons and equipment of the era.

Other Attractions

Normandy has a long history. William the Conqueror was born in Falaise and buried in Caen. The Bayeux Tapestry is well worth a visit. This is a seaside holiday area, and the resorts from Deauville to Port-en-Bessin have the attractions and activities that can be expected. The River Orne estuary is a nature reserve.

The region is well known for its cuisine, which makes heavy use of cream and apples. Seafood is a speciality of the area. Courseulles is a centre for oyster farming, and Gold and Juno Beaches are covered in mussel beds.

Appendix A

Artillery Technical Terms and Glossary

Ammunition and its effects

The weapon of artillery is the ammunition not the gun, which is merely the means of projecting the round. The illustration shows three types of ammunition. The predominant round used was the High Explosive (HE) shell (1). This was a steel container filled with a high explosive and detonated by a fuse to create a cloud of supersonic splinters and a blast wave of hot gas that could suffocate, crush and burn. Different fuses could function on impact (2) to create a wall of supersonic splinters from the point of impact; after a short delay, to allow for penetration of light cover or collapse trenches; or after a set time to burst the shell in the air (3). Some fuses permitted combination of effects, e.g. functioning after a set time or on impact. Colouring could be added to the explosive to create marker shells to indicate targets. The splinter pattern varied with the ammunition nature, trajectory of the round and whether a ground or air burst. However, most of the splinters would be forward and to the side of the point of impact (4). A significant proportion of splinters would travel a couple of hundred yards, and one or two big fragments might travel 600 yards. Smoke shells (5) provided clouds of smoke to blind an enemy or screen movement. This could be provided by a filling of White Phosphorus shell (6). The 25-pounder smoke round functioned by ejecting smoke pellets from the base of the round (7). Star shells released a flare on a parachute to illuminate a target at night (8). Armour-piercing rounds were also available to engage tanks.

Field artillery is an area weapon. The rounds from the same gun do not fall in the same place. Instead, they are scattered in a cigar-shaped, normal distribution along the line of fire. If a 25-pounder gun fired at a target 10,000 yards away, half fall within 40 yards either side of the mean point of impact and all within 120 yards. A battery of eight 25-pounders firing at the same target would be expected to cover an area around 150 × 150 yards with a pattern of shell splinters. The fire from a regiment of twenty-four guns would cover an area around 250 × 250 yards. The fire of seventy-two guns of a divisional artillery would cover an area around 350 × 350 yards. The Royal Artillery had a regimental standard concentration to engage linear targets such as a road or hedge-line, or to provide the lines in a barrage. Each of the twenty-four guns in a regiment would fire at one point.

Artillery fire achieved its effects in three main ways. Interference was to cause casualties, shake the enemy's morale and interfere with his mobility. Neutralization was to stop the fire of enemy weapons, while destruction was to destroy enemy defences and material. The most important tactical effect of field artillery was to neutralize the effects of enemy weapons while its own fire continued. Direct fire weapons could be neutralized by fire or blinded by smoke (1). Enemy guns could be prevented from firing by counter-battery fire (2). 'Defensive Fire' could anticipate

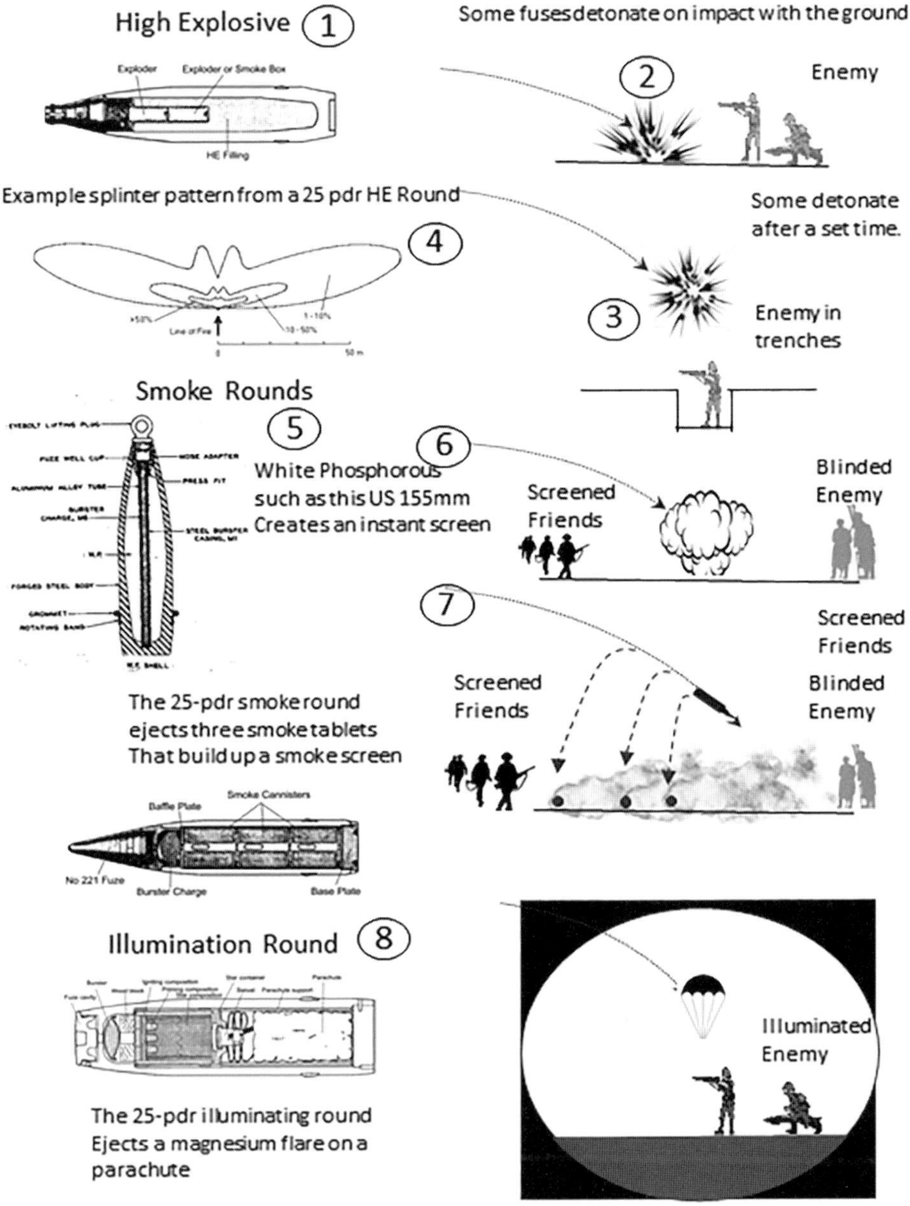

Field Artillery Ammunition.

positions enemy might occupy or move through to counter-attack (3). Some targets were important enough to be destroyed. This might require a lot of ammunition and heavy guns. In Normandy there were few places offering good observation, and obvious ones such as church towers (4) and factory chimneys were the targets for destruction. Artillery was also used to interfere with enemy movement and to inflict

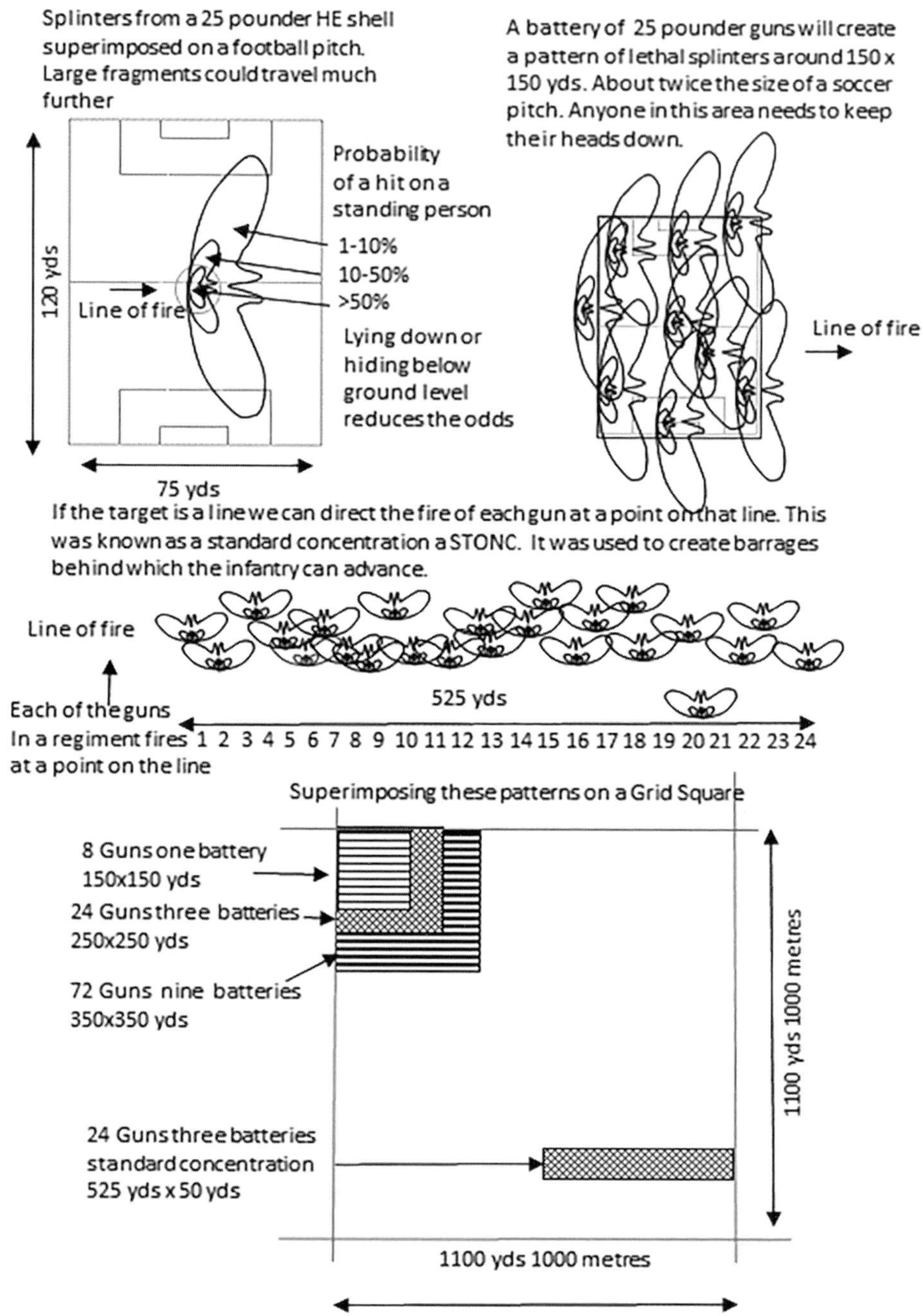

Artillery splinter patterns

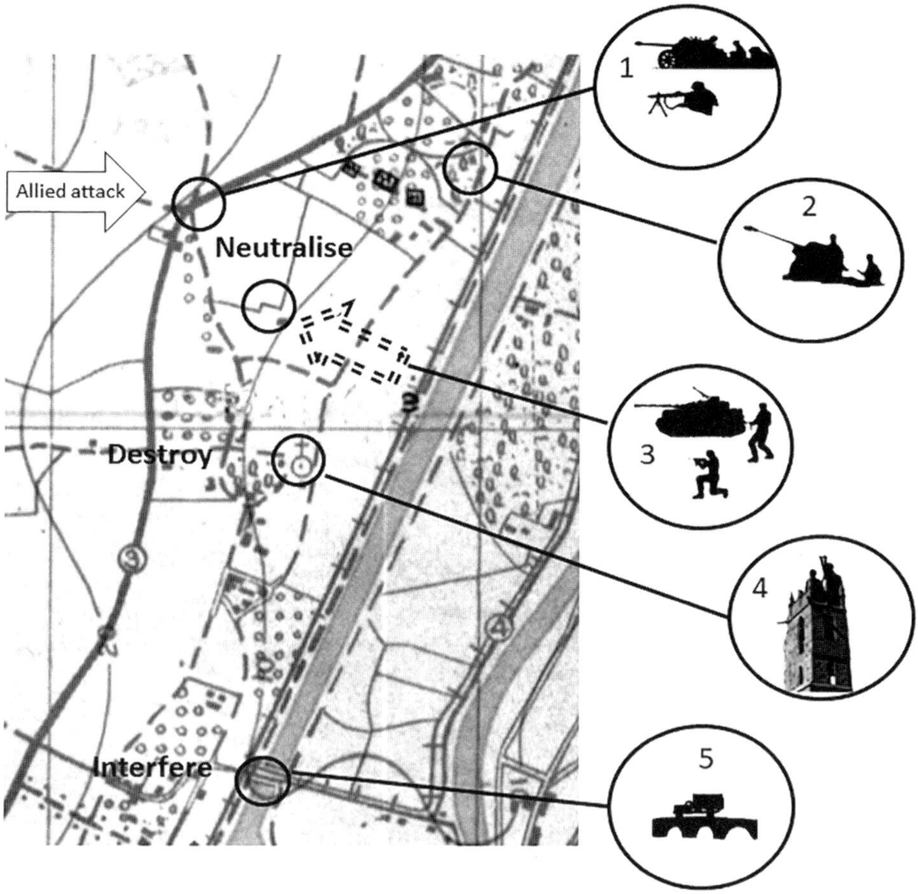

Effects of Artillery

casualties. Targets might include suspected HQs and, as shown, choke points on supply routes (5).

The main type of anti-tank ammunition used was Armour Piercing Capped (with Ballistic Cap, APCBC). Adding a soft metal cap to armour piercing shot improved the penetration of the round. However, the shape of the cap reduced the aerodynamic quality of the round, so a thin metal cap was added to improve this. A minority of ammunition was Armour Piercing Discarding Sabot. A central penetrating plug of dense material such as tungsten was surrounded by a lighter 'sabot'. This resulted in the central plug achieving a very high velocity. There were only 10,000 rounds of 6-pounder APDS available on D-Day.

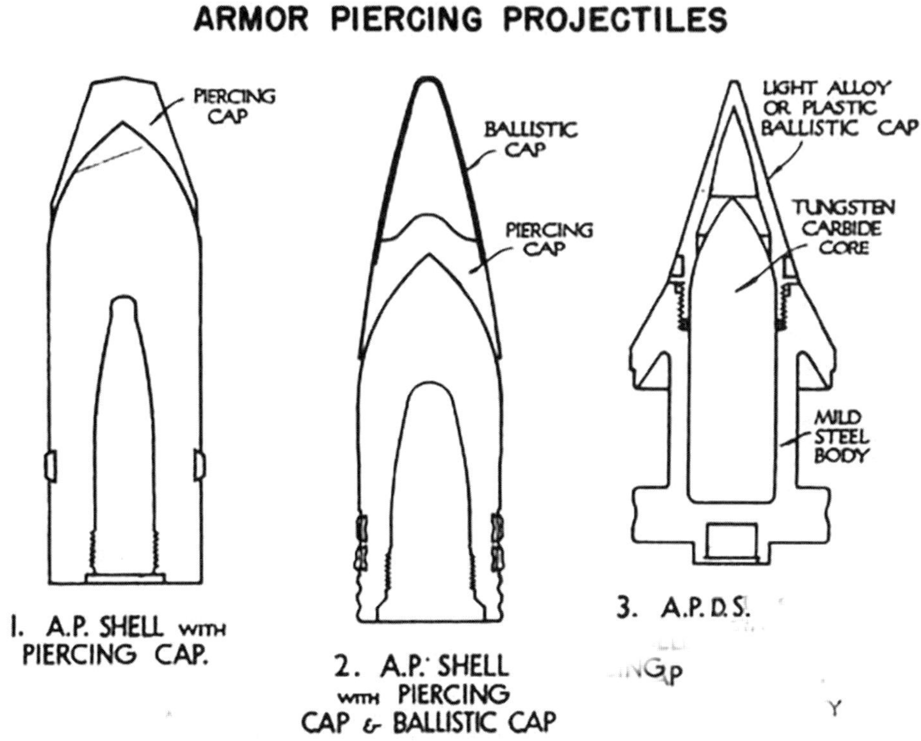

Anti-Tank Ammunition

17-pounder Armour Piercing Discarding Sabot Ammunition.

Organization and deployment of a Self-Propelled Battery

A self-propelled artillery battery was a big organization: ten officers and 200 men, including six Army Catering Corps (ACC) Cooks and five craftsmen from the Royal Electrical and Mechanical Engineers (REME). The establishment of a 25-pounder

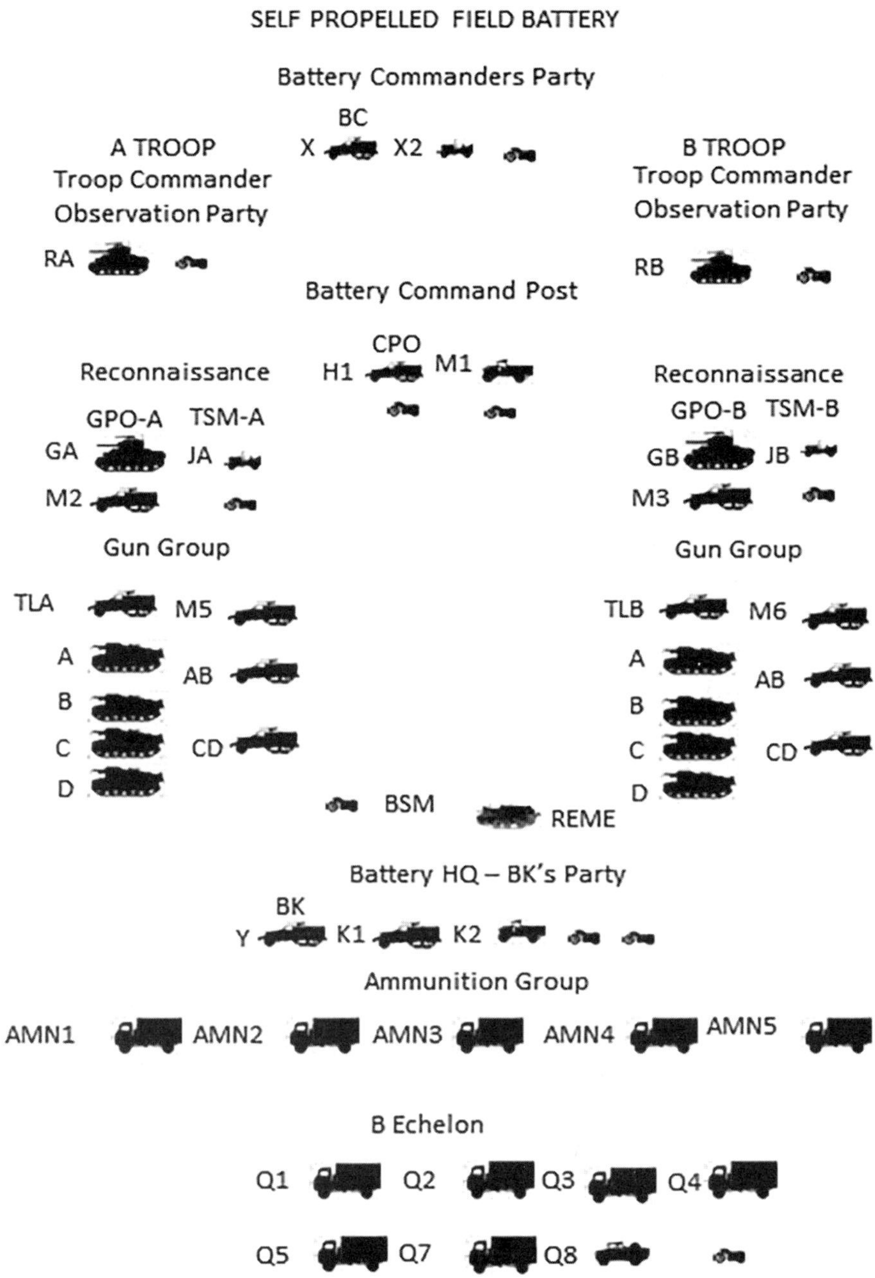

SP Battery Vehicles and Grouping.

SP battery (War Establishment II/190A/2. May 1944) included four medium tanks and ten armoured half-tracks, around twenty unarmoured vehicles and eleven motorcycles, all to support the eight self-propelled guns that delivered its main effect.

The battery was grouped into echelons for deployment. Each vehicle was lettered, indicating its role in the battery. 'X' was the Battery commander, and 'X2' his liaison jeep. 'RA' and 'RB' were the Armoured OPs for the troop commanders of A and B troops. They had a motorcycle for liaison. The battery commander and the troop commanders would deploy with the infantry battalion or armoured regiment to which they provided direct support.

The Battery Command Post group was commanded by the Command Post Officer in 'H' which contained the computational centre for the battery and the signals sergeant's 'M1' for communications. The CPO was responsible for the overall gun position including its gunnery and local defence.

Each troop had a Gun Position Officer (GPO) in 'GA' and 'GB', responsible for technical gunnery, and troop sergeant major 'JA' and 'JB' for ammunition as well as signals vehicles. When the guns deployed, the Regimental 2IC would allocate an area to the senior subaltern or command post officer for each battery. The CPO would recce the area to site the two four-gun troops and the Battery Command post. The troop GPOs would do their own recces, selecting individual gun platforms. These would be in an irregular pattern to provide a troop frontage of 70–110m.

The Gun Groups were the guns and ammunition vehicles as well as a troop leader and signals vehicle. The Gun Group for each troop consisted of the four SP Guns lettered A–D, a half-tracked ammunition limber for each pair of guns, and two half-tracks, one for the Troop Leader (TLA) and one for the Troop signals NCO (M5 and M6). Each 25-pounder SP carried 103 rounds, with sixty-four carried in each half track. The GPO would appoint an officer, warrant officer or NCO to act as section commander and supervise each section in the troop in addition to their other duties.

The senior officer on each battery position was the (battery) captain, known as the BK because 'BC' was the abbreviation for the Battery Commander. The BK had responsibility for administration and was not involved in firing the guns. The BK was also the second in command and would replace the BC if he became a casualty.

The Battery Sergeant Major was responsible for ammunition re-supply. The two 3-ton 4x4 ammunition trucks each brought 152 rounds to the gun position, and could be supplemented by ammunition vehicles from the Royal Army Service Corps prior to major fire plans. Batteries equipped with the M7 Priest were issued three more 3-ton 4x4 trucks as the 105mm ammunition was larger. The Priest only carried seventy-two rounds, a half-track forty-four and a 3-ton 4x4 ninety-four.105mm rounds.

Batteries equipped with towed 25-pounder guns would have similar grouping, but the M5 half-tracks and Gun Position Officers' tanks would be replaced by 15cwt trucks fitted for wireless. Troop commanders would be mounted in Universal Carrier Armoured OPs.

Appendix B

Artillery Equipment

Field Artillery Equipment

Gun	Calibre mm/in	Shell Weight	Rate of Fire per minute	Weight in action	Muzzle velocity	Range	Detachment
75mm	75/2.95	14lbs	3–6	653kg (1,439 lbs)	381 m/s (1,250 ft/s)	9,600yds (8,778m)	6
25-pounder	87.6/3.45	25 lbs	6–8	1,633 kg (3,600lbs)	198 to 532 m/s (650 to 1,750 ft/s)	12,253m (13,400yds) (HE shell)	6
105 mm M7	105/413	33 lbs		50,640lbs (22.97 metric tons	472m/s (1,550ft/s)	11,270m (7.00 mi)	8
4.5-inch BL	114/4.5	55 lbs	2–3	12,879lbs (5,842kg)	2,250 ft/s (686 m/s)	20,500yds (18km)	10
5.5-inch BL	130/5.5	100 lbs 80 lbs	2–3	13,647lbs (6,190kg)	100lb shell: 1,675ft/s (51 m/s) 82lb shell: 1,950ft/s (590m/s)	100lb shell: 16,200yds (14,813m) 82lb shell: 18,100yds (16,550m)	10
M1 155 mm	155/6.1	95 lbs	40 rds per hr	13,880kg (30,600lbs)	853m/s (2,799ft/s	23.7km (14.7 mi)	14
7.2-inch		200 lbs	1–3	38,580lbs (17,500kg)	1,925ft/s (587m/s)	19,667yds (17,984m)	10
German capabilities for comparison							
10.5 cm leFH 18/40	105/4.1	14.81/ (33 lbs)	6–8	1,900kg (4,180lbs)	540m/s (1,770ft/s)	12,325m (13,434yds)	6
15.0 Cm sFH 18	149/5.9	43.5/ (95.7lbs)	4	5,512kg (12,126lbs)	520m/s (1,706ft/s)	13,325m (14,522yds)	7
17.cm K18	172/6.8	68kg/(150lb)		17,510kg (38,522lbs)	860m/s (2,821ft/s)	28,000m (30,520yds)	10
21cm Mrs18	211/8.3	113kg (249lb)		16,700kg (36,740lbs)	565m/s (1,850ft/s)	18,700m (20,380yds)	10
15cm *Nebelwerfer* 41	159/6.3	2.5kg warhead	6 in 10 secs	540kg (1,188lbs)	342m/s (1,120ft/s)	6,900m (7546yds)	6
21cm *Nebelwerfer*	215/8.5	10.2kg HE warhead	6 in 10 secs	550kg (1,210lbs)	320m/s (1,000ft/s)	7,850m (8,585 yds)	4

Anti–Tank Artillery

Comparative penetration of anti–tank weapons

'Perforation of homogeneous armour at 30° Strike', ranges in yards.

Weapon	Ammo	600	1000	1600	2000
British 6-Pdr	APCBC	81	74	64	58
	SABOT	130	118	101	90
US & Br 75mm	APCBC M61	100	93	82	77
German 75mm PAK 40	APCBC	110	102	92	86
PAK 41	AP	137	100	?	?
KWK 42	APCBC	119	100	95(a)	89
US & British 3″ M–10	APC M62	97	90	80	74
US 90mm	APC M77	111	103	93	86
British 17-pdr	APCBC	127	120	112	107
	SABOT	183	172	155	145
German 88mm					
KWK 36 (f)	APCBC	108	102	94(a)	87
KWK 43 (f)	APCBC	178	140	131(a)	121

AA Artillery

Equipment	Calibre	Weight of shell lbs	MV f/sec	Weight in action/ tons	Rate of fire r.p.m	Max ceiling ft
British						
3.7 inch HAA	3.7″	28	2600	7.5–8	8/10	41,000
40mm Bofors	1.58″	2	2700	2.0–2.5	120	23,600
20mm Polsten	20mm (0.79″)		2700	2.0–2.5	450rpm cyclic 150–180 practical	6,500
German						
8.8cm Flak 36	3.46″ (88mm)	20	2690	5.5	15/20	34,773
3.7cm Flak 36	37mm	1.4	2610	1.53	140	13,775
3.7cm Flak 43	37mm	1.4	2610	1.2	150	13,775
2cm Flak 30	20mm (0.79″)	120gm/4.25 oz	2,950	0.45	450 cyclic 120–180 practical	7,000

Wireless Communications

Type	Mode (1)	Freq (MHz)	Power (watts)	Range (miles)	Using Antenna	Weight (lbs)
No.18	W/T R/T	6–9	0.25	W/T 4 R/T 2.5	6ft rod	34
No.19A	W/T R/T	2–8	12	W/T 15 R/T 10	8ft rod	
No.19B	R/T	229–241	3	1	half–wave	
No.19HP	W/T R/T	2–8	30	R/T 25–50	12ft rod	
No 22	W/T R/T	2–8	1.5 W/T 1 R/T	W/T 20 R/T 10	12ft rod	
No 38	R/T	7.3–8.8	0.2	0.75	4ft rod	22
No 46	W/T R/T	3.4–9.1 crystals	1.5	R/T 4–10	6ft rod	
TR 1143	R/T	100–120	4	50	dipole	

Notes

(1) W/T = Wireless–telegraphy, i.e. Morse code. R./T = Radio Telephony .i.e. voice communications

(2) The main radios used by the artillery were as follows:

(a) The No 18 set was a man-pack radio designed for use in infantry battalions between companies and battalion HQ. It was issued to artillery observers (and others) for communication with infantry. Canada produced it as the No.58. No.68 was a modified version for longer-range use. This had a range of 5 miles for voice and 10 miles Morse.

(b) The No. 19 set was the standard radio in armoured vehicles, including armoured OP carriers, and it could operate on the move. However, it was also used for many other purposes, for example, it could be fitted with an amplifier to produce a high-power set used in HQ armoured command vehicles, and sometimes fitted to Air OP and other aircraft. In its full configuration it was actually two radios, one HF (A set) and the other UHF (B set), used for short range inter–tank communications. It could be used to send Morse code as well as voice communications. It could have a handset remotely connected by cable to about half a mile away. HF range could be up to about 20 miles with a suitable antenna.

(c) The No.22 Set could be vehicle mounted or dismounted into a trench or building and was portable as a three-man load. It had remote control facilities that enabled the operator to be connected by cable to the radio up to half a mile away or to connect the radio to a line switchboard. It could also be directly connected to another radio, using a short multi-core cable, for re-broadcast operating (i.e one radio received a message and it was simultaneously re-transmitted by the second radio, which worked in both directions). It could transmit Morse as well as voice. The range could be 10–15 miles in close country and up to 40 miles in open country with a suitable antenna.

(d) The No.38 set was a short-range man-pack radio only operating in R/T mode and used mainly within infantry companies and by artillery forward observers. Each observation party (OP) received one in 1943 for FOO use, whilst tank OPs used them to communicate with infantry.

(e) No.46 was a special crystal-controlled and waterproofed radio for use in amphibious landings; some artillery observers probably used it. It had a range of 3–5 miles in close country, 10 miles open country and 20 across water.

Appendix C

Artillery on the British Beaches and Landing Grounds

BRITISH

21ST ARMY GROUP

SECOND BRITISH ARMY

1st British Corps

62 ATk, 102 LAA, 9 SvyRegts

3 Div	7, 33, 76 Field Regiments, 20 Anti-Tank Regt, 92 LAA Regt
3 Canadian Division	12, 13, 14, 19 Field Regt RCA, 3 Anti Tank Regt RCA, 4 Light AA Regt RCA
6 AB Div	53 AL Lt Regt, 3, 4 AL Anti-Tank Btys, 2 AL LAA Bty
51 (Highland) Div	126, 127, 128 Field Regiments, 61 Anti-Tank Regt, 40 LAA Regt
4th Army Group Royal Artillery	150 & 191 Field Regiments, 53, 65, 68, 79 Med Regts, 51 Hy Regt, 319 Coy RASC
30th British Corps	
50 (Northumbrian) Div	74, 90 (SP), 124 Field Regiments, 102 (NH) Anti-Tank Regt, 25 LAA Regt
49 (West Riding) Div	69, 143, 185 Field Regiments, 55 Anti-Tank Regt, 89 LAA Regt
7 ArmdDiv	3 RHA, 5 RHA (SP), 65 Anti-Tank Regt, 15 LAA Regt
5th Army Group Royal Artillery	7, 64, 84, 121 Med, 52 Hy Regt, 987 US FAB (SP), 725 Coy RASC

ARMY TROOPS

4RHA 86 and 147 FdRegts

1 COBU

3 COBU

16 Fire Control Unit

76 AA Brigade	99, 112, 113, 146 HAA Regiments, 120, 125, 127, 320/93, 62/20LAA Regts, 356 SL Bty
80 AA Bde	86, 103 HAA Regiments, 73, 113, 114, 139, 321/93 63/20 LAA Regts, 474 SL Bty

GERMAN

This lists the artillery in contact with the British Second Army on D-Day and the first week afterwards

Seventh Army

1st SS Panzer Corps

12 SS Panzer Division

SS Artillery Regiment 12

- I/SS-Artillerie Regiment 12: 12 × 10.5 cm (SP) Wespe; 6 × 15cm (SP) Hummel
- II/SS-Artillerie Regiment 12:1 8 × 10.5 cm FH18
- III/SS-Artillerie Regiment 12: 4 × 15 cm sFH; 4 × 10 cm K 17
- IV/SS-Artillerie Regiment 12: Nebelwerfer

21 Panzer Division

Panzer Artillerie 155

- I./Artillerie Regiment 155 : 4 × 12.2 cm Russian Howitzers
- 2./Artillerie Regiment 155 :4 × 12.2 cm Russian Howitzers
- 3./Artillerie Regiment 155 :4 × 10 cm K 18
- 4./Artillerie Regiment 155 : 6 × 10.5 cm le FH 18 auf Lorraine
- 5./Artillerie Regiment 155 : 6 × 10.5 cm le FH 18 auf Lorraine
- 6./Artillerie Regiment 155 : 6 × 15 cm le sFH13 auf Lorraine
- 7./Artillerie Regiment 155 : 6 × 10.5 cm le FH 18 auf Lorraine
- 8./Artillerie Regiment 155 : 6 × 10.5 cm le FH 18 auf Lorraine
- 9./Artillerie Regiment 155 : 6 × 15 cm le sFH 13 auf Lorraine
- 10./Artillerie Regiment 155: 2 × Nebelwerfer (sf) Reihenwerfer

Sturmgeschütz–Abteilung 200

- I./Sturmgeschütz–Abteilung 200:4 × 7.5cm Pak; 6 × 10.5cm cm le FH16 auf Ho
- 2./Sturmgeschütz–Abteilung 200:4 × 7.5cm Pak; 6 × 10.5cm cm le FH16 auf Ho
- 3./Sturmgeschütz–Abteilung 200:4 × 7.5cm Pak; 6 × 10.5cm cm le FH16 auf Ho
- 4./Sturmgeschütz–Abteilung 200:4 × 7.5cm Pak; 6 × 10.5cm cm le FH16 auf Ho
- 5./Sturmgeschütz–Abteilung 200:4 × 7.5cm Pak; 6 × 10.5cm cm le FH16 auf Ho

Panzer-Lehr-Division:

Panzer Artillerie 130

- I/Artillerie Regiment 130:12 × 10.5 cm (SP) Wespe; 6 × 15cm (SP) Hummel (Arrive 20 June)
- II/Artillerie Regiment 130: 12 :12 × 10.5 cm FH18
- III/Artillerie Regiment 130: 12 × 12.2 cm Russian Howitzers

Flak abteilung 130 18 × 8.8cm flak

LXXXIV Corps

Artillery Battalion 989: 12 × 12.2 cm s.F.H.396(r) heavy howitzers

716 Infantry Division

I./1716: HQ: Colomby-sur-Thaon

- 1./1716 : 4x 10cm leFH 14/19 (t) - Merville
- 2./1716 : 4x 10cm leFH 14/19 (t) - Colleville-sur-Orne (Wn16)
- 3./1716 : 4x 7.5cm FK16 n.A. - Bréville
- 4./1716 : 4x 15.5cm sFH 414 (f) - Ouistreham (Château d'Eau/Wn12)

II./1716 :HQ : Crépon (Wn35b)

5./1716 : 4x 10cm leFH 14/19 (t) - Wn36a

6./1716 : 4x 10cm leFH 14/19 (t) - La Mare-Fontaine (Wn32)

7./1716 : 4x 10cm leFH 14/19 (t) - Bény-sur-Mer

352 Infantry Division

Artillerie-Regiment 352

III./352: HQ: La Noé

7./352 : 4x 10.5cm leFH 18/40

8./352 : 4x 10.5cm leFH 18/40 –Sommervieu

9./352 : 4x 10.5cm leFH 18/40 - Beauvals

Fifteenth Army

LXXXI.Armeekorps:

Artillery Abteilung 1151 12 × 12.2cm s.F.H.396(r) heavy howitzers

346 Infantry Division

Artillerie-Regiment 346

I./346 : 12 × 7.62cm Russian howitzers

II./346 : 12 × 10.5cm French howitzers

IIII./346 : 12 × 12.2cm s.F.H.396(r) heavy howitzers

711.Infanterie-Division:

Artillerie Regiment 1711

I./346 : 16 × 7.62cm Russian howitzers

II./346 : 16 × 15.5cm French howitzers

COASTAL DEFENCE ARTILLERY

Heeresküstenartillerie-Abteilung1255: HQ: Blonville-sur-Mer

1./1255 : 6 × 15,5cm K420 (f) - Villerville

2./1255 : 6x15,5cm K420 (f) - Mont Canisy; OberleutnantSondam

3./1255 : 6x15.5cm K420 (f) - HoulgateTournebride

4./1255 : 4x10,5cm K331 (f) - Hennequeville

Heeresküstenartillerie-Abteilung126 : HQ: Arromanches

1./1260 : 6x 15,5cm K418 (f) - Riva-Bella

2./1260 : 6x 15,5cm K418 (f) - Pointe-du-Hoc

3./1260 : 4x 12,2cm K390/1 (r) - Mont Fleury

Index

Airborne Bridgehead, 208
Air defences of the beachhead, 81
Air OPs, 56, 78
Airborne landings:
air landed battery, 70
artillery observation and liaison landings, 68
artillery support from seaborne landing, 93
artillery support plan, 67
battle for Le Port, 103
dispersion, 91
German D-Day counter-attack, 99
Allied aircraft, 14, 55, 56, 63, 153, 196
Allied artillery equipment:
Anti-aircraft radar, 24
20mm AA guns, 95, 105, 116, 239
20mm calibre Oerlikon cannon, 25
20mm Polsten, 28, 255
25-pounder, 4, 6, 47, 40, 48, 55, 70, 95, 119, 181, 220, 241, 246, 253
3.7-in heavy AA guns, 83, 149
6-pounder, 18, 20, 58, 68–9, 90, 93, 97, 115, 179, 233, 235, 236
17-pounder anti tank gun, 18, 20, 58, 68–9, 90–1, 95, 97, 115, 140, 235–6, 252
40mm L60 Bofors Gun, 95
5.5-in gun, 13, 94
75mm US Pack Howitzer, 67, 220
Crusader SP AA tanks, 95
M1 155mm 'Long Tom', 13
M7 Priest, 48, 118, 252
M12 US 155mm SP Gun, 57, 179–80
M10 SP anti-tank gun, 18–19, 20, 57, 126, 141–2, 144, 149, 179, 202, 235–6
British Equipment:
AA Artillery, 255
AA Radar No3 Mk II, 24
Anti-tank Artillery, 255
Bofors Crusader SP, 18, 20, 25, 28, 126, 130
Coventry Clock, 44, 123
Wireless communications, 9–10, 256
Allied intelligence assessment of defences, 63
Amfreville, 217, 220
Post-D-Day battles, 220
Ammunition and its effects, 246–52
Anguerny, 230
Ardenne Abbey, 229
Arromanches, 81, 84, 172, 174–6, 179, 207, 238–41, 243, 245, 260
air defence of Mulberry Harbour, 239
360° Museum theatre, 245
Asnelles, 76–7, 175, 179, 187, 198, 202, 207
Authie, 229–30, 232

Banville, 147, 151, 171
Bas de Ranville, 215
Basly, 227, 230
Bayeux, 32, 59, 76, 80–1, 83, 147, 153, 170–1, 176, 180, 193–4, 196, 198, 229, 230, 232, 234, 235–7, 243, 245
Bayeux Tapestry, 245
Bayeux War Cemetery, 196, 236–8
Bayeux War Museum, 235
Bazenville, 196
Beauregarde, 224
Bénouville, 78, 88, 92–3, 100–101, 103, 105, 110, 116, 215, 223
Bény-sur-Mer, 78, 80, 147, 151, 163, 230
Bény-sur-Mer Canadian War Cemetery, 170
Bernerville, 87
Bernières-sur-Mer, 77–8, 80, 145, 147, 153–4, 159–61, 163–5, 169–70, 227
Biéville, 79, 100, 141–2, 224
Brécy, 194

Bretteville-l'Orgueilleuse, 83, 147–8, 232–3, 235
  battle 8–10 June, 232
Bréville-le-Mont, 83, 92–3, 97, 208, 215–17, 221–2
  12 June battle, 221
British Formations:
  21st Army Group, 1, 59, 79, 80, 86–7, 101, 109, 142, 153, 181, 196, 216, 229, 230, 258
  Second Army, 3, 31, 52, 58, 258
  Army corps:
    I Corps, 59, 112,150,258
    XXX Corps, 57, 59, 83, 179, 180
  Divisions:
    3 British Infantry, 7, 69, 80–1, 83, 90, 92, 109, 112, 114, 118, 126, 129, 148, 225
      Post- D-Day summary of actions, 83
    6th Airborne, 49, 51, 56, 67–8, 87, 89–94, 97–8, 101, 109–10, 114, 220-1, 237, 245
    50 (Northumbrian) Infantry, 76, 177, 178, 181, 183
    51 (Highland) Infantry, 216, 217, 220
  Brigades:
    1 Special Service, 75, 78, 89–90, 97, 110, 110, 114–15, 124, 215
    3 Parachute, 68–9, 86–7, 90–1, 96
    5 Parachute Brigade, 68–9, 88, 90–2, 97
    6 Air Landing Brigade, 69, 88, 103
    8 Armoured Brigade, 178
    8 Infantry Brigade, 51, 78, 83, 103, 105, 109, 112, 114–15, 118, 125, 147, 151, 161, 168, 173, 175–6, 201, 214, 225, 227, 229, 234, 244, 253–4, 259
    8 Armoured Brigade, 81, 178–9
    9 Infantry Brigade, 83, 110, 115
    27th Armoured Brigade, 110, 243
    56 Infantry, 81, 84, 176, 178–9
    69 Brigade, 76, 81, 176, 178, 183–4, 194–5
    151 Brigade, 81, 176, 178, 203
    185 Brigade, 78–9, 83, 110, 114–15, 141, 223
    231 Brigade, 76, 80, 81, 84, 176, 178–9
    76 Anti Aircraft, 259
    80 Anti Aircraft, 259
    Royal Marines Armoured Support Group, 55, 76–7, 94, 99, 112, 128, 148–9, 151, 155, 159, 161, 168, 177, 227
British Units:
  Commandos:
    No 3, 88–9, 212
    No 4, 69, 75, 77, 87–90, 109–10, 115, 118, 144, 148, 206, 238
    No 6, 89, 92, 98
    No 41 Royal Marine, 75, 77, 109,115, 129, 132–3, 135, 148
    No 45 Royal Marine, 89
    No 47 Royal Marine, 81, 176
    No 48 Royal Marine, 77, 148, 168
  Infantry battalions:
    5th Black Watch, 217
    1st Devonshire, 204
    12th Devonshire, 220
    1st Dorset, 81, 199, 202–4
    6th Durham Light Infantry, 203
    8th Durham Light Infantry, 203
    2nd East Yorkshire, 74, 78, 107, 122, 125, 143
    5th East Yorkshire, 176, 184–5
    2nd Essex, 236
    6th Green Howards, 81, 176, 184, 186, 191, 194
    7th Green Howards, 176, 184, 194
    1st Hampshire, 81, 199, 201–2, 204, 207
    2nd Hertfordshire, 183
    2nd King's Shropshire Light Infantry, 79–80, 141, 142, 225
    1st Norfolk, 79, 124, 139, 225
    2nd Oxford and Buckinghamshire Light infantry, 88
    7th Parachute Battalion, 92
    8th Parachute, 87, 92
    9th Parachute, 87, 91–2, 211–12, 216–17
    12th Parachute, 220–1
    1 Royal Ulster Rifles, 88, 97, 215
    1 South Lancashire, 75, 127, 129
    1st Suffolk, 78, 139–41
    2nd Warwickshire, 224–5, 237

Royal Armoured Corps:
4/7th Dragoon Guards, 81, 184, 194, 196
13/18 Hussars, 109, 122, 144, 220
East Riding Yeomanry, 110
Sherwood Rangers, 199, 202, 207
Staffordshire Yeomanry, 79, 110, 140–2
Westminster Dragoons, 184
61st Recce Regiment, 81
Other corps:
5th Assault Regiment Royal Engineers, 109, 122
No 9 Beach Group, 183
101 Beach Maintenance Area, 116
969 Port Floating Equipment Company RE, 239
Operations Research Section, 70
British Army Royal Artillery *see also*
Order of Battle, 257
Royal Artillery formations:
4 AGRA, 90, 112, 152, 257
5 AGRA, 57, 177, 180
76th AA Brigade, 179, 239
80th AA Brigade, 112, 130, 149–50, 239
O AA Assault Group, 150
Regiments, field:
4 RHA, 112, 114–15
6th Field, 151, 257
7 Field, 76, 79, 112, 114, 121–2, 138, 141, 224, 257
10th Field, 51
25th Field, 238
33rd Field, 69, 75, 79, 93, 112, 114–15, 122, 131, 135, 141, 196, 227, 257
74th Field, 178
76th Field, 69, 75, 78, 90, 93, 107, 112 122–5, 130, 137, 144, 257
86th (Hertfordshire Yeomanry) Field, 43, 48–9, 77, 81, 94, 177–8, 180–1, 193–4, 200, 236, 238, 257
90 (City of London) Field, 76,177–8, 199, 201–3, 196, 199, 206, 238
124th Field, 178
147th (Essex Yeomanry) Field, 81, 177–8, 181, 196, 199, 200–201, 205, 207, 258
150 Field, 112, 115, 220, 257
191st Field, 151, 257
Regiments, air landing light:
53 Air landing, 49, 56, 68–9, 89–90, 97, 215, 222, 257
Regiments, anti-tank:
20th, 98, 112,115–16, 130,238
61st Anti–tank, 99
62nd Anti Tank, 112, 115, 149, 196, 235
73rd Anti–tank, 177
102nd (Northumberland Hussars), 179, 258
Regiments, heavy:
51st, 227
Regiments, Heavy AA:
86th (HAC), 150
103 HAA, 48, 214, 242
113 HAA, 177, 179
Regiments, Light AA:
25 LAA, 177, 179, 196
73rd LAA, 48
92 (Loyals) Light AA, 103, 112, 116, 130, 237
93rd Light AA, 150,177
110th LAA, 238
114th LAA, 48, 150, 189, 257
120 LAA, 177, 180
127th Light AA, 237, 239, 257
139th Light AA, 180, 239, 257
Regiments, medium:
14 Medium Regiment, 237, 257
53 Medium, 112, 115, 257
65 Medium, 93, 112, 115, 257
79th Medium, 151, 257
107th Medium, 237, 257
Regiments, survey:
4 Survey, 177, 257
9 Survey, 112, 115, 149, 151, 257
Miscellaneous Royal Artillery Units, 253
No 16 Fire Control Unit, 119, 242
Maritime Regiments, 128
1st Forward Observation Unit, 56
Batteries:
Anti-tank:
3 Air Landing, 68–9, 258
4 Air Landing, 68–9, 258

45 Anti-tank, 115
245th Anti-tank, 196
Field:
342nd, 180
462nd Field, 185, 193
light AA:
2 Air landing light AA battery, 68, 90, 257
318 Light AA, 105, 116
Royal Artillery:
Anti-aircraft equipment and organization, 21
Anti-aircraft Radar Equipment, 24
Anti-tank Command and Control, 18
Anti-tank Equipment, 18
Developing Air Landing Artillery, 49
Field Artillery Command and Control, 5, 10
Field Artillery Organisation, 5, 251
Field Artillery Survey and Target Acquisition, 13
Firing from Landing Craft, 44
Organization, 5, 14, 18, 21, 24, 25
Training, 45
Batteries:
Field:
9th (Irish) Field, 224
210 Air Landing Light, 69
211 Air Landing Light, 69, 89, 97, 215, 217, 220, 257
212 Air Landing Light, 69, 85
302 Field, 107, 125, 130, 143
341st, 44, 183
342nd, 44, 184
357th Field, 203
358th Field, 203
431st Field, 201
431st Field, 201
432nd Field, 175
454 Field, 130
462nd Field, 184
465th Field, 203
511st Field, 205
Heavy:
420 Heavy, 177
Anti-tank:
3rd Air landing anti-tank, 90
4th Air landing anti-tank, 90
41st Anti-tank, 142
45 Anti-tank Battery, 116
67 Anti-tank, 115, 144
193rd Anti-tank, 99
198th Anti-tank, 179
234th Anti-tank, 179
245 Anti-tank, 112
246th Anti-tank, 149, 235
288th Anti-tank, 179
Heavy AA:
273rd Heavy AA, 150
356 Heavy AA, 177
362 Heavy AA, 177
366 Heavy AA, 179
383rd Heavy AA, 150
391 Heavy AA, 179
Light AA:
2 Air landing light AA, 68, 90
318th Light AA, 103
320 Light AA, 177, 180
321st Light AA, 150
375th Light AA, 150
394 Light AA, 177
395 Light AA, 177
82 Light AA, 177, 179, 196
British Military Units:
1 Combined Operations Bombardment Unit (COBU), 112
2 Combined Arms Bombardment Unit, 149
152 AA Operations Room, 177, 180
652 Air OP Squadron RAF, 112
652 Squadron AOP RAF, 151
662 Air OP Squadron RAF, 177
No 83 group RAF, 239
Brooke, Field Marshal Alan, 125
Buhot, 81, 180, 196, 202
Bures, 87, 92
Buron, 83, 229, 230, 232
7 June battle, 229, 230

Caen, 32, 33, 52, 59, 69, 70, 74, 76, 78, 79, 81, 83, 87, 89, 93, 100, 101, 109, 110, 113, 117, 141, 143, 147, 153, 170, 176, 180, 194, 209, 214, 216, 223, 225, 227, 229, 230, 232, 234, 242, 243, 244, 245
Cambes, 83
Canadian Army divisions:

3 Canadian Infantry, 80–1, 83, 109–10, 147–8, 230, 258
summary of battle with 12 SS Division 7–10 June, 83
Canadian Army brigades:
7th Canadian Infantry, 147–8, 153, 234, 235
8th Canadian Infantry, 147–9, 151
9th Canadian Infantry, 83, 148, 227, 234
Canadian Army Units:
1 Canadian Parachute Regiment, 92
1st Canadian Para Battalion, 87
27th Armoured Regiment (the Sherbrooke Fusiliers), 227, 230
6th Canadian Armoured Regiment (1st Hussars), 155, 157
Canadian Scottish, 77, 80, 153, 155, 232, 235
Fort Garry Horse, 161
Le Régiment de la Chaudière, 165
North Nova Scotia Highlanders, 168, 227, 230
North Shore Regiment, 169, 230, 232
Regina Rifles, 153, 232–3
Royal Winnipeg Rifles, 77, 80, 153, 155, 232, 234–5
The Queen's Own Rifles of Canada, 160–1
Canadian artillery units:
Regiments RCA:
Field:
12th Canadian Field, 77, 148–9, 151, 155, 157, 233, 234
13th Canadian Field, 77, 148–9, 151,157, 159, 170–1, 23–4
14th Canadian Field, 78, 80, 149, 151, 160–1, 163, 166, 170, 227, 230, 257
19th Canadian Field, 78, 80, 149, 151, 160, 168, 170, 257
Anti-tank:
3rd Canadian Anti-tank, 149, 227, 233, 235, 257
Light AA
4th Canadian, 149, 257
Batteries RCA:
44th Field, 159
105th Canadian Anti-tank, 149
32nd Canadian Light AA, 149
52nd Canadian Anti-tank, 149
81st Canadian Field, 170
94th Canadian Anti-tank, 235
Carpiquet, 83, 148, 227, 229, 230
Chateau St Come, post-D-Day battle, 216
Colleville-Montgomery, 117, 121, 125
Colleville-sur-Mer, 78
Collins, Gunner, 98
Colombelles, 87, 223
Courseulles-sur-Mer, 77, 145, 147, 151, 153–5, 157, 159–60, 171, 174, 227, 238, 245
Crépon, 81, 147, 176, 179, 189, 193–4
Creully, 81, 147, 176, 179, 194, 196
Cussy, 229, 230, 232
Cuverville, 92

D-Day
Advance inland, 78
Gold Beach Jig Sector, 81
Gold Beach King Sector, 80
Juno Beach, 80
Sword Beach, 78
Naval and aerial bombardment, 61
Operation Overlord – D-Day summary, 59
D–Day Academy, Rots, 245
Dempsey, Lieutenant General Miles, 52
Dives River, 3, 31–2, 52, 68, 87, 92, 96, 121, 211, 214, 216
Douvres-la-Delivrande, 83, 148
defence and capture, 227
Dutch Princess Irene Brigade, 216

Eisenhower, 1, 133
Espace Robert Kiln, 180–1

Falaise, 33, 59, 109–10, 245
Feuchtinger, 31, 33, 35, 100–1, 141
Fire plan, iv, 51–2, 63, 77, 109, 140, 153, 173, 193–4, 202, 220, 221, 224

Georges Leygues, 241
German artillery order of battle units, 260
German Artillery units *see also* Order of Battle:
155 Artillery Regiment, 34, 141
12 SS, Artillery Regiment, 42

352 Artillery Regiment, 241, 260
1716 Artillery Regiment, 78, 87, 144, 147, 176, 189, 193, 209, 212, 236, 242
1255 Army Coastal Artillery Battalion, 31, 259
1260 Coastal Artillery Battalion, 31, 117, 189, 241, 260
989 Heavy Artillery Battalion, 32, 80, 147
200 Sturm-Artillerie Abteilung, 200, 35, 259
305 Flak Battalion, 109
Artillery Battalion 260, 346
Artillery Battalion 352, 260
Heavy Artillery Battalion 189, 259
SS Artillerie Regiment 12, 259

German Artillery equipment:
2 cm Flak 30/38, 40, 210
3.7 cm Flak 38, 40
3.7 cm anti-tank gun, 37, 175, 199
5cm PAK38/KwK anti-tank gun, 37, 108, 124, 143, 147, 157,161, 167, 175–6, 183, 185–8, 198–9, 215, 242, 227, 259–60
7.5cm PAK 40 anti tank gun, 37–8, 77, 198, 209
7.5cm field gun, 157, 227
7.5 cm Pak 39 L/48, 235
7.5 cm SP Guns, 109
7.5cm anti-tank, 121, 124, 143, 147, 168, 176
7.5cm field gun, 147
7.5cm Howitzers, 36
8.8cm PAK 41/43 anti–tank guns, 37, 119
8.8 cm, 138, 173, 183, 186, 205, 241, 255
8.8cm Flak, 36–8, 40, 74, 108–9, 118–19, 120, 125, 147, 164, 171, 173, 175, 183, 242, 259
10 cm leFH 14/19(t), 87, 210
10cm K 18, 109
10.5cm Field Howitzers, 36
10.5cm SP Howitzers, 109
15cm Howitzer, 36, 230
15cm TbtsK C/36 150 mm (5.9″) naval gun, 241
15.5cm Howitzers, 87
155mm K 418 (f) gun, 118
Multiple rocket launchers firepower demonstration, 133
Nebelwerfers, 37
Sturmgeschützen, 81

German armed forces:
Artillery organization and methods, 35
Defensive deployment, 32
Defensive dilemmas, 32
Field Artillery Equipment, 253

German Formations:
I SS Panzer Corps, 259
LXXXIV Corps, 101, 194, 259
12th SS Panzer Division, 33, 83, 208, 229, 234–5, 259
21st Panzer Division, 32–4, 37, 79–80, 86, 101, 109, 119, 134, 141–2, 216, 230, 259
346th division, 216, 221
352nd Infantry Division, 32, 36, 76, 175, 198, 236
711th Infantry Division, 52, 87, 212, 260
716th Infantry Division, 31–2, 37, 76, 86, 92, 108, 141, 147, 154, 170, 236, 245, 259
Army Group B, 31–2, 100–1
Fifteenth Army, 211, 260
Kampfgruppe Meyer, 194
Kampfgruppe von Oppeln, 142
Panzer Gruppe West, 37
Seventh Army, 31, 37, 61, 259

German Units:
22 Panzer Regiment, 35
26 SS Panzer Grenadier Regiment, 233
53 Luftwaffe Signals Regiment, 147
125 Panzer Grenadier Regiment, 35, 86, 92, 100
192 Panzer Grenadier Regiment, 109, 227
200 Panzerjäger Battalion, 109, 141, 147, 200
441 Eastern (Ost) battalion, 147, 176, 185, 199
642 Eastern (Ost) battalion, 86
726 Grenadier Regiment, 32, 80, 147
736 Grenadier Regiment, 32, 78, 80, 86, 108–9, 125, 139–40, 147, 154, 170, 175,185, 227
916th Grenadier Regiment, 176, 198
KG Meyer defeat on D-Day, 81

German Artillery:
Anti-aircraft equipment, 38
Anti-tank equipment, 37
Coastal Artillery Organization, 31
Communications, 37
Organization, 29
Shortcomings, 37
German defensive positions:
Longues-sur-Mer battery, 63
Merville Battery, 63, 209
Strongpoint Douvres, 147
Stützpunkt Orne, 214
WN05 Overlooking Sword Beach, 210, 214, 241–2
WN08, Riva Bella, 63, 120,123
WN12 'Daimler', 109, 144
WN14 'Sole', 143–4
WN16 Morris Battery, 6, 78, 109–10, 138, 140
WN17, Hillman bunker, 78–9, 109–10, 125, 139–41
WN18, 76, 108, 121, 123–4
WN19, 76
WN20, 'Cod', 75, 78, 108, 122, 123, 125–6, 128
WN21 'Trout', 75, 108, 129
WN22, 108, 147
WN27, 147
WN29, 147, 155, 160
WN30, 147, 155
WN31, 147
WN32, 176, 189
WN33, 175, 183, 185, 188
WN 33A (Le Buisson), 155, 173
WN33A, 155
WN34, 175, 180, 185, 189
WN35, 175, 183, 188
WN36, 76, 175, 198–9
WN36B, 189
WN37, 76, 176, 199, 201, 204
WN38, 176, 198
WN39, 207
German plans, 29
Gold Beach, 3, 55, 57, 76, 77, 78, 81, 119, 173–7, 179–80, 183, 186, 198, 206–7, 239, 241, 243, 245
assault narrative, 76
D-Day allied artillery order of battle, 177
D-Day assault anti-aircraft artillery plan, 179
D-Day assault anti-tank artillery plan, 179
D-Day assault field artillery plan, 178
D-Day assault fire plan, 177
D-Day assault Jig Sector, 198
D-Day assault King Red Sector, 183
D-Day assault plan, 176
D-Day assault, Sergeant Palmer at Le Hamel, 205
D-Day inland from King, Creully, 194
D-Day King Red, Crepon, 193
Geography, 175
German defences, 175
Gold Beach tour, 174, 180
Jig Sector, 76–7, 81, 175–6, 178–80, 198–201, 206, 243
King Sector, 76–7, 81, 173, 175–6, 178–181, 183–8, 191, 193, 200–201, 203, 206, 243
landing the guns., 76
US 987th Field Artillery Battalion, 180
Gooseberry artificial breakwater, 129
Gray-sur-Mer, 80
Gun Position Jane, 170

Hauge, 97
Hermanville-sur-Mer, 75–6, 79, 108, 117, 125, 128–9, 135, 137–8
Herouvillette, 108
HMCS *Algonquin*, 161
HMS *Ajax*, 241
HMS *Arethusa*, 90
HMS *Belfast*, 174, 227, 230
HMS *Bulolo*, 241
HMS *Dacres*, 121
HMS *Grenville*, 207
HMS *Jervis*, 204
HMS *Largs*, 112, 180
HMS *Mauritius*, 90
HMS *Orion*, 17, 81, 194, 196
HNoMS *Svenner*, 130
Horsa Bridge, 96, 101, 105, 243
Houlgate, 87, 243

Jarmain, Major, 99
Juno Beach, 3, 55, 77, 80, 83–4, 98, 110, 130, 133, 145, 147, 151–4, 157, 168–9, 172–3, 175, 183, 239, 243, 245

14 Canadian Field Regiment under fire, 163
AA Plan, 149
Allied Field Artillery plan, 148
Allied plan, 147
Artillery regrouping, 149
assault narrative, 77
D-Day fight for Tailleville, 169, 170
D-Day Gun Position Jane, 170
D-Day Gun Position Mary, 171
D-Day Rhino ferry fire, 169
Evaluation of fire plan, 153
Field artillery deployment, 151
Juno Beach Centre, Courseulles, 245
landing the guns, 78
Mike Sector, 77, 80, 145, 147, 151–3, 155, 157, 170, 172–3, 233
Nan Green Sector events, 157
Nan Sector, 77, 96, 145, 147, 148–9, 151–2, 155, 157, 159–61, 168, 170
Nan Sector Red, 145, 151, 155, 167, 168
Nan Sector White, 145, 151, 160–1, 170
tour, 153

La Londe, 83
La Rivière, 76–7, 81, 174–7, 179–80, 183–6, 188
Lagrune-sur-Mer, 77, 94, 148, 168
Landing Craft Tanks (A), 55
Laurent-sur-Mer, 242
Lavatory Pan House, 187, 189, 191
LCG, 185
Le Hamel, 76, 77, 175, 176–7, 179, 201–202, 204, 207, 239
Le Havre, 121, 216, 242
Le Port, 92, 103, 105
Lebisey Wood, 80, 142, 223–4
Les Buissons, 229–30
Logistics, 84
Lion-sur-Mer, 75, 117, 129, 132, 134–5
Strongpoint Trout, 132–3
Longues-sur-Mer, 81, 84, 208, 241
Longues-sur-Mer battery, 176, 241
Longueval, 97, 215
Luc-sur-Mer, 110, 129, 133

March-Phillipps, Major Gustavus Henry, 1, 242
Mary Gun Position, 171
Memorials:
14th Canadian Field Regiment (Bernières-sur-Mer), 163
1st Battalion Suffolk Regiment (Hillman Bunker), 139
1st Special Service Brigade (Riva Bella), 124
27th Cavalry Regiment (Sherbrooke Fusiliers) (Buron), 229
2nd Battalion Kings Shropshire Light Infantry & 3rd Division (Lebisey Wood), 225
2nd Battalion the Hertfordshire Regiment (Ver-sur-Mer), 183
3rd Division Artillery (Hermanville-sur-Mer), 130
4/7 Dragoon Guards (Creully), 194
50th Division Artillery (Ver-sur-Mer), 181
6th Airborne Division (Bréville-les Monts), 221
86th (Hertfordshire Yeomanry) Field Regiment (Ver-sur-Mer), 181
9th Battalion the Parachute Regiment (Chateau St Come), 216
Allied casualties (Periers-sur-Dan), 141
Ardenne Abbey victims, 232
Bayeux War Memorial, 238
British Normandy Memorial (Ver-sur-Mer), 193
Canadian DD Tank memorial (Courseulles-sur-Mer), 157
Canadian Scottish Regiment (Juno Beach), 153
Capture of Bayeux, 236
Church Ruins (Bréville-les-Monts), 221
Combined Operations Pilotage Parties (Hermannville-sur-Mer), 129
Commando Memorial (Lion-sur-Mer), 133
Dutch Princess Irene Brigade (Chateau St Come) 216
Essex Regiment (Bayeux), 236
Field Marshal Montgomery Memorial (Colleville-Montgomery), 125
Gooseberry Breakwater (Hermannville-sur-Mer), 129
Green Howards (Crépon), 193

HMoNS *Svenner* (Hermannville-sur–Mer), 130
Juno Beach Centre, 153
North Shore Regiment (Authie), 232
Ranville Landing Zone (Ranville-sur-Mer), 96
Regina Regiment (Bretteville-l'Orgueilleuse), 234
Regina Rifles (Juno Beach), 153
Royal and Merchant Navy (Hermannville-sur-Mer), 128
Royal Winnipeg Regiment (Juno Beach), 153
The Queen's Own Rifles of Canada (Bernières-sur-Mer), 160
United Nations memorial (Lion-sur-Mer), 133
Merville, 13, 68, 87, 91, 96, 208, 209, 211, 212, 214, 216, 238, 242, 245, 260
Merville battery, 68, 87, 91, 96, 208, 209, 212, 214, 238, 242
tour, 209
Meuvaines, 81, 175–6, 187, 189
Meuvaines Ridge, 175–6, 187, 189
Meyer, Standartenführer Kurt, 208
Mont Fleury, 175–7, 185, 189, 191, 260
Mont Fleury battery, 191
Montgomery, General Bernard, 1, 5, 117, 125, 138–9, 166, 194, 196
Mulberry Harbour, 25, 84, 180, 239–40, 245
Museums:
Mur de l'Atlantique, 117
360° Museum, 239
Le Grand Bunker Musée du Mur de l'Atlantique, 245
Mémorial de Caen Museum, 245
Memorial Museum of the Battle of Normandy, 245
Musée de la Batterie de Merville, 209, 245
Musee du Debarquement Arromanches, 245
Musée No 4 commando, Ouistreham, 245

Naval Gunfire firepower, 14–15
Norrey-en-Bessin, 232, 234

O'Brennan, Lieutenant, RCA, 232
Omaha Beach, 155, 239–41
Operation Overlord, 1, 52, 83
planning, 1, 43
fire plan, 58
preparations, 43
Order of Battle British Artillery, 257
Order of Battle German Artillery, 258
Orne bridgehead, 85, 93, 208, 216
1st Special Service Brigade deployment, 89
6th Airborne Division deployment, 87
6th Airborne Division Artillery plan, 89
Airborne artillery communications issues, 90
air defence of the Orne bridges, 101, 105
Airborne landing plan, 87
Airborne Landings, 85
D-Day Exploitation plan, 89
Geography, 86
German deployment, 86
Post-D-Day summary of action, 83
Orne Canal, 1, 78, 86, 105, 210
Ouistreham, 59, 63, 75, 86, 108, 110, 117, 119, 120–2, 143–4, 210, 214, 216, 239, 242–3, 245, 260
viewing point, 242

Parham, Brigadier H. J., 51–2, 56, 58
Pegasus Bridge, 93, 103
Museum and exhibits, 93, 245
Peltz, Luftwaffe General, 214
Périers-sur-Dan, 79–80, 98, 109–110, 141–2
Plumetot, 109, 110, 135, 138
Point 61, 141
Pooley, Major John, 212, 238
Port Winston, 239
Port-en-Bessin, 3, 59, 76, 81, 84, 175–6, 178, 239, 243, 245
Post-D-Day Tour, 208
Putot-en-Bessin, 59, 77, 83, 147, 148, 232–5

Queen Red, 75, 109, 121, 125, 127, 131, 133

Ranville, 69, 83, 88, 92–3, 96–101, 110, 116, 215, 217, 223
  Battle Landing Zone post-D-Day battles, 215
  Artillery deployment and defence post-D-Day, 97
Ranville War Cemetery, 98
Ring Contour, 100
Riva Bella, 75, 108–9, 117, 120–1, 123–4, 144, 242
River Dives, 3, 68, 86–7, 89, 101, 242
River Orne, 1, 3, 31, 59, 68, 75, 78, 83, 85–8, 90, 92–3, 95–6, 100–101, 105, 109–10, 114, 119, 122, 139, 208, 210, 212, 214, 216, 239, 242, 245, 260
Robehomme, 87
Rommel, Erwin, 31
Rots, 232–3, 245
Royal Air Force, 54
  Bomber Command, 52, 63, 83
Royal Navy, 15
  Fleet Air Arm, 55, 63
Ryes, 176, 179, 196, 203, 204
Ryes War Cemetery, 196

Sanders, Brigadier D.C.M, 99
Seaborne landings, 70
Seine Estuary, 121
St Aubin d'Arquenay, 88, 109
St Aubin-sur-Mer, 78, 80, 88, 108, 109, 145, 153, 155, 155, 160, 166–70, 198
St Croix, 80, 147, 151, 171
St Leger, 176
St Manvieu, 233
Sword Beach, 3, 55, 69, 74, 76–8, 80, 83–4, 86–7, 91, 101, 107–108, 112, 117, 121, 124, 128, 130, 133, 147–8, 168, 212, 214, 239, 242–3
  3rd Division Plan, 109
  allied anti-aircraft plan, 116
  allied artillery order of battle, 112
  allied field artillery plan, 113
  allied anti-tank plan, 115
  artillery landings, 75
  battle for Strongpoint Hillman, 139
  capture of WN 12 Daimler, 144
  capture of WN 14 Sole, 143
  fire plan for the assault landing, 112
  geography, 107
  German defences, 108
  German D-Day armoured counter-attack, 142
  Sword Beach visit, 107
  tour, 107

Tailleville, 80, 147, 154, 166, 169, 170
Training, 45
Troarn, 86–7, 215

US Army Formations:
  1 US Division, 81
US Army Units:
  987th Field Artillery Battalion, 57, 177, 179–80, 186, 258
US Army Air Corps Formations:
  Eighth Air Force, iv, 63, 189
  Eighth US Air Force, 52, 153
  Ninth US Air Force, 63
USS *Arkansas*, 241

Varaville, 68, 86, 87, 89, 92
Vaux, 179, 189
Ver-sur-Mer, 81, 174, 176, 179–81, 183, 186–7, 189, 191
Vierville, 119
Villers Bocage, 59, 76, 80–1, 84, 176, 179
Villers-le-Sec, 194
Villerville, 87, 260
von Rundstedt, 29, 31